FEMINIST INTERPRETATIONS OF SØREN KIERKEGAARD

RE-READING THE CANON

NANCY TUANA, GENERAL EDITOR

This series consists of edited collections of essays, some original and some previously published, offering feminist re-interpretations of the writings of major figures in the Western philosophical tradition. Devoted to the work of a single philosopher, each volume contains essays covering the full range of the philosopher's thought and representing the diversity of approaches now being used by feminist critics.

Already published:

Nancy Tuana, ed., *Feminist Interpretations of Plato* (1994)

Margaret A. Simons, ed., *Feminist Interpretations of Simone de Beauvoir* (1995)

Bonnie Honig, ed., *Feminist Interpretations of Hannah Arendt* (1995)

Patricia Jagentowicz Mills, ed., *Feminist Interpretations of G. W. F. Hegel* (1996)

Maria J. Falco, ed., *Feminist Interpretations of Mary Wollstonecraft* (1996)

Susan J. Hekman, ed., *Feminist Interpretations of Michel Foucault* (1996)

Nancy J. Holland, ed., *Feminist Interpretations of Jacques Derrida* (1997)

FEMINIST INTERPRETATIONS OF SØREN KIERKEGAARD

EDITED BY CÉLINE LÉON AND SYLVIA WALSH

THE PENNSYLVANIA STATE UNIVERSITY PRESS
UNIVERSITY PARK, PENNSYLVANIA

Library of Congress Cataloging-in-Publication Data

Feminist interpretations of Søren Kierkegaard / edited by Céline Léon
and Sylvia Walsh.

    p. cm. — (Re-reading the canon)
    Includes bibliographical references and index.
    ISBN 0-271-01698-1 (cloth : alk. paper)
    ISBN 0-271-01699-X (pbk. : alk. paper)
    1. Kierkegaard, Søren, 1813–1855. 2. Woman (Philosophy)
  3. Feminist theory. I. Léon, Céline, 1942– . II. Walsh, Sylvia,
  1937– . III. Series.
  B4378.W65F45   1997
  198'.g—dc21   96-49105
                                              CIP

It is the policy of The Pennsylvania State University Press to use acid-free paper for the
first printing of all clothbound books. Publications on uncoated stock satisfy the minimum requirements of American National Standard for Information Sciences—
Permanence of Paper for Printed Library Materials, ANSI Z39.48-1992.

IN MEMORIAM
MIYAKO MATSUKI
a dear friend

Contents

Preface

Take into your hands any history of philosophy text. You will find compiled therein the "classics" of modern philosophy. Since these texts are often designed for use in undergraduate classes, the editor is likely to offer an introduction in which the reader is informed that these selections represent the perennial questions of philosophy. The student is to assume that she or he is about to explore the timeless wisdom of the greatest minds of Western philosophy. No one calls attention to the fact that the philosophers are all men.

Though women are omitted from the canons of philosophy, these texts inscribe the nature of woman. Sometimes the philosopher speaks directly about woman, delineating her proper role, her abilities and inabilities, her desires. Other times the message is indirect—a passing remark hinting at woman's emotionality, irrationality, unreliability.

This process of definition occurs in far more subtle ways when the central concepts of philosophy—reason and justice, those characteristics that are taken to define us as human—are associated with traits historically identified with masculinity. If the "man" of reason must learn to control or overcome traits identified as feminine—the body, the emotions, the passions—then the realm of rationality will be one reserved primarily for men,[1] with grudging entrance to those few women who are capable of transcending their femininity.

Feminist philosophers have begun to look critically at the canonized texts of philosophy and have concluded that the discourses of philosophy are not gender-neutral. Philosophical narratives do not offer a universal perspective, but rather privilege some experiences and beliefs over others. These experiences and beliefs permeate all philosophical theories whether they be aesthetic or epistemological, moral or metaphysical. Yet this fact has often been neglected by those studying the traditions of philosophy. Given the history of canon formation in Western philosophy, the perspective most likely to be privileged is that of upper-class, white males. Thus, to be fully aware of the impact of gender biases, it is imperative that we re-read the canon with attention to the ways in which philosophers' assumptions concerning gender are embedded within their theories.

This new series, *Re-Reading the Canon,* is designed to foster this process of reevaluation. Each volume will offer feminist analyses of the theories of a selected philosopher. Since feminist philosophy is not monolithic in method or content, the essays are also selected to illustrate the variety of perspectives within feminist criticism and highlight some of the controversies within feminist scholarship.

In this series, feminist lenses will be focused on the canonical texts of Western philosophy, both those authors who have been part of the traditional canon, as well as those philosophers whose writings have more recently gained attention within the philosophical community. A glance at the list of volumes in the series will reveal an immediate gender bias of the canon: Arendt, Aristotle, de Beauvoir, Derrida, Descartes, Foucault, Hegel, Hume, Kant, Locke, Marx, Mill, Nietzsche, Plato, Rousseau, Wittgenstein, Wollstonecraft. There are all too few women included, and those few who do appear have been added only recently. In creating this series, it is not my intention to reify the current canon of philosophical thought. What is and is not included within the canon during a particular historical period is a result of many factors. Although no canonization of texts will include all philosophers, no canonization of texts that exclude all but a few women can offer an accurate representation of the history of the discipline as women have been philosophers since the ancient period.[2]

I share with many feminist philosophers and other philosophers writing from the margins of philosophy the concern that the current canonization of philosophy be transformed. Although I do not accept the position that the current canon has been formed exclusively by power relations, I do believe that this canon represents only a selective history of the tradition. I share the view of Michael Bérubé that "canons are at once the location, the index, and the record of the struggle for cultural representation; like any other hegemonic formation, they must be continually reproduced anew and are continually contested."[3]

The process of canon transformation will require the recovery of "lost" texts and a careful examination of the reasons such voices have been silenced. Along with the process of uncovering women's philosophical history, we must also begin to analyze the impact of gender ideologies upon the process of canonization. This process of recovery and examination must occur in conjunction with careful attention to the concept of a canon of authorized texts. Are we to dispense with the notion of a tradition of excellence embodied in a canon of authorized texts? Or, rather than abandon the whole idea of a canon, do we instead encourage a reconstruction of a canon of those texts that inform a common culture?

This series is designed to contribute to this process of canon transformation by offering a re-reading of the current philosophical canon. Such a re-reading shifts our attention to the ways in which woman and the role of the feminine is constructed within the texts of philosophy. A question we must keep in front of us during this process of re-reading is whether a philosopher's socially inherited prejudices concerning woman's nature and role are independent of her or his larger philosophical framework. In asking this question attention must be paid to the ways in which the definitions of central philosophical concepts implicitly include or exclude gendered traits.

This type of reading strategy is not limited to the canon, but can be applied to all texts. It is my desire that this series reveal the importance of this type of critical reading. Paying attention to the workings of gender within the texts of philosophy will make visible the complexities of the inscription of gender ideologies.

Notes

1. More properly, it is a realm reserved for a group of privileged males, since the texts also inscribe race and class biases that thereby omit certain males from participation.

2. Mary Ellen Waithe's multivolume series, A History of Women Philosophers (Boston: M. Nijhoff, 1987), attests to this presence of women.

3. Michael Bérubé, Marginal Forces/Cultural Centers: Tolson, Pynchon, and the Politics of the Canon (Ithaca: Cornell University Press, 1992), 4–5.

Acknowledgments

WANDA WARREN BERRY, "The Heterosexual Imagination and Aesthetic Existence in Kierkegaard's *Either/Or*, Part One," is reprinted by permission of Mercer University Press from *International Kierkegaard Commentary: Either Or, Part I*, ed. Robert L. Perkins (Macon: Mercer University Press, 1995), 201–8. Copyright 1995 by Mercer University Press.

BIRGIT BERTUNG, "Yes, a Woman *Can* Exist," is reprinted with revisions by permission of the author and C. A. Reitzel Publishers from *Kierkegaard Conferences I: Kierkegaard—Poet of Existence*, ed. Birgit Bertung (Copenhagen: C. A. Reitzel, 1989), 7–18. Copyright 1989 by Birgit Bertung.

Selections from SYLVIANE AGACINSKI, *Aparté: Conceptions and Deaths of Søren Kierkegaard* (Tallahassee: Florida State University Press, 1988), 152–56 and 167–80, are reprinted with corrections by permission of the University Press of Florida. Copyright 1988 by the Board of Regents of the State of Florida.

SYLVIA WALSH, "Subjectivity Versus Objectivity: Kierkegaard's *Postscript* and Feminist Epistemology," is reprinted with revisions by permission of Mercer University Press from *International Kierkegaard Commentary: Concluding Unscientific Postscript*, ed. Robert L. Perkins (Macon: Mercer University Press, 1997). Copyright 1997 by Mercer University Press.

SYLVIA WALSH, "On 'Feminine' and 'Masculine' Forms of Despair," is reprinted with revisions by permission of Mercer University Press from *International Kierkegaard Commentary: The Sickness unto Death*, ed. Robert

L. Perkins (Macon: Mercer University Press, 1987), 121–34. Copyright 1987 by Mercer University Press.

LESLIE HOWE, "Kierkegaard and the Feminine Self," is reprinted with revisions by permission of the author from *Hypatia* 9, no. 4 (Fall 1994): 131–57. Copyright 1994 by Leslie Howe.

TAMSIN LORRAINE, "Amatory Cures for Material Dis-ease: A Kristevan Reading of *The Sickness unto Death*," is reprinted with revisions by permission of Indiana University Press from *Kierkegaard in Post/Modernity*, ed. Martin Matuštík and Merold Westphal (Bloomington: Indiana University Press, 1995). Copyright 1995 by Indiana University Press.

JULIA WATKIN, "The Logic of Kierkegaard's Misogyny, 1854–1855," is reprinted with revisions by permission of the editors from *Kierkegaardiana* 15 (1991): 79–93. Copyright 1991 by *Kierkegaardiana*.

The editors express gratitude to their respective spouses, Albert Mittal and Robert L. Perkins, for the loving support they have provided throughout the planning and preparation of this volume. Thanks are also due Grove City College and Stetson University for the support services these institutions have provided for the project.

Abbreviations

AN   *Armed Neutrality* and *An Open Letter*. Edited and translated by Howard V. Hong and Edna H. Hong. Bloomington: Indiana University Press, 1968. (*Den bevæbnede Neutralitet*, written 1848–49, published 1965; "Foranledigt ved en Yttring af Dr. Rudelbach mig betræffende," *Fædrelandet*, no. 26, 31 January 1851.)

C   *The Crisis [and a Crisis] in the Life of an Actress*. Translated by Stephen Crites. New York: Harper and Row, 1967. (*Krisen og en Krise i en Skuespillerindes Liv*, by Inter et Inter. *Fædrelandet*, nos. 188–91, 24–27 July 1848.)

CA   *The Concept of Anxiety*. Edited and translated by Reidar Thomte in collaboration with Albert B. Anderson. Princeton: Princeton University Press, 1980. (*Begrebet Angest* by Vigilius Haufniensis, edited by S. Kierkegaard, 1844.)

CD   *Christian Discourses* and *The Lilies of the Field and the Birds of the Air* and *Three Discourses at the Communion on Fridays*. Translated by Walter Lowrie. London: Oxford University Press, 1940. *Christelige Taler*, 1848; *Lilien paa Marken og Fuglen under Himlen*, 1849; *Tre Taler ved Altergangen om Fredagen*, 1849.)

CI   *The Concept of Irony with Continual Reference to Socrates*, together with "Notes on Schelling's Berlin Lectures." Edited and translated by Howard V. Hong and Edna H. Hong. Princeton: Princeton University Press, 1989. (*Om Begrebet Ironi*, 1841.)

COR   *The Corsair Affair.* Translated by Howard V. Hong and Edna H.
        Hong. Princeton: Princeton University Press, 1982. (Articles
        by Kierkegaard and others relating to the *Corsair* affair.)

CUP   *Concluding Unscientific Postscript,* 2 vols. Edited and translated
        by Howard V. Hong and Edna H. Hong. Princeton: Princeton
        University Press, 1992. (*Afsluttende uvidenskabelig Efterskrift,* by
        Johannes Climacus, edited by S. Kierkegaard, 1846.)

EO   *Either/Or,* 2 vols. Edited and translated by Howard V. Hong and
        Edna H. Hong. Princeton: Princeton University Press, 1987.
        (*Enten/Eller* I–II, edited by Victor Eremita, 1843.)

EPW   *Early Polemical Writings.* Edited and translated by Julia Watkin.
        Princeton University Press, 1990. (*Af en endnu Levendes Papirer,*
        1838, and early writings from before the "authorship.")

EUD   *Eighteen Upbuilding Discourses.* Translated by Howard V. Hong
        and Edna H. Hong. Princeton: Princeton University Press,
        1990. (*Opbyggelige Taler,* 1843, 1844.)

FSE   *For Self-Examination* (published with *Judge for Yourself!*). Edited
        and translated by Howard V. Hong and Edna H. Hong.
        Princeton: Princeton University Press, 1990. (*Til Selvprøvelse,*
        1851; *Dømmer Selv!* 1852.)

FT   *Fear and Trembling* (published with *Repetition*). Edited and trans-
        lated by Howard V. Hong and Edna H. Hong. Princeton:
        Princeton University Press, 1983. (*Frygt og Bæven,* by Johannes
        de Silentio, 1843; *Gjentagelsen,* by Constantin Constantius,
        1843.)

JC   *Johannes Climacus.* See *PF.*

JFY   *Judge for Yourself!* See *FSE.*

JP   *Søren Kierkegaard's Journals and Papers,* 7 vols. Edited and trans-
        lated by Howard V. Hong and Edna H. Hong, assisted by Gregor
        Malantschuk. Bloomington: Indiana University Press, vol. 1,
        1967; vol. 2, 1970; vols. 3 and 4, 1975; vols. 5–7, 1978. (From
        Papirer I–XIII; and *Breve og Akstykker vedrørende Søren Kierke-
        gaard,* 2 vols., edited by Niels Thulstrup [København: Munks-
        gaard], 1953–54.)

KAUC   *Kierkegaard's Attack upon "Christendom."* Translated by Walter Lowrie. Princeton: Princeton University Press, 1944. (*Bladartikler 1–21, Fædrelandet, 1854–55; Dette skal siges; saa være det da sagt, 1855; Øieblikket 1–10, 1855; Hvad Christus dømmer om officiel Christendom, 1855.*)

LD   *Kierkegaard: Letters and Documents.* Translated by Henrik Rosenmeier. Princeton: Princeton University Press, 1978. (*Breve og Aktstykker vedrøende Søren Kierkegaard, vol. 1, edited by Niels Thulstrup.*)

LY   *The Last Years.* Translated by Ronald C. Smith. New York: Harper and Row, 1965. (From *Papirer* XI^1–XI^2.)

OAR   *On Authority and Revelation: The Book on Adler, or a Cycle of Ethico-Religious Essays.* Translated and edited by Walter Lowrie. Princeton: Princeton University Press, 1955. (*Bogen om Adler,* written and twice rewritten, 1846–47; unpublished except for one section, "Om Forskjellen mellem et Genie og en Apostel" ["On the Difference between a Genius and an Apostle"], *Tvende Ethisk-Religieuse Smaa-Afhandlinger,* by H. H., 1849.)

P   *Prefaces: Light Reading for Certain Classes as the Occasion May Require.* Translated by William McDonald. Tallahassee: Florida State University Press, 1989. (*Forord. Morskabslæsning for Enkelte Stænder efter Tid og Leilighed,* by Nicolaus Notabene, 1844.)

PAP   *Søren Kierkegaards Papirer,* 2d enlarged ed. 16 vols. Edited by Niels Thulstrup, with index, vols. 14–16 by N. J. Cappelørn. Copenhagen: Gyldendal, 1968–78.

PC   *Practice in Christianity.* Translated by Howard V. Hong and Edna H. Hong. Princeton: Princeton University Press, 1991. (*Indøvelse i Christendom,* by Anti-Climacus, edited by S. Kierkegaard, 1850.)

PF   *Philosophical Fragments* (published with *Johannes Climacus*). Edited and translated by Howard V. Hong and Edna H. Hong. Princeton: Princeton University Press, 1985. (*Philosophiske Smuler* by Johannes Climacus, edited by S. Kierkegaard, 1844; "Johannes Climacus eller *de omnibus dubitandum est,*" written 1842–43, unpublished, *Papirer* IV C I.)

PV   *The Point of View for My Work as an Author: A Report to History and Related Writings*, including " 'The Individual': Two 'Notes' Concerning My Work as an Author" and "My Activity as a Writer." Translated by Walter Lowrie. London: Oxford University Press, 1939. Reprint edited by Benjamin Nelson. New York: Harper and Row, 1962. (*Synspunktet for min Forfatter-Virksomhed,* posthumously published 1859; *Om min Forfatter-Virksomhed,* 1851.)

R   *Repetition.* See *FT.*

SLW   *Stages on Life's Way.* Edited and translated by Howard V. Hong and Edna H. Hong. Princeton: Princeton University Press, 1988. (*Stadier paa Livets Vej,* edited by Hilarius Bogbinder, 1845.)

SUD   *The Sickness unto Death.* Edited and translated by Howard V. Hong and Edna H. Hong. Princeton: Princeton University Press, 1980. (*Sygdommen til Døden,* by Anti-Climacus, edited by S. Kierkegaard, 1849.)

SV   *Søren Kierkegaards Samlede Værker.* 1st ed. 14 vols. Edited by A. B. Drachmann, J. L. Heiberg, and H. O. Lange. Copenhagen: Gyldendalske Boghandels Forlag, 1901–6.

TA   *Two Ages: The Age of Revolution and the Present Age: A Literary Review.* Edited and translated by Howard V. Hong and Edna H. Hong. Princeton: Princeton University Press, 1978. (*En literair Anmeldelse: To Tidsaldre,* 1846.)

TDIO   *Three Discourses on Imagined Occasions.* Translated by Howard V. Hong and Edna H. Hong. Princeton: Princeton University Press, 1993. (*Tre Taler ved tænkte Leiligheder,* 1845.)

UDVS   *Upbuilding Discourses in Various Spirits.* Translated by Howard V. Hong and Edna H. Hong. Princeton: Princeton University Press, 1993. (*Opbyggelige Taler i forskjellig Aand,* 1847.)

WL   *Works of Love.* Translated by Howard V. Hong and Edna H. Hong. Princeton: Princeton University Press, 1995. (*Kjerlighedens Gjerninger,* 1847.)

Introduction

Where does Kierkegaard stand on the subject of woman and the sexual relation? What value does a feminist re-reading of his writings have for contemporary feminists? Do these works have anything to impart to us today in a cultural situation whose trends are at once global and atomistic? Few writers have been so prolific as the Danish philosopher Søren Kierkegaard (1813–55), who produced more than thirty works as well as voluminous private journals in the short span of thirteen years. In a philosophical tradition that, written by men and for men, had little or no interest in sexual difference or the sexual relation, it is remarkable that Kierkegaard should have chosen to dedicate a considerable portion of his writings to these questions. Yet, his attitude toward women, the feminine, and the rapports between men and women is at best ambiguous. On the one hand, he insists on an ultimate and fundamental equality of the sexes before God—even, in some instances, the greater perfection of woman—and singles out the feminine as the paradigm of religious existence. On the other hand, insofar as his entire production is bestrewn with stereotyped, degrading, and patriarchal remarks about woman, a positive reading of his views appears highly problematic for feminism. In fact, his very first publication, "Another Defense of Woman's Great Abilities," a short, satirical piece opposing the emancipation of women, written while the author was still a university student, was truly a harbinger of things to come.

Any assessment of Kierkegaard's position on the issues that interest us here is immensely complicated by the fact that his production—often designated as "authorship"—follows two parallel paths that sometimes converge, sometimes diverge, and by the fact that no two critics see eye to eye when it comes to the question of deciding where the congruences and the disagreements begin. Because the philosopher frequently wrote and published under the guise of pseudonyms, from whose viewpoints he sought to distinguish himself as author and/or editor, a major interpretative difficulty of the authorship concerns the degree to which Kierkegaard's own views are reflected in the pseudonymous writings. Although no one in Denmark had any doubt as to who was the actual author of the works he published pseudonymously, Kierkegaard, who more than once felt tempted to doff the disguise altogether, maintained—almost to the very end of his life—what he termed his "indirect communication" concurrently with edifying discourses that he published under his own name. The whole question of pseudonymity is an interesting one that requires, as Kierkegaard himself enjoins us to do, that we deal with the pseudonyms and not read their perceptions of women and the sexual relation as his own. Through these personae Kierkegaard aimed at protecting his personal identity from the distraction and embarrassment of publicity, but his primary concern was to establish distance: to release the creatures of his imagination from himself and maieutically to free the reader from the author's authority.

If the fictitious authors are all masculine, and if the overall perspective is that of the masculine equated with the universal, women, (re-)presented through the eyes of men, are the object of a doubly indirect communication. Because it is not always easy to distinguish the socially constructed from the naturally given, or positive criticism from negative constructs, a problem recurrently faced by Kierkegaardian critics is that of differentiating between irony and literalness, and of respecting the intended dialectical ambiguity of the works. Do Kierkegaard's writings reflect the traditional, negative stereotypes of his time on the issues of woman and gender, or do they—if only potentially—manifest a progressive (even feminist) thrust concerning these and other matters? Are the socially inherited prejudices concerning women and gender embedded there independent of, and thus theoretically excisable from, the philosophical framework of Kierkegaard's thought?

Attempts at feminist interpretations of Kierkegaard are complicated in yet another way. The pseudonymous production is divided into three spheres: aesthetic or immediate, ethical or universal, and religious. As the higher spheres are reached, the content of the authorship itself changes with regard to woman and the sexual relation: Beginning with arbitrary and offensive judgments on "Woman" and the difference that separates her from "Man," it advances to a more ambivalent position wherein a persistent revindication of equality in the ethical-religious is puzzlingly conflated with belief in the existence of sexual differences, together with an inveterate and persistent opposition to woman's emancipation. In addition, although woman's relativity/relatedness is proclaimed in all three spheres, the concept is radically altered as higher thresholds are reached. It may in fact be claimed with no exaggeration that each sphere can best be understood by the specific way in which it expresses the sexual relation. The first, or aesthetic, sphere is that of seduction, where a single man seduces many women, or concentrates his negative attentions on a single one. The second (ethical) has to do with marriage, namely, the committed relationship to one woman. The third, or religious, sphere is that of "the exception," namely, that in which man abstains from any commerce with women.

Therefore, because of the many-layered aspect of the Kierkegaardian edifice, the essays in this volume have had to think both with and against the grain of Kierkegaard in their readings; they have also had to apply the same optic to the pseudonyms and to the relationship between pseudonyms and author. It is easy not to take as emblematic of Kierkegaard the point of view of the aesthetic personalities; as progress is made, however, to the higher spheres of the ethical and the religious, the temptation to identify author and pseudonyms increases, with the consequence that—in an apparent but nonexistent paradox—greater caution must concurrently be exercised. Furthermore, greater too becomes the temptation to view all the negative statements as problematic for a feminist reading, as the feelings directly expressed in the journals or in the communications that Kierkegaard wrote under his own name appear undeniably closer to the author's truth.

Because feminist philosophy is monolithic neither in method nor in content, we have striven to give in this volume a fair representation of its various approaches and to highlight some of the controversies that have arisen within feminist scholarship on Kierkegaard. We have organized the essays dialectically so as to reflect these strains, proceeding from rather positive readings where tensions between existentialist and essentialist views of woman are registered, through the negative criticism of essentialist trends, followed by a synthesis of critique with commendation, and finally to a reclamation of the feminine.

The first four articles are by critics (Berry, Bertung, Watkin, Perkins) who oppose the perception that Kierkegaard was a common misogynist;

emphasizing the indirect, ironic, and paradoxical character of his production, they contend instead that—even when at his most offensive—he is negatively maieutic so as dialectically to encourage women (and men) to self-activity. On the horizon of these readings, a variety of existential options become available for both sexes: full humanity/selfhood, same-sex relations, single life, as well as heterosexual love and marriage genuinely and reciprocally experienced. These essays thus convey a sense that the dialectical tensions existing between author and pseudonyms yield a message that feminists should heed, and that, on this score, the philosopher, vastly concerned with sexual equality, had much to impart to women—and, in some instances, to men as well. What remains significant here, rather than a (neo)feminist reclamation of difference, is the presentation of alternative choices by which the actual lives of women (and men) could be enhanced.

The next three essays, by two critics (Léon, Agacinski) influenced by postmodernism, underscore the ambivalence of the masculine position—pseudonymous and/or authorial—in Kierkegaard's writings and conclude that, as long as ambiguity abides, woman, equated with nature, is excluded from culture, which remains the privilege of one sex. As sexual difference is emphasized, so are time-honored distinctions between passive versus active, unconscious versus conscious, outer versus inner, body versus soul, with female/male on either side of the divide. Acknowledging the difficulty, nay, impossibility, of woman's existence as a human being once her lack of (self-)consciousness has been/is assumed, these articles recognize the odd circularity whereby cultural prescriptions are made regarding determinations imputed to woman's nature. According to these critics, there is an implicit danger in the celebration of woman as marginal and in the reinscription of sexual difference. For both, the fear, at once cultural and biographical (although the latter term should be taken figuratively, rather than literally), is not so much *for* the woman (as the males tend to claim) as it is *of* woman—and particularly of the feminine within.

Aiming primarily at helping women achieve personal identity and at proclaiming, as well as bringing about, the equality of rights between the sexes, the third set, in the classical tradition of feminism, not only attends to negative strains in the authorship but also perceives the tensions arising within pseudonyms, or between pseudonyms, or between pseudonyms and author, or within the author himself as being favorable to women and their liberation. According to two of these critics (Taylor,

Walsh), derogatory comments about women in the authorship stem, at least in part, from a belief in the existence of empirical differences between the sexes, rather than from assumptions of biological or innate capacities. Less favorably, however, another critic (Howe) objects to such a perception, feeling that ultimately the pseudonyms who appear supportive of women's liberation, and Kierkegaard himself, are irretrievably given to essentialist assumptions. Other essays seek—at once more, and less, radically—to establish a feminist discourse of empowerment by urging both a condemnation of inappropriate male behavior and a reappropriation of specifically womanly qualities through an emphasis on connectedness (Duran), subjectivity (Walsh), silence (Berry), or devotedness (Lorraine) in the texts. Shifting attention away from Kierkegaard's treatment of women to the role of the feminine in his metaphysics, they read the specifically feminine commended in his works as inscribing qualities that all—males and females—can equally benefit from developing.

We do not mean for these distinctions to be rigid. Often it has been difficult to delineate between trends, as, say, no maieutic is ever without some potential for empowerment, and no reclaiming of specific qualities without its dangers of exclusion. Appropriately, given the dialectical character of the authorship, many of the themes treated in the volume could be organized as a series of diptychs: essentialism/existentialism, speech/silence, sexual and gender differences (either fostered or canceled)/indifference, objectivity/subjectivity, married life/single life, heterosexuality/homosexuality, social/spiritual equality. This variety reflects the multiplicity of Kierkegaard's concerns and also his fascination with alternate existential possibilities; to an amazing extent, it anticipates problems that, as rifts between the personal and the public have intensified, have become increasingly acute in our own century.

The Kierkegaardian authorship traditionally has been the object of a bipartite, or a tripartite division. The former arrangement reflects the separation between aesthetic and religious productions or between pseudonymous and acknowledged writings. As for the latter, or tripartite schema, it distinguishes between the philosopher's early pseudonymous (1843–44), middle transitional (1845–48), and late religious (1849–55) writings. We have striven to maintain a balance between these conventional divisions; not all, but certainly a substantial number, of Kierkegaard's writings in each division/period are subjected to feminist analysis and critique in the pages that follow.

The first essay in the volume, by Wanda Warren Berry, begins where

Kierkegaard himself began, to wit, with the aesthetic production upon which he embarked in the wake of the rupture with Regine Olsen, the young girl to whom he became engaged on 11 October 1941, only to realize one day later that he had made a mistake—not because he did not love her but because of inner conflicts that prevented him from marrying. Berry's focus is the first volume of *Either/Or* (1843), which, in her view, raises the problematic of "the heterosexual imagination," or the envisioning of erotic relationships as being limited to rapports with the opposite sex. Observing that ironically the females depend upon the males for their (literary) existence, Berry nonetheless notices progress in the work in that, over against Johannes the Seducer, Kierkegaard's paradigmatic reflective seducer, A, the anonymous scriptor of the volume, is not only aware of the falsifications of the sociocultural—including the role and significance of class—but also able to experience the lives of the women from the interior, and to project for them what looks like real possibilities beyond their reflective sorrow, beyond their aesthetic despair. Yet, the understanding and the hope are short-lived; A, animated by his own aesthetic heterosexual imagination, projects antithetical views of/for the other sex.

In Berry's opinion, Kierkegaard uses the difference between the sexes to denounce as masculinist and sexist certain attitudes current in mid-nineteenth-century Denmark: By subverting fixed or stereotyped ideas of masculinity and femininity, the philosopher shows the limitations and the risks inherent in emphasizing difference and in depicting each sex as being fulfilled only through the other. To the stereotype of woman as "being-for-others" corresponds that of man as "being-for-self," with the result that, if man is able to separate himself from the "for-other" moment of his own self, or relationality, woman is granted no "for-self." When the stress is placed on the difference between the sexes rather than on their common humanity, nefarious consequences are to be expected: (1) Aversive reactions to same-sex relations (women loving women and/or women identified with women); (2) victimization of women; (3) sado-masochism. Why, asks Berry, is aesthetic existence always a source of suffering for women? By being "for-others," women, whose self-image is essentially "for man," are victims of an enemy whose views they have internalized. Yet, they are no more ontologically "for-other" than men are ontologically "for-self": Both man and woman are equally "before God." For a fuller treatment of these questions, Berry directs the reader to *The Concept of Anxiety* (1844) where, although emphasized, the "generic

difference," or inherent differences between the sexes, is declared ultimately irrelevant within the context of the religious.

As for the first volume of *Either/Or*, Berry argues that, insofar as its
perspective is that of the romanticized aesthetic consciousness, it embraces dualistic distortions and grants preferential treatment to heterosexuality. In Johannes the Seducer's pathological masculine
heterosexuality, Berry discerns not so much a hyperbole as an accurate
representation of what typically happens within romanticized patriarchy
with its dualistic distortions and its express repugnance to same-sex relations. By creating in this work an author and characters who cause an
aversive reaction to heterosexist stereotypes, Kierkegaard forewarns
against giving universal extension to this type of imagination and provides a negative maieutic that challenges gays and lesbians to acquire
ethico-religious selfhood, just like heterosexuals, yet, not through "penetrating the generic difference," but through "penetrating the generic
sameness."

In Chapter 2, Birgit Bertung, who turns her attention to one of Kierkegaard's most important later writings, *The Sickness unto Death* (1849),
chooses to concentrate on the concept of human being and on the analysis of despair provided by Anti-Climacus, the pseudonymous author of
this work. A human being is a synthesis of finitude and infinitude, necessity and freedom, temporality and eternity, in which, through God, the
self relates to itself. Any imbalance in these elements generates despair.
True despair, which alone is aware of being in despair, expresses itself in
two ways: that of not willing to be oneself (identified as "feminine") and
that of willing to be oneself (termed "masculine"). Yet, no more than the
latter is limited to males is the former restricted to females. In Bertung's
opinion, feminine despair is to be understood as an empirical or a cultural
phenomenon, not as a biological determination of something specifically
womanly. Emphasizing the equality mandated by the concept of love,
Bertung shares Berry's awareness of the necessary cancellation of the
man-woman distinction in the relationship to God. According to the
interpretation of the text given by the Danish critic, a woman can be in
two relations—a spiritual relationship to God, and a body-soul relationship to her husband—with the consequence that a problem for her at the
ethical level is often that of confusing the two relationships. As with the
awareness manifested by A in Berry's essay, the misinterpretation, Bertung is careful to point out, is not grounded in anything biologically
necessary, or absolute, but merely in an empirical, historical, hence alter-

able, reality. Both critics agree on the internalization of the negative process by women themselves; whereas, however, Berry envisions the possibility of new modes of relating, Bertung concentrates on what a clear delineation of concepts might signify for women, as well as for men—Kierkegaard included—who refuse the patristic and patriarchal notion of the subjugation of one sex by the other.

In *The Concept of Anxiety*, taking up a direction indicated by Berry, Bertung finds that, if woman is more anxious than man, it is because of her greater inclination to abandon freedom, and to satisfy herself with "being-for-others." Of special significance to Bertung is the absolute difference in the body-mind-spirit synthesis that, constitutive of each sex, distinguishes it from the other. Both in intercourse and in childbirth, where she exists almost merely for the sake of the new individual, woman is at the extreme end of the synthesis; that is, at a point where one element (*soma*) prevails at the expense of the other two and where the distance between the components is greatest. Far from deeming Kierkegaard—even at his most vituperative, as in the direct attack on women in the last years of his life—complicit with the system within which his thought is embedded, Bertung reads his method as a maieutics meant to encourage women to reaction and self-activation. Evident in the two important texts analyzed here is not an opposition to woman's personal liberation, or to woman herself, but a disallowance of the stereotypically deficient creature that society has made of woman—an irony at the very heart of the Kierkegaardian project.

Julia Watkin (Chapter 3) also feels the need to address the question of the extremely negative polemic of Kierkegaard's later years (1854–55). For her as well, the offensive stance adopted by the philosopher must be read as a maieutics: not specifically as an attack on woman, but as an alarm sounded against those for whom Christianity is in a smug, complacent, comfy-bourgeois collusion with the world. To the question of knowing whether Kierkegaard's harsh comments regarding women (and marriage) referred only to his sociocultural situation, her answer is an unqualified yes. Yet, between her position and Bertung's there are substantive differences regarding both the content and the method of Kierkegaard's message. For Watkin, as for Bertung, the philosopher's misogyny is only apparent, but for a different reason: It is in fact a "misogamy," or an attack on marriage as that institution was understood by the society of his day. This critic rejects a psychological-pathological explanation; more radically than Bertung, she propounds that the extremism of the strategy adopted by Kierkegaard is not a later development, but is perfectly consistent with other fundamental assumptions of the authorship. Far from becoming "distorted in his later writings about marriage and sexuality," Kierkegaard moves to an affirmation of asceticism, not as an epiphenomenon, but as a logical consequence implied from the very beginning of his production.

Addressing the same question of whether Kierkegaard was a misogynist and/or a misogamist from a different angle, Robert Perkins (Chapter 4) acquits him of both charges and argues, on the contrary, that Kierkegaard was at once a critic of aesthetic expressions of misogyny and an apologist for, rather than an antagonist toward, the institution of marriage. Examining "In Vino Veritas," the first part of *Stages on Life's Way* (1845), Perkins interprets this piece as a modern reinscription of Plato's *Symposium*. Whereas Plato's symposium is concerned with male homosexual relations, Kierkegaard's focuses exclusively on heterosexual rapports (another example of "the heterosexual imagination" at work in the authorship?) and is intended as an indirect refutation not only of ancient and modern forms of misogyny but also of the intellectual, transcendent vision of Plato that leads away from love of the individual to "that great sea of beauty" which is the ultimate object of Platonic eros.

Emphasizing the importance that the category of the individual and concrete human relations held for Kierkegaard, Perkins bases his interpretation primarily on the last scene of the piece, whose predominant feature is the surprise appearance of a married couple, Judge William and his wife. Perkins understands the introduction of these figures as a defense of "the Christian-Lutheran heritage of gender relations as defined by the nineteenth-century bourgeoisie" in opposition to the egoistic, abstract, aggressive misogyny of modern, masculine aestheticism that sets itself against marriage and the possibility of any meaningful (mutual and equal) relationship between the sexes. Although Perkins recognizes that the Judge, as shown elsewhere in the authorship, "is not entirely liberated from the patriarchal views of woman and of the relation between the sexes prevalent at the time," he nevertheless finds an authentic expression of human intimacy in the marital love of this couple that is foreign to and utterly lacking in the modern aesthetic view of relations between the sexes.

In the process of illuminating Kierkegaard's negative stance toward aesthetic expressions of misogyny and misogamy, Perkins also brings to bear a brief but revealing Marxist/feminist critique of the lavish and self-indulgent social setting of the two symposia, which are designed as "extravaganzas sponsored by men of the wealthy upper classes for their own exclusive titillation and entertainment." Concerning the plight of women, in unity with all the previous critics Perkins finds that, if the five speakers in Kierkegaard's symposium are right in observing that women tend to misinterpret the concept of existence more often than men, it is because of the constraints society places on them. With Berry, he is sensitive to the differences among women and to women's tendency within patriarchy to oppress one another with self-definitions that are as exclusionary as those created by men. Women come from different races, ethnic groups, and economic backgrounds, differences that often seem more striking than the shared identity of belonging to one gender, or one sex.

Céline Léon (Chapter 5), in the first of two contributions to this volume, shows the rift of woman being perceived as either aesthetically immediate, or immediately religious in the writings where Judge William, Kierkegaard's paradigmatic ethicist and married man, figures prominently: *Either/Or*, Part II, and "Some Reflections on Marriage in Answer to Objections" in *Stages on Life's Way*. Against Perkins, for whom the judge's marriage signifies an ironic refutation of misogyny (and misogamy), Léon argues that, since ethical existence requires independence, woman's intrinsic relationality to her husband renders highly problematic her inscription within Kierkegaard's second sphere. In effect, the Judge's ethical realm is also that of a re-marking of the contrasting pairs of opposites that have traditionally legitimized the lower status imputed to woman: Weak, she is strong, yet strong in her weakness, she is less than a human being. Giving herself, she is inferior to man, because she does so naturally; not giving herself, she is unfeminine, with the consequence that, either way, she loses. She is more herself by not being herself, yet, not being herself, how can she be a self as required of ethical (and religious) existence? Whereas Kierkegaard's original disjunction, his Either/Or, encodes man's choice between the aesthetic and the ethical life, woman's is a nonchoice between aesthetic existence, to which she is said naturally to belong, and emancipation, against which both pseudonym and author prescribe. Feminine, she is less than ethical, (a) feminist, she is less than a woman. Léon's contention, in sharp contrast with all four preceding critics', is that sexual difference is everywhere inscribed (aesthetically, ethically, and religiously) for/by the ethical, and that this inscription, far from pointing to the force of circumstances, registers the endorsement of essentialism. Never mind the contradiction of enjoining women to remain/become that which they are naturally!

Having noted the telling dichotomy between the quantitative (female reproduction) and the qualitative (masculine creativity), Léon's essay ponders the rationales undergirding the dread of feminine achievement in a progression that, because of the recurrence of the associations made between independence and sexuality (expressed or repressed), reveals that the fear is not so much *for* the woman, as it is *of* the woman, and of what she signifies for the conception males have of themselves as men— whether the unease be linked to misgivings concerning the risk of (a) general effeminization, or, more threateningly, to apprehensions vis-à-vis one's own ambivalence. For Léon, the Judge's homophobic panic at the thought of woman's emancipation betrays unexplained and unresolved inner tensions.

These tensions reproduce at the higher level of the ethical those by which an aesthete, like A, is inwardly divided. But, recognizing the same ambivalence in Kierkegaard himself, Léon finds it difficult to subscribe to the notion that the philosopher is an ironical feminist bent on rectifying the wrongs done to women, or to the claim that his thought lends it-self to an affirmation of same-sex relations. Struck by the ubiquitousness of the misogyny, she argues that the place allocated to woman by the ethical permits (even at this relatively early stage), not an assessment of possibilities granted woman toward her liberation, but rather an incursion into what constitutes man's fear, namely, that of (the) woman without and of the feminine within.

Using primarily three Kierkegaardian texts—two pseudonymous ones, *Repetition* (1843) and *The Sickness unto Death* (1849), as well as the non-pseudonymous discourse, *The Woman Who Was a Sinner* (1850)—as dis-seminating pivots, postmodernist Sylviane Agacinski (Chapter 6), following in Derrida's footsteps, embarks on a "double session" of her own. Along with pondering the sexual difference, her essay also inscribes the biographical encoded in the anguish of biosexual fantasies. Alluding to Kierkegaard's first published piece, Agacinski notes that woman was his first reason for coming to writing. Here, however, she is concerned with drawing out the interconnections between writing, woman, and rep-etition (or the lack thereof), the aesthetic/religious movement whereby one is reborn or receives oneself again, which she sees as occurring in Kierkegaard's texts through a masculine appropriation of the powers of women, or the feminization of writing. Ironically, the males, who depend on women for their literal existence, have reversed the situation by having the women depend on them for their literary existence (as already noted by Berry) or, as Agacinski argues here, for their existence in literature. Having (re-)marked (on) the hierarchical oppositions that divide reality in favor of one sex, Agacinski notices their duplication in the form of double binds that, by conforming to biblical injunctions, appear to glorify the feminine—the reappropriation of which she opposes. For one thing, this is not the way in which women are portrayed in their daily lives; for another, these privileged positions are said to be constitutive of woman's essence, and, because of their constant association with certain negative qualities (tears, weakness as strength or virtue, submission, renunciation) they reinscribe stereotypes that have always harmed women and have traditionally been used as a way to control their sexuality, their reproduction, their beings. Whichever way one looks at it, woman's relationality to man abides throughout the authorship as a major and inalterable impediment on the road to self-fulfillment. The feminine, in other words, is the reinscription of qualities that men are praised for acquiring, and women are blamed for not manifesting—although these perfections are allegedly inherent in their nature. What others have seen as grounded in historical circumstances, Agacinski perceives as essentialist, innate, ineradicable traits. Sardonically, were woman to be "better" than man, she would be, if not "worse," at least not as "good" as he, because she would be so *naturally*. Agacinski finds irony in the most injurious, delirious deprecations, as Bertung has; in her view, however, the irony is not in favor of women, but at their expense.

Whereas for Julia Watkin the single life represents a valid option, consistently embraced by Kierkegaard, for Agacinski the conspiracy Kierkegaard imagined to have existed between the state, the Lutheran Church, and the family is a way to exclude woman, sexual difference, and to proclaim (masculine) indifference in their stead. Incidentally, over against Perkins, Agacinski re-reads Kierkegaard's re-reading of Plato's *Symposium* as the glorification of heavenly pederasty. Far from being a misogamy, the antagonism toward marriage is attendant upon the misogyny, and the erection of masculine indifference upon the eradication of the sexual difference/woman. By contrast with Berry and Bertung, for whom the cancellation of the generic difference in the religious is empowering to woman, Agacinski sees that in man's chosen castration lies woman's unwilled demotion.

In a second contribution to the volume (Chapter 7), Céline Léon notes, as does Agacinski, the contradictions said to reside in woman's being: her "double nature" and the double binds in which she is caught because of the constraint of opposite and contradictory demands placed on her being. Whereas, however, Agacinski dwells on a series of "apartés" thematically linking various Kierkegaardian texts, Léon turns her attention to two works—*Fear and Trembling* (1843) and *Stages on Life's Way* (1845)—that elucidate each other. In Léon's essay, as in Agacinski's, sexual difference figures prominently, as does the eventual inscription of (masculine) indifference, by way of the abolition of the alternative / sex / woman / the difference. However, rather than having the rejection of sex presented as Kierkegaard's Christian solution, as in Agacinski's postmodern approach (True Christianity requires virility, hence castration), or in Watkin's more traditional one (True Christianity favors the single state), Léon reads the Christian solution to which Kierkegaard came as sublimation. For her, the anguish is not of bisexual fantasies, but of the feminine within epitomized and reproduced in the feminine without. Also explored in these pages are the positions of woman, yet not so much—as with Agacinski—of the possibilities woman represents for man as of those with which he is willing to invest her. Here too it can be seen that, by ideally co-opting woman's literal aptitude for impregnation, man bars her from an ideal (re-)appropriation of her *proprium,* to wit, the "feminine." Over against Berry and Bertung, for whom cancellation of the generic difference in the religious is everything for women, Léon views the establishment of indifference *hic et nunc* as a (frightened) man's way to confront/dispense with feminine difference.

Having begun with the dissimilarities that exist between Quidam and Quaedam, the anonymous male and female lovers in *Stages on Life's Way*, Léon ponders the odd twist whereby, in an authorship that celebrates the ethical quality of an engagement just as much as it does that of marriage, no room is made for a successful turn of events where the betrothed are concerned. In the many instances presented, this sidestepping of the ethical-universal is linked to a young man's acknowledgment of the sexual difference and/or of the existence of a secret, and is effected by means of the idiosyncratically Kierkegaardian concept of "the exception." Whether aesthetically or religiously understood, such a notion allows a man to discard the woman in his life and to achieve self-actualization precisely through the removal.

For an elucidation of that which allows the drama to unfold, one must

turn, Léon claims, to the earlier *Fear and Trembling*, where the pseudonymous Johannes de Silentio envisages, through a series of ethico-religious
conflicts, the disjunctions that can result from various combinations of
the dichotomies speech/silence and marriage/the single life. A close examination of the crucial moment that, in each one of these sketches,
justifies embracing the alternative silence/the single life, reveals something of Quidam's—and beyond him, Kierkegaard's—secret. Léon notices that the chasm which lies between lover and beloved—according to
Silentio, a chasm so vast as to amount to a language difference—typifies
the sexual difference. Since an essential distinction presented in the same
work is that which separates the knight of faith (Abraham) from the
knight of resignation, Léon considers the fiancés in light of these two
movements. Knights of faith, Quidam/Kierkegaard would have married,
confident that God would remove the difficulty that lay between them
and the beloved. But knights of faith they were not, merely knights of
infinite resignation; that is, men with just enough faith to let go of the
beloved, yet not enough to believe that she would be restored to them in
this life. In other words, the predilection manifested by pseudonym and
author for silence and the single life is tied to the necessity with which
they are faced of having to deal with the other('s) sex.

Also finding thematic links between texts, Mark Lloyd Taylor's (Chapter 8) analysis of *Concluding Unscientific Postscript* (1846) leads to the
recognition that this volume, ascribed to the pseudonym Johannes Climacus, is typical of other Kierkegaardian works in that, like them, it
unfolds a threefold pattern of critique, relativization, and commendation,
not merely of women but also of the feminine. Taylor agrees with Bertung
and Watkin that the Kierkegaardian polemic is to be read ironically; he
is, however, more nuanced in his assessment—if only because he discovers a greater complexity in the very structure of the ironic intent.
Exploring the autobiographical texture and architecture of the text as a
way of attending to its "gendered body," Taylor sees the pseudonym's
tripartite critique unfolding as follows: (1) a critique of bourgeois man
and his values manifested through criticism of woman and of womanly
qualities; (2) a relativization of the difference between man and woman
by virtue of their common relationship to God; (3) a commendation of
qualities typically bestowed upon women (sympathy, relationality)—
qualities that, religiously manifested as faith, love, piety, and trust, constitute exemplars for the highest sphere, that is, models that all, females
and males alike, would do well to (re-)appropriate. This reappropriation

Taylor perceives as occurring in at least three ways in Climacus's book: in his concept of writing; in his characterization of the dominant male culture of mid-nineteenth-century Europe; and in his view of Christian faith, which, like feminine inwardness, is directed outward to an other.

In detecting a critique of bourgeois complacency by the pseudonym, Taylor is very close to Bertung and Watkin; in perceiving a relativization of differences in the text, he echoes Berry's criticism of the heterosexist imagination and anticipates the next essay by Walsh; and in noticing the commendation of the specifically feminine here and elsewhere in Kierkegaard's authorship, he prefigures the gynocentric re-readings of Duran, Walsh, Berry, and Lorraine. Unlike Léon and some other interpreters for whom the authorship inscribes Kierkegaard's autobiography, Taylor reads the text strictly as an account of Climacus's intellectual development. From one end of the book to the other, Taylor traces the pseudonym's (self-)perceived advance from a youthful, feminine self infatuated with renowned male figures to a more mature, independent, masculine self: that of a dialectician with no woman in his life and whose sole relation to the erotic is through abstractions.

The next essay (Chapter 9), by Sylvia Walsh, returns us to *The Sickness unto Death* for an analysis of the continuum of despair, whose extremities are constituted by feminine despair (unwillingness to be oneself, despair of weakness), and masculine despair (willingness to be oneself, despair of defiance). Whereas feminine despair indicates a lack of masculine self-assertion, masculine, or defiant, despair "results from an individual's unwillingness to adopt a feminine mode of selfhood." That the distinctions are not rigid in an absolute sense is evident on two accounts: (1) Anti-Climacus gives mostly male examples to illustrate feminine despair; and (2) both modalities—although they are so in different, and usually inverse, proportions—are always simultaneously present in every human being. If woman needs to become more masculine, man needs to become more feminine; what is desired is a balance of both masculine and feminine "modes of relating" to oneself and to others (including the divine). It would therefore appear that the ideal of human selfhood is one of psychological androgyny, a cultivation of both feminine and masculine characteristics in men and women, a complementary wholeness that holds feminine and masculine qualities to be equally valuable and equally necessary to the formation of a fully developed and healthy human individual, of either sex.

Do Anti-Climacus's observations about feminine despair in women apply to women in general? Do they imply beliefs about woman's nature? Or was he only criticizing the women of his time, as contingently unrealized selves? Do sex roles result from natural differences between man and woman, or does Anti-Climacus believe them to be constructed in large part by empirical factors? Like Bertung, Walsh stresses the necessity to differentiate between that which is absolutely inevitable in woman, and that which is only relative or contingent; that is, socially constructed, culturally informed, and historically produced. In Walsh's opinion, Anti-Climacus praises woman's devotedness—a quality he understands as a natural characteristic—but cautions against woman's tendency to lose herself in giving herself to others (in his view, a culturally or historically acquired trait). Finding the thrust of his analysis quite liberating for women, Walsh feels that Bertung does not go far enough in showing the potential for selfhood that, in her opinion, Anti-Climacus links to changes in the historical condition.

Yet, less optimistically than Taylor and more in tune with Agacinski, Walsh guards against the danger of falling back (if only unwittingly) on traditional stereotypical views of femininity. Pointing to Carol Gilligan's model for women's development—a model in which both individuality and relatedness are included—Walsh maintains that Kierkegaard does not sufficiently recognize the interdependence of these factors in females. She warns also against the danger inherent in the cultivation of the latter, a stance that has traditionally favored and justified male dominance by means of the subjugation of women. With Berry and Taylor, she sees a contradiction emerge. On the one hand, Kierkegaard declares that, since the basic structure of selfhood is presumably the same for both sexes, essentially (before God, religiously), human beings are metaphysically and morally equal. On the other hand, he maintains that substantive differences exist between woman, in whom are embodied relatedness and self-giving, and man, who epitomizes self-awareness and individuation.

Walsh's claim that Kierkegaard, in persona Anti-Climacus, advocates something like psychological androgyny in his view of selfhood is expressly challenged by Leslie A. Howe (Chapter 10), in whose opinion woman, repeatedly and systematically associated with the finite, the sensuous, the relative, and a lack of reflection or self-consciousness, could never carry out the ethico-religious task of realizing selfhood, or at least not so well as man. Because of hierarchical assumptions about the relative value of certain human characteristics, because of the superior value ascribed to self-consciousness (male) as a mode of relating over the natural and the instinctual (female), and also because of woman's relating to God only through the male, Howe finds it impossible not to conclude that woman is, and remains, a lesser self in Kierkegaard's authorship. Furthermore, were her empirical reality to become altered, woman, whose synthesis strongly leans to one side, could not be significantly different from what she is.

Nevertheless, Howe shares Walsh's feeling that, even if one assumes—as Bertung does—that Kierkegaard was using women to teach a lesson to the complacent Danish Church, the difficulty remains of a stereotypical linking of women to degradation. In addition, she argues that, even if one feels that Kierkegaard points to an androgynous ideal of selfhood, as Walsh claims, he fails to present such an ideal, and maintains instead essentialist characterizations regarding the respective natures of men and women. If these were to be abandoned, she concedes, then Kierkegaard would provide "much of the necessary conceptual apparatus" on which to build a truly balanced or androgynous view of the self; but whether such an account could be called "Kierkegaardian," Howe thinks, is questionable.

Jane Duran (Chapter 11), whose inspiration is from Lorraine Code, Lynn Nelson, Nancy Chodorow, Dorothy Dinnerstein, and Susan Bordo, sees specificity and connectedness—elements central to Kierkegaard's philosophy—as emblematic of gynocentric thinking. Although aware of the problematic aspect of retrieving the work of Kierkegaard for feminist theorizing, she argues that there are at least two grounds on which the authorhip can be read as an attempt to subvert masculine values of discourse and be perceived as consistent with feminist principles. What, in her opinion, distinguishes the thought of Kierkegaard from typical androcentric styles of thinking—divorced, detached, and objectifying, such as those found in Kant or Descartes—is, on the one hand, its emphasis on specificity, individuality, and a holism that emphasizes connectedness, and on the other hand, its predilection for devoted commitment and passionate attachment to others. To Duran, this gynocentric bent is evident in all three stages of existence delineated by Kierkegaard: (1) in the aesthetic, for example, in *Either/Or*, Part I, where—notwithstanding the re-creation and reification of women that obtain everywhere within that sphere—an individual as offensive as Johannes the Seducer introduces the notion of reflectivity and evinces interest (however perverted) in a woman (Cordelia) in her particularity;

(2) in the ethical, for example, in *Stages on Life's Way*, through the "ledger of responsibility" referred to by Judge William, namely, a "devoted commitment, based on a passionate devotion to a given particularity held under ethical laws, rules, and obligations" characteristic of the Judge's sphere; and (3) in the religious, for example, in *Philosophical Fragments* (1844), where the same female-centered aspects are evinced—only even more so—through the parable of the King and the Maiden.

Like Duran, Sylvia Walsh, in her second contribution to the volume (Chapter 12), discovers in Kierkegaard's *Concluding Unscientific Postscript* an attitude compatible with epistemologies developing out of some contemporary feminist theorists and reads him reconstructively as offering a perspective that contains at least five ingredients useful to feminists in their attempt to reject dichotomous thinking: (1) a nonrelativist and nonsubjectivist awareness of the limitations of objective knowledge; (2) an emphasis, even from an epistemological standpoint, on the subjective and the existential; (3) a prodding to individual self-assertion; (4) an invitation to the cultivation of passion and subjectivity; (5) a dialectical, rather than dichotomous or dualist, understanding of the relation between objectivity and subjectivity.

While Walsh finds much to admire in this text, she also casts a critical eye on what she regards as a glaring inconsistency and, from a feminist standpoint, anti-woman mentality in the philosophy of Johannes Climacus. Subjected to her feminist critique is the distinction the pseudonym makes between subjective truth—a truth he privileges qua hidden inwardness and passion—and "feminine inwardness," which in his opinion is not true inwardness because it is momentary, emotional, and externally directed. Here a point of disagreement emerges between Walsh and Taylor, as the former interprets Climacus's understanding of religious inwardness as consisting fundamentally in hidden inwardness—a hidden inwardness that is not transcended in outward relations to other human beings until Kierkegaard's later religious writings, for example, *Works of Love* (1847). Both critics take note of Climacus's identification of feminine inwardness as a lesser inwardness, but Taylor is unwilling to take the negative characterization of women altogether seriously inasmuch as the pseudonym "commends a re-appropriation of womanly qualities, while rejecting inappropriate male demeanors." Whereas, for Taylor, the ironic discrepancy, or interplay of critique and commendation, evident in the *Postscript*, permeates all of Kierkegaard's writings, Walsh locates the tension in this instance between the pseudonym and Kierkegaard himself in the knowledge that the philosopher expressly rejects hidden inwardness in his pseudonymous as well as nonpseudonymous, specifically Christian writings.

Wanda Warren Berry's second article in this volume (Chapter 13) explores the theme of "the silent woman" as it is woven in three of Kierkegaard's late religious writings: *For Self-Examination* (1851), *Judge for Yourself!* (1851–52), and *The Lilies of the Field and the Birds of the Air* (1849). Berry takes Kierkegaard to task on two accounts: (1) his having adhered to an uncritical biblical hermeneutic that counsels women to be silent; and (2) his lapses into an essentialist categorizing and a romantically patriarchal view of woman strangely at odds with his religious existential hearing/reading. Yet, having criticized these incongruencies, she reaffirms the liberatory potential of his religious existentialism and, in total disagreement with Agacinski and Léon, for whom silence is incontrovertibly tied to submission, obedience, and inaction/passivity, she uncovers a positive significance in his recurrent use of such controversial images as those of the silent woman and the seamstress. Although she concedes the culture-bound aspect of the imagery and its ties to the heterosexist imagination, she argues in its favor, at least inasmuch as one returns to it with a chosen mode of religiousness in mind useful to all within the context of a gender-neutral interpretation. By relying on the lilies of the field and the birds of the air to teach us the meaning of silence as an expression for an awareness of the transcendence of God, Kierkegaard, according to Berry, uses the concept of jest, also associated with the silent woman, to point to "religious existence as continual reliance upon a Meaning/Power beyond all finite achievement."

Unlike Howe, and in fact most of the critics of this volume, in whose opinion Kierkegaard devalues nature and woman because of her association with natural processes, Berry praises his awareness of "the interconnected harmony of being" taught by the lilies and the birds. In Kierkegaard's "jesting" silence, in the jest whereby the lilies and the birds (nature) are linked to silence, just as much as in his criticism of the rough and noisy ways of the world and his synthesizing of the finite and the infinite, she hears/reads an interesting adumbration of contemporary ecofeminism, such as is epitomized in the writings of the historical theologian Rosemary Radford Ruether. Lamenting Kierkegaard's lack of awareness of the slave woman in the fields and the proletarian woman in the sweatshop, Berry, whose Marxist/feminist critique echoes that of Perkins, deems as racist, sexist, and classist a stance that, ignoring real women's lives, rationalizes oppression.

Are women more grounded than men in the everyday world of the particular, the world of immanence? Giving this question a positive answer, Tamsin Lorraine (Chapter 14) ascertains that, in *The Sickness unto Death*, the pseudonym Anti-Climacus enables us to discover, through the feminine, a form of subjectivity of primary importance for the development of all human beings. Transforming the "being-for-others," which Berry (for good reasons) viewed negatively, into a "being-with-others," Lorraine argues in favor of a transformation whereby we come to understand our possibilities, our capacities to change ourselves. Sensitive to resonances between Anti-Climacus's Danish Lutheran depiction of self-hood and Julia Kristeva's Lacanian interpretation, she espies a model of selfhood whereby traditional gender stereotypes are challenged, and innovative possibilities tendered for humane ways of living and relating to one another. Her Kristevian reading of Anti-Climacus has despair and sin relating to an imbalance in the semiotic (unconscious/pre-Oedipal/imaginary, maternal) and symbolic (conscious/Oedipal/patriarchal) modalities of subjectivity. But because, in Lorraine's opinion, Kristeva's psychoanalytic model reinforces gender in a way problematic for a feminist cause, the critic favors the paradigm offered by religion, at least as it is understood in Anti-Climacus's concept of the God-relationship.

Observing, as Bertung and Watkin have, that Anti-Climacus appeals to women for examples of what approaches his conception of the appropriate role for a human being vis-à-vis God, and recognizing, with Walsh, a feminine positioning (or at least one that transcends the boundaries of a traditionally masculine self) of that relation, Lorraine believes the feminine will enable us to escape atomistic individualism. Her ideal, however, is not androgynous, as for Walsh and Howe, but rather starts from womanly qualities whose development she wishes to foster. In her view, Anti-Climacus's religious discourse is an amatory discourse of self-transformation, a "liberating 'cure,' " such as the one wished for by Kristeva, inasmuch as the pseudonym's depiction of the God-relationship adumbrates Kristeva's portrayal of a relationship to a loving (imaginary) father. Faith in an infinite other, beyond the Oedipal situation and the paternal Law, Lorraine argues, suggests possibilities inconceivable within the boundaries of the Oedipal frame; to wit, unprecedented configurations of the self in relationship whereby multiple differences can be acknowledged and our understanding of sexual difference re[de]fined. Witnessed by this infinite Other (Anti-Climacus), the self-in-world (Kristeva) will encounter the stranger within, as well as without; effectively transform itself by incorporating disturbing, inconvenient, or contradictory aspects of its own reality; and by enacting reciprocal attentiveness, recognize alternative systems or possibilities, and build ethical community. Although Lorraine is careful to sound a note of warning against reinscribing essentialism, she believes that the risks involved in such a re-reading of Kierkegaard are outweighed by the possibilities proffered for feminist politics.

Made evident from the above is not only the uncontested male bias of Western philosophy, but also the reality of feminist interpretation as a contested ground. Was Kierkegaard a feminist maieutically pretending otherwise? Was he a good father who, with a little help from a feminist re-vision, can bring an important message of liberation to culturally conditioned women? Or do his very limitations make him a father whose insights should be carefully sorted out? Is he, rather, just another "dead-beat dad," who fails to deliver on the promise of freedom made to women? When all is said and done, does Kierkegaard teach us anything that can be useful for feminist theorizing, or for women interested in finding themselves outside the maze of patriarchal constructs? The answer is yes, insofar as his writings expose prejudices against women, subvert typically masculine modes of behavior and discourse, and, by privileging existence, singularity, plurality, and continuity as well as rejecting a disembodied, authorial voice, not only value, but also inscribe, the feminine. But it is also yes when emancipation is opposed, when equality is in(de)finitely postponed, when woman is depreciated, dichotomized, discarded, excluded, or spoken for, when stereotypes and essentialist statements about her nature are taken up and embraced. For, whether we agree, or disagree, much can be learned from an exposure whereby, either way, what is awakened is "dead or sleeping consciousness." In the words of Adrienne Rich: "This awakening . . . has already affected the lives of millions of women, even those who don't know it yet. It is also affecting the lives of men, even those who deny its claims upon them."[1]

In the wake of this exposure, we are faced with the same multiplicity of questions repeatedly posed by feminists/women everywhere: Should women become self-assertive and independent like men, or should they seek to preserve their difference(s)? Should the differences between man and woman be reduced to a minimum, or should they be cultivated? Do women, by virtue of the qualities with which they have been traditionally invested, have in fact the advantage of a privileged situation regarding new models of existence? Can the development of such traits as devotedness, sympathy, and so forth, provide an antidote to despair and isolation, and to the diremption of materialism? The complex of questions raised ultimately points to the difficult, but enlivening, relation between postmodernism and feminism, and between feminist theory and feminist practice.

Dangers threaten on all sides, as women/feminists must navigate between the Scylla of abstraction, and the Charybdis of distortion/misreading: While feminism began with an identity politics that often did not take differences among women into account, postmodernism, leaving us with either a cultivation of difference, or a multiplicity of "differences," tends to abandon feminist politics for the high road of theory. Some feminists, concerned about postmodernism's often inaccessible and esoteric language, view with suspicion the authority it has progressively acquired. Wary of what they perceive to be essentialist tendencies, they fear a discourse, an *écriture* that, "pure" and confined to academic circles, can remain divorced from practice, and have very little to do with the reality of women's lives. On the other hand, the unrestrained admiration for a writer (male, in this case), often manifested as the determination to exonerate him by placing him in a context he would never have acknowledged as his own, can be a perilous ventriloquism that, putting words into the mouth of the father, prevents a full assessment of the biases that inhabited him and his culture. By minimalizing the damage done to women, the reappropriation risks falling short of the express intent of being at their service.

Should feminism concern itself with establishing ideals grounded in the acknowledgment of traditionally feminine qualities; that is, a relational mode of being that tends to value self-sacrifice? Are ideals appropriate? How can one articulate a "feminine" mode of being without grafting this project upon essentialist characterizations? Does the use of stereotyped characterizations of the sexes risk perpetuating dangerous cultural identifications of women—and men? Do the feminists who oppose femininity to masculinity ultimately reinscribe Western dichotomous thinking, even when they do not associate these terms with women and men? By propounding a common ideal for all, does androgyny, by combining traditionally masculine traits with traditionally feminine ones, constitute a problem for feminism?[2]

No simple answers are propounded, nor are they likely to be forthcoming. As Tina Chanter perceptively underscores: "The fact that what unites women is also at the same time what women seek to overcome—namely their marginalization—produces a contradiction that feminism must confront."[3] What can be hoped for is the conceptualization of woman's subjectivity as a form of intersubjective recognition (a relation between self and other) that allows for—in Kierkegaardian dialectical fashion—both identity and concrete differences. This relation between self and other, this search for (a group) identity should not deny differences among women (class, race, ethnicity, religion, sexual preference) nor those between women and men. Neither should it let these differences rule out the possibility of solidarity among women and a recognition of our common humanity and rightful equality, both social and spiritual, with men. The tensions between the need for unity, or togetherness among women and between women and men, and the need to leave room for difference, or alterity, can be addressed through vigilance against collapsing difference into sameness, or, for that matter, sameness into difference. Teresa de Lauretis longs for a "house of difference" that has room for all.[4] It is our hope that the essays in this volume may lead us closer to its door.

Notes

1. Adrienne Rich, "When We Dead Awaken: Writing as Re-Vision (1971)," in *The Norton Anthology of Literature by Women: The Tradition in English*, ed. Sandra M. Gilbert and Susan Gubar (New York: Norton, 1975), 2045.

2. Cf. Janice Raymond, *The Transsexual Empire: The Making of the She-Male* (Boston: Beacon, 1979).

3. Tina Chanter, *Ethics of Eros: Irigaray's Rewriting of the Philosophers* (New York: Routledge, 1995), 30.

4. Teresa de Lauretis, "Upping the Anti [sic] in Feminist Theory," in *Conflicts in Feminism*, ed. Marianne Hirsch and Evelyn Fox Keller (New York: Routledge, 1990), 266.

1

The Heterosexual Imagination and Aesthetic Existence in Kierkegaard's *Either/Or*, Part I

Wanda Warren Berry

Kierkegaard's pseudonymous authorship is populated with "fictive lover figures" who Kresten Nordentoft says share the concept of erotic love which is formulated in the essay on "The Immediate Erotic Stages" in *Either/Or, 1*. Nordentoft characterizes this view of eros as "now fixed upon sexual differentiation, that is (from the essay's masculine point of view) upon 'the idea of the feminine.' "[1] This analysis encourages us to look at *Either/Or, 1* in terms of the questions we have been learning to raise about fixed or stereotyped ideas of masculinity and femininity. It also implies that we might improve our understanding of this volume by placing its "masculine point of view" more inclusively, emphasizing what I am calling "the heterosexual imagination" which it expresses. By claiming that *Either/Or, 1* expresses "the heterosexual imagination" I am calling for courage to enter the very controversial space surrounding contemporary discussions of sexual preference as well as sexual identity. Tensions are high in this arena and the following analysis will be misunderstood if careful attention is not given to certain important aspects of my approach.

First, for the purpose of this essay, it is essential that the reader note carefully my definition of its key phrase: *the heterosexual imagination is the conscious or unconscious tendency to express dualities, polarities, or dialectics found in human existence in terms of imagery of the two sexes.* In heterosexual imagination the "otherness" (*heteros,* "other") of a meaning to its dialectical partner is made concrete in terms of male-female imagery. For much of human history and in most cultures the tendency toward such imagery has been unnamed and unrecognized as a specific form of imagination, since heterosexuality was presumed to be universal or, at least, normative. Recently, however, scientific research as well as social movements have relativized heterosexuality by making it clear that a significant number of human beings are erotically oriented to the same sex by factors usually considered not subject to moral decision.[2]

Next, it is important to note that "the heterosexual imagination" is not always "hetero*sexist.*" For this reason, my exegeses of *Either/Or, 1* are entered through the former term, rather than the latter, since I do not want to prejudice the reading of this complex text. Heterosexual imagery can manifest healthy, nonoppressive existential dynamics so long as it is acknowledged as expressing a specific form of imagination, rather than assumed to be universally and exclusively relevant. A heterosexual imagination that tends to rule out the possibility that authentically human existence also might be imaged through relations between members of the same sex could be called heterosex*ist.* In a parallel way, I think that what we might call "the sexual imagination" becomes sex*ist* when it uses human sexuality to image existence in such a way as to deny full humanity to one sex or the other. In the following analysis it will become clear that I view both sex*ist* and heterosex*ist* imaginations as pathological, since they tend to fixate human development and obviate healthy existential dialectics.[3] Kierkegaard himself may not have supported this view; but I believe it to be a contemporary appropriation of his fundamental emphasis on human becoming through the concrete synthesis of freedom and necessity.

In addition, it is important to keep in mind that I intend to treat *Either/Or, 1* as an artistic construct. Kierkegaard creates in this work a particular kind of aesthetic consciousness that should be seen as characterizing the pseudonym/anonym, A, rather than Kierkegaard himself. I shall make judgments about Kierkegaard's own attitudes toward sexual identity and sexual orientations only through comparisons to other works considered closer to his own point of view. Initially, I am only asking my readers to entertain the interesting possibility that the heterosexual imagery was consciously developed in this "novel" as a way to express an aesthetic consciousness. It can be argued that Kierkegaard himself transcends heterosexism in *Either/Or, 1* by creating an author and characters who cause an aversive reaction to such stereotyping. This, however, probably was not his conscious purpose, but followed from his concern to encourage a leap away from aesthetic existence (*PV*, 74–75).

In *Either/Or, 1*, Kierkegaard created a massive, diverse volume that he intended to unify in what he called the aesthetic point of view, a mode of existing that is properly called a "stage," both because all humans begin in it and because there can be development beyond it. The question is whether this unity coordinates with the fact that each section of the volume in some way establishes its meaning through pictures of male-female relations. Indeed, starting with Victor Eremita's prefatory warning to "the reader of the fair sex" (*EO*, 1:14–15), the whole volume has much of its dynamic in the "fixation upon sexual differentiation" that Nordentoft identifies. In some essays this dynamic surfaces only in passing similes or brief examples used to develop literary, psychological, or philosophical comments (see, e.g., *EO*, 1, "Diapsalmata": 25, 26, 27, 29, 32, and so forth). In such segments of the volume as "The Seducer's Diary," "The Immediate Erotic Stages," and "Silhouettes" the picture of heterosexual relations is central to the whole project. While it might be argued that this preoccupation with the difference between the sexes only expresses the conventional and romantic manner of writing literary essays in the nineteenth century,[4] there are aspects of the volume which suggest that Kierkegaard may have been self-consciously using this custom in order better to express the problematics of certain kinds of aesthetic orientation.[5]

I shall isolate the relation between the aesthetic orientation and the heterosexual imagination by first examining Part I's last unit, "The Seducer's Diary," which epitomizes the stereotyped masculine heterosexual imagination. As examples of A's efforts to present women's experience of the heterosexual imagination, I shall consider next (a) the letters of the Seducer's object, Cordelia, (b) "Silhouettes," and (c) the treatments of

Antigone in "The Tragic in Ancient Drama Reflected in the Tragic in Modern Drama" and of Emmeline in "The First Love." Finally, Kierkegaard's self-consciousness about heterosexuality as image of the aesthetic will be corroborated by looking at the analysis of the emergence of heterosexual desire in the volume's first essay, "The Immediate Erotic Stages." This movement backward through the volume, both in order of pages and in psychological development, seems most likely to expose quickly the relation between aesthetic existence and heterosexual imagery. Starting with the picture of the most reflective, methodical aesthete (Johannes the Seducer) will facilitate recognition of the role of heterosexual imagination in the presentation of the less self-conscious feminine figures of aesthetic despair as well as in the interpretation of immediate, nonreflective aesthetic existence in the volume's first essay.

Stereotyped Male Heterosexuality as Victimizer: "The Seducer's Diary"

The fact that Johannes the Seducer is the last speaker at "The Banquet" in *Stages on Life's Way* supports the view that his ultimate place in *Either/Or, 1* is not randomly determined. In both of these writings, the final image of aesthetic existence (when posed by a heterosexual imagination that is poetically fascinated by the topic of "woman") is the reflective seducer. That the seducer is placed so as to epitomize the issues raised by the aesthetic is also indicated when, at several places in *Either/Or, 1*, the more immediate stages of the erotic are delineated by comparison with this reflective possibility (see, e.g., EO, 1:90, 98–101). Thus the issues implicit in the whole volume's male-female imagery are crystallized in Johannes's theory and practice. In Johannes the Seducer Kierkegaard presents an imagination that is completely heterosexualized; his fixation on sexual difference expresses his formulation of aesthetic existence. As the reflective seducer he is the paradigm of aesthetic existence in which the subject, a unit of conscious response to stimuli,[6] is defined in reaction to an object which is grasped as *essentially* other, that is, as not-subject.

There are two climaxes in the Diary's development of this figure, both having been long in preparation. The *dramatic* climax, in which the *practice* of the seducer culminates is the "offstage" *physical* act of intercourse, which Johannes's last two diary entries as well as Cordelia's letters imply took place on the night between 24 September and 25 September. The *philosophical* climax, in which the *theory* of aesthetic existence is formulated in terms of heterosexuality, occurs in Johannes's "categorical" treatment of woman; this is entered in the Diary at the point where he had won Cordelia *psychologically*, since she is ready to break the engagement because of her conviction, newly learned through Johannes's manipulation, that marriage is "ordinarily human," rather than superior to unconventional sexuality (*EO*, 1:427–28). Once he has written this logical analysis of woman, Johannes sees even more clearly the congruence of his theory and his practice (*EO*, 1:432). Thus it might appear that his "idea of the feminine" establishes his identity as seducer/aesthete. Nevertheless, the real culprit is the view of himself that needs this view of the other. As an aesthete, Johannes views himself as an isolated subject whose interests define whatever meaning various objects might have. This aesthetic orientation is fixated by absolutizing the difference between him*self* as male and the *other* as female.

We here deal with no casual "Vive la différence!" However, that slogan is often used to rationalize the kind of ideological, stereotyped heterosexuality seen in the Diary. Johannes's operating premise about the essential difference between men and women controls his perceptions and his analyses. Thus Johannes perverts the Hegelian logic of the two moments of any concrete entity ("being-in-itself" and "being-for-other") by adopting the determination of those aspects in which the "something" and the "other" dualistically separate or "fall apart." Hegel himself allows for another "determination" or way of thinking in which being-in-itself and being-for-other are unified in determinate being, each containing the other moment in itself. Criticizing the option that Johannes chooses, Hegel says: "But their truth is their relation" (*EO*, 1:658, n. 204); that is, the truth is that neither being-in-itself nor being-for-other subsist except as "determinations which are relations." They are dialectically related to one another. The unexpressed corollary of Johannes's stereotype of woman as "being-for-other" is his stereotype of man as "being-for-self"; he is unable to know the truth about himself because his imagination is captive to the idea of the absolute difference of the other sex. By categorizing woman as "being-for-other," he is able to separate himself from the "for-other" moment of his own self, that is, from his relational reality. This is significant for his whole orientation, and not just his treatment of Cordelia and other particular women, as is clear in his subsumption of "woman" within the larger category of "nature." All of nature is denied the intrinsic, "end-in-itself" meaning granted to men, who are apparently "spirit" (the "for-self"), the consummating end of nature (the "being-for-other") (*EO*, 1:430).

This theory is expressed throughout the Diary whenever Johannes reveals his need to see woman as different from man; of course, it is also expressed in his practice of calculating seduction, which grants no "for-self" to the sexual object. Not only is man capable of "existence" whereas woman is only "being" (*EO*, 1:431), but in many more specific ways, woman is characterized as essentially different from man. Thus woman's development "requires isolation," whereas man's "requires contact" (*EO*, 1:339). She is characterized by beauty and not by intellect (*EO*, 1:362, 428). Her very substance is "innocence," whereas naïveté is a negative factor in a man (*EO*, 1:445). If one can speak in some sense of her "freedom," it is really only her capacity for "devotion" (*EO*, 1:340). A "feminine leap" has a different character from a "masculine" plunge over the abyss of infinity; it is negotiated with a "beautiful," "soulful," "swinging" confusion of "poetry and actuality" (*EO*, 1:391–92). Woman is fulfilled in "absolute devotedness" and, thus, is "invisible" in herself, being seen only by virtue of her relation to a male. She has no real choice, and is only free aesthetically; that is, she does not have freedom in herself but by virtue of that which is not herself, the initiative of the male (*EO*, 1:431). Woman becomes free only through a man, with whom there lies the power to propose freely.[7] Whereas man is "reflection," she is "substance"; he is "questioning," she is "answer" (*EO*, 1:430–31). A male needs to be "interesting"; but a female ought not to be interesting, but simply beautiful (*EO*, 1:339–40); that is, attractive to the male. She really "loves only once" (*EO*, 1:377), while it is questionable whether Johannes ever really loves as he practices multiple seductions, each of which consumes up to six months (*EO*, 1:368).

For this essay, all of this culminates in Johannes's aversion to the association of women with one another:

> there is nothing more corrupting for a young girl than associating a great deal with other young girls. . . . The woman's fundamental qualification is to be company for the man, but through association with her own sex she is led to reflection upon it, which makes her a society lady instead of company. . . . If I were to imagine an ideal girl, she would always stand alone in the world and thereby

be assigned to herself, but mainly she would not have friends among the girls. (*EO*, 1:340)

However *seductive* this last picture of the feminine ideal as "standing alone in the world" and "assigned to herself," it clearly does not intend to grant a woman existential authenticity, as she is fundamentally "company for the man." Within the historical-cultural context of nineteenth-century conventions (which created a "society lady" as unattractive to many of us as it was to Johannes), it is easy to slide into sympathy with his strategy of isolating the feminine object. However, Romanticism's masculine ideal of the feminine, which denies human empowerment to actual women, is an issue throughout this volume. This suggests that Kierkegaard himself must have had some awareness of the problems posed for women by this passage. Moreover, its undertone suggests the incredulous and offended emotional reaction now familiar as the characteristic homophobic response to the idea of lesbianism, that is, of women-loving-women and/or identified with women. While I do not assume that Kierkegaard wrote this with prophetic recognition of a heterosexist response to manifest lesbianism, the passage does suggest that he was self-consciously developing Johannes in terms of a pathological masculine heterosexuality as an image of aesthetic existence. This interpretation is supported by Johannes's passing comments on "the kiss": not only is he convinced that a "perfect kiss" requires "a girl and a man," he asserts that "A man-to-man kiss is in bad taste" (*EO*, 1:416).

In addition to these explicit expressions of aversive reactions to same-sex relations, Kierkegaard's conscious recognition of the dualistic distortions encouraged by stereotyped heterosexuality is suggested when he depicts Johannes's theory of woman as based on a clear misuse of Hegel's logical analysis of the determinations of concrete being. This can be recognized if one keeps in mind the contrasting emphasis on the truth of relation expressed later by Kierkegaard in *Works of Love*. Of course, the emphasis on "equality before God" in Kierkegaard's analysis of neighbor love allows no dualistic separation of subject and object in human relations.

The image of the Seducer intentionally formulates the aesthetic mode of existence in terms of its implications for other human beings. This figure, of one who consciously manipulates the other to gain satisfaction of desire without respect for the intrinsic concerns of the desired object, sets the stage for the ethical character who speaks in the second volume.

Indeed, one way to place this volume's predominant heterosexual imagery within the authorship is to say that it allowed Kierkegaard to highlight the *moral* issues posed by the aesthetic. This might be contrasted, for example, to the more epistemological issues stressed by the intellectual forms of aestheticism considered in other volumes (e.g., *Philosophical Fragments* and *Concluding Unscientific Postscript*). Of course, the ethical man of Part II of *Either/Or* also imagines existence primarily through heterosexuality, albeit through use of the imagery of marriage between male and female to invoke a mode of existence no longer conditioned only by reactions to stimuli. In both volumes, the attention given to ways of managing human sexuality emphasizes the issues involved in human relations. However, this might not be recognized if one were not encouraged to take the point of view of the women involved in these stories. Without the point of view of the seduced, the seducer can be treated only in terms of his interesting irony and his metaphysical despair, rather than his impact upon other beings in the world, including nature (the "for-other") and both men and women (e.g., Edward Baxter, the ridiculed cousin who sincerely loves Cordelia, as well as Cordelia herself).

It is important to notice that "The Seducer's Diary" is presented only after A's prefatory interpretation both of Johannes and of Cordelia, as well as after his transcription of her pained letters. As in Mozart's *Don Giovanni*, where the opening scene makes it impossible to embrace the unbridled erotic desire that Don Giovanni represents without the anxiety that comes from knowing that he has committed rape and murder, so here: A makes sure that we enter the Diary only after attending, however briefly, to the experience of the seduced.

Stereotyped Female Heterosexuality as Victim: Cordelia, the Silhouettes, Antigone, Emmeline

Any attempt to speak of a woman's point of view in this volume must carefully note that even when female characters seem to be directly present (e.g., in Cordelia's letters as well as in "Silhouettes"), they are shadows seen only through several layered screens consisting of male interpretations. The final screen, of course, is the mind of Kierkegaard himself, which is almost completely hidden outside the volume. Within the volume, Cordelia, for example, is presented in the Diary itself only through the sensibilities of Johannes the Seducer. In addition, as is noted above, A's interpretation precedes Johannes's entries, providing another screen. While we are led to feel that A gives us direct access to Cordelia's voice in her four letters, we cannot be sure that this is the case, since A makes a point of the fact that he has transcribed them.

In like manner, the characters in "Silhouettes" not only are derived from dramas written by men, their experience is screened from us by A's deliberate development of them beyond the play/opera itself. A analyzes in turn Marie Beaumarchais from Goethe's *Clavigo*, Donna Elvira from Mozart's *Don Giovanni*, and Margarete from Goethe's *Faust*. The sections toward the end of each silhouette wherein A imagines the women themselves speaking (which directly parallel Cordelia's letters in their function) should not mislead us: We have here at every point images of women's experience as created by men and filtered through several screens constituted by the imaginations of men. Wittingly or not, Kierkegaard has constructed an essay that represents the problematics of women's studies within patriarchal history and culture; those who seek to know women's experience often have available only the "shadowgraphs" formed by both light (ways of knowing) and screens (particular minds) that may well be alien to the lives that are pictured.[8]

A himself develops at length his reasons for speaking of "silhouettes." He announces his intent to uncover the concealed "interior picture that does not become perceptible until I see through the exterior" (*EO*, 1:173). The exterior in each case is a female character in a drama in which she is known publicly to have been betrayed by the man whom she loves.[9] What, then, is the concealed element which A seeks? The fact that these characters have been deceived, forsaken, betrayed, seduced, is a matter of exterior record; his discussions of these facts do not uncover something formerly concealed. Instead I believe that his conviction that he is revealing that which has not been seen before derives from the fact that attention has rarely been given to the "interior" life of such characters, as they are secondary to the males for whom the dramas are named. They are the shadows cast by aesthetic heroes. Therefore, in spite of the distortions of his masculine lens, A's enterprise in "Silhouettes," as well as with Cordelia, is remarkable. Unlike the Seducer, his method at least presupposes the intrinsic dynamics of the lives of others, here specifically, of women. He avoids sexism to the extent that his studies of reflective sorrow through these women imagines them as sharing human experience with him.

Cordelia Wahl and the literary figures treated as "silhouettes" are shadow-images cast by aesthetic heroes and have in common the syndrome today called "victimization." The anonym finds in Marie Beaumarchais, Elvira, and Margarete the same form of aesthetic despair that he discovers in Cordelia, whom he explicitly identifies as a "special kind" of "victim" (*EO*, 1:307). Like the women in "Silhouettes," she is distinguished from victims who are unfortunate by virtue of a specific "objective sorrow" (*EO*, 1:171, e.g.), such as being cast out by a society. Such clear wrongs, apparently, can be resolved once and for all through intense grief; or they can be "ventilated in hate or forgiveness" (*EO*, 1:307). But no such resolution is possible for a woman who has been deceived by the one she loves, as in A's view, "a woman's life" is "her love" (*EO*, 1:172). The reflective sorrow that A studies in the silhouettes and sees in Cordelia cannot be resolved within the aesthetic realm of moods and feelings. A indicates that there are ethical and religious possibilities for transformation of such futility to which he cannot attend because of his aesthetic point of view. But he also argues that these alternative modes of existence are less available to women. Nevertheless, one of the remarkable aspects of A's studies of these characters is that he occasionally projects for these women fully human possibilities. This is clearest in his treatment of Marie; in two different places he notes that reflective sorrow will spin its wheels forever in its ambivalence between her passion and the lover's deception, unless there is a radical shift into the ethical, that is, into an existence determined by will, rather than feelings. Of Marie's tortured inner dialogue he says: "This path of thinking is infinite and does not end until the individual arbitrarily breaks it off by affirming something else, by a determination of the will; but the individual thereby enters into ethical qualifications and does not engage us esthetically" (*EO*, 1:179–80; see also 1:188).

A also observes that Goethe might have conceived of Marie Beaumarchais differently than he did, as having "sufficient strength" so that she "severed all connections with others in order to consume the sorrow in herself and to consume herself in the sorrow" (*EO*, 1:180). That is, remaining within the aesthetic, she might have been imagined as heroic herself, rather than dependent. But Goethe chose the more sexist path, and so does A. When A imagines a different development for her, he suggests that she could have attained "masculine maturity," if she had totally lost Clavigo (i.e., apparently, through death) (*EO*, 1:189). In that case, she would have experienced objective sorrow, which then could have been resolved through grief and expressed as despair. A's association of this possibility with masculinity may derive from the fact that Romanticism pictures women within patriarchy as protected from full exposure to such loss, expressing *class* bias as well as masculine bias.

In addition, A cannot imagine that there might be a different kind of maturity more characteristic of those who are powerless and, thus, especially vulnerable not only to natural evil, but to devastations caused by misuse of human freedom. By starting with the shadows of aesthetic heroes, he does not see images of women developing special strengths as they cope with powerlessness within patriarchy. The aesthetic, when expressed through a romanticized sexist imagination, presents pictures of women who are finally denied the full experiences of humanity: "Their lives were not cracked or broken, as others' were, but were bent into themselves; lost to others they futilely sought to find themselves" (*EO*, 1:307).

As A deals with Donna Elvira in Mozart's *Don Giovanni*, he again projects a way beyond reflective sorrow, only to deny it to her in the end. He delineates her choice as between the aesthetic (continuing in her love for Don Giovanni) and entering into ethical/religious categories, in which case the former nun would face the "great demands" of a second entrance into the religious through "repentance and contrition" (*EO*, 1:198). Revealing his heterosexual imagination, A allows that "no girl makes as brilliant a match as she who espouses heaven" and continues to picture women's possibilities as mediated by men, saying that it is questionable whether she can find "a priest who can proclaim the gospel of repentance" so as to challenge Don Giovanni's advocacy of pleasure. Finally, in his view, Elvira has no way to deal with despair except by "clinging" to her love for Don Giovanni (*EO*, 1:198–99). While A credits himself with "gallant" willingness to imagine her as stronger than Don Giovanni, he does so in terms only of the stereotyped feminine virtues: that is, of the full "vitality of her beauty," of "youthful luxuriance," and of "energetic firmness of feminine passion" (*EO*, 1:196).

These women whom A chooses to study are lost in futility because they are victims of an enemy that has come to reside in themselves: the idea of woman as essentially "for-other"; that is, her self-image is as "for-man." Stereotyped heterosexuality within patriarchy has often damaged women precisely in the ways pictured here. When this ideology is internalized by women, so that the love of men is the only imaginable meaning of their lives, women tend toward the patterns that recur in Cordelia and the silhouettes. Six recurring characteristics reveal a syndrome that is derived from their victimization and tends to perpetuate it. Close analysis of Cordelia's letters, for example, reveals her as *(1) totally vulnerable* to Johannes, whose intellect at times "annihilates her as a woman" and whose passionate desire and changing moods leave her insecure and trembling (EO, 1:309–10). Cordelia's mind is now *(2) totally dependent* upon Johannes; such dependence is emphasized particularly in Margarete as well, since Faust created her much as Johannes deliberately reshapes Cordelia (EO, 1:309, 212). Marie is described as so dependent upon Clavigo that she cannot stand alone when he is gone, but collapses in the arms of friends (EO, 1:180). Each of these women is defined by *(3) total love for and identification with the man;* that is, with the very one who has seduced and betrayed as well as deceived and abandoned her. While Elvira is strongest in her capacity for anger and for action toward vengeance, she finally also is bound totally by her love for Don Giovanni. Aside from Elvira, the women are *(4) only reactive*, rather than active; incapable of direct action, their lot is only to wait, to hope, to "take the veil of . . . sorrow" (EO, 1:183). By the time one hears Margarete's "voice" expressing her absolutely dependent love, which lacks the capacity to be angry or to seek revenge, one wishes to return to the relative strengths of Marie, Cordelia, and Elvira. However paralyzed these others are by the *(5) ambivalence* that all of the characters manifest, they at least manifest various degrees of angry indignation during the moments when they dare see the wrong done them. All of the women manifest the *(6) self-reproach/self-abnegation* now known to plague the oppressed, who have internalized the negative images projected upon them by the dominant culture. Some even plead to be forgiven for loving still the one who has abandoned them (EO, 1:213, 313).

I have been arguing that these six characteristics place all of these women together as victims. Although A's picture of Elvira may seem to lack not only passive reactivity, but also vulnerability and dependence, his emphasis on the ruling power of Elvira's love for Don Giovanni finally places her within the whole syndrome. Indeed Elvira expresses the self-reproach of the victim in stronger tones than the others and does so explicitly in terms of the patriarchally conditioned heterosexual imagination. Manifesting ambivalence, with self-blame alternating with moments of hatred during which Don Giovanni is held to be the guilty one, she ends in self-hatred:

He was no deceiver; he had no idea of what a woman can suffer.
If he had had that, he never would have forsaken me. He was a
man who was to himself enough. . . . Why, then, do I complain
because a man is not like a woman. . . . Did he deceive me? No!
Did he promise me anything? No! . . . He did not ask my hand in
marriage; he stretched out his hand, and I grasped it . . . he opened
his arms, I belonged to him. I clung to him. . . . I rested my head
on his breast and gazed into that all-powerful countenance, with
which he ruled the world. . . . Can I demand more? Was I not his?
(EO, 1:203)

Here women are presented in terms consistent with A's deceptively
benign formulation of Johannes's theory of woman as being-for-other. To
appeal to the idea of a being for whom love is so absolute that no other
value supersedes is demonic if this idea is not developed through the
ethico-religious, wherein it culminates in an experience of human equality before a transcendent absolute love. Stereotyped heterosexuality,
which emphasizes the complete difference between the sexes rather than
their common humanity, encourages sadomasochism. To say that "a
woman's happiness" is identical with her love, and then to picture this
love as total identification with a particular man in spite of his abuse, is
to express the idea of woman as "being-for-other" in especially dangerous
terms. Such a theory of woman isolates her not only from other women
and the communities of support they might provide, but from the children upon whose nurturance the idea of the feminine is often built. It is
interesting that children have no place in these stories, except for Margarete's child, whom she murders. Instead, the images are of women psychically patterned to love only the male *as male*, not even as child. At
least when they are "for-other" in the sense of being for their children,
women have the possibility of valuing femaleness in their daughters, and
eventually, perhaps, in themselves.

I have noted that A's studies of these women are self-consciously limited by his aesthetic point of view. In spite of the fact that he is not
comparably reflective about his masculine perspective, he uncovers literary images of the peculiar forms of aesthetic despair that plague women
who are victims of patriarchally conditioned stereotyped heterosexuality.
Within aesthetic existence, the meaning of life is established by the interaction between one's conscious subjectivity and that which is "other

than" this consciousness. Aesthetic despair arises in the unavoidable frustration of our interests by this "other," this "given," this "way things are." Patriarchy defines power and value as male and, therefore, as "other" than women. When combined with stereotyped heterosexuality, which defines the sexes as absolutely different from each other and as fulfilled only through the other, it predisposes a woman's existence toward the futility that A somehow recognizes: its meaning depends in no way upon self-activity; except insofar as she pleases the "other" who holds all the power in the relationship, her life is despair.

This futility characterizes even A's interpretations of Antigone and Emmeline, who are not victimized by male lovers like the others. Our knowledge from outside this volume, both of how deeply Kierkegaard himself identified with Antigone and of the Sophoclean image of her as an ethico-religious heroine, ought not to obscure for us the fact that A imagines her *aesthetically* in the essay on the tragic in ancient and modern drama (EO, 1:153–64). In defending his use of Antigone as an image of reflective sorrow, A appeals to a woman's advantage in preserving enough "substantiality for the sorrow" (EO, 1:153); thus he suggests the same truncated use of the Hegelian analysis of the dialectic between being-in-itself (substantiality) and being-for-itself (subjectivity) as we found in Johannes the Seducer. Unlike the Seducer, however, he treats this woman as uniting in herself both determinants of being, both finitude and infinitude, but does so in terms of an aesthetic orientation. She is not seen in terms of her freely chosen action, but in terms of her fatedness; the meaning of her life hinges upon the "other," the sum of all those factors that are not subject to her will. A presents Antigone in terms that express his romanticized heterosexual imagination and that render her existence paralyzed in reflective sorrow, rather than confronted with the limitations of the aesthetic. He says that as woman she can only "concern us" when imaged as "bride," since this is her destiny. Ironically, then, this "bride of sorrow" is an image of A himself, who, like *his* Antigone, "does not even know the idea that animates" him (EO, 1:157–58), that is, his masculine aesthetic heterosexual imagination.

The anonym may seem to confound this whole analysis, however, by including in the volume an essay on modern comedy that reviews the Danish translation and production of Scribe's *The First Love*.[10] The only female character in this one-act comedy, Emmeline, contrasts with those considered above in the way she is presented as well as in her character and her situation. Emmeline is presented as the center of this play (*EO*, 1:253), rather than a shadow of its hero. She is interpreted by a female actor (*EO*, 1:278) rather than only layers of male authors.[11] Although A suggests comparison to the silhouettes by speaking of a "shadow play" (*EO*, 1:277), he does not interpret Emmeline's hidden inner life, but presents her empty silliness through the comic situations.

There is less to suggest a sexist functioning of heterosexual imagination in this essay than elsewhere in the volume, since A self-consciously emphasizes the play's "equally witty mockery" (*EO*, 1:261) of both male and female. Nevertheless, the romantic ideas being satirized tended to be associated with women and it is an aunt who was addicted to novels and became the teacher in the "education by novels" that determined the characters of both Charles and Emmeline. In analyzing the different forms sentimentality takes in Emmeline and in Charles, A sees congruences with their sexual identities (*EO*, 1:250). Emmeline's "faith in illusion" is implied to be less mature than Charles's reliance on his own power to mystify; she is called more "fortunate" for not having had to feel the "pinch of actuality." Nevertheless, A vehemently opposes the assumption that Emmeline is sentimental and Charles "worldly" (*EO*, 1:252). Although brief expressions of assumed differences between male and female are scattered through the essay (e.g., *EO*, 1:252, 259, 272) and A clearly finds Charles the more interesting character (*EO*, 1:251–52), male and female here are presented as equally distorted by a falsifying culture.

A's interpretation of this comedy of manners, therefore, reveals his awareness of sociocultural factors in aesthetic despair. The "novel-nurturance" which is satirized locates the source of meaninglessness in human culture, not nature. A even manifests sensitivity to the role of economic class in the specific forms of "spiritlessness" (*SUD*, 41) created by romanticized patriarchy in both male and female. Emmeline is said to have been able to continue undisturbed in her romantic illusions because of "her father's wealth" (*EO*, 1:249); and throughout the play the father paternalistically coddles her whims, rendering her infantile. Charles's poverty and maleness, by contrast, send him out into a world (*EO*, 1:249–50) that his childhood education has encouraged him to believe can be dealt with through trickery rather than transparency (*SUD*, 14).

On the surface, Emmeline does not have many of the characteristics of victimized consciousness analyzed above: she is *not* vulnerable and dependent in the usual sense, but wins her way in the "sly" (*EO*, 1:266) ways often necessitated by lack of real power. Although the play opens with her depression and pretended illness, A makes it clear that she is *not* a figure of reflective sorrow, but is "invulnerable" (*EO*, 1:272) to actuality because her consciousness has been shaped completely by the romantic novels that were the soap operas of her day. Emmeline lacks enough reflection to be self-reproaching and her "fixed idea" of "first love" means that she is not at all ambivalent. While she seems, like Cordelia and the silhouettes, to have total love for one man, she actually is a "parody of faithfulness" (*EO*, 1:274), since she does not love a partic-ular man, but the romantic aura of moonlit nights and youthful ring exchanges. In order to stress her lack of real passion, A emphasizes the importance of the ring to Emmeline. Surprisingly, he ignores her early statement that she learned from novels that the indelible impression of a woman's first love determines her to love only one man in her life.[12]

In spite of the many ways in which Emmeline is presented as different from Cordelia and the silhouettes, she also is a victim of romanticized patriarchy. Here comedy reveals the truth that specific cultures encourage immediate, nonreflective aesthetic existence, preventing maturation through existential dialectics. Patriarchal cultures have tended more often to encourage such infantilism in privileged-class women than in men. In contrast to the talk of "woman's essential nature" in other parts of *Either/Or*,[13] in this essay it is because of her nurture rather than her nature that a woman's passion is "inane" (*EO*, 1:279), her talk is "prat-tle" and "drivel" (*EO*, 1:276), and she is "infinitely silly" (*EO*, 1:257).

A's own ironic aestheticism is completely at home in this play's "luna-tic" situation of "aimless jest" (*EO*, 1:277) at the end of which "nothing but nothing remains" (*EO*, 1:273). But Emmeline, like Charles, lacks reflection and is "irony's darling," rather than herself ironic (*EO*, 1:252, 271). As female, she thus tends to provide A with an Other, an object for his laughter that deflects radical appropriation of despair over himself. Throughout most of A's "The First Love" both sexes are seen as victim-ized by romanticism and comedy's delicate touch allows no blame (*EO*, 1:266); there is only ironic laughter "that does not issue from any one person but is the language of a world force" (*EO*, 1:273). Finally, how-ever, the inanity is identified as "Emmeline's" (*EO*, 1:179) and the au-thor's masculine heterosexual imagination allows him ironic distance from the theme of *Either/Or*'s "Ultimatum."

"The Immediate Erotic Stages" and the Origins of Pathological Heterosexuality

The socially constructed, nonreflective aesthetic orientation analyzed in "The First Love" is different from the immediate (nonreflective) erotic stages treated in the first essay of the volume. *Either/Or, 1* differentiates the *immediate* and the *reflective* stages within aesthetic existence. The essay on the musical erotic pictures a natural epigenesis of aesthetic immediacy rather than education into cultural constructs. In this essay A intends to delineate "the different stages" that "collectively make up the immediate stage" and that are all present in Don Giovanni, the character epitomizing the whole "richness" of nonreflective erotic immediacy (*EO*, 1:74, 124–25). Contrasting forms of the aesthetic are pictured in the calculating reflection of Johannes the Seducer, the reflective sorrow of Cordelia and the silhouettes, and the nonreflective artificial sentimentality of Emmeline and Charles.

Heterosexuality is an issue throughout the analysis of the "awakening" of consciousness[14] that A traces in his essay on music through characters in Mozart's operas. In Cherubino of *The Marriage of Figaro*, who represents the first stage of erotic immediacy, A sees an original unity of "desire and desired" indicated by the fact that the music for this male character is arranged for a woman's voice. Here human desire emerges as a "dreaming . . . intoxication with erotic love": "the desire is so vague, the object so little separated from it, that what is desired rests androgynously in the desire, just as in plant life the male and female are in one blossom. The desire and the desired are joined in this unity, that they both are *neutrius generis* [of neuter gender]" (*EO*, 1:77–78). A's emphasis here is not pursued in terms of the dramatic action, which, indeed, stresses the ambiguity of the Page's sexual identity, but more in terms of his music and lines. In this first stage of the erotic, desire is not fully conscious and its object is not yet fully separated from itself. Nevertheless, A presents "femininity" as Cherubino's object; the Page is pictured as "rocked by an unaccountable inner emotion" in which he is oriented vaguely toward women without conventionally justifiable specificity (*EO*, 1:76).

In the second stage consciousness, having become more separated as "desire from its object," is interpreted as "seeking that which it can desire"; that is, it seeks its concrete object. Through his music, Papageno, the bird catcher of *The Magic Flute,* is interpreted as "exuberant, merrily twittering, bubbling over with love" (*EO*, 1:81). A does not pause even to develop some aspects of Papageno that might support his interpretation; just as in his treatment of Cherubino, A is apparently too anxious to get on to his beloved *Don Giovanni* to do so. For example, he does nothing with the interesting fact that, when Papageno finally discovers that which he desires, it is a female figuration of himself: Papagena. Here heterosexual desire is for the complementary other who is the missing feminine self, without even the concrete definition of her own name.

This interpretation of Papageno/Papagena supports A's summary analysis of the third immediate erotic stage, which he says is the starting point of his whole analysis of desire (*EO*, 1:84). The third stage, represented by the figure of Don Giovanni, is that of complete separation between consciousness and its object, since in it desire is absolutely oriented toward particular objects, but in sequential, rather than categorical, multiplicity. Whereas Papageno seeks the particular as the woman for him ("the particular in the category of multiplicity" [*EO*, 1:85]), Don Giovanni desires particular women, one after another.

> In the particular, desire has its absolute object; it desires the particular absolutely. In this resides the seductiveness that we shall discuss later. In this stage, therefore, desire is absolutely genuine, victorious, triumphant, irresistible, and demonic. (*EO*, 1:85)

> Don Juan . . . is a downright seducer. His love is sensuous, not psychical, and, according to its concept, sensuous love is not faithful but totally faithless; it loves not one but all—that is, it seduces all. (*EO*, 1:94)

A could have developed this argument in terms of the interesting fact that in the opera particular women with their own specific names are Don Giovanni's objects: Anna, Elvira, and Zerlina. This, of course, contrasts with the vagueness of Cherubino's desire and with Papageno's discovery of an*other* who is the feminine form of himself. Neither of these characters expresses the seductive power of desire, whereas Don Juan is a seducer, but in a special sense. A argues that Don Juan is not a reflective, conscious seducer. Instead he seduces by virtue of the power of desire: "he does not seduce, he desires, and this desire acts seductively" (*EO*, 1:98). Because ethical categories do not apply to Don Juan at all, he is best understood as a seducer only insofar as he is a deceiver. Apparently, the fact that his desire in each moment is for a particular woman deceives each woman into thinking that he loves her in particular in the absolute way that she longs for him. Nevertheless, Don Giovanni is not himself so much an individual as a "force of nature"; therefore, it "is the power of the sensuous itself that deceives the seduced, and it is rather a kind of nemesis" (EO, 1:99). The seduced, then, also exist aesthetically, as much so as does Don Juan. His desire for each woman stimulates sensuous desire in her. This is her *nemesis;* she suffers the consequences of living aesthetically, of being totally vulnerable to the other/heteros, *because* she lives aesthetically; that is, she lives as a response to the other as stimulus, rather than in terms of choosing herself through the power of will.

The question might well be asked: Why is this aesthetic existence always imagined as a source of suffering for women, while for Don Juan the emphasis is simply on the exhilarating vitality of sensuousness, passion, desire, intoxication, and pleasure? (EO, 1:90). Don Juan is pictured as going on and on through his thousands of momentary loves without becoming reflective. The possibility of a female figure of such elemental sensuousness (EO, 1:101) apparently is ruled out by A's view of women as responding with total love to one particular man. Elvira is said to represent all of the seduced in terms of her "offended womanhood" (EO, 1:114), which is described as her only weapon. And this is not pictured as moral offense, but as "raging" and "obsessive" passion through which the power of Don Giovanni himself "resonates" in her (EO, 1:121–22). As in the silhouettes, the determining motive in terms of which Elvira represents womanhood is her desire for Don Giovanni. A is not interested in the less romantic alternative theory that women are oriented more monogamously than men by their biological role in the normal consequences of heterosexuality (i.e., human reproduction: pregnancy, childbirth, lactation, nurturance, and so forth). He does not develop the difference between male and female that might be implied when he says: "Don Juan is capable of everything, can withstand everything, except the reproduction of life, precisely because he is immediate, sensate life, of which spirit is the negation" (EO, 1:113). The context for this correlation of the tension between the "sensate" and the "spiritual" with that between immediacy and reproduction is A's interpretation of the Commendatore as spirit (EO, 1:112). A's interest is in the fact that musically the Commendatore represents with "aesthetic lightness and metaphysical truth" that which dialectically opposes Don Juan. As ghost, as apparition, the Commendatore transcends sensuous immediacy by being a "coming again" or reproduction.[15] A does not pay direct attention to the fact that the Commendatore does so not just as a victim of murder, but as an offended *father* (of a daughter) and, thus, as a male image of responsibility for future generations. A's masculine heterosexual imagination here pictures the ethico-religious challenge to aesthetic existence in terms of a male alternative (the father). Such an imagination, working within an artistic heritage expressive of its own orientation, cannot picture the ethical in female images. The role of culture as well as psychology in sexist expressions of heterosexual imagination here is indicated, as it is in the essay on *The First Love*: when inherited mythologies and literatures encourage fixed images of sexual differences, maturation through the existential dialectic can be blocked.

The Concept of Anxiety analyzes some of the existential tensions involved in the heterosexuality of *biological* reproduction or procreation of life with some attention to sexual difference (CA, 62–73). However, in *Either/Or, 1,* A's aesthetic and romanticized perspective is shown in his strong identification with Don Juan and makes it impossible for him to imagine women's sexuality in terms of its usual association with human reproductive processes. This perspective also imagines women as suffering within erotic immediacy simply because of the singleness of their passion for the male, rather than also by virtue of their roles in human reproduction.

Conclusion: A Way from Aesthetic Heterosexuality

A's association of "reproduction of life" with "spirit" as opposed to "sensate" immediacy helps to clarify the existential dialectic central to the essay on "The Immediate Erotic Stages." According to A, the very "idea of the elemental originality of the sensuous" (*EO*, 1:85) was posited by Christianity's testimony to the possibility of its dialectical opposite: to exist as "spirit." But when that which sensuous immediacy (Don Juan) cannot "withstand" is defined as "reproduction of life," the intended meaning of "spirit" is clarified as not simply the nonphysical/nonbodily. Rather, *spirit is the power to exist so as to bind time through self-activity, rather than to be determined by immediate sensation.*[16]

Kresten Nordentoft characterizes as historical and psychological, rather than normative,[17] A's argument that Christianity is the source of the Don Juan image of "the flesh" as split from "the spirit" (*EO*, 1:89). In Nordentoft's view, in "The Immediate Erotic Stages" A's discussion of the historical development of a dualistic separation of sensuality and spirituality correlates with the psychological analysis in *The Concept of Anxiety*. Thus Nordentoft uses the interpretation of Christianity in the later text as a key to the earlier essay, calling attention to a passage important to any consideration of the place of A's heterosexual imagination within Kierkegaard's own views of the existential dialectic:

> In Christianity, the religious has suspended the erotic, but not merely as sinful, through an *ethical* misunderstanding, but as indifferent, because in spirit there is no difference between man and woman. Here the erotic is not neutralized by irony, but it is suspended because the tendency is to bring the spirit further. When in modesty, the spirit becomes anxious of and shy of putting on the generic difference, the individuality suddenly leaps off and, instead of pervading the generic difference ethically, seizes an explanation from the highest sphere of the spirit. This is one side of the monastic view, whether it is more particularly determined as ethical rigor or as predominantly contemplation. (*CA*, 70–71)

Nordentoft goes on to explore in depth the psychological significance of what he identifies as Kierkegaard's view here: "that sexuality ought to be something indifferent, i.e., that it ought not, in anxiety-laden abstinence, lay special claim to an individual's emotional life."[18] Nordentoft interprets Kierkegaard as arguing that the development which can liberate emotional life from the demonic power given to sexuality by repression of libido is not religious asceticism, but ethico-religious transformation of the "generic difference." When religiousness is not passed through the ethical stage, it endangers the whole person; by perverting religiousness into fantastical abstraction from concrete existence (*SUD*, 32), it also perverts sexuality into sensuality.

It is important to note that in the quotation above (*CA*, 70–71) *The Concept of Anxiety* recognizes the critical role of sexual difference in psychological development at the same time as it affirms that sexual identity is finally religiously irrelevant. Through the psychologist Vigilius Haufniensis, Kierkegaard pictures the difference between male and female in the aesthetic "stage," wherein all humans begin, as the vehicle for development of self-conscious individuality; awareness of "self" is heightened through erotic desire for the other/*heteros*. In aesthetic immediacy, heterosexuality embodies the subject-object dialectic in terms of which meaning is a function of the desires of the individual for that which is other than the individual.

This recurrence of emphasis upon "the generic difference" in *The Concept of Anxiety*, a text considered an important resource for Kierkegaard's own anthropology, formulates psychological insight in terms of heterosexuality. Future interpretations of the human significance of *Either/Or* need to avoid assuming the universality of such an imagination. Modern knowledge that some persons are erotically oriented toward the same sex might suggest to the Kierkegaardian thinker a need for additional artistic creations that provide a maieutic to meet gays and lesbians where *they* are in the aesthetic in order that the challenge of ethico-religious selfhood be powerfully presented to them. While the move "away from the aesthetic" for heterosexuals is accomplished through "penetrating the generic difference ethically," the comparable step for gays and lesbians would seem to require "penetrating the sexual sameness ethically." Same-sex erotic desire can present an aesthetic cleavage between subject and object just as can heterosexuality; seduction and victimization can be implied in its dynamics as well. But it also can be transformed by an ethico-religious intersubjectivity realized through freedom and commitment. Kierkegaard avoids heterosex*ism* when he finally interprets Christianity as rendering sexual difference irrelevant in aiming to bring the "spirit further." Today this needs to be recognized as providing equality "before God" not only for women and men, but also for homosexuals and heterosexuals.[19]

The content of *Either/Or, 1* has enabled more frequent attention in this essay to the implications of the heterosexual imagination for heterosexual women than for homosexual persons. Indeed, one way to formulate the purpose of *Either/Or* is in terms of heterosexuality: to provide a maieutic so that the self (male *or* female) appropriates the ethical task of pervading the "generic difference ethically." It can provide an existential maieutic for heterosexual women *if* Victor Eremita's "charming reader" in some way overcomes the romanticized and stereotyped masculine heterosexual imagination that informs the volume's pictures of women's possibilities. Indeed, the volume provides for both male and female readers encounters with images of women victimized by patriarchal aestheticism. These pictures of the oppressive consequences of fixation on sexual difference when one sex holds power and value categorically can stimulate a leap "away from the aesthetic." Johannes the Seducer's discussions of women seem contrived to cause this aversive reaction.

In Kierkegaard's own view women are not ontologically "for-other"; men are not ontologically "for-self." Finally both are equally "before God." Nevertheless, the given, finite, necessary aspects of the self that are to be integrated with the "for itself" through reliance upon "the power that established it" (*SUD*, 14) include the generic difference of sexuality. Each woman, like each man, must develop through ethical choice of the concrete self and its tasks. Whatever one's erotic orientation, sexual identity is existentially important, since biological reality is fundamental to one's concretion.[20]

Therefore, when A says of Antigone: "our heroine is on the point of wanting to leap over an element of her life; she is beginning to want to live altogether spiritually, something that nature does not tolerate" (*EO*, 1:162), his interpretation of Antigone points toward the analysis of the erotic that we have noted in *The Concept of Anxiety*. Here A deepens his treatment of Antigone; the collisions involved in her drama are reinterpreted by focusing upon her loves. Antigone is seen as fated, not only into a collision between her love for her father/family and her love for herself, but also into a collision between her love for family and her erotic love for her betrothed (which she is on the verge of "leaping over"). A introduces a critique of inauthentic spirituality through evaluating Antigone's temptation to deny erotic love. This allows us a glimpse behind the screen of the anonym's consciousness to the scrim curtain of *his* author's own mind. But the possibility of a final transformation of the heterosexual imagination, not only through ethico-religious development of the erotic but also through awareness of sin and forgiveness, lies far beyond this volume in the direct expression of *that* mind in *Works of Love*.[21]

In *Either/Or, 1*, however, the heterosexual imagination tends to depict the subject-object dialectic characteristic of the aesthetic sphere in pictures of male-female relations. When it points toward the tension between the aesthetic and the ethical, this dialectic is pictured in terms of male-male relations (Don Juan and the Commendatore, Don Juan and Socrates, A and Judge William, and so forth). Thus this volume functions for heterosexual women, and to a lesser extent for homosexual persons, as a negative maieutic. Of course, this is to say that these individuals experience, even more intensely than heterosexual men, the "wound from behind" involved in the book's indirect communication. The woman whose consciousness has been formed within patriarchy can be educated by the text if she reads it by identifying with the women pictured, rather than ignoring them. The same might be said for the male reader. Those who read with existential concern might find that one cannot identify for long as either a victim or a victimizer—or even as one who is ignored—without asking for an alternative mode of existing.

Notes

1. K. Nordentoft, "Erotic Love," *Kierkegaard and Human Values*, vol. 7 of *Bibliotheca Kierkegaardiana*, ed. Niels Thulstrup and M. Mikulova Thulstrup (Copenhagen: C. A. Reitzels, 1980), 89.

2. Scientific evidence supports the view that sexual orientation, as distinct from sexual activity and self-understanding, results from a complex interplay of genetic and sociocultural factors at such an early age that it cannot be described as a choice. Recent studies are summarized by Chandler Burr in "Homosexuality and Biology," *Atlantic Monthly* 271, no. 3 (March 1993): 47–65.

3. Some have asked whether there can be a pathological homosexual imagination that could be called homosex*ist*. Inasmuch as homosexual persons are keenly aware that they are a minority, they do not tend to absolutize their own imagery or deny the humanity of those who are heterosexual; later I shall indicate that there can be pathological homosexual behavior.

4. Sylvia Walsh, in her response to an earlier draft of this paper at the AAR Kierkegaard Seminar (1988), indicated that it was "perfectly normal" (rather than "a fixation on his part") for Kierkegaard to focus "on male-female relations in this work," given the historical context in Danish literature as well as the "reserve" of the culture. I do not attribute the "fixation" to Kierkegaard, but see it as created by him to characterize the aesthetic existence of the pseudonym. I agree with Walsh that Kierkegaard seeks "ironically to expose romanticism as masculine and sexist in spite of its avowed championing of the feminine."

5. This also suggests a new approach to *Either/Or, 2*. While my essay "Judge William Judging Woman: Existentialism and Essentialism in *Either/Or*, Part II" (*International Kierkegaard Commentary: Either/Or, Part II*, ed. Robert L. Perkins, 33–57 [Macon: Mercer University Press, 1995]) was developed independently of the present work, in retrospect I think it reveals that the Judge's views express the heterosexual imagination in terms of a certain kind of ethical orientation, paralleling *Either/Or, 1*'s expression of certain forms of the aesthetic.

6. As A introduces the Diary he twice pictures Johannes's aestheticism in the stimulus-response mechanism: "As soon as actuality had lost its significance as stimulation, he was disarmed, and the evil in him lay in this" (*EO*, 1:306). "For him, individuals were merely for stimulation" (*EO*, 1:308).

7. Thus Cordelia's surname, "Wahl," cannot be her real name, according to A; one assumes this is due to the fact that the Germanic roots of the name imply choice (*EO*, 1:305).

8. Sylvia Walsh has argued that the maleness of the author did not obviate the possibility that he accurately expresses the experiences of women (AAR Kierkegaard Seminar, 1988). I do not deny this, but think the volume's self-conscious devices suggest that Kierkegaard himself recognized the irony of our dependence upon male authors for knowledge of female experience.

9. The case of Cordelia differs slightly in this respect, as the seduction itself may not have

been publicly known, except to A. Nevertheless, her relationship to Johannes, including the broken engagement, was in the public arena.

10. *Den første Kjærlighed*, Johan Ludvig Heiberg's translation of Augustin-Eugène Scribe, *Les Premières Amours ou Les Souvenirs d'enfance* (Repertoire of the Royal Theater, 1832). See also *First Love: A Comedy in One Act* by Eugène Scribe, adapted from the French by L. J. Hollenius (New York: Robert M. De Witt, 1869).

11. In early nineteenth-century France most novels were written by men. Exceptions to this rule would have been the two novels of Germaine de Staël.

12. Hollenius, *First Love*, 4. Comedy treats this theme lightly, but patriarchal ideologies, in their focus upon virginity and "defloration," usually have treated "first love" as biologically and psychologically determinative for women more than men.

13. See the discussion above of the Seducer's "category of woman" and my "Judge William Judging Woman: Existentialism and Essentialism in *Either/Or*, Part II."

14. That the issue is consciousness is indicated through the repeated use of the image of "awakening" (e.g., *EO*, 1:76, 79).

15. The passage from Hegel cited in the notation to the above quotation suggests that its connection of "spirit" with reproduction is an important clue to Kierkegaard's project in this volume; see *EO*, 1:620–21.

16. That "spirit" is "freedom" is manifest in *SUD*, where "willing" is the power to accomplish imagined possibilities in synthesis with the necessities of concrete existence (*SUD*, 29–35).

17. Kresten Nordentoft, *Kierkegaard's Psychology*, trans. Bruce Kirmmse (Pittsburgh: Duquesne University Press, 1978), 53.

18. Nordentoft, *Kierkegaard's Psychology*, 58. In the English translation cited, the Lowrie translation of *The Concept of Dread* (Princeton: Princeton University Press, 1946) is used for the passage quoted above from the Thomte translation of CA.

19. Kierkegaard's inattention to homosexuality is somewhat surprising, given the keenness of his psychological observations and his knowledge of classical Greek materials. Respondents have reminded me of the ways in which mid-nineteenth-century Danish culture would have limited his ability to express any awareness he might have had of the reality of same-sex erotic desire.

20. Lesbians and gay men do not deny the importance of their sexual identities; they simply are erotically oriented toward their own sexes.

21. See my essay "Finally Forgiveness: Kierkegaard as a 'Springboard' for a Feminist Theology of Reform," in *Foundations of Kierkegaard's Vision of Community: Religion, Ethics, and Politics in Kierkegaard*, ed. George B. Connell and C. Stephen Evans (Atlantic Highlands, N.J.: Humanities Press, 1992), 196–217.

2

Yes, A Woman *Can* Exist

Birgit Bertung

The stress in the phrase "Kierkegaard as the poet of existence" may well be placed on the word "poet," because what he writes about women are *not* theoretical deductions about the concept of woman as an object of science, but more or less poetic provocations or rebuffs. The fundamental conflict between "the medium of poetry" and "the medium of existence" is not merely a conflict, but also a possibility for communication. By *definition* it is impossible to theorize about existence. The ethical and the religious *can* only be expressed in language by *means* of the aesthetic.

My title—Yes, a woman can "exist"—is the answer to a question that nearly everyone has answered pretty much in the negative, at least to the extent that it is felt to be somewhat of a provocation to answer it in the affirmative. But that is far from what is intended here. I take my stand on the most unremitting scholarly efforts to prove the correctness of the assertion, as far as this is at all possible with Kierkegaard, whose method in all his works, taken separately or as a whole, was existential challenge. Therefore unlike other philosophical authors, he is to be neither read nor argued with *directly*, or at least one does so at one's own risk. Conversely, if one never dares to take a risk, one never wins anything.

Even in the very concept of "existence" there is a duality that immediately puts the focus on Kierkegaard's special handling of the Danish language. It is necessary to realize that his use of language is an *integral* part of his philosophy. At the same time Kierkegaard himself maintains that as a means of communication language is unsuitable for directly conveying existential messages; that is, in this context too, we are faced with a philosophy of paradox. The paradoxical is to Kierkegaard both means and end. Everything is written *in order* to draw attention to the religious paradox, and it is done with the aid of a paradoxical vehicle: indirect communication. Therefore it ought not to take anyone by surprise that when dealing with the special problems posed by women, Kierkegaard also employs indirect communication.

Now time does not permit us to dwell at length upon the method in his indirect communication, but one thing *must* be made clear: that an understanding of its main ideas is necessary if we are going to profit from Kierkegaard scholarship. Furthermore, readers of translations in particular must be aware of the serious aesthetic game that is going on when for instance Kierkegaard speaks of the Romantic idea of *taedium vitae*[1] and then puts the word "a dose of" in front of it. Theoretically it says the same, but in reality an artistic, comic element has been added that totally alters the situation. We shall encounter insurmountable problems if, without reflection, we take all his statements at their face value; for example, that "cannibals should enter the Kingdom of God before clergymen and professors,"[2] or the quotation more relevant to my context, that "the greatest distance from the ideal emanates from family life, from the lioness, or to put it in another way which is also sometimes true, from the farrowing sow."[3] Utterances of this type both should and should not be taken literally. They are to be grasped dialectically. All the forays against clergy, pedagogues, and husbands, are of course directed against those who presume to tutor others in existential affairs, or those who believe that head-knowledge is the meaning of life; that is, those whose existential relationship is in some way incorrect, who do not do the one good thing: become themselves or rather "a Self." For this means that we do not teach but we respect the other person's freedom to choose for himself or herself; we make room for our own self, and in common parlance that will mean that we act charitably. Without love—no self. If one has become oneself, one loves God, and thus implicitly one's neighbor. Then one does not moralize, and does not judge, but presupposes love in the other person. Love does not change the other person, but oneself.

Kierkegaard's apparent attacks upon women are of a similar character to those on clergymen and professors, and so they have their particularly well-warranted *function* in Kierkegaard's works. The primary aim of his writings is precisely that they should be usable for an existential purpose, not that they should have conferences held about them; that is our responsibility.

I am, however, of the same persuasion as Kierkegaard, that without the listeners or readers being personally involved to some extent, that is, having a minimum of interest in the matter at hand, any speech is in vain, and therefore without meaning. In such a case the most that could be claimed is a certain degree of intellectual understanding, not existential appropriation, but in Kierkegaard's terminology one does what one has understood.

I have chosen to deal with his view of women in particular, of course, because it concerns me. I well realize that men may not care so much about the problem, but that does not mean that they have to swallow it all uncritically.

The conscious ambiguity that makes Kierkegaard employ several meanings of nearly all central concepts like "existence," "spirit," "self," is both a philosophical necessity and an existential challenge, a form of action; he picks out the very collocations of concepts that can be misunderstood. For that reason he gives, for example, pietistic concepts new specifically existential-philosophical significations. He consciously aims at the reader's misinterpreting him, at least at first, and taking him to be a hopelessly conceited hidebound pietist.

Something similar applies to what he says about women. He does not wish to stand in the way of any woman's *own* resolution of her existential situation, so he wishes to be misunderstood, and he must be said to have succeeded overwhelmingly. The use of this method, he thinks, is the only way he can make people react, and that is the whole aim of all his works, to get one to act for oneself, even if he has to trick the reader cunningly into the truth.

It is essential to mention one more fact about the technique of indirect communication or dialectic, and that is the use of pseudonyms. This is due to Kierkegaard's unwillingness to use the didactic form. So he is obliged to make use of fictitious characters between whom the dialogue may proceed and with whom the reader may enter into dialogue. In Kierkegaard's opinion authority can only arise from the reader's own self-understanding. But at the same time he has to find some way of presenting the topic of discussion; that is the paradoxicality. So the pseudonyms are existential roles, but *none* of them should or *can* indeed merely be adopted, not even those which are apparently ideal; as a point of *principle* no list of the correct answers is supplied.

The role of Kierkegaard is rather that of the stage director. He stages his pseudonyms, or rather altogether they make up the performance, the unfinished dialogue about the possibilities and impossibilities of human life. He was also himself a personal participant in—and spectator to—the existential crises or alienation of humanity. Kierkegaard was a dialectician and the confrontation still works: no two of us are today completely agreed about what he meant: we are still uncertain about what existence is—and that was precisely his intention.

After this necessary introduction, which unfortunately is far from adequate, I shall move on to present a close reading of those texts that, with the reservations mentioned, provide relevant information about Kierkegaard's view of a woman's possibility of "existence." These are mainly *The Sickness unto Death* and *The Concept of Anxiety*. For practical reasons and despite what I have just said, I shall take the liberty of calling the authors of both works Kierkegaard; it is indeed he who is pulling the strings.

The essential thing is that a human being, unlike nature's beasts, *can* become spirit and *can* obtain existence, Kierkegaard thinks. For Kierkegaard, to be human is to be a relation (most frequently, however, a misrelation, lacking harmony).

On the immediate level a human being is only body and soul, that is, merely has being or exists in the commonplace sense of the word. In this context what appertains to the soul does not differ from what a psychologist would call "the physical." On this level Kierkegaard speaks about "the continuity of the states of soul";[4] that is, we are within the psychological area in which one thing follows straight from another. The person is not sufficiently self-aware to make existential choices. Only two elements of the person are present, and as such there is no self at all, no spirit from any point of view, no Kierkegaardian existence. One cannot begin to speak of a self until one is aware of oneself as a relation, and that may be on two superior levels, or from two points of view that are simultaneous. There is no question of a theory of development, but of choices. First, one can understand oneself as "the self whose yardstick is humanity." Second, "as a self seen from a specifically *Christian* viewpoint," or the self being before God, the theological self where God enters directly into the self-understanding and is not something external. This is designated a "deeper self," but means deeper down in the same Self, at the same moment in time (see diagram below). (When one catches sight of the elements of infinity in oneself, then we can speak of a deeper self, for God.)

On the purely psychical level the person only exists in a commonplace sense, as divided from other things. But when one becomes oneself or a Self, one becomes able to recognize that one has been created or established by a something other. Through this first relation, this same recognition becomes, understood Christianly, a challenge and the person becomes conscious of being a self before God, acquires existence in the

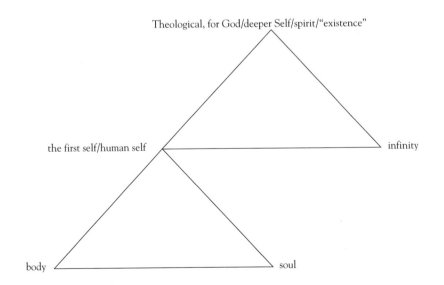

true sense. The concept of awareness or consciousness is thus used by Kierkegaard both as a concept of cognition theory and as an ethical and religious concept having to do with the *will*. It might also be termed self-knowledge, for it implies a reflection upon the awareness of the self, a reaction. In the ambiguous terminology of Kierkegaard, a double reflection is thus an act of consciousness *plus* the adoption of an attitude, a relating to this consciousness; the same word is used simultaneously in the two senses, about the same phenomenon.

The right attitude or balance in the structure of the synthesis is a presupposition for being oneself or achieving existence. If there is not equilibrium among the elements, then anxiety or despair appears. As an existing being, the person may also be described as a synthesis of finitude and infinitude, the temporal and the eternal, necessity and possibility, which can be actualized as freedom (see diagram). If one does not see that only *by* one's relationship to the other or to God one can be in equilibrium, one is, existentially, still in despair and is only working oneself deeper down into one's despair, and one must *at each instant* fully recognize this state of affairs.

Despair may have three main forms: (1) in despair not to be conscious of having a self (unactual despair); (2) in despair not to *will* to be oneself; (3) in despair to will to be *oneself*, or defiance.

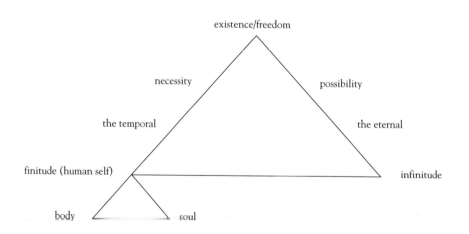

The idea behind describing the person as a synthesis is that every time there is a misrelation between the components of the synthesis there is existential despair, but not necessarily also psychological despair that may be observed by other people. A deficiency in one of the components implicitly means that there is too much of its opposite, for they are in inverse proportion, and imagination is the medium in which the lack of balance or misrelation finds expression. Both too much and too little imagination is evil; the imagination is identical with the will to see the possibility of good. To assume responsibility for the components in the synthesis is to relate correctly to them, and God is that everything is possible.

If we look at despair from the viewpoint of consciousness, there are many degrees, depending on the reflection upon self-awareness, that is, on self-knowledge and thus on choice. First, true despair is aware of being in despair, and that can manifest itself in two ways: in despair not to will to be oneself, to be unliberated, what Kierkegaard calls "the despair of weakness,"[5] or "so to speak the despair of femininity," and this "so to speak" is very important, for it signifies that there is really no question of anything feminine in an absolute sense, but only of a "lower synthesis"[6] in general. The other way is termed "despair seen from the qualification of spirit," and Kierkegaard designates it "masculinity's despair" or defiance. Only relative opposites are involved here, for no despair is quite without defiance nor is it without weakness. Kierkegaard himself uses the word relative, and the character whom he describes as someone in despair in a typically feminine way is in actual fact a man!

But in order to hold our attention captive and stretch us to the limit, Kierkegaard in the same passage in *The Sickness unto Death* speaks of two relations a woman can be in: her temporal relationship to her husband, and over against that, her existential relationship, her relation as spirit. A confounding of these two relationships is, for a woman particularly, a very common but nonetheless disastrous existential error.

In bodily surrender, woman is female, that is her nature as a sex; she is being herself in the ordinary commonplace sense. There is no question here of surrender to God, the spiritual aspect of the human being, of the person's personality, but of that which is bodily. But, continues Kierkegaard (and I quote): "In the relationship to God, in which the distinction of man-woman vanishes, it holds for men as well as for women that devotion is the self, and that in the giving of oneself the self is gained. This holds equally for man and woman, although it is probably true that in most cases the woman actually relates to God only through the man."[7] But this final damning addition only applies to the empirical reality that surrounds Kierkegaard and that, for instance, he describes in "In Vino Veritas," where all the men in various ways view woman as a thing without independent identity. Even the judge's wife has not even a name, while he has both a name and a title. Kierkegaard's attack is not, of course, aimed at anything nonhistorical, biologically necessary, or absolute. Elsewhere he uses the expression "according to order,"[8] by which he means "according to society's order." That is what he is aiming at, because only the order of society can be changed, not the order of how men and women are created: Kierkegaard's whole concern is to be the occasion for human beings to change. The reason for Kierkegaard's calling the lower synthesis of spirit that of "femininity" is thus merely that he can observe in society that women apparently more frequently misinterpret the concept of existence and that the five speakers are right in this. This leads to the equation: "being for God" = being nothing in oneself, becoming identified with the situation "being for one's husband," so that without warrant he is given the place of God.

If one dares venture upon a biographical digression, that is precisely what Kierkegaard personally wished to avoid. He was afraid that the conventions of society, which are indeed appallingly strong, would affect him so that he would come to treat his wife as if she should be submissive to her husband, as the marriage ritual actually said at that time, and that was a monstrosity which he had to renounce. In Kierkegaard's opinion only God may demand submission.

This conventional attitude with the husband in the place that should be God's is of course inherent in the patriarchal system, and that cannot be harmonized with Kierkegaard's talk of "the individual." He does not think (unlike, say, Hegel) that a line runs from the government of the world to the government of the state to the government of the family. To Kierkegaard, God is something qualitatively different from human beings, and that is what justifies the demand made upon them to be nothing before God. But precisely in that way man and woman become of equal worth, just as, mathematically, the concept of infinity nullifies finite differences.

That a human being should be "nothing before God" does not mean that one should merely focus upon oneself. On the contrary. "To love God" = to love one's neighbor, but God must be the middle term, as Kierkegaard calls it, otherwise we have attempts at subjugating the other person or at self-subjugation. The road runs via God to one's neighbor, and both movements are necessary. Kierkegaard is not self-centeredly pietistic. Some misunderstandings arise from the Danish language, where the word *selvbevidsthed* (self-consciousness or self-awareness) to most people nowadays means arrogance, but not for Kierkegaard in his Hegelian age. If a person is submissive to another person, that is self-subjugation and not love (regardless of any marriage certificate there may be); in Kierkegaard's view the concept of love includes the idea of equality, and a human being has a duty to obey the personal demand. On Kierkegaard's premises, one can by no means relate to God through another human being, for then it is not God one is relating to, and that is idolatry. So he also says: "A relationship to God at second hand is just as impossible and as completely nonsensical as being in love at second hand."[9]

Kierkegaard's differentiation between what is absolutely inevitable in woman, and what is only relative or contingent (e.g., culturally determined), is very important. For there is no question at all of the despair of femininity being specifically feminine; it is merely a description applicable to all humans of how one tries to keep the problem of the self, the spirit, and so reality at bay. Both men and women try to avoid being what they should be—themselves. But for cultural reasons men are most often guilty of the sin of trying to dominate. Very few people at all become actually "existent," says *The Sickness unto Death;* elsewhere there is talk of "not a single one." So it is far from something that all men succeed in doing. The problem is not primarily a question of intellect but of will, of self-knowledge in the face of annihilation of egoism, or capitulation in the face of love.

It is likewise particularly important to grasp that in Kierkegaard's opinion it is *not* a matter of becoming abstract spirit as much as possible. The despair of masculinity is seen under the qualification of spirit, but this only means that, as regards the concept of spirit, it is in a defiant position. The self in the despair of masculinity will, in very defiance, not begin by losing itself, which is the first step toward becoming concretely oneself, but wishes, in defiance of its own self-awareness, to be its own self. In its despairing striving it works in the opposite direction. In despair it wishes to be its own fantastic abstract self.

This is therefore called the demonic position, and its most extreme form is identical with the very concept of the devil, who is characterized as "sheer spirit."[10] That means that his self is absolutely transparent *to himself* as God's adversary, and therefore is also absolutely selfish, whereas the good of becoming spirit is to become something transparent *to God*, to capitulate. Not until then does a person exist in the Kierkegaardian sense.

It is not spirit in itself as an abstract phenomenon that is the ideal, but to become oneself concretely as spirit, to achieve balance in one's synthesis, to reach equilibrium, and not be in a misrelation to what one is. To exist is to be the right *relation*.

The relative concept of femininity's despair is thus only a matter of "an empirical state or average," as Kierkegaard says himself. But in *contrast* to this he does call into service an absolute relationship in two senses. One I have already mentioned: the relationship to God. As possessors of personalities that in principle are responsible, man and woman are, in an absolute sense, equal. The other absolute relationship derives from a bodily difference, of principle or absolute, between man and woman, a difference in the syntheses *themselves*, not that the syntheses are relatively higher or lower.

The one kind of synthesis cannot be said to be better than the other. The good is simply to adopt the actuality which one happens to have, and it is precisely this actuality that differs between man and woman. This differentness is elaborated upon in *The Concept of Anxiety*, where Kierkegaard/Vigilius Haufniensis also asserts that "woman is more anxious than man." Anxiety is also the precondition for the reality of sin, for there can be no question of sin until one is aware of the possibility of becoming oneself. For not until then can there be any question of an alienation from oneself, and *that* is what is tantamount to sin. Anxiety both attracts and repels, and it is positive insofar as it shows that the person is at least glimpsing the possibility of being able to become spirit or personality and is not preoccupied solely with the mundane or temporal side of the synthesis, thus being out of balance.

We shall return to the syntheses and combine them into one (see diagram). The relation between the elements in them is such that if there is "a disorganisation of the one, it manifests itself in the rest."[11] Furthermore, sexuality is the extreme point of the bodily, that is, right out on the edge of the synthesis. This means that the various elements cohere in such a way that even the slightest influence at one point will have an effect on the others, so that, for example, sexuality is an expression of pure sensuousness but at the same time an expression of the personality or the spirit, and it may be the trigger that leads one to see oneself as cut off from other things. If, for instance, sexuality is not in

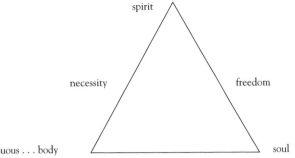

balance with the other elements, that is to say, conceived as an integral part of the self, then one cannot become fully "existent." A disorganization is tantamount to an imbalance or an overprioritizing of one element. If one element is hypostasized, it becomes indeed an independent power that threatens to destroy the personality, which really should be integrating the various parts in such a way that a whole person emerges. Therefore such a substantiation is a sin—and not sexuality in itself. "Here, as everywhere," says Kierkegaard, "I must decline every misunderstood conclusion, as if, for instance, the true task should now be to abstract from the sexual, i.e., in an outward sense to annihilate it. . . . The task, of course, is to bring it under the qualification of the spirit."[12]

This issue arises in the complex of problems concerning man and woman, because the concept of "the sexual" is for Kierkegaard very broad, also including the particular functions that separate the concepts of male and female, like suckling and childbearing. In the ordinary sexual relationship the man and the woman invest equal amounts of their personalities, but the birth comes as a something *more* for the woman. She is more subject to necessity; that is, her bodily functions constitute a "something more" compared to those of the man. Word for word he says therefore: "In childbirth the woman is *again* at the furthest point of one extreme of the synthesis. Therefore the spirit trembles, for in this moment it does not have its task, it is as if it were suspended."[13] The spirit trembles, because the birth proceeds whether the woman wills it or no—not even the strongest personality can stop it. A birth is not an area of will, therefore it is a demanding undertaking and it is this *again* that, to Kierkegaard, makes the whole difference between man and woman.

Birth means that when the task facing a person is, for instance, to identify with one's sensuousness for the sake of balance in the synthesis, then greater demands are made upon the woman; it is she who has to bear the children. That implies that her synthesis is different from the man's; her actuality or necessity is different; it is of necessity and not by chance that it is she who has to give birth. Both a sexual relationship and a birth are to Kierkegaard tantamount to being placed right out on the outermost point of the extreme of the synthesis, where a person is almost on the way across into the sheerly animal and is thus moving away from becoming spirit, and so away from being master of one's own personality, or from the balanced synthesis. That this is so is manifested by both situations being language-less, and language is the spirit's highest medium of expression.

These greater demands upon the woman, of twice having the necessity to find herself at the one extreme of the synthesis for every time the man does so, make themselves felt in a greater anxiety, because anxiety was precisely an expression of having problems with one's personality. Greater demands are thus made upon the woman's personality and upon her sense of responsibility. This may also be phrased thus: "in freedom's possibility anxiety will find a greater scope";[14] that is, there are larger interstices between the components of the synthesis in woman; it requires greater effort to hold them *together; therefore* a woman is more anxious than a man.

But the more there is to live up to, the greater is the perfection if someone does it; so Kierkegaard can also say that woman is more perfect than man. But if any woman should be tempted to give priority to one side of the synthesis and try to reduce herself to something bodily by mainly living as a birth-machine, as a "farrowing sow," then freedom is suppressed and it will be very difficult for her to obtain real existence. Man's synthesis differs in an absolute sense from woman's, because it does not afford the same opportunity for the bodily manifestation of the personality or the spirit. A woman is more at risk of falling victim to an existential crisis, an alienation, because she is more sensuously or somatically conditioned. This makes greater demands upon her sense of responsibility, as the drive or the somatic is in itself something impersonal, something originally immediate that cannot express the spirit, for this first immediacy is the opposite of relating to one's consciousness. Therefore a woman is more inclined to abandon freedom and thus anxiety, to repudiate true existence, and to be content with what is called "being for others." This position may indeed be said to be a characteristic of the birth situation. In this situation she is almost exclusively there for the sake of the new individual, *therefore* it is taxing for the personality or the spirit. "Being for others" is, in this connection, tantamount to "not being anything in oneself," to self-effacement in relation to other people, and that is disastrous from an existential viewpoint.

Self-effacement, or "dying from finitude," is only a category that may be utilized over against God. It means that one is surrendering the finitely determined synthesis as the only possibility and adopting the other one, the deeper understanding, but the former is contained in the latter. Thus it does not mean that the life of this world has no value, that everything is staked upon an eternal life in the commonplace sense. For Kierkegaard always speaks about this world; he considered himself unable to make any statement about any other world there might be. What is being said is that a human being must die from the egoism or selfishness of this world, from the overprioritizing of self-absorption. This does not of course mean that one is not to think about oneself at all—that is not feasible—for then one would die for instance of hunger and thirst instead of achieving existential joy. The bodily is a *factor* in the synthesis, it should not and *cannot* be destroyed. One must love one's neighbor *as* oneself; that is, it is fully legitimate, not to say a duty, to love oneself.

The overprioritizing of self-love has to pass away, but true self-love (loving God) lies at the basis of all love. Kierkegaard did not advocate asceticism but synthesis. The body (including sexuality) must just be an integral part of our self-understanding. In Kierkegaard's view, it is important to own up to what we are, to take ourselves over, not to weed anything out first, and not in general to choose any other people we would rather be. The negative definition of the concept of spirit is precisely "not to be like the others,"[15] and the positive definition is "to have the conception of an infinite consistency in oneself, to stake everything on the one thing," that is, to become "nothing before God."

For that very reason the Virgin Mary is an ideal figure, and it has given rise to many misunderstandings that she is indeed a virgin. But that does not mean that sexuality is to be denied. What makes Mary something ideal is that her "marriage relationship" and her God-relationship in this context are identical. That entails that we can speak of absolute surrender in both relationships, while for an ordinary woman in an ordinary marriage this is precisely what must not be the case; here the husband is of course a human husband. If a woman misinterprets her situation in that she confuses her body-soul relationship to her husband with her existential relationship, her relationship to God, thus becoming nothing for her *husband's* sake, then she errs. For then she becomes unreal and alienated from herself; then she does not exist in Kierkegaard's sense, and that is what Kierkegaard reproaches women for doing. The Virgin Mary, on the other hand, represents the thoroughgoing consistent attitude that does not normally occur. She is the perfect human being, because existence is a matter of consistency. Mary does not ask any silly questions of a scientific nature. At the same time, she is to the highest degree a woman. This notwithstanding, Kierkegaard has only commendatory words to spare for her. So nothing suggests that he is antiwoman in any commonplace sense.

The reason that this label has often been applied to him is to be found in the failure to understand Kierkegaard's idea and means of expression. For instance, his criticism of the first Danish feminist, Mathilde Fibiger, has been taken to be general antifemininity, which is quite wrong. What Kierkegaard reprehends in Clara Raphael, the main character in Fibiger's *Twelve Letters*[16] is precisely that she, unlike the Virgin Mary, relates exceedingly inconsistently to her idea, and *for that reason* she has no true existence.

Her idea is, first, that she will not marry—and then she does anyway. Second, she does not live up to the idea of marriage; she reduces it, being content with a brother-sister relationship to her husband. In brief, she does not fully exist, and that is what is wrong with her in Kierkegaard's opinion, not her being a woman. Mathilde Fibiger herself commits the mistake of believing that one can become oneself through a collective cause, the cause of feminism, that is, through "the others"—but one can only become oneself through God. As straightforward phenomena "the others" stand in the way of the individual.

But conversely, this does not mean that someone just has to be self-absorbed in a commonplace sense; the concept is given new content by Kierkegaard. First, in becoming oneself, one becomes able to be something for others, but the way lies through God, not through the other person (as it does, for example, in Hegel). Not until the encounter with "love itself" is it possible in love to love another person as oneself. In Kierkegaard, the love concept contains the equality concept. Without equal worth being given to people, love simply does not exist.

This is far from meaning that all people are the same, only that they have equal value. As human beings they are of equal worth, or equally little worth, because when set over against love they do not of course make the grade. So the only thing they can do is to will to choose love and thus equality; no more can be required of human beings, thinks Kierkegaard. But to communicate such a message at a time when the words of the official marriage ritual said that the wife should be submissive to her husband was a difficult undertaking; thus he had to communicate indirectly.

Kierkegaard was attacking the general behavior of human beings in the entire period. But the people who seemed to Kierkegaard to be the most oppressed, the most subjugated in the actual society of the time were, very understandably, women. At all society levels their personalities were in general dominated by their husbands, and therefore he spends such a large proportion of his writings in being ironical about marriage and women—in depicting them as completely ludicrous—partly to show that women themselves had the decisive blame for this. It is just as great a sin to allow oneself to be subjugated; one has a duty to exist properly and not, spiritually, to perish in a merely immediate routine life. This sin was most widespread among women, and therefore Kierkegaard speaks so vehemently to them. But that does not of course mean that he was an opponent of women's personal liberation, or that he did not consider they *could* obtain existence; in that case it would not make much sense to write in the way he does. Kierkegaard was not a descriptive writer of history, but an indirect communicator of religious questions.

Kierkegaard wrote as he did about women in order to point out that both women and men are equally significant; all in principle are able to become themselves, and that is the sole truly significant thing, that which has existential value. A woman *can* therefore exist in Kierkegaard's opinion; whether she does so is her own responsibility, and, strictly speaking, other people can know nothing about it.

Now it is not necessarily the case that because something can be deduced from Kierkegaard's philosophy, it was lived out by him personally. It may perhaps be thought that he was unable to follow out his own ideas in practice, but actually this is not a very interesting question. For Kierkegaard did not indeed desire the role of an authority. He *could* not be an example for imitation, for that would be contrary to his method. In my view, his philosophy implies the possibility of existence for women.

But, as already mentioned, it requires a modicum of personal involvement or interest in the matter to be able at all to read Kierkegaard and therefore to understand his view of women. That is why so many have misinterpreted so much. Either because, being men, they were less concerned, or because they were filled in advance with so many prejudices about his view of women and sexuality that they did not give their imagination the scope it needs to grasp anything. Thus the fault is to be found in the reader himself. But Kierkegaard's feat as regards feminine policy is that back at that historical juncture he was pointing out that human beings vary, but are in principle of equal worth. What he indirectly points to are but the still current misjudgments that will not disappear as long as bringing babies into the world is not valued more highly. And Kierkegaard will not be understood so long as his concept of reflection is identified merely with intellectual reflection. For the existential joy that is attained after despair has been surmounted is indeed quite *without* reflection.

Any discrimination against women is in my opinion a projection by the reader. Kierkegaard in his entire philosophy tried to draw attention to this misunderstanding, but we can never arrive at a conclusive result. As regards his personal standpoint, Kierkegaard himself is located somewhere between sane insanity and insane sanity. Sanity is a questioning and erring human being. I consider, like Kresten Nordentoft, that "Kierkegaard's onslaught upon his own hypocrisy holds its own against the hypocrisy"[17] in this context too.

His dialectic of communication may be seen in the light of an old Jewish proverb that the Czech writer Milan Kundera quotes: "Man thinks—God laughs." God laughs at the sight of the thinking human being, because the truth is slipping away precisely while the person is thinking. "The art form," says Kundera, "which was created by God's laughter, does not disseminate ideological convictions, it rather contradicts them. Like Penelope, every night it unravels the cloth which theologians, philosophers, and scholars have woven the day before."[18] That is the art of Kierkegaard.

Notes

Sources consulted include *Søren Kierkegaards Samlede Værker*, 3d ed., ed. A. B. Drachmann, J. L. Heiberg, and H. O. Lange (Copenhagen, 1962), here cited as *SV*; and *Søren Kierkegaards Papirer*, 2d enlarged ed. by Niels Thulstrup (Copenhagen, 1968–78), here cited as *PAP*.

1. SV 19:298.
2. PAP XI, 1-A100.
3. PAP XI, 2-A271.

4. *PAP* II-A163.
5. *SV* 15:105.
6. *SV* 15:121.
7. *SV* 15:107.
8. *PAP* VIII, 2-B154.
9. *PAP* XI, 1-A464.
10. *SV* 15:98.
11. *SV* 6:205.
12. *SV* 6:169.
13. *SV* 6:162.
14. *SV* 6:155.
15. *SV* 18:130.
16. *PAP* X, 3-A678.
17. Kresten Nordentoft, *Kierkegaards Psykologi* (Copenhagen, 1972), 488.
18. "Politiken" (Copenhagen), feature article, 15 June 1985.

3

The Logic of Søren Kierkegaard's Misogyny, 1854–1855

Julia Watkin

When one reads the *Journals* of the last two years of Kierkegaard's life, one cannot help being struck by the negative expressions about women. We read that "woman is personified egoism. Her burning, hot devotion to man is neither more nor less than her egoism," whereas man "is not originally an egoist," he does not become that until "he is lucky enough to be united to a woman," when he becomes the thorough egoist in the union "commonly known as marriage . . . the proper enterprise of egoism."[1] We learn that woman's characteristic fault is "cunning, subtlety and lies," she is "the weaker sex," expected to "wail and scream."[2] Man "was structured for eternity" but woman "leads him into a digression." Woman in her relation to the religious "explains nothing," her devotedness "is essentially related to interjections, and it is unfeminine if it is more than that."[3] For she relates to things directly, "breathes the air of directness"; she "participates in religion at second hand, through the man."[4] So "at the greatest distance from the ideal is: mother, madam. The real fury against the ideal comes from family life, from the lioness, or, to say it another way . . . from the suckling sow."[5] Parallel to these statements are Kierkegaard's many comments (often invoking the authority of Saint Paul)[6] praising celibacy and rejecting the sexual drive with its begetting of children as something anti-Christian, as in the piece headed "Propagation of the Species, Christianity wants to bar the way."[7]

Several reasons have been given as to why Kierkegaard in his last years seems to make a violent attack on women, sex, and marriage—an attack that seems all the more strange when one considers his positive attitude earlier toward marriage.[8] Most obvious is a psychological-pathological explanation. One can suggest that Kierkegaard could not fulfill his engagement in the reality of marriage to Regine Olsen;[9] over the years he developed a vicious "sour grapes" attitude concerning women and sex. Eduard Geismar considers that Kierkegaard's struggle with his "thorn in the flesh" is an element in the situation when he develops his view that the philosophy of Schopenhauer is to blame. Kierkegaard, who was already leaning in a similar direction, developed "an asceticism hostile to life" because he was influenced by Schopenhauer's cynical disgust with life. Schopenhauer's thought encouraged Kierkegaard to relieve his feelings in the *Journals* from 1854 and in several numbers of "The Instant."[10]

Yet another possibility is that advanced by Birgit Bertung, who sees in Kierkegaard's statements about women a "poetical provocation or repulsion." By using such negative language Kierkegaard aims at a dialectical attack on, not women, but on the mixing up of a temporal relationship to the husband with the spiritual relationship to God, something that they are in risk of doing, since woman as the child-bearer is in danger of falling into the role of existing only as "being for others," of becoming a victim to the animal-temporal side of human nature and thus moving away from spirit and the command of her own personality. On this view, Kierkegaard is not an ascetic, but is ironizing over the domination of women by men to which women give their assent. By using such language he hopes to provoke Society, and especially women, into an insight into the situation and to movement toward the proper preservation (in this world) of the equality of men and women before God through the relation to God.[11]

From the above it can be seen that an important consideration must influence an assessment of Kierkegaard's final statements about women. It has to be decided whether or not he means his attack to be taken at face value. Linked to this question is the problem of Kierkegaard's description of women. Is it meant to apply to women only in the cultural situation of his time, or does he regard it as a true account of women in every age? Is it the case, as Sylvia Walsh suggests in her article "On 'Feminine' and 'Masculine' forms of Despair," that in his use of "stereotyped characterizations of the sexes" he reflects and helps perpetuate such characterizations, even though his analysis of the self rests on a common structure of selfhood for both sexes?[12]

With respect to the second question, I am inclined to think that even in his last years, Kierkegaard was describing Society the way he observed it around him, and that he probably never considered the question of cultural conditioning on personality the way we understand that question today, even though he realized that each individual starts out from an historically conditioned situation. Although he respects and idealizes women and asserts a fundamental equality of the sexes before God, Kierkegaard, like many other authors of his generation and later, also perceived fundamental external and natural differences between the sexes, seeing woman as frail, as needing the support of the man, and as instinctive and intuitive in intellectual matters. Thus one must try as far as possible to distinguish between Kierkegaard's nineteenth-century view of women—a view that includes the above-mentioned and very modern emphasis on fundamental equality—and the extreme polemic of his final years.[13]

Regarding the first and main question, I here develop the view that Kierkegaard's attack is to be taken directly at face value, but that it is not aimed exclusively at women and that it makes sense in terms of the structure of his authorship as well as of the cultural situation of the time. The extreme statements of the last years are in agreement with the logic of basic metaphysical assumptions in the authorship.[14] In this connection I shall be taking a look at Kierkegaard's view of God, the world, and humankind, with special reference to the significance of marriage, before finally turning to his cultural situation.

Kierkegaard makes it clear many times in his authorship that he presupposes the existence of the personal God of Christianity, a God who is pure personhood, "pure subjectivity," and who "creates out of nothing."[15] As Kierkegaard explains in a Journal entry from 1846, in the act of creating from nothing God withdraws himself so that creation may come into being. He withdraws himself in order to give himself, because it is by so doing that he "makes the recipient independent." That is, in finite relationships, the recipient of a gift is not independent because he is obligated to the giver, who, in turn, lacks the power to give without creating obligation. Although God omnipotently creates human beings "out of nothing" in that humankind is not already in independent existence prior to creation, he renounces the obligation established through humanity's factual total dependence on him in order that human beings may truly be free.[16] Kierkegaard's thought here is very like Simone Weil's "creative renunciation of God,"[17] and already comes to expression in the early years in his criticism of Solger in the comment that "in that God sacrifices himself, he creates."[18]

God's self-giving, self-sacrificing creativity has two expressions. On the one hand, the divine omnipotence is "able to create the most fragile of all things—a being independent of that very omnipotence"; on the other, it is also able to create "the most impressive of all things—the whole visible world."[19] This latter is directly dependent on God; it is the realm of nature, of the aesthetic, where life in its immediate state unconsciously fulfills its development according to God's design.[20] The former, since the individual is independent while partaking of the substance of visible creation, is a synthesis, not only of psyche and body, but also of the temporal and the eternal. The individual is animal, but also spirit.[21] God has created humankind in his own image and since the eternal God is spirit, to be spirit is a person's "invisible glory."[22] Yet, as Judge William points out in *Either-Or*, the individual is "finite spirit" assigned to temporality, which latter is the possibility of that spirit's glorification.[23] Within the realm of temporality each person is as yet only finitely "like God" and must use the period allotted to him to fulfill and make real his God-given potentiality or possibility.

For Kierkegaard, then, there are two realms, temporality and eternity, with eternity transcending all time—past, present, and future.[24] These two realms stand in an inverse relation to each other, and "God is always the inverse of man" because of the character of the nature of God and of eternity. For Kierkegaard, God's realm is the realm of the intensive, whereas temporality is the realm of the extensive.[25] In the temporal world, it is the nature of all existence to extend and assert itself. Creation is Being, opposite God, as it were, and humankind in its self-consciousness is actively ego opposite God in freedom and not passively so like animals and the rest of nature, which follow instinct according to God's will. To the world of temporality belong progression and assertion of self-hood, quantity, expansion; to the realm of eternity belong self-denial, quality, renunciatory withdrawal. The opposite of the extensive life of the world is the intensive life of the spirit.[26]

Such a life can be lived in the world and is expounded by Judge William to the young man in *Either-Or*. For Judge William temporality "exists for the sake of humankind and is the greatest of all the gifts of grace," because in it each member of the community can relate to the Christian God, "the eternal Power who omnipresently pervades the whole of existence." Authentic community is formed by each individual living unselfishly in relation to God and neighbor. The aesthetic world-order of human nature in the raw is brought under control of the ethical-religious.[27] This thought is expanded in the Journals where Kierkegaard regards the individual in his relation to God as being "decisive as the presupposition for forming community," true neighbor love being "self-denial, rooted in the relationship to God."[28] "Earthly love . . . at its highest is love only for one single human being in the whole world," "spiritual love . . . loves more and more people, has its truth in loving all." "Erotic love and friendship are preferential," but in authentic love to the neighbor there is an equality belonging to eternity.[29]

In this way, the individual can live the life of eternity now, within the context of human relationships. Instead of living the competitive life of the temporal world in the manner of the animal kingdom, he dies to self-centeredness and lives the life of fellowship with God and the transcendent kingdom of heaven, something that is everlasting in that at death the individual enters into full membership of that realm.[30]

Yet just because the realm of eternity is the end and aim of existence, marriage and physical continuity of the race are treated ambiguously in Kierkegaard's writings. For Judge William, if the temporal is the realm where the individual is placed by God, then, as we have seen, the individual's duty is to aim at the highest within the finite sphere by living a self-denying and hence eternally orientated life within finite relationships. Marriage must be the highest and a duty in the finite sphere because otherwise the physical and spiritual structure in which individuals make up families and the social whole would disappear. In this sense marriage unites the spiritual and the physical, providing the spiritual and physical continuity of the race. Yet the Judge's outlook is not to be confused with that of one for whom this life is all. Marriage does not exist merely for the sake of continuing the race, but as the necessary presupposition for the possibility of ethical-religious life in temporality. The temporal world remains the sphere of humankind's unavoidable self-orientation as the individual extends himself in space and time, and even the Judge can see that this is what gives marriage—"the deepest form of life's revelation" and "the beautiful mid-point of life and existence"—a natural egocentricity from which it cannot be freed by the most unselfish love.[31]

For what hampers the God-like self-renouncing life in the temporal order is the unavoidable fact of natural preference. In concrete terms, a man or woman who neglects partner and children in order to give the appropriate love and care to others is hardly the paragon of love. There is a sense in which individuals must put the selfhood of the family unit first, however unselfishly they live. Similarly, even where a nation has an idealistic democratic constitution, it is impossible to escape conflict of interest, not only within the state but between nations where a government must put the interest of the nation before that of other nations.[32] Viewed in that light, the state, as Kierkegaard points out, functions as a "higher egoism" with the task of controlling personal egoisms[33] and cannot be regarded as Christian. Instead, the best government aims at the greatest happiness of the greatest number as best it can, with emphasis on protecting posterity.

This fact of natural preference is thus the reason why Johannes Climacus in *Philosophical Fragments* points out that "self-love" is "the ground in all love," the basic starting-point of all human relationships before they are transformed into something higher, while Judge William in *Stages on Life's Way* says that "from the essentially religious point of view . . . it makes no difference whether or not a person has been married" and that not marrying is "higher" than marrying, the Judge's revision of his earlier statement being a necessary consequence of a standpoint that has the transcendent realm of God as the ultimate goal. This is seen clearly in Climacus's discussion of "Religiousness A" in *Concluding Unscientific Postscript*, where the individual is shown as directing his attention more profoundly toward the transcendent. Here, "self-annihilation is the essential form of the God-relationship." The individual concentrates on his God-relationship with greater detachment from human relationships, though paradoxically participating in them more effectively because of aiming to do so on a totally non-self-regarding basis.[34] The movement of the authorship is away from any form of self-orientation to a God-centeredness that requires an ever-increasing self-denial and self-renunciation.

At this point, it is useful to take a look at Kierkegaard's view of human-kind's place in creation in connection with the Christian doctrine of the Fall. For the factor of unavoidable natural self-concern must be taken into consideration when looking at Kierkegaard's later statements that treat procreation as a fall into sin. The "ideality" preceding the Fall is for Kierkegaard here the God-intended ideal state in which humankind is like God through a totally self-denying God-relationship. The Fall itself is the human race "lost" or separated from God, this state of affairs seen as occurring when self-conscious man first failed to be willing to renounce everything for God and thus consciously asserted himself. In that sense, procreation is particularly "the Fall" as the assertion of the human ego in physical existence. From this standpoint, every child and generation is lost and fallen through being born, the child sharing in the parental egoism insofar as it is a part of it.[35] As early as 1844 we learn from Vigilius Haufniensis in *The Concept of Anxiety* that if Adam had not sinned—that is, by his disobedience stressed mankind's opposite relation *to* God as opposition to God—he would have become eternal immediately, "would in the same moment have passed over into eternity."[36] Instead of which, the emphasis on man as separate ego means that the sexual, because of sin, becomes "the centre of human egoism," a propensity to carry human-ity further away from God. In a *Journal* note from the draft of *The Concept of Anxiety*, Kierkegaard's pseudonym even goes as far as to state that "first with sin time actually comes into being," implying that temporality originates through sin, a thought that occurs in the *Journal* entries of the final years. Adam asserts himself, and expands his ego self-assertively on the horizontal plane of history, instead of relating in total self-denial to God on the vertical plane of eternity. Sexuality leads to the fact of human history, and with the advent of human self-consciousness, procre-ation becomes a purposive instead of an instinctive activity. Viewed in that light, existence can be described by Kierkegaard as "crime" and "punishment" in that humankind, having defied the divine purpose, will-fully continues in a situation that tends to isolation from God.[37]

God can therefore be seen as self-denyingly creating nature so that man in freedom can choose between two ways of being like God or having "kinship with the Deity." The individual can either be a physical creator in giving life or he can surrender himself to an existence of total self-denial: he can propagate the species as "animal creature" or as "man of spirit"—choose to be naturally self-asserting in creation to a greater or lesser extent, or, in utter self-denial can be an example encouraging others to follow the pattern of God's nature, Jesus, incarnate God and suffering, atoning servant, who gives up everything, even life itself.[38]

Humankind, however, interprets God's omnipotence as self-assertive monarchic power. The individual wishes to be the independent lord of creation. Hence his first idea is to propagate his kind. He expresses his egoism through reproduction: "Man wants to dabble in the creator's activity, if not by creating man, at least by giving life," says Kierkegaard, but "to create is reserved for God . . . the giving of life is a weak analogy to this . . . human egoism culminates at this point." In humankind, "the instinct for the propagation of the race" is in fact as strong as "the instinct of self-preservation," because through the strength of numbers it is part of self-preservation, while family life centered round the mother with her children becomes, as in the animal kingdom, a species of egoism, in which "woman most certainly does not love herself foremost but through (egoistically) loving her own she loves herself."[39]

For this reason, Kierkegaard points out that "the way marriage is regarded is decisive for every religious view of life" and that "propagation of the race is a substitute for immortality."[40] All life-views—even religions that presuppose a personal God and advocate individual self-denial for the sake of others—are rejected by Kierkegaard if they postulate a false "unity of the divine and this life." Humankind in defiance of God wishes to remain within the realm of temporality. It establishes family life as "a form of godliness," centering its hopes on this world in terms of extension of the human ego in the form of race, relationships, and goods. There is a tendency to identify the natural order of existence with the religious, nationality with religion, and to recast God in the image of man.[41] Not willing himself to be a real Christian, the individual turns Christianity into "Christendom" when he "undertakes to beget children who shall become Christians and these children in their turn behave in the same way" thus turning Christianity into enjoyment of life in "the ordinary human sense."[42]

It can thus be seen that Kierkegaard does not become distorted in his later writings about marriage and sexuality. It is his metaphysical assumptions about God and creation, the eternal and the temporal, that make it difficult, if not impossible, for him to reconcile marriage and procreation with an ideal likeness to God that demands total self-renunciation. Thus his attitude to marriage shifts when he moves from discussing how the Christian individual relates to God in and through the temporal world to how he relates to God from the temporal world in the light of the demand of Christian ideality. In the writings of the Judge, marriage is the important relationship sanctifying the temporal under God, though he is careful to emphasize it as a relationship rather than in its aspect of continuing the race. Later though, when Kierkegaard begins to speak of the exception and of self-annihilation before God, marriage becomes viewed not just as something one may give up under certain circumstances, or as something one has no time for if one intends to serve the Absolute absolutely, but as something one must normally give up in order to fulfill the divine command totally, especially where the human emphasis on marriage is on having children and on the continuation of the race. If the true spiritual path consists of dying to selfishness, denying the natural self, expansion of the ego in space and time in one's descendants can be seen as a form of the assertion of selfhood difficult to reconcile with self-denial when absolute ideality is demanded.[43]

The ideality of the renunciation of marriage is in a sense implied at the beginning of Kierkegaard's authorship because Kierkegaard does not have a closed definition of Christianity. Judge William does not set up his ethical-religious way as ultimate perfection, but puts it forward as the path of development, after which the situation is seen as being between God and the individual.[44] Even toward the end of the authorship, however, when Kierkegaard as the "corrective" scornfully rejects the thought that "everyone is duty-bound to marry and that marriage is the genuinely ennobling life," he still allows the permissibility of marriage, in "the Moral" in *Training in Christianity*. In the last years, side by side with demands for a "stop" to procreation and a rejection of Christian "epicureanism," he points out that there are exceptional dialectical situations where the ideal of total renunciation may in fact require the individual to marry, as in the case of Luther. There are times when to keep "the things of the world does not signify that one wants to keep them—no, but that one wants to do something still higher than to give them away."[45] Also, although Kierkegaard regards the Christian injunction to hate one's life in this world as a principle logically "so asocial that it cannot constitute community" and says that he is "unable to comprehend how it can occur to any man to unite being a Christian with being married," he points out that he is "not thinking of the case of a man who was already married and had a family, and then at that age became a Christian" but of the one who "is unmarried and says he has become a Christian."[46] In retrospect he believes that his own desire to marry was a mistake, and it is surely his own situation he is describing when he speaks of letting the loved one go "in order to love God."[47] The New Testament's "hatred of men" thus does not mean "conceitedly and arrogantly" wanting to "despise man and love God," but is a rejection of temporality whenever and wherever it becomes divorced from God.[48]

We can now return to the statements about women with which we started, having ascertained that Kierkegaard's misogyny is rather a "misogamy" or attack on marriage in which both male and female roles are sharply criticized. Here, it should be noted that the bulk of the negative statements, and especially those dealing mainly with women, appear in the *Journals* and not in the *Works*, and that there is nothing to suggest that the *Journal* entries in question were sketches for a proposed special "attack" on women only, dialectical or otherwise.[49] We should therefore see Kierkegaard as dealing here, not with the relationship between men and women, but with the attitude toward marriage current in the society of his day in the light of his view of Christian ideality. Certainly one can regard Kierkegaard's published "anti-marriage" statements of the last years as shock tactics, as a part of his attack on "Christendom," but these and the *Journal* entries on marriage and women ought also to be viewed in the light of other *Journal* entries that tell us not a little about attitudes in society toward married and single persons.

We learn from a number of *Journal* entries that, whereas celibacy was regarded as belonging to holiness in the Middle Ages, after the Reformation the reverse has become the case: "Fasting, celibacy, etc. is ridiculous extremism, madness, unreasonable worship of God. But marriage is the true and reasonable worship of God." Under the influence of Protestantism, marriage has not only come to be "well-pleasing to God," it now also "constitutes the meaning of life." This has affected attitudes toward the unmarried. We thus also learn that "the unmarried girl who is not lucky enough to marry . . . is overlooked and minimized." Whereas the married are regarded as the only "genuine citizens in this world," the single person "is an alien," "ridiculous." Married people regard such a person as "selfish," and just as families prefer their doctor to be married because "they are afraid that an unmarried man will be lecherous," so the congregation "will have no confidence in someone as a spiritual adviser etc. if he is not married." Even Kierkegaard's brother, Peter Christian, has, by 1848, come to believe that "the blessing of God does not rest upon an unmarried person."[50]

Even if we must consider Kierkegaard's harsh comments about women and marriage as having reference only to the situation of his time, can they say anything to us today in our cultural situation where both men and women concentrate their energies on career and family? I think they probably can. To the extent that we live in a time of overemphasis on the pursuit of sexuality in various forms, Kierkegaard's statements ought to give us pause for thought, for the "abstainer" is still regarded with suspicion as selfish and as a deviant from the "norm,"[51] while various forms of self-denial and self-renunciation tend to be understood only in relation to this-worldly goals, for example, fasting as a political protest in China. As we have seen, Kierkegaard's statements are to be understood as being linked to the basic point that he is making in his authorship, his definition of Christianity and Christian ideality, with final emphasis on asceticism in relation to the traditional hope of eternal life. It can be argued that this is still something that we can take into consideration as a possibility, instead of taking it for granted that it is "ridiculous extremism" about something untrue because it goes against our natural inclinations and our current assumptions about the nature of existence.

Notes

This essay was presented at the Eighteenth World Congress of Philosophy, Brighton, England, August 1988.

References are to the following works:

Kierkegaard's Collected Works: Søren Kierkegaards Samlede Vaerker, 14 vols., 1st ed., ed. A. B. Drachmann, J. L. Heiberg, and H. O. Lange (Copenhagen: Gyldendal, 1901–6); here cited as SV.

Søren Kierkegaards Papirer, vols. 1–13, 2d ed., ed. P. A. Heiberg, V. Kuhr, E. Torsting, and N. Thulstrup (Copenhagen: Gyldendal, 1968–70); index, vols. 14–16, ed. N. J. Cappelørn, 1975–78; here cited as Pap.

Søren Kierkegaard, *Kierkegaard's Writings*, ed. and tr. Howard and Edna Hong et al., general editor Howard V. Hong (Princeton: Princeton University Press, 1978–); here cited as KW. Other translations are named in the appropriate notes.

Søren Kierkegaard, *Søren Kierkegaard's Journals and Papers*, vols. 1–7, ed. and tr. Howard and Edna Hong (Bloomington: Indiana University Press, 1967–68); here cited as JP.

1. Pap. XI, 1 A 226 cf. 281 1854 (JP IV 5000, 5003).

2. Pap. XI, 1 A 228, 233 1854 (JP III 3175, IV 5002).

3. Pap. XI, 1 A 426 1854, XI, 2 A 70 1854 (JP IV 5005, 5006).

4. Pap. XI, 2 A 192 1854 pp. 207–9, cf. SV XI 163 ft. (JP IV 5007, cf. KW XIX *The Sickness unto Death* SUD 50 n).

5. Pap. XI, 2 A 271 1855 (JP II 1823 p. 306).

6. I Cor. 7:7–9; cf. e.g. Pap. XI, 1 A 157, 169, 313, 1854, SV XIV 199, 254, 261 (JP III 2908, 2618, 2621 p. 138, Søren Kierkegaard, *Kierkegaard's Attack Upon "Christendom"* 1854–1855, tr. Walter Lowrie (Princeton: Princeton University Press, 1968 ed.) AX 165, 213, 220).

7. Pap. XI, 2 A 150 1854, cf. XI, 1 A 129, 150, 169, 253, 295, 313, 1854, XI, 2 A 153, 154, 160, 172, 176, 231, 238, 241, 1854, 372, 1854–55 (JP III 2622, cf. 2616–2621, 2623–2631).

8. See Pap. XI, 1 A 210 n.d., SV II 5-140, VI 85–74, V 204–25 (JP VI 6882, KW IV EO II 5–154, KW XI *Stages on Life's Way* SLW 87–184, Søren Kierkegaard, *Thoughts on Crucial Situations in Human Life*, Three Discourses on Imagined Occasions, tr. David F. Swenson (Minneapolis: Augsburg Publishing House, 1941) TDIO 43–74, "On the Occasion of a Wedding," where Kierkegaard refers to, for example, "the sacred vocation of marriage," SV V 219, TDIO 65 (*Ægteskabets hellige Kald*).

9. In a paper to the Søren Kierkegaard Society Denmark (Vartov, Copenhagen, 24.3.1988) psychiatrist Dr. Thorkil Vanggard suggests that Kierkegaard was very scared of a close relationship with a woman and could not cope with the physical side of marriage.

10. Eduard Geismar, *Søren Kierkegaard*, I–II (Copenhagen: G. E. C. Gads, 1927) II, section VI 40–45. For the references to comments involving women in "The Instant" see SV XIV 175, 197, 252–56, 260, 265 (AX 145, 163, 212–16, 219–20, 223).

11. Birgit Bertung in her paper "Yes, a Woman *Can* Exist," in *Kierkegaard Conferences I "Kierkegaard Poet of Existence."* (Copenhagen: C. A. Reitzels, 1989). See also her book, *Om Kierkegaard, Kvinder og Kærlighed* en studie i Søren Kierkegaards kvindesyn (Copenhagen: C. A. Reitzels, 1987).

12. *International Kierkegaard Commentary: The Sickness unto Death,* ed. Robert L. Perkins, (Macon: Mercer University Press, 1987), IKC 19: 121–35.

13. On the individual's historical context see, for example, SV I 123, II 193–94, 231, IV 301 (KW III EO I 145, KW IV EO II 216, 258, KW VIII *The Concept of Anxiety* CA 28–29). On the assertion of spiritual equality of men and women before God mentioned with their external and psycho-physical differences, see, for example, SV IX 133–34, Pap. III A 234 1842, V B 53:25 1844, XI, 1 A 231 1854, XI, 2 A 192, 193 1854 (Søren Kierkegaard, *Works of Love,* tr. Howard and Edna Hong [New York: Harper and Row, 1962] WL 139–40, JP I 95, IV 4989, 5001, 5007, 5008). In the last two *Journal* entries women are depicted as relating directly to things, as unable to "endure a dialectic." It is interesting to compare Kierkegaard's entries here with a statement by J. L. Heiberg in 1833, when he went as far as to invite women as well as men to attend his philosophy lectures. He observed that "although men usually have a sharper and more consistent reason, a greater capacity for dialectic, women usually have a surer, more infallible feeling for immediately grasping truth." J. L. Heiberg, lecture programme: *Om Philosophiens Betydning for den nuværende Tid* (Copenhagen: 1833), 53.

14. In this I shall be following up the thought of Gregor Malantschuk in his essay, "Kierkegaard's View of Man and Woman" in his *Controversial Kierkegaard,* tr. Howard and Edna Hong, The Kierkegaard Monography Series, ed. Alastair McKinnon (Waterloo, Ontario: Wilfred Laurier Press, 1980), 37–61. Malantschuk sees Kierkegaard in the last years as looking at everything from an "extreme Christian point of view, consequently as one who in his thinking and in his life earnestly tried to break with this world." From such a viewpoint, "the whole earthly enterprise looks different than when one feels altogether bound to it." Kierkegaard now looks at woman from the "plane of the solitary hermit." See esp. pp. 58–59.

15. Pap. XI, 2 A 54 cf. 97 1854, II A 359, 758 1838, VII, 1 A 181 1846, X, 2 A 563 1850, XI, 1 A 491 1854, XI, 2 A 3 1854, SV I 210, IV 352 ff. VI 118, VII 220 (JP III 2570, IV 4571, 4412, II 1310, 1251, 1299, 2099, 1224, KW III EO I 236, KW VIII CA 83 ft., KW XI SLW 122, Søren Kierkegaard, *Kierkegaard's Concluding Unscientific Postscript,* tr. David F. Swenson and Walter Lowrie (Princeton: Princeton University Press, 1941) CUP 232–33. See also on God as creator out of nothing in the church fathers, Anselm, Aquinas, Augustine, references in e.g. F. C. Copleston, *Aquinas* (Great Britain: Penguin Books, 1955) 70–71, 141–48, and Copleston, *A History of Philosophy* I–VIII (London: Burns Oates and Washbourne, 1946–66), II:74–77.

16. Pap. VII, 1 A 181 1846 (JP II 1251).

17. Simone Weil, *Waiting on God—The Essence of Her Thought* (England: Collins, Fontana, 1959), 113–14, 102.

18. SV XIII 382, Søren Kierkegaard, *The Concept of Irony*, tr. Lee M. Capel (London: Collins, 1966), CI 329.

19. Pap. VII, 1 A 181 1846 (JP II 1251).

20. See e.g. Søren Kierkegaard, *Edifying Discourses in Different Key*, "What we Learn from the Lilies of the Field and the Birds of the Air," SV VIII 245–96, esp. 269, cf. SV II 201, 161, 172 (Søren Kierkegaard, *The Gospel of Suffering and the Lilies of the Field*, tr. David F. and Lillian M. Swenson [Minneapolis: Augsburg Publishing House, 1948], GS 165–236, esp. 197, cf. KW IV EO II 225, 178, 191).

21. SV II 38, IV 355, 358, VII 258, XI 127–31, II 224 cf. 238, Pap. XI, 1 A 408 1854 (KW IV EO II 41, KW VIII CA 85, 88, CUP 267, KW XIX SUD 13–17, KW IV EO II 250 cf. 265, JP I 87).

22. SV VIII 278–79 (GS 210–11).

23. SV II 224 (KW IV EO II 250).

24. SV IV 360 (KW VIII CA 90).

25. Pap. XI, 2 A 123 1854, XI, 1 A 402 1854 (JP IV 4814, II 1807). Thought about opposition of the intensive and the extensive is repeated a number of times in Kierkegaard's authorship: Pap. IX A 126 1848, X, 4 A 219, 392, 1851, X, 4A 541 1849, X, 5 A 26 1852, XI, 1 A 189, 402, 414, 468, 500, 1854, XI, 2 A 64, 76, 123, 146, 1854 (JP III 2640, II 2100, 2101, 1852, 2102, 2056, 1807, III 2448, IV 4810, II 2103, 2104, IV 4813, 4814, III 2994).

26. Pap. XI, 2 A 123, 51, 53–55 1854 (JP IV 4814, III 3099, II 1444, III 2570–71).

27. SV II 224, 152, 133, 229, 235, cf. 18 (KW IV EO II 250, 167, 147, 255–56, 262–63, cf. 19).

28. Pap. X, 2 A 390 1850, VIII, 1 A 196 1847, X, 2 A 351 1850, VII, 1 A 20 1846, cf. SV IX esp. 58–60 (JP III 2952, 2410, IV 4170, 4110, WL esp. 68–70).

29. SV II 57, IX 54, 59–60 (KW IV EO II 62, WL 65, 70).

30. On Kierkegaard's view of death see my article: "Kierkegaard's View of Death," in *Journal of the History of European Ideas* II, no. 1 (1990).

31. SV II, 56–57, 224, 270, VI 97–98, 162–63, VII 214, Pap. IV A 234, SV VI 44–45, 112–14 (KW IV EO II 60–61, 250, 302, KW XI SLW 101–2, 171, CUP 227, KW XI SLW p. 42–43, 117).

32. As, for example, in the "cod war" between Britain and Iceland in the seventies.

33. Pap. XI, 2 A 108, cf. 111 (JP IV 4238, cf. 4501).

34. SV IV 206, 215, VI 104, 161, 164, VII 401, 335–484, IX 135 (KW VII PF 39, 48, KW XI SLW 107, 169, 172, CUP 412, 347–493, WL 141).

35. Pap. XI, 2 A 154, 201 1854, SV XIV 267, Pap. XI, 1 A 289 1854, XI, 2 A 150 1854, XI, 2 A 439, 434, 420, 1855 (JP III 2624, II 1818, AX 226, JP III 3643, 2622, VI 6969, II 1940, Søren Kierkegaard, *The Last Years Journals, 1853–55*, ed. and tr. Ronald Gregor Smith [London: Collins, Fontana, 1968] JRGS 346–47). In following up Kierkegaard's thought about Fall-doctrine, I will also be following up a comment by Eduard Geismar, *Søren Kierkegaard* II, section VI, 45, "that if one believes that most people are eternally lost, fallen, it is difficult to look positively at procreation."

36. SV IV 363, 348, 319 (KW VIII CA 93, 79, 49).

37. Pap. XI. 2 A 154, 150 1854, V B 55:12 1844, XI, 2 A 176, 202 1854, XI, 1 A 289 1854, XI, 2 A 439 1854, SV XIV 265, 267, Pap. XI, 2 A 434 1855 (JP III 2624, 2622, cf. KW VIII CA 198, JP III 2627, IV 3970, 3643, VI 6969, AX 223, 226, JP II 1940).

38. SV XIV 330, cf. 256, Pap. XI, 2 A 150 1854, XI, 1 A 194 1854, X, 3 A 150 1850, XI, 1 A 158, 22, 358, 115, 1854 (AX 265 cf. 215, JP III 2622, II 1803, I 1061, II 1929, 1925, I 83, IV 4980).

39. Pap. XI, 2 A 154 1854, XI, 2 A 439 1855, SV XIV 199, Pap. XI, 1 A 141 1854 p. 99 (JP III 2624, VI 6969, AX 165, JP IV 4998).

40. Pap. XI, 1 A 150 1854, XI, 2 A 154, 176 1854, SV XIV 262 (JP III 2617, 2624, 2627, AX 221).

41. Pap. IX A 424 1848, X, 3 A 293, 139 1850, XI, 1 A 139, 151, 184, 1854, X, 3 A 426 1849, X, 3 A 157 1850 SV VII 38–9, 349, Pap. XI, 2 A 183 1854, SV XI 209–10, 226–38, Pap. XI, 1 A 168 1854, XI, 2 A 164 1854, XI, 1 A 552, 524, 1854 (JP II 2217, 2221, 2218, 2224, 2225, 2227, I 843, II 2219, CUP 49, 360, JP II 1766, KW XIX SUD 99, 117–29, JP II 2054, I 370, III 3209, IV 4352).

42. SV XIV 255–56, 53, 252, Pap. XI, 1 A 259 1854, XI, 2 A 222 1854, XI, 1 A 295 1854 (AX 215–16, 38, 212, JP IV 3969, III 2337, 2620).

43. SV XIII 359 ft., SV XIV 252–56, 259–63, Pap. X, 2 A 181 1849, XI, 2 A 231, 226, 1854 (CI 305 ft., AX 212–16, 219–22, JP III 2608, 2628, IV 5000).

44. See e.g. SV II 306–18, VII 100, Pap. X, 3 A 509 1850 (KW IV EO II 341–54, CUP 110, JP II 1789).

45. Pap. X, 4 A 15 1851, XI, 1 A 226 1854, SV XII 64–65, Pap. XI, 1 A 295, 313, 1854, XI, 2 A 150, 153, 1854, XI, 1 A 552, 546, 1854, XI, 2 A 301 1853–54 (JP I 708, IV 5000, Søren Kierkegaard, *Training in Christianity*, tr. Walter Lowrie [Princeton: Princeton University Press, 1941] TX 71, JP III 2620–23, 3209, I 602, III 2543). On the duty of marriage it is interesting to note a fairy story recorded by Carl Ewald in his *Eventyrskrinet* Gamle Danske Sagn og Eventyr I–V (Copenhagen and Kristiania: Gyldendalske Boghandel Nordisk, 1906–7) IV p. 35–45. "Præstekonens Synd" (The pastor's wife's sin), where because the wife deliberately marries when she is too old to have children she is regarded by the heavenly powers as having murdered her unborn children.

46. Pap. XI, 1 A 190 n.d., 313 1854, SV XIV 253–54 (JP II 2057, III 2621, AX 213). On hating and forsaking the temporal in the New Testament see Matt. 10:37, 19:19 and 29, Mk. 10:29, 13:12, Lk. 12:52–53, 14:26, 21:16–17, Jn. 15:18.

47. Pap. XI, 1 A 226 1854, SV XIV 197 (JP IV 5000, AX 163).

48. Pap. XI, 1 A 279 1854 (JP III 2443).

49. See notes 1–2 and 11 above.

50. Pap. XI, 1 A 129 1854, XI, 2 A 154, 238 1854, XI, 1 A 169 1854, VIII, 1 A 190 1847, X, 1 A 440 1849, IX A 245 1848, X, 3 A 293 1850 (JP III 2616, 2624, 2629, 2618, 2569, 2605, 2601, II 2221).

51. I have encountered this outlook as late as autumn 1988 in Copenhagen, where a married man with a university education described Mother Teresa of India as "selfish" for not marrying. The reason given was that she had "run away" from the responsibilities and difficulties of marriage.

4

Woman-Bashing in Kierkegaard's "In Vino Veritas":

A Reinscription of Plato's *Symposium*

Robert L. Perkins

Plato's *Symposium* and Kierkegaard's "In Vino Veritas," the first part of *Stages on Life's Way*, are important contributions to the understanding of love, woman, and gender relations. The two works invite comparison for obvious reasons.[1] Both are symposia and have elaborate settings. Apollodorus, who was not present, reports that Agathon's party took place the day after his play had won first prize in the annual contest. That was a year before Alcibiades convinced the Athenians to undertake the disastrous Sicilian campaign, which led to the end of "the glory that was Athens," and before his trial for sacrilege. Things were never to be the same in Athens again. The party outside Copenhagen, reported by William Afham, who was present, occurs during the "Golden Age of Danish literature," just before the changes of the constitution of 1848, which marked the transition from absolute monarchy to constitutional monarchy and after which the cultural, political, and economic hegemony of Copenhagen over the rest of the country dramatically declined. Things were never to be the same in Copenhagen either.

Kierkegaard constantly forces us to note the literary dependency on and philosophic difference of his dialogue from Plato's. For instance, Kierkegaard, in the persona of Johannes the Seducer (*SLW*, 74), and Plato, in the persona of Agathon, refer to Hesiod's myth of the origin of woman (195c).[2] After the exit of the flute-girl from Agathon's party the two symposia exhibit a likeness in the sexual makeup of the symposiasts: no woman is present for the speeches. However, both Plato and Kierkegaard manage to introduce a woman who rather takes charge of the situation. The speech of Diotima (203c–212c) is central to the *Symposium*; it sets out the central thrust of Plato's own view of love. The (unnamed) wife of Judge William in "In Vino Veritas" also takes control of the conversation (*SLW*, 82–85), and, though she is no Diotima, her persistent questioning requires the Judge to note (again) the centrality of his wife in his life and happiness.

More ambiguously, there are women present and women absent in Plato's *Symposium*. First, at the suggestion of Eryximachus, the flute-girl is sent away (176e) so the guests can engage in conversation. The entrance of another flute-girl in the company of Alcibiades marks the beginning of the drunken denouement to Agathon's party (212c). While the flute-girls are absent, the influence of Bacchus is nil, and philosophy progresses dialectically. Yet, in another sense, *in vino veritas*; the highest truth and meaning of it all babbles forth in the drunken ravings of Alcibiades (215a–222c). There are apparently two ways into philosophy for Plato, dialectic and divine madness, the latter providing at least the passion for philosophy.

A third woman who is both absent and present is Diotima, a woman of Mantinea and Socrates' teacher in all matters of love (201d–212c), whose metaphor of the ladder of ascent from the love of the beauty of one body to the love of all beauty, truth, and goodness, a love that is a vision of a single sea of beauty, is one of the most powerful figures in the history of Western philosophies and religions.

These figures, the flute-girls and Diotima, testify to the complexity of the presence of woman in Plato's philosophy. Whatever limits his views have, and they are several, his effort to improve the condition of women seems clear. The education of qualified women (*Republic*, 445b–457b) and Diotima's instruction of Socrates, an episode that seems to assume that the recommendation for women's education has been followed and that also reverses the line of intellectual authority in Athenian society, radically revision the role of women. Athenian customs, law, and the propensity of Aristotle to describe and justify the status quo rather than to judge it by the ideal, and other factors, too many to name, blunted whatever positive effect Plato's philosophy might have had on behalf of women.[3]

Plato's *Symposium* ends in the triumph of philosophy and Kierkegaard's "In Vino Veritas" in the triumph of marriage, but along the way homosexual love has been variously interpreted, praised, and transformed into a metaphor for the love of wisdom, while woman and heterosexual love have been bashed and defamed by both Plato's and Kierkegaard's banqueters. However, both woman and marriage are existentially and ironically rehabilitated in the surprise ending of Kierkegaard's "In Vino Veritas."

Plato's *Symposium*, literally a drinking party, becomes such only after the serious business of the speeches (but one) is over, while Kierkegaard's symposium is a drinking party from the start and the speakers are required to feel the influence of the wine before they speak (*SLW*, 26, 28, 30). Music is played at both banquets, although in the *Symposium* it is stopped early on. The banqueters in "In Vino Veritas" are greeted with strains of dance music from Mozart's *Don Giovanni* upon arrival, and more music follows an encomium on Mozart by Victor Eremita (*SLW*, 28). One interesting difference is that Agathon's drinking party is either a continuation or a repetition (with a slight change of characters) of one held the previous evening while, by contrast, the party in the forest outside Copenhagen is organized suddenly with the understanding that it will never be repeated and that the setting will be demolished (*SLW*, 23), a circumstance that suggests that Constantin, who provided the banquet and the setting, has considerable wealth.

The economic bases of the settings of the symposia suggest another interesting similarity from the standpoints of both a feminist and a Marxist analysis, for both are lavish, self-indulgent extravaganzas sponsored by men of the wealthy upper classes for their own exclusive titillation and entertainment. In both, the distinctions of wealth and labor are apparent. Plato's *Symposium*, reflecting the social conditions of Athens at the time, has slaves as servants. The fact that the party can continue for at least two nights suggests the ostentatious consumption of the upper classes in

Athens. The upper classes have it at least as good in Denmark's Golden Age. Everything is done lavishly. The banqueters and the workers who are to destroy the expensively decorated dining room as soon as the banquet is finished arrive simultaneously. The gross self-indulgence enjoyed by the empowered men in the environs of Copenhagen is even more extreme than in Athens.

Kierkegaard repeatedly provokes us to contrast the dialogues. Here are three instances. First, the most important link between the two symposia is that the title of Kierkegaard's piece, "In Vino Veritas," is a phrase gaily sung out by the intoxicated Alcibiades in the *Symposium* (217e). Second, both dialogues exhibit surprise and humorous denouements laden with sexual overtones. The drunken Alcibiades' recitation of his attempt to seduce Socrates reveals all he ever understood about the Socratic search for the virtuous life through eros and also how little of it he appropriated. Kierkegaard presents his view of the truth of love through the playful yet passionate sunrise tryst of two married lovers in a hidden bower. Third, in the opening speech of "In Vino Veritas," the Young Man explicitly distinguishes his intent from that of the *Symposium* by declaring that his speech is about heterosexual gender relations in contrast to "Eros in the Greek sense" (*SLW*, 33).

One may wonder why Kierkegaard chose Plato's *Symposium* for his foil. I shall hazard the thought that Kierkegaard wished to comment upon a trinity of ideas on love: the debate in Athens about the nature of eros, the darker significance of modern subjectivism and eroticism, and, as an alternative to both, the glimpse of bourgeois married love and intimacy he briefly presents in the personae of Judge William and his wife. Kierkegaard connects the misogyny in Western life and thought to "Greek love." In his *Symposium* Plato permits women and heterosexual love to be demeaned by two famous homosexual lovers. Emphasizing the moral benefits of homosexuality, Phaedrus demeaningly says that "even a woman" could die for a lover (179b). Bisexuality is not even an option for Plato's next speaker, Pausanias, who characterizes heterosexual relations and relations with boys as a "lower" form of love and as "vulgar," while homosexual relations, when they follow the conventions of the Athenian upper class, are "higher." Pausanias introduces the metaphors of a higher and lower Aphrodite, and adds that, though both gods are to be honored, these two forms of love must be kept apart (180e–181b). We note that by the end of these speeches, Aristophanes develops a severe case of hiccups, a logographic necessity not to be overlooked. By contrast, Kierkegaard takes his point of departure from heterosexual relations and attempts to show connections between ancient misogyny and the more extreme aspects of modern aestheticism and male chauvinism.

When he wrote "In Vino Veritas," Kierkegaard had long been interested in Plato's *Symposium*, which he had discussed in his dissertation and commented upon briefly in his journals.[4] His treatment of the *Symposium* in the dissertation is subordinate to its general thesis, namely, that the position of Socrates is "infinite absolute negativity." Because of this bias, the climax of the dialogue in Diotima's speech is seen to have ended in an abstract idealism, not in a positive vision of the unity of eros and philosophy (CI, 46). Kierkegaard entirely changed his position regarding Socrates between the writing of the dissertation and the *Philosophical Fragments, Concluding Unscientific Postscript,* and *Stages on Life's Way.* In the *Fragments* Socrates is presented as the paradigm of religious humanism and as the opposite of the Teacher (a stand-in for Jesus Christ). In the *Postscript* Kierkegaard differentiates between Socrates and Plato by saying that Plato remains speculative by pursuing the lure of recollection and immanence (CUP, 1:206 n) while Socrates, by contrast, becomes the paradigm of the subjective, existing thinker.

Kierkegaard's dialogue in *Stages on Life's Way* examines the relation of eros and the ethical within the dual context of modern egoism and bourgeois religiosity. I shall not present a detailed comparison of the dialogues, but rather concentrate on one issue in Plato's thought, the significance of the individual, and on Kierkegaard's reinscription of that issue as it applies to gender relations in bourgeois Copenhagen. The concept of the individual is crucial in determining the central feature of love as understood by both authors. I argue that Plato's view of eros directs us toward "that great sea of beauty" (219d) and away from love of the individual. This neglect of the existing individual is the feature common to Plato and the modern forms of woman-bashing that Kierkegaard depicts. The historic rejection of Plato's first steps in the revisioning in the figure of Diotima and in the *Republic* lead finally, after many twists and turns, to an imaginary banquet in a wood outside Copenhagen.

As one examines these works one should take care not to interpret the speeches of all the characters as representing the authors' own views of woman and gender relations. For Plato, the pursuit of eros until one sees "that great sea of beauty" renders any claim for the ultimate value of sexual desire moot. The misogynous utterances of Kierkegaard's literary creations express forms of alienation and despair that the philosopher rejects and believes can be and are overcome in marital love.

A major issue in Plato's philosophy of love is whether individuals are loved in any final sense. It is very difficult to distinguish the Socratic and the Platonic in Diotima's speech, where the ultimate object of love is the form of the beautiful. Gregory Vlastos suggests that all that follows the reference to "birth in the presence of beauty" (206c) is Plato's (Vlastos 1981, 21 n. 58). This distinction accentuates the issue of the love of an individual for his or her own sake, and Vlastos thinks that such love is not possible in Plato. The ambiguous status of the individual as the object of love is, for Vlastos, the main difference between Plato and the Hebrew-Christian heritage. Irving Singer (1984) agrees, at least in part, when he writes:

> The Platonic lover does not love *anyone*: he loves only the Good, either in abstraction or in concrete manifestations. But then, I insist, there is at least one kind of love that Plato's philosophy neglects. That is the love of persons, the love between human beings who bestow value upon one another, each responding to the uniqueness of the other, each taking an interest in the other as a separate individual, regardless of imperfections and apart from the satisfactions that also accrue. (1:84)

In the Christian story, Vlastos argues, God does not love the class of sinners, or the universal in each person; rather, God loves each in his or her irreducible individuality. There is a radical heterogeneity in the universe between God and persons, and an ideal, an absolute, or a universal cannot unite these individuals. These two—the fundamental ontological entities, God and a person—simply encounter and respond to each other. This view is in utter contrast to loving the ideal, the form, or the idea in Plato's particular sense of the immaterial and eternal object of thought, which is at the same time in the fullest sense real and the goal of all eros. For Plato the universal is the only fully adequate object of love, but for Kierkegaard such a love object is not available to an existing human being. Plato does not present us with a God who loves human beings as such.[5] Love, for Kierkegaard, is a very complex concept and an existential relation, but it is, minimally understood, a shared and mutual response of persons to each other, even if, or especially if, one of the "persons" is God.[6]

Kierkegaard's insistence on the irreducible individuality of the person and the impossibility of reducing the individual to an instance of a universal form may appear as a rejection of reason itself. However, such a view can only appear as irrational from the standpoint of Greek philosophy and metaphysics. Rather, Kierkegaard challenges us to encounter individuality as posited by Christianity and learn to think it with an eye toward existing.[7] Kierkegaard calls this "subjective thinking," and it requires us to enter into human and humane relations, be concerned for the ethical integrity of others, and expand the ordinary epistemological concept of truth beyond objectivity to include what can be personally appropriated. Plato struggled with the requirement of the appropriation of the ethical categories through the persona of Socrates, but he did not further develop a notion of the participation of the person in the form. His language about "participation" refers to an object's relation to the form. His difficulty is founded in the very abstraction and separation of the form from the particular. The speakers in "In Vino Veritas," by contrast, have encountered the ethical individuality of Christianity but have failed to think it existentially, and they have also failed to appropriate it in their human relations. The result is alienation and despair.

In "In Vino Veritas" Kierkegaard is interested in heterosexual love. This is a striking contrast to the *Symposium*, where only Aristophanes admits the legitimacy of heterosexual love, along with gay and lesbian love (189d–91d), and where only Diotima suggests that the production of children is "a godly affair" (206d). Heterosexual relations are held in low regard by the other speakers. The first speaker, Phaedrus, simply assumes the normative nature of homosexual love and ignores heterosexual love altogether. Pausanias, the second speaker, speaks of the love of women and boys as a lower kind of love, lower, that is, than homosexual love between a mature man and a youth. Woman is thus devalued even as a sex object, which culturally means that she has no intrinsic worth or value in herself except in the roles of household manager and child bearer. In Pausanias's speech Greek homosexuality is presented as an aggressive misogyny. However, Aristophanes, as noted, makes heterosexual love and both forms of homosexual love normative for humankind.

In Kierkegaard's Lutheran culture, by contrast, marriage, the home, and family are considered to be the normative form of love. Yet, these forms of patriarchal love, whatever their shortcomings, and they were many, were the bearers of the common life and were being subtly assailed by powerful social and cultural developments, among them an egoistic aestheticism. In "In Vino Veritas" Kierkegaard presents a set of character sketches that reveal the dark underside of modern egoism and hedonism as his first move in his defense of the positive aspects of the Christian-Lutheran heritage of gender relations as defined by the nineteenth-century bourgeoisie.

The first speaker in "In Vino Veritas" is the unnamed Young Man (*SLW*, 31–47), who introduces the theme of heterosexual relations as the subject of his speech. The subsequent speakers follow his lead. The Young Man, who also appears to be more knowledgeable of Plato than any of the other speakers at the banquet, remarks that Greek love was "beautifully eulogized" by Plato and, following Pausanias, notes that the love of women was considered to be "imperfect" in comparison to the love of young men. However, he says, to make his own point of departure clear, "By love, I understand here the relation between man and woman" (*SLW*, 33). This understanding that the normative love relation is heterosexual is never challenged in "In Vino Veritas." Homosexual relations are not so much rejected as they are simply historically and temporally relativized as "Greek eroticism" (*SLW*, 39).

The Young Man suggests that the normative love relation is between a man and a woman, and this view makes his speech an important critique of the assertions of some speakers in the *Symposium*. Moreover, he argues that if we agree with Plato that one should love the good, then "one has overstepped in a single step the whole sphere of the erotic" (*SLW*, 34). However, the Young Man, no less than Plato, finds in love an infinite, but for the Young Man the infinite does not relate to an ideal form, rather to the infinity of the passion of love itself in the human personality.

The Young Man has idealized the object of love just as completely as Plato, except that, unlike Plato's, his idealization is psychological rather than ontological. For him love is "an imaginary construction in thought" (*SLW*, 32). In Plato no single material representation of the form can manifest the form completely, any material representation being both more and less than the form itself (*Timaeus, 49a–52c*). The Young Man, by contrast, idealizes and infinitizes his imaginative idea of love; as a result, it is impossible for him to love a finite human being. The reason is that no individual can ever incarnate all the ideals and fantasies the human imagination can dream. The psychological abstraction and idealization of love are much more damaging to the Young Man than the homosexuality of the speakers at Plato's banquet could ever be to them. The latter are experienced lovers, related to particular individuals, and knowledgeable of the flesh and passions. Homosexuality is a human relation, whereas the Young Man can and does love only his idea of love. Finally we must conclude that the Young Man loves only himself as the creator of his idea of love.

The psychological idealization is the result of the hyperintellectualism of the Young Man. Though no ordinary rationalist, he claims he relates primarily to his "thought" (SLW, 32), a radically overblown claim. When the Young Man admits that he has no experience with love, Constantin objects and attempts to stop his speech. Sophistically, the Young Man replies that the lack of experience is not a limitation on his speech but rather enables him to speak about "the whole sex and not about individuals." Here we note again the disposition of rationalism to seek the universal of which the particular is a mere specimen. For the young man, however, the construction of the imagination, which he identifies with his "thought" (SLW, 45, 46), supplants the empirical and mathematical foundations of knowledge.

This sort of "intellectualism" is egocentric in spite of its pretensions to objectivity. Classical rationalists, such as Descartes, made various moves to restore the world in their thought. But there is no "other" in the thought of the Young Man. In a peculiar adaptation of Descartes's notion of clear and distinct ideas, he has determined never to love anyone before he has understood the idea of love. He objects that love is "something that exercises its power everywhere, and yet cannot be thought" (SLW, 38). The difficulty of love, and all the passions for that matter, in a rationalist world is better put nowhere: "If I cannot explain to myself what it is that I am doing, then I will not do it; if I cannot understand the force to whose power I am surrendering, then I will not surrender to that power" (SLW, 40). As a result, he does not, cannot love. For the Young Man, love remains an irrational passion, a view that legitimizes modern subjectivism in its more undisciplined, disordered, and egocentric forms.

Because of the imaginative, as opposed to experiential, source of his conceits, love is ludicrous to the Young Man, who seeks a commensurability between the power and importance of the passion and its expression. Thus he laughs over the discrepancy that he thinks lies between the loftiest and most spiritual protestations and words regarding love and its expression in the sensual: "Two loving souls assure each other they will love each other for all eternity; thereupon they embrace each other and seal this eternal pact with a kiss." The Young Man understands this to be a "contradiction" (*SLW*, 39). He is also aware that the "lovable" is indefinable and can mean one thing to one person and the opposite to another (*SLW*, 34–35). He laughs at the phenomenon of "falling in love," because not a single criterion can be produced to determine when, if, or with whom anyone will fall in love (*SLW*, 36). For him love is both a natural necessity and the act of rationally free persons (*SLW*, 41), and that, again, is a contradiction which makes it comic.

After his failure to understand love, the Young Man turns to marriage, where he also finds contradiction and the comic. He rejects "the collo-quialism that a woman is only a half a person," for then "she would not be at all comic in erotic love" (*SLW*, 43). Two persons, a man and a woman, both of whom are whole, become halves by falling in love, and think they can become whole or complete again only in marriage. The comic and the contradiction is that these wholes think of themselves as halves. However, they think that as a result of the union of one-half and one-half they become one, and then, oops, they produce another whole (a child) who, by falling in love later, will become a half just as they did. After parodying marriage, the Young Man turns to the child and there again finds contradiction and the comic. This offspring is an "eternal soul," but it is a contradiction that an eternal soul can be born (*SLW*, 42–44). However the Young Man approaches love, he finds that it is full of contradictions and, hence, comic.

The unity of the comic and the tragic, so casually introduced as Plato's *Symposium* ends, is as casually and ironically appealed to here. The Young Man, in a passing remark, states that "the comic and the tragic are always connected" (*SLW*, 36). In the *Symposium* Socrates is the embodiment of the unity of the comic and the tragic. Here, the unity of the comic and the tragic is the Young Man himself. But the Young Man is no Socrates. Comic in his slavishness to his rationalistic "imaginary constructions," he rejects immediacy, love, the inexplicable, and wishes to be faithful only to his thought (*SLW*, 46–47). The result is the tragic half-life he lives: Barren of any exercise of the passions, he confuses "imaginary con-structions" with the earned products of reason. The unity of the tragic and the comic is not to be found in the Young Man's speech but in the fact that he existentially embodies the half-life of the subjectivist and egotist—paraded as the life of the intellect. His confession that he is afraid of love because it is unknown to him (*SLW*, 32) shows that he is the parody of both the intellectual who passionately seeks the unknown in order to grasp it or be grasped by it (*PF*, 47) and the philosopher who erotically seeks the truth (210a–d) in the belief that we should not fear the unknown, even if that unknown is death (*Apology*, 40–42a).

At the end of the speech William Afham, the reporter, says that the Young Man was "almost more beautiful than he was before the meal" (*SLW*, 47). He is, rather, the self-centered parody of the beauty transfigured in Socrates at the end of Alcibiades' speech. One wonders if William Afham has scales on his eyes.

Constantin, the next speaker (*SLW*, 47–56), sees things more clearly than William Afham; he says the Young Man is bewildered and "does not know whether he should laugh or cry or fall in love" (*SLW*, 47). We have met Constantin before; he is the author of *Repetition* and is an experimenting psychologist. Rather than constancy, his name suggests immovability and doggedness. He has found repetition impossible, and so he is as he is. He cannot change. Constantin constantly harps upon woman's inconstancy. He reminds one of Professor Higgins in *My Fair Lady* expressing his frustration through the question, "Why can't a woman be like me?" The contradiction between Constantin's name and the inconstant creature he demeans constitutes the comedy and the irony in his discourse. Constantin is an Aristophanic character in "In Vino Veritas." Yet his comedy is not hilarious; it is bitterly ironic.

Toward the end of his speech, the Young Man creates the transition to Constantin by echoing the ancient theme that woman is "a temptation that wants to lure" men, not into sin, but "into becoming ludicrous" (*SLW*, 46). Constantin agrees and subsumes woman "under the category of jest." By placing woman under this category, Constantin announces his determination not to take woman seriously as a moral being of equal value with a male. This is misogyny. After all, a "man's function is to be absolute." Woman, by contrast, "consists in the relational"; thus Constantin denies the independence of a woman's personhood. That is male chauvinism. Mocking 1 Timothy 2:14, he says that "jest entered the world through woman" (*SLW*, 48). Thus he robs woman of ethical, personal, and religious significance.

Jest, Constantin claims, is an incipient ethical category. A man, however, cannot enter into ethical relations with a woman, at least not with a woman "constructed in one's imagination," that is, with a fiction. This is quite similar to the portrayal of woman found in the speech of the Young Man. There the result was that such a "woman" could not be loved. Here, the result is that she is incapable of the earnestness of the ethical (SLW, 48). Both speakers' views are flawed in that an imaginatively constructed woman is not an existent, actual woman, the only kind capable of being loved and having ethical relations. But Constantin unwittingly ironizes himself: having discussed an imaginatively constructed woman, he then proceeds to criticize existing women for living in an imagined ideality.

A woman is inconstant, Constantin continues, in everything she does: saying one thing one day and the opposite the next, all the while emphatically meaning and honestly believing both. A man fails in his constancy, absoluteness, and morality if he attempts to relate to this inconstant creature. As long as one refuses to take woman seriously, however, "the amusement is incalculable." One begins to wonder whether man ever, as Constantin claims, "aims at her with an ethical category" (SLW, 48). It appears, rather, that not only is woman ridiculed in Constantin's speech, but the ethical is also. Existence, not an imaginary construction, is the place of the ethical, and Constantin rarely encounters existence.

Constantin also discusses the relation of the cosmic and the tragic in order to ridicule woman further and to invalidate the distinction between these categories. A cuckold, he says, is as ludicrous as a woman, but the tragedy is that the pain he suffers is meaningless. We sympathize with the cuckold so long as he is present in order to laugh at him when he has departed. There simply can be no tragedy where woman is concerned; she has no ethical significance and is beneath the concern of men. If, however, woman is considered under the category of jest, the "tragedy" of infidelity evaporates into comedy (SLW, 50). Whereas the Young Man attempted to keep the categories of tragedy and comedy in place, Constantin's concept of jest obliterates the distinction and flattens out the texture of art and existence.

Constantin's view is different from that of the speakers in Plato's *Symposium*, who, however great or small their self-deception, their denigration of women, their bad faith, the division of love into a higher and a lower expression, the putdowns they offer each other, their bad logic, and so forth, at least do love and do not deny the power of the god to move them. More dangerously, morally and psychologically, Constantin demeans the capability of the human heart to love anything but the fictions imaginatively constructed in one's own likeness. Significant otherness is denied, with the consequence that Constantin is locked into a destructive egotism, not realizing that he is the victim of his own jest; without actual otherness, eros becomes egotism. By relegating imaginatively constructed woman to the status of jest, Constantin makes her the mirror image of himself.[8]

We are also already acquainted with the next speaker, Victor Eremita (SLW, 56–65), the editor of Either/Or, who puts forth the thesis that woman's "misfortune is that her life in the romantic consciousness has become meaningless" (SLW, 56). Victor says that, for one reason or another, since Plato men have thanked the gods that they were not born women. This remark, which cannot be traced to any of Plato's dialogues, is a far stronger statement than any found in the Symposium.[9] Victor's remark acknowledges the demeaned position of women, whatever the causes, in ancient Greek and modern bourgeois societies. Further, since men have traditionally controlled society, it is also, for us at least, a criticism of male domination. Victor, however, does not take this tack. Rather than criticizing modern society, he simply appears to accept the view of woman in the "romantic consciousness." Although Victor does not offer a gradation of love as Plato did in the Symposium, he does distinguish love and marriage and characterizes the latter as betraying the higher aspirations of man.

Throughout Victor's speech there is a sustained polemic against life-long relations, specifically marriage, between man and woman. Thus he contrasts the youthful and adored Juliane with the Mrs. Peterson whom Juliane becomes and who resides on the corner of Bathhouse Street (SLW, 57–58). Marriage provokes the "bourgeois-philistine mentality," and it looks "most ridiculous when it is decked in ideality" (SLW, 60). Marriage is, rather, the end of ideality, and so, if a man marries, he can again attain the benefits of ideality only if the woman dies or is unfaithful, and if the latter, the sooner the better (SLW, 61–63). Of course, it is best not to marry at all.

For Victor Eremita, marriage is a bundle of contradictions: self-willed and spontaneous, partially pagan and partially Christian, something sacred and something secular, both erotic and obligatory (SLW, 63). So complex is marriage that it cannot be accomplished spontaneously, with the result that erotic immediacy dies within it (SLW, 64).

Man's nature, according to Victor, is to be reflective. A man's thought must then be reduplicated in his life and action, a view that Kierkegaard confirms (JP, 6:6224). Victor's example of reduplication, however, is a deception in which a man appears to be a faithful husband while seducing girls all around. This, we recognize, is just a garden variety of unfaithfulness and adultery, not the reduplication of the thought of a husband in action and life. Victor then appears to be rather like Alice who thought that words can mean anything one wants them to mean.

The situation of a woman is different; being unreflective, she cannot reduplicate her thought in her life and action (*SLW*, 64–65). What is she to do? How is she to live? She must live immediately under the authority of the man.

Throughout Victor's speech, woman continues to be the intellectual construction introduced by the Young Man. Given the significant histori-cal differences between the later symposium and the earlier one, Victor's speech appears to be an exegesis of the misogynous assertions of some of Plato's speakers who reduce the love of woman to a level inferior to male homosexual love. The demeaning of heterosexual love is modified here, however, to praise the romantic enjoyment of woman while avoiding commitments and promises by denying the ethical seriousness of mar-riage, a point also implicit in the *Symposium*.

The next speaker, the Fashion Designer (*SLW*, 65–71), will have none of even the romantic enjoyment of women as sexual objects. In fact, it is woman as a sex, single or married, who is the object of his misogyny. Building on the views of woman held by the previous speakers, the Fash-ion Designer exploits his occupation and his considerable talents to make fools of his female customers and the bill-paying husbands or lovers. The Fashion Designer's stress upon the importance of fashion in gender and class relations has no parallel in Plato's *Symposium* and constitutes a major innovation in Kierkegaard's views of love and women. The Fashion Designer uses all the means of huckstering and manipulation then known (but much better known and used by the advertising industries today): creation of artificial need, beguiling, flattery, fantasy, love of ostentation, class pride, and bullying, to name just a few. Kierkegaard has begun to think through the connection of fashion, illusion, escapist fantasy, and class competition—still used by television and produced for the masses through, for instance, the voyeurism of "Lifestyles of the Rich and Fa-mous."[10] The aggressive misogyny that denies woman full humanity in Plato's *Symposium* and in "In Vino Veritas" here reaches its extreme ex-pression. However, the connection between misogyny and economic ex-ploitation and domination is untouched by Plato in the *Symposium*. Through the depiction of unauthentic and dehumanized human relations created by the economic manipulation of undisciplined and neurotic eros, Kierkegaard makes an important contribution to the understanding

of the economic exploitation of eros and the sexual competition it generates between women.

With Johannes the Seducer, the last speaker (*SLW*, 71–80), Kierkegaard offers a comic speech which rivals that of Aristophanes in the
Symposium (189e–194e). We first met Johannes as the autobiographical
author of "The Seducer's Diary" in *Either/Or*, Part I. Here Johannes presents the theory of woman (or persons) that underlies the practice of a
successful seducer. Johannes takes his fellow banqueters to task for the
shoddy attitudes they display toward women, criticizing each speech in
turn (*SLW*, 72–73). Johannes, in contrast, praises woman, though, of
course, he does so only to demonstrate the presuppositions of seduction
to the banqueters. He is, of course, an exhibitionist.

Johannes's speech refers to the myth of the creation of woman in Hesiod's *Theogony* (calling attention to the connection to Aristophanes'
speech) and also in the second chapter of Genesis (calling attention to
the fact that he speaks in a historical and cultural context different from
that of Aristophanes). Johannes challenges the traditional reading of
Genesis by saying that Adam, not Eve, is the seducer. Further, he urges
that Hesiod's *Theogony* and Genesis agree in saying that in the beginning
there was only one sex, the male sex. Woman is derived, secondary.
"Woman, even less than the god, is a whim from a man's brain, a day-
dream, something one hits upon all by oneself and argues about *pro et
contra*" (*SLW*, 73). Johannes, then, like the rest of the speakers at the
banquet, thinks of woman as an imaginative construction, a sexual fantasy, and not as an existent, actual person.[11] Given that Johannes is not
dealing with phenomena, it may be thought that his syncretistic literary
allusions are a mere literary conceit. Yet Johannes's position needs to be
taken seriously as a social comment about the sexism of Western societies, for the *image* of woman served up by the entertainment, advertising,
and other industries today is a footnote on his views.

With as much prissiness and braggadocio as Phaedrus and Pausanias
display in defending homosexual love, Johannes defends his own practice
of seduction, suggesting that women want to be seduced (*SLW*, 78), that
a seduced woman is a better wife than one never seduced, and that it is a
great misfortune for a woman never to be seduced (*SLW*, 79). Woman,
"the most seductive of the God's most cunning thought" (*SLW*, 75) was
created to prevent the rebellion of men against the gods. But the Seducer
eats the bait and cheats the gods, a rebel still (*SLW*, 79). All the mystifi-

cation, glitter, and self-alienation apparent in "The Seducer's Diary" of *Either/Or*, Part I, are present again here in Johannes's speech. The brutality, violence, and injury inflicted on actual victims of exploitative male sexuality are here passed over as beating the gods at their own game. Johannes thinks he has won in a more serious issue against the gods than that for which they punished Prometheus, suggesting modern aestheticism's preference for sexual fantasy in contrast to knowledge. Johannes does not recognize that victimizing women is not quite the same as defying the gods by stealing fire.

In many ways this is the most imaginative and unhistorical speech in the lot, but even Johannes cannot entirely escape history and time. He defends himself against both married men and his victims by saying that the fate of a seduced woman is of no concern to him (*SLW*, 73). Marriage, he continues, is the victory of the gods' strategy to deflect man's soaring imagination and mind from challenging them and to trap man in finitude and time. The seducer thinks he has won a victory over time by his repeated activity of seduction. "With a husband she [a wife] becomes temporal and he through her" (*SLW*, 80). With this denial of the constitutive power of time in human existence, the speech and the speeches are nearly over. The end of the speeches and the banquet, being temporal events, demonstrates that the seducer is self-seduced. He too is temporal, though without a woman. All he has is women, but each of the several victims of his seductive powers may well be as much an experimental construction as "woman" is, "a dream, the highest reality" (*SLW*, 80). Whatever the case may be, the banquet is over, and his effort to escape time rings false as the glasses of the last toast shatter against the wall and the carpenters who are to destroy the hall begin their work.

Had Kierkegaard written no more, not a single word, he would have been immortal, for his literary picture shows a whole range of ancient and modern views and sentiments from the (highly disputed) Greek rationale for homosexuality to the modern romantic imagination with its all too apparent male chauvinism, sexual fantasy, and effort to exalt flesh over spirit. As must be apparent to all, Kierkegaard's sympathies are with the Athenians; at least they loved.

Still, he wrote one more scene, a scene about heterosexual love, and that scene is the rebuttal to all the speeches given at Constantin's party and to the speakers at Agathon's celebration as well. In this last scene (*SLW*, 82–85) Kierkegaard presents a brief dialogue that reveals more of love than do all the speeches we have examined.

As day breaks and while the banqueters wait for the carriages to be hitched up, they wander through a wood and come upon a scene of domestic bliss. Judge William and his wife are discovered in an arbor having an early morning tea, but the presence of the voyeurs is not suspected by the lovers. Tenderness and solicitude abound as the wife teases her husband, finally forcing a language game he has successfully avoided until that moment. She asks whether he would not have been a greater man had he not married her, and this time she will be answered. One whimsical and courting remark deserves another, and so Judge William, while he lights a cigar, hums a tune about cutting switches and then reminds her that Danish law permits him to beat her, a threat at which she only smiles. His response is neither clumsy nor impatient, but is rather the inverse and indirect language of love playfully yet passionately spoken.[12] Parrying her insistence that he answer her question, he judiciously asks, "What sort of person was I supposed to be?" The Judge is apparently just the sort of person he desires to be: husband, lover, beloved; that is, he is happy. He is so content in these occupations that he can only smile at the suggestion that there is something greater he could be. What is better than happiness? She has her victory. The Judge kisses his wife on her forehead; they fold their arms together and disappear down a path, poetically expressing "the quiet and contented security of married life" (SLW, 128).

The banqueters are astounded that their speeches have been refuted by the love shared between a man and a woman. The very flesh and blood individuality of Judge William and his wife, their mortality, their frailty, their teasing and tenderness, all conspire to refute the banqueters' imaginative constructions. These men's despair, cynicism, cowardice, and hopelessness are founded, first, in the fact that their ideas are even more distant from existence than Plato's forms. Their ideas of women, if I may adopt Platonic language, "participate" in no material actuality at all. Second, they despair because they have cultivated habits of mind and personal characteristics that leave no room for the uniqueness of an other, and in so doing, each one has become invisible to himself.

Although it is clear in his letters (EO, 2:5–333) and essay (SLW, 87–184) that the Judge is not entirely liberated from the patriarchal views of woman and the relation of the sexes prevalent at the time, at least in love his wife and he are equal, mutual in their teasing and tenderness. Together they rebut the trivialization and mockery of the deepest human intimacy presented by the banqueters, be they at Constantin's or at Agathon's party. For Kierkegaard, the Judge and his wife are far closer to the ethical in the sense of the universally human than Socrates complaining of Xanthippe's bad temper. Over against the divinized and transfigured Socrates at the end of the *Symposium*, Kierkegaard offers the mortal and incarnate love of a man and a woman as the expression of their humanity. Against Diotima, Kierkegaard shows that the vision of beauty is not an intellectual and mystical vision transcending the senses and existence but is rather in the face, voice, and presence of the beloved. Not *in vino*, but in the banter of lovers at early morning tea—*veritas*. Judge William and his wife, rejuvenated and nourished by the tender teasing that manifests their love, step together, arm in arm, from their protected bower into their universally human tasks as understood in Golden Age Denmark. By contrast, at the end of the *Symposium*, Socrates leaves alone to pursue his singular task: the philosophic education of his fellow citizens.

I conclude with one other statement, slightly expanded, about banquets, the well-known line of Auntie Mame: "Life is a banquet, but most poor suckers"—Athenians and Copenhageners alike, even if they have banqueted lavishly all night—"are starving to death."

Notes

1. Feminist investigators have recently discussed Plato's *Symposium*. Some of their results have been gathered in Tuana 1994. See especially, "Sorcerer Love: A Reading of Plato's *Symposium*, Diotima's Speech" by Luce Irigaray (181–95) and "Irigaray and Diotima at Plato's Symposium" by Andrea Nye (197–215). For a brief discussion of Irigaray's discussion of the *Symposium* in the context of her thought, see Tina Chanter, *Ethics of Eros: Irigaray's Rewriting of the Philosophers* (New York: Routledge, 1955), 159 64.

2. I quote the *Symposium* from the recent translation of Nehamas and Woodruff (Plato 1989), but I refer (without sigla) to the Stephanus edition of Plato's works first published in Geneva in 1578. *Hesiod's Theogony*, 69–70, lines 590–617.

3. For a brief study of woman in Aristotle, and a select bibliography of recent studies, see Nancy Tuana, *Woman and the History of Philosophy* (New York: Paragon House, 1992), 23–33.

4. For a summary of the development of "In Vino Veritas" and references to the journals, see Croxall (1956) 101–2. See also the valuable monograph by Chaplain.

5. For a critique of Vlastos's interpretation of the problem of the love of the individual in Plato, see A. W. Price, *Love and Friendship in Plato and Aristotle* (Oxford: Clarendon Press, 1989), 1–14. Price places his critique of Vlastos in an interpretation of the *Lysis*.

6. Kierkegaard writes of nothing more than love, its uses and abuses. See his *Either/Or*, *Stages on Life's Way*, and *Works of Love*. For a more complete statement, see the Hongs' summary in the "Historical Introduction" to *Works of Love*, x–xi.

7. See Letwin (1977), 137. This is a singularly significant article.

8. It must be painfully puzzling to some readers that I have so scrupulously avoided Freud's analysis of narcissism, in spite of how much Freud has taught us. I have avoided his analysis,

first, because if one uses it, then one requires the reader to penetrate Freud's density before going on to understand Kierkegaard, who is difficult enough. Second, I wish to avoid issues of interpretation of Freud in this essay, which is directed to Plato. There is ample opportunity for further readings of "In Vino Veritas" by others on this subject. See the important recent study by Vincent McCarthy (1995), which is a Freudian interpretation of the aesthetic stage.

9. See *SLW,* 688 nn. 155, 156. The Hongs quote the textual evidence of this attribution to Socrates; none of it is earlier than Lactantius and Diogenes Laertius. The prayer is also found in Rabbinic Judaism. See Tosephta Berakoth 7, 8. Cited in Swidler (1979), 155. Swidler indicates that the prayer is repeated in Talmud pBerakhoth 13b and Talmud bMenakhoth 43b. It was recommended not as a seasonal prayer or for certain occasions, but as a *daily* prayer.

10. For a brief analysis of the importance of fashion in the modern productive process, see Avineri (1973), 193–215; and Perkins (1973), 216–19.

11. See the excellent analysis of "The Seducer's Diary" by Dewey (1971), 1–24. This article is briefly summarized in Dewey (1995), 182–90.

12. On the language of love and lovers, see Walsh (1988), 250–54.

References

Avineri, Shlomo. 1973. "Labor, Alienation, and Social Classes in Hegel's Philosophy." In *The Legacy of Hegel,* edited by J. J. O'Malley, K. W. Algozin, H. P. Kainz, and I. C. Rice, 193–215. The Hague: Martinus Nijhoff.

Chanter, Tina. 1995. *Ethics of Eros: Irigaray's Rewriting of the Philosophers.* New York: Routledge.

Chaplain, Denise. 1964. *Etude sur "in vino veritas" de Kierkegaard.* Paris: Les Belles Lettres.

Croxall, T. H. 1956. *Kierkegaard Commentary.* New York: Harper and Brothers.

Dewey, Bradley R. 1971. "The Erotic-Demonic in Kierkegaard's 'Diary of the Seducer.' " *Scandinavica* 10:1–24.

———. 1995. "Seven Seducers: A Typology of Interpretations of the Aesthetic Stage in Kierkegaard's 'The Seducer's Diary.' " In *International Kierkegaard Commentary: Either/Or, Part I,* edited by Robert L. Perkins, 159–99. Macon: Mercer University Press.

Hesiod. 1953. *Hesiod's Theogony.* Translated by Norman E. Brown. New York: Liberal Arts Press.

Letwin, Shirley Robin. 1977. "Romantic Love and Christianity." *Philosophy* 52:131–45.

McCarthy, Vincent. 1995. "Narcissism and Desire in Kierkegaard's *Either/Or,* Part One." In *International Kierkegaard Commentary: Either/Or, Part I,* edited by Robert L. Perkins, 51–72. Macon: Mercer University Press.

Perkins, Robert L. 1973. "Kierkegaard's Epistemological Preferences." *International Journal for Philosophy of Religion* 4, no. 4:197–217.

Plato. 1989. *Symposium.* Translated by Alexander Nehamas and Paul Woodruff. Indianapolis: Hackett.

Price, A. W. 1989. *Love and Friendship in Plato and Aristotle.* Oxford: Clarendon Press.

Singer, Irving. 1984. *The Nature of Love.* 3 vols. Vol. 1, *Plato to Luther.* 2d ed. Chicago: University of Chicago Press.

Swidler, Leonard. 1979. *Biblical Affirmations of Women.* Philadelphia: Westminster.

Tuana, Nancy, ed. 1994. *Feminist Interpretations of Plato.* University Park: The Pennsylvania State University Press.

Vlastos, Gregory. 1981. *Platonic Studies*. 2d ed. Princeton: Princeton University Press.
Walsh, Sylvia. 1988. "Forming the Heart: The Role of Love in Kierkegaard's Thought."
    In *The Grammar of the Heart: New Essays in Moral Philosophy and Theology*, edited
    by Richard H. Bell, 234–56. San Francisco: Harper and Row.

5

(A) Woman's Place Within the Ethical

Céline Léon

Unlike an aesthete who oscillates between envy and commiseration, Judge William (B), in the second volume of *Either/Or* (1843) and in *Stages on Life's Way* (1845), praises women and declares himself against altering them for self-enjoyment or self-aggrandizement. In effect, not only does Kierkegaard's paradigmatic ethicist and married man invest women with new strengths, he finds them just as capable as men of realizing the universal human: "My brief and simple opinion is that woman is certainly just as good as man—period. Any more discursive elaboration of the difference between the sexes or deliberation on which sex is superior is an idle intellectual occupation for loafers and bachelors" (*SLW*, 124). Having probed elsewhere the favorable aspect of William's attitude regarding woman, I concentrate here on the negative sentiments he con-

comitantly and paradoxically expresses on this issue and on that of liberation (Léon 1997). It is indeed surprising—albeit not atypical of his
century—that William should compliment woman for her ability to help
man achieve ethical self-realization and for being less than she can be—
less than *he* is—and also embrace the delineation of the "other sex" as
relational, dependent, and oriented toward finitude and immediacy.
Once coupled with the immediate religiosity also assumed to be characteristic of woman, such claims made regarding her essential nature are
bound to have significant repercussions for her inscription—even the possibility of that inscription—within the sphere which the Judge epitomizes. Only emancipation would free woman of some of these fetters, yet
no one is more opposed to its enactment than the Judge.

Critics, whether they agree or disagree regarding the congruence of
Judge William's ethical position and Kierkegaard's own on the issue of
marriage, have tended to agree that, even when he does so by negative
prodding, the philosopher is favorable to women. Yet, on the two issues
considered here—that of woman's essence and that of her emancipation—the thoughts of pseudonym and author are in remarkable consonance. After more than a half-century of man's asking: "What is it that
(a) woman wants?" the time has come for us to ask: "What is it that (a)
man fears," when he forbids woman to move from nature to culture?

Essential Differences between the Sexes

Judge William's claim that a woman is a composite being, whose essence
(*Vaesen*) is "that she is simultaneously more perfect and more imperfect
than the man," shows his belief in the existence of sexual differences
and his unquestioned acceptance of the notion that woman, with her
admixture of frailties and special characteristics, represents "the different":

> If we wish to characterize the most pure and perfect, we say "a
> woman"; if we wish to characterize the weakest and most fragile,
> we say "a woman"; if we want to convey a conception of the
> spirituality elevated above the sensuous, we say "a woman"; if we
> want to convey a conception of the sensuous, we say "a woman";
> if we want to characterize innocence in all its uplifting greatness,

we say "a woman"; if we wish to characterize the depressing feeling of guilt, we say "a woman." Thus in a certain sense woman is
more perfect than man, and Scripture expresses this by saying she
has more guilt. (*EO*, 2:92, 1 Tim. 2:14).

What this passage reveals is that, whether it is perceived as special
orientation toward the finite and the temporal, or as relationality and
dependency, or as immediate religiosity, woman's difference has potential
ramifications in all three spheres.

The aesthetic difference

Let us, to begin with, (re-)consider the extraordinary manner in which
woman is allegedly able to explain (through her work) the inexplicable
(time). Resorting to an extended bird metaphor to express the insipid
character of a woman's life, Judge William contends that a wife is "always
busy" with graceful "minutiae" because she lacks the capacity for "vigor-
ous and sustained work that a man has" (*EO*, 2:307). Their pedagogical
import notwithstanding, her occupations remain a game, an idle way to
while away the time, a "riddle," whose significance eludes a husband's
mighty powers of intellection (*EO*, 2:307). Like the moth, which flutters
about the flame, oblivious of its former existence as a caterpillar, a wife
counters by a senseless activity remembrance of the time that has preceded her metamorphosis through the agency of man. Not unlike the
busybody of a tale he tells in the second volume of *Either/Or*, the passive
vessel the Judge is married to "buzzes about" the living room, sanctimoniously spreading the "matrimonial music" (*EO*, 2:308). "Created to deal
with little matters," she trains others in consequence (*EO*, 2:68). Thus,
in *Stages on Life's Way*, this enemy of silence is shown spending most of
her time discussing trivial issues, such as the settling of accounts, the
cook's sweetheart, or the maid's legroom (*SLW*, 134). Thanks to daily
contacts with his wife, the Judge has developed a remarkable sense of
humor and learned how to expatiate on chatty, domestic themes, such as
the propriety of bringing the subject of a young girl's corns to the attention of her prospective lover (*SLW*, 129). An actress's success—such as
Mme Nielsen's—depends on her ability adequately to express the eternal
feminine, to be Everywoman, to wit, to portray woman in her vapid and
inessential essence (*SLW*, 131).[1] Not even motherly love is exempt from

this glorification of the trivial; what makes it "essentially beautiful" is its residing "precisely in what is insignificant" (*SLW*, 140). Either way—either as point of origin, or as destination—the stereotype of the "other sex"'s incidental essence is emphasized and women's subordinate status reinforced.

A wife and her husband relate to time in different—not to say opposite—ways. Whereas continuity and historicity (ethical determinations) characterize a husband's temporal existence, busyness, repetition (aesthetic determinations) best describe a wife's daily intercourse. Were she actively engaged in life, as her husband is, she would soon forget the trivia that weave the tapestry of her life, but, seeing little change about her, compelled by the vacuity of her humdrum tasks, she concentrates on petty cares. Over against the phallic principle by virtue of which one remembers one's experiences, the axiom that guides a woman's life is that of accumulation and reserve, with memory a mere receptacle for time. In the passage from *Stages* where he underscores, for the man, woman's regenerative role in later years, William remarks on the simplicity, the sweet (com)pliancy of woman *quod matrem*: "A man never finishes his life in this way, ordinarily his accounts are more complicated; but a housewife has only elementary events, the everyday distresses and the everyday joys" (*SLW*, 134). Undergirding the irony with which the laud of woman's humdrum tasks is sung is the dichotomy that favors the qualitative aspect of creation over the quantitative feature of reproduction (a woman can give birth more than once). For, as William contends at the beginning of the second volume of *Either/Or*: "The greater the probability that something can be repeated, the less meaning the first has" (*EO*, 2:40). Furthermore, unlike a man, who always has something of significance to do with his time, a woman, "assigned the least significant tasks," cannot wait to get rid of hers, in other words, to get rid of herself (*SLW*, 144). Even though it is true that time can also stand still for a husband, it is for the opposite reason: he thinks best when he is least occupied. A truly ethical man, in the manner of William, draws from silence and stillness increased awareness and continual maturation. His indifference to questions of detail, his obliviousness to his surroundings at once testify to his virile strength and to the inherent superiority of his aspirations.

Are we to believe William divested of irony when he contends that woman "is more perfect than man, for surely the one who explains something is more perfect than the one who is hunting for an explanation" (*EO*, 2:311; *SV* II, 279)? Do not his wife's facile solutions demonstrate her inability—rather than uncanny insight—to see further than the tip of her nose? Did not Kierkegaard himself acknowledge Mrs. B's ineffectuality: "But on the other hand she does not explain anything" (*JP*, 4:5006)? Would A, William's aesthetic counterpart, not be entitled to a good laugh at the expense of the Judge? After having heard B protest ad nauseam the ethical invalidity of chance and accident, could he not force the inconsistent assessor to swallow his words and berate him for praising Mrs. B's collusion with chance and irrationality?

Nor is there any significant difference between William's views and those of the aesthetic personalities regarding the matter of woman's intellectual inferiority: "A woman in understanding is not a man in understanding" (*SLW*, 166). Yet, that this is as it should be is confirmed by the Judge, for whom women are "not supposed to know the anxiety of doubt and the agony of despair . . . not supposed to stand outside the idea" and must remain nonreflective and unaware of their situation in that respect (*EO*, 2:311)[2] In other words, the inferiority of the "other sex" is not merely descriptive, but also prescriptive: "A feminine soul does not have and *should not* have reflection the way a man does" (*SLW*, 166; my emphasis).[3] Here indeed is a perfect example of the double bind whereby woman is commended for at once cultivating lesser qualities and repressing traits that would enhance her status (intelligence, independence, creativity, and so forth). Sanctimoniously, patronizingly, lip service is paid to the artlessness of the immediately lived existence, but truly, deeply, and earnestly all praises go to the tormenting complexities of the life of mind and spirit. Therefore the valuational opposites that traditionally have split humanity not only remain, but acquire greater impact within Kierkegaard's second existence-sphere. In a more trivial—albeit not altogether insignificant—way, Judge William's awareness of how little his wife's nose is shows that, despite his many protestations of indifference to her aesthetic difference(s) from others of her sex, he is not adverse to subsuming her under merely aesthetic categories (*EO*, 2:9). In fact, not only does he commend woman for providing man with aesthetic enjoyment, he paradoxically tends to ground most of the tributes he pays to her on purely aesthetic qualifications. Even more disturbingly, although, unlike the aesthetic, the ethical standpoint does not depict woman as coming into being/becoming visible through the interposition of man, the emphasis the second existence-sphere places upon the relational characteristics of her being suggests that the "Or" of her aesthetico-ethical disjunction may be problematic.

The ethical difference

Over against an aesthete who wishes to alter (a) woman, an ethicist will take her as she is; yet, in either instance, as Leslie A. Howe (1994) perceptively shows in "Kierkegaard and the Feminine Self," she is "first and foremost a 'helpmeet' to man's existence—she enhances his life in one way or another, but thus she is always seen as an instrument, an addendum, whether aesthetically, or as the occasion for an ethical decision on *his* part" (142). Thus both spheres, although they do so differently, equally accentuate feminine characteristics of being-for-other and the confinement of woman to what is deemed to be her natural condition. Nonetheless, rather than showing (a) man transformed by the presence of (a) woman by his side, the ethical standpoint depicts woman as becoming elevated from her position of inferiority by virtue of her association with man. What William's paternalistic promotion of his wife's derived status succeeds in conveying is little more than (its discreet charm notwithstanding) the dependency of this bourgeoise's existence (*EO*, 2:67; for another example, see *Prefaces*, xxvi).

Ironically, the dubious compliment a husband publicly pays his wife for the enhancement—ethical or even aesthetic—of his own life resembles the deferential and condescending gesture of the victor to the vanquished. As with gallantry—this sin for which he so vehemently berates the Aesthete—William is willing to let his wife believe that she is more than he is because of his conviction that at bottom she is infinitely less (cf. *SLW*, 145–46). In fact, insofar as it is directed from a higher perspective, the encomium is more insidious and more damaging to women than the contempt that undergirds the aesthetes' attention (*EO*, 2:209). At any rate, because a wife is not supposed to display the strength she has acquired through her husband's interposition, Judge William, not unlike many men of his generation—and later—insists that she adopt a meek and supportive stance in public. He congratulates a wife on her willingness to protect her spouse's self-esteem and on her ability to disguise her strength, or more accurately, the strength she has acquired at his hands: "She loves her husband so much that she always wants him to be dominant, and this is why he appears to be so strong and she so weak, for she uses her strength to support him, uses it as devotedness and submission" (*SLW*, 144). Mrs. B, he expects, will continue subordinating her freedom to his own and bending to his heart's desire (*EO*, 2:81). Why, after all, should a married man deprive himself of the self-serving belief that marriage—that *his* marriage—is "formed from the strength of the man and the frailty of the woman" (*SLW*, 118)? It is therefore clear that William fills and empties this vessel at will, letting either weakness or strength predominate according to the strategic need of the moment (*SLW*, 144). Either woman is envied for raising no expectations, or she is commended for hiding her strength: Conveniently the Judge equates the former with necessity and chance, and the latter with virtue and choice. In sum, whether he declares woman's weakness an essential, or an existential, truth of her being, William makes sure that all revolves around him and that, either way, there occurs no transgression of his power to believe in himself.[4]

More disturbingly, beyond William's commendation of a wife's ability to conceal her strength, beyond his lauding her supporting role, lies an even greater mystification: his claiming that "She *chooses* her task, *chooses it gladly, and also the joy of continually equipping man with the conspicuous strength*" and thus "freely" embraces her instrumentality (*SLW*, 144; my emphasis). Will woman truly appreciate the tribute paid to her being like the "silk cord," which, over against the iron chain, chooses to remain invisible, chooses "to be deceived," in the knowledge—as indicated by the motto which the Judge uses as epigraph for his "Reflections on Marriage"—that "the deceived is wiser than the not deceived" (*SLW*, 142)? It is doubtful—although the facile and immediate gratifications concomitant with such praises can often constitute an enticing, well-nigh irresistible, snare. Thus, ethically speaking, (a) woman's options lie between the Scylla of enforced femininity and the Charybdis of denied humanity: Either she chooses the former ("chooses her task, chooses it gladly"), or she ventures another way. Yet, as we soon shall see, she only does the latter at the price of her femininity equated with her self-identity (*SLW*, 144). In brief, her options are either not to exist, or to exist for the sake of another—which is another way of not existing. Louis Mackey (1971) aptly sums up her schizophrenic plight: "[A woman is] all freedom *qua* human, and all nature *qua* woman and wife" (85–86).

Even more striking is the realization that, if the Bs have but one like fashion of seeing things, the felicitous conjunction is owing to the fact that Mr. B's views are unquestioningly accepted by Mrs. B—this being whose essential right is that of approval (*EO*, 2:218, 91). It is little wonder then that his love for her should keep on increasing. With a chauvinism typical of his century (and which is indeed far from having died out), William expresses the conviction that, since "she loves him in this she has her life," and that since he is "everything to her," Mrs. B, wholly immersed in her devotion to him, will remain by his side (*EO*, 2:55, 81). The underlying assumption is that, without a man, a woman would never come to herself and that, once she has tied herself, she, who cannot give herself without putting her whole self into the endeavor, has nothing left for higher considerations. Not only is a wife at her husband's service, but, unable to rise higher than her devotion, she gives herself absolutely to this relative end. Although the same thing could be said of some males, it is not true of the whole masculine gender; as a rule, a male lives for the idea, that is, for something that transcends woman's purely immediate category and does not give himself absolutely to anything finite (*SLW*, 373).[5]

Some critics have further remarked on the inner contradiction of saying, on the one hand, that one's wife is free, that she has chosen herself in her eternal validity (*Gyldighed*), that is, in the concerned responsibility of an eternal commitment and, on the other, that her freedom is consonant with her husband's choices, that her " 'absolute' self is identical with her relationship to her man" (Mackey 1971, 84). Awareness of the difficulty has prompted Christine Garside to answer in the negative the question she poses in a 1971 article: "Can a Woman be Good in the Same Way as a Man?" In Garside's view, Mrs. B's "choice" of the ethical life is a nonchoice and therefore unethical: "Since reflection is demanded before the resolution of marriage, and before becoming ethical, a woman cannot enter into marriage from the same motive. It is not a real choice for her in the sense that it is a real choice for a man" (534–44, 539–40). This raises the important question of the place the ethical can allocate to a being whose dependent and relational status it ubiquitously proclaims.

No pseudonym senses the precariousness of the Judge's position more than Johannes Climacus, for whom feminine devotion is flawed to the extent to which it depends on others for its fulfillment. Whereas man's necessity, Climacus argues in *Concluding Unscientific Postscript*, is an inner necessity, whereas his relation is a relation to self, woman's is always a "relation with" or "to." Therefore, although inwardness is said to be present in all, men and women, it is always so in different degrees and expresses itself differently for each sex: "A feminine inwardness as devotedness is lesser inwardness [than that of man—Quidam, in this instance], because the direction is obviously *outward, toward*" (*CUP*, 1:291; my emphasis). Incidentally, the discrepancy seems to justify Birgit Bertung's contention that, for Kierkegaard: "If a woman misinterprets her situation in that she confuses her body-soul relationship to her husband with her existential relationship, her relationship to God, thus becoming nothing for her *husband's* sake, then she errs" (Bertung 1989, 15). What is left open, however, is the question of deciding whether or not woman's tendency to self-obliteration is acquired and rectifiable, or innate and inalterable. Because, however, any attempt at an answer would be premature until the highest sphere of the religious is reached, what can only be re-marked at this juncture is that from the standpoint of the ethical, woman is once again caught in a double bind: Even when she "has deliberated with her conscience about having this man"—an issue raised in *Works of Love*—she has no better option than that of having him "for a master" (*WL*, 139).

To what extent does the new picture of woman, it must be asked, actually differ from Piloty's aesthetic representation that William means to counter? Portray to yourself the Judge's version—a version touched up by the brush of the ethical:

> She is, then, not kneeling adoringly, for the difference that is fixed in the immediacy of erotic love, the man's strength that gives him the advantage, is sensed to be raised into a higher unity, into the divine equality of the religious. *She is only sinking down; she wants to kneel in the admiration of love, but his strong arm holds her upright. She is drooping,* yet not before the visible but before the invisible, before the excessiveness of the impression; then *she grasps him, who is already holding her supportively.* (*SLW*, 168; my emphasis)

Should the Judge not be reprimanded for indirectly (through his wife's reliance on him) relying on despair, namely, *"a condition that either lies outside the individual or is within the individual in such a way that it is not there by virtue of the individual himself"*? (*EO*, 2:180; author's emphasis; see also, *EO*, 2:182; 235–36). Should the contradiction not puzzle critics who, like Gregor Malantschuk, affirm total consonance between Kierkegaard's position and that of his paradigmatic ethicist (1980, 47–48; *JP*, 4:4987–5008)? Should the conclusion that a woman cannot be good/ethical in the same way as a man not complicate the stance of the male ready for union within that sphere? Or will such difficulties be obviated by means of her religious "difference"?

The religious difference

By an interesting nemesis, the "less" in autonomy and intellect with which woman has been invested is considered by Judge William a "plus" that will serve her well both to reach the religious and to exist within that sphere. Concerning existence within the highest sphere, a first advantage identified by William in the letter with which he opens the second volume of *Either/Or* is that, inasmuch as she is nonreflective, abstract (in the sense that this can be said of nature), woman has God's ear and is much closer to Him than man is (*EO*, 2:53). This closeness to the divinity is also evident in a second gift—a point made by William in the letter that follows—by virtue of which woman's prayer is superior to man's: "It is a woman's nature to pray for others . . . as a rule you will find her praying for others, for her parents, for her beloved, for her husband, for her children, always for others. Man by nature prays for himself" (*EO*, 2:315). The superiority of (a) woman's prayer lies in its inherent faith and unselfishness: "In this respect man and woman form, so to speak, two ranks. First comes woman with her intercessory prayer; she moves, as it were, the deity with her tears. . . . Intercessory prayer is so essentially her nature that even in that case her intercessory prayer for man will be different from his own prayer" (*EO*, 2:315). A third disparity that, according to William, gives woman the advantage from the point of view of the religious is that which distinguishes her from man on the matter of trust: While a male believes that "for God something is impossible," woman tends to "give up on herself," but remains confident that "for God all things are possible" (*For Gud er Alt muligt*), from which it appears that she has more faith (*EO*, 2:315). A fourth talent of woman lies in her intrinsic devotion—a devotion that makes her more God-fearing, hence more pious than man, whose superior powers of intellect tend to act as a screen between him and his commitment to the divinity (*SLW*, 166–67).

As far as women's transition to the religious is concerned, the conviction that she develops toward faith immediately, without reflection, is more boldly and more explicitly stated in *Stages* than in *Either/Or*, Part II; it is not until the later text that Judge William argues that "swiftly as a bird [a woman] comes from esthetic immediacy to the religious" and that "feminine romanticism is in the next moment the religious" (*SLW*, 166–67). In the Judge's opinion, woman's faith has a directness, a trusting simplicity, a moving force—well-nigh impossible for (a) man, whose thoughts are complex and whose nature is torn by contradictions and conflicts. Insofar as a female does not involve herself in the ethical questions by which a male is plagued, hers is the childlike candor required by the Gospel:

> [In (a) woman] the transition to the religious occurs without reflection. That is, when an intimation of the thought, the content of which the man's reflection ideally exhausts, passes through her consciousness, she faints, while her husband hurries off and, equally moved but also through reflection, is not overwhelmed; he stands firm, the beloved leaning on him until she opens her eyes again. In this swooning, she has transferred from the immediacy of erotic love into that of the religious, and here they meet again. (SLW, 166, 167)

But here, as elsewhere, the advantages ascribed to woman reveal themselves to be egregious marks of inferiority. It is immediately apparent that, precisely because of her being naturally more religious than man, woman is always less religious than he is. First of all, women's lesser degree of (self-)consciousness renders them far more uncomfortable with questions of a theological nature, such as the thought of God, than their masculine counterparts, whose natural inclination is to embrace infinitude and complexity.[6] Second, women's tendency to resort to prayers and miracles not only shows their inability to confront a reality that eludes their grasp, but also reveals their magical collusion with the lower forms of existence. Or worse even: Mrs. B's being is in thrall to a strange witchcraft; her "arts" are "genuine magic" (EO, 2:308).[7] In other words, women glide into faith as they do into superstition: In either instance, they frivolously depend on forces that lie beyond their control, forfeit interiority, and reproduce the inarticulate interjections of blind fate. With, behind them, a long practice of unquestioningly embracing all they are told, they are more likely than men to "believe against the understanding," to believe that the impossible is always possible and to effect with greater ease and levity the transition to the religious (CUP, 1:232–33; see EO, 2:315).[8] Third, although the Judge declares woman to be better than man at addressing prayers to God for the benefit of someone else, he recognizes the infinite superiority of man's prayer—self-directed, resigned to God's will, and absolute: "Then comes man with his prayer; he halts the first rank [woman] when in fear it wants to run away; he has another kind of tactic that always brings victory. This, again, is because the man pursues the infinite. If woman loses the battle, then from man she must learn to pray" (*EO*, 2:315). Moreover, in the Judge's view, the same thoughts that cause a wife to faint and emphasize her helplessness, do not "overwhelm" her husband (*SLW*, 167). Therefore, despite the promise of an eventual cancellation of differences in the religious, woman's faith, which "occurs without reflection," is only a first immediacy that lacks the solidity and maturity of that of the male, whose immediacy is a second immediacy, a new spontaneity grounded in an ethical development (*SLW*, 166). As Christine Garside (1971) perceptively remarks: "A man must pass through the ethical stage before becoming religious, while a woman passes directly from the aesthetic to the religious" (540).

From this we can see that, from the vantage point of William's ethical sphere, not only are the sexes differently religious, not only do they reach the religious differently, but man does so better—which plainly shows that in effect only *he* is truly religious. Therefore, notwithstanding its postulate of existential equality for all, the second existence-sphere has the gap, not diminishing, but actually widening between the sexes, as it superimposes substantive ethico-religious discrepancies upon the dissimilarities already deplored within the psycho-biological sphere. Also quite perplexing is the realization that, both more aesthetic and more religious than man, woman tends to exist beneath, and beyond, the category of the ethico-universal.[9] It is little wonder then that "a married man, a genuine husband," who has to face not only the "turtle" of marriage, but also a being both higher and lower than himself, must himself be "a wonder" (*SLW*, 166). What miracle will enable two partners so disharmonious, so unequally bound by love to achieve a temporally anchored relationship? More bafflingly perhaps, when the religious immediacy of the "other sex"—clearly of a lower order than the religiousness of man—is coupled with its unquestioning acceptance and its intrinsic relationality, it becomes difficult to envision what can truly be meant by the proclamation of the sexes' ultimate equality.

Hence there resurfaces with(in) the ethical—with, as can already be sensed, powerful consequences for the religious—that which the need to seduce proclaimed within the aesthetic realm, to wit, the desire to assert masculine hegemony by underscoring the differences alleged to lie between the sexes. Thus, patriarchy, typically eager to maintain a hierarchy that works to the advantage of the more favored, insists on depicting women as immediate, dependent, and gullible, while jealously converting reason and broadness of scope into exclusively male preserves. In a paradox of which the ethical makes no mention, the reasonable woman is she who uses her reason to maintain herself within the natural sphere. What is shown here is that, even when ethically inscribed, masculine praise continues to enfold woman within representation: By reiterating cultural myths that negate her autonomy and deprive her of intellect, it sustains and remakes patriarchy which, retroactively, satisfies itself that it did not err in the choice of predicates it initially attributed to her. As with all stereotypes, circularity obtains insofar as, if representation confirms reality, it is because reality has already been preordered by (masculine) representation.

In sum, if man's disjunction consists of the *Either* of aesthetic existence and the *Or* of the ethical choice, woman's is more accurately expressed by/in the opposition: femininity/emancipation. This difference between the masculine-universal alternative and the feminine one urges us to inquire into the fate which the ethical—unexempt from the biases of a culture traditionally ambivalent to women—has in store for the women who have managed to escape the roles traditionally ascribed to their sex. How does Kierkegaard's second existence-sphere look upon these creatures who, by being either unable/unwilling to hide their personal talents, or loath to behave as dutiful wives and mothers, or merely disinclined to exhibit worshipful compliancy and unconditional devotion to the males, have to a certain extent appropriated masculine prerogatives?

Woman's Emancipation

The cleverest, the acutest men are often under an illusion about women. They do not read them in a true light; they misapprehend them, both for good and for evil: their good woman is a queer thing, half doll, half angel; their bad woman almost always a fiend.

—Charlotte Brontë, *Shirley*, chap. 20.

And she who scorns a man must die a maid
—Alexander Pope, *The Rape of the Lock*, Canto 5, line 28

In his first letter to the Aesthete, in the second volume of *Either/Or*, Judge William declares himself against female emancipation, in his view, "one of the many unbeautiful phenomena of which the men are guilty" and for which he holds responsible certain male Romantics—Byron among others—with their advocacy of free love (EO, 2:22). The antagonism persists in the book's second letter, where the Judge proclaims his hatred of "all that detestable rhetoric about the emancipation of women" and even prays to God that its advent be prevented, asking that "the serpent" never "tempt her [woman] with seemingly delightful fruit" (EO, 2:311, 311–12). Although woman's liberation covers a variety of evils, the anomalous figures by/for whom it has become a reality are accused of being unfaithful to their nature, of falling short of "femininity"; they are scorned with just as much intensity as their more "feminine" counterparts (the mother, the woman of years, and so forth; SLW, 134–40 and 133–34) are praised, in a dichotomy that brings to mind the angel-and-monster imagery identified by recent feminist criticism.[10] These creatures, whom either defiance, or ignorance, of the masculine script have emboldened to forget their place, comprise either inappropriately desirous types depicted as sources of distrust and opprobrium, or reflective figures with minds of their own ridiculed as the instigators of the most unsightly confusion. But the categories do overlap, with the consequence that it is not always possible to extract/abstract in their purity the paradigms by which each one is epitomized.

For Judge William, two embodiments of the highly sensual type are the creature bold enough to resist marriage and the one brazen enough to marry a much younger individual. As far as free love is concerned, the Judge's feeling is that, although the conceit of a relationship outside marriage would betray a like "light-mindedness bordering on depravity" in the man and the woman, it would be "especially [so] on the part of the female participant in the association" (EO, 2:23; also 53). A seducer flees matrimony; he seeks to free himself by multiplying either his conquests or his variations on a theme. Conversely, a woman, whose essence has been universally/masculinely defined as lying neither in such a proliferation of objects of desire nor in such chromatic explorations, can only be seductress by virile identification. As for the age discrepancy, in a fashion that was to outlive his own century, William perceives it to be an anomaly, an excusable foible or weakness in the male, but the unacceptable mark of deviant behavior in the female. Thus, he comments in Stages:

> It is bad enough for a man who is tried and experienced in the erotic—indeed, is a burned-out case—brazenly to take a young girl for a wife in order to be rejuvenated a little and to have the

best nursing care now that he is beginning to become old; *but it is revolting for an elderly woman, an experienced spinster,* to marry a young man in order to assure herself of a safe shelter and a sophisticated stimulation. (*SLW*, 155; my emphasis)

In his second epistle, the Judge equates woman's emancipation with the adoption of shorter hairstyles. By such unseemliness, a woman dooms herself to ostracism and alienation—dooms herself to "run like a crazy person, a criminal, to the terror of the people" (*EO*, 2:313). Faithful to the letter of Scriptures, William sees long hair as a reminder that, whereas man is "an-thropos," or "he who looks up," heavenward, woman is, and should remain, earth-bound; alleging that "within the definition of man "she would [never] become more perfect than man," he enjoins her to abide by the "perfection of her imperfections" (*EO*, 2:312; see 1 Cor. 11:5ff.). Incidentally, in not even so trite a matter can woman escape the series of double binds in which she is imprisoned: Whether she (abiding by the New Testament) wears her hair long as a sign of her imperfection and allows her subservience to man to be proclaimed, or (ignoring biblical injunctions) cuts these "heavy chains" and publicizes the shamelessness of her impertinence; either way, her inadequacy is equally divulged (*EO*, 2:312–13).

More generally, sameness worries the Judge, who is bent on maintaining difference, complementarity, and symmetry between the sexes: Will both sexes merge into one? Will they wear the same clothes? When it comes to expressing antipathy for the idea of unisex clothing, William's rhetoric reaches hyperbolic heights, yet not even on so trivial an issue does he think of consulting his wife, or imagine, in his passionate indignation, that she might speak for herself (*EO*, 2:311–13). He dwells on the unseemliness of liberation, depicting it alternately as either an improper mixing of categories, or a deplorable attack upon women perpetrated by hybrid individuals—who belong neither to one sex nor to the other. A firm believer that men should be men and women women, William worries about the men "not much good at being men," the "half-men" who, indifferent to their own sexual identity and to the Other('s) sex, strive in effect to corrupt women by transforming them into homologues (*EO*, 2:311–12; also 22, 53). According to the Judge, these nomen, emblematic of all that is bankrupt in the society of his day, both suffer from feminization and are true misogynists whose self-hatred—a

self-hatred that longs to annihilate the masculine aspect of their nature—is compounded by hatred for the other sex.

Two years later, in *Stages*, Judge William, now echoing Constantin, no
more approves of the indecent attempts to emancipate women than he
did in *Either/Or* (*SLW*, 56, 124). The "away with emancipation" that
resonates throughout William's writings implies that either a woman remains submissive, worshipful, and unconditionally devoted to man, or
that, doffing the feminine role, she becomes a madwoman with characteristics of both sexes, a hermaphroditic monster, a parody of Plato's glorious
androgyne. Although they are often obsfucated by hyperbole, a few truths
emerge nonetheless from the contrast the emancipated woman provides
with the usual characterization of the "other sex" as a bland sea of benign
compliance. On the one hand, it is clear that, insofar as they take on
illusory strength from the dichotomous presentation, these alarming pro-
totypes, these grotesquely exaggerated negative exceptions not only sustain, but also strengthen, the dominant ideology by hideously
exacerbating what could happen in the eventuality that it should become
subverted (*SLW*, 78). The exception in fact lapses precisely to the extent
to which it reinforces the rule. Here indeed is a case when exception
should be taken to exceptions that only camouflage themselves as such
the better to justify unjust decrees and to legitimate unfair rationalizations. On the other hand, seeing in some women (the mother, the vener-
able woman, and so forth) a higher type of humanity confirms, rather
than invalidates, the assumption that woman belongs to an inferior caste.
Either a woman remains unchanged, true to herself in being true to man,
or she risks losing everything in renouncing man for the uncertain com-
pensations of liberation. Either way, the assessment made of her person
is function of her faithfulness—or unfaithfulness—to the comportments
expected of her sex. When they consider this wager of liberation versus
adherence to the status quo, the males fail to understand why anyone
would wish to pay a high price for a solution to a problem that, as far as
they are concerned, does not exist. Why should a woman want to acquire
qualities whose very absence enhances her status?

Significantly, Judge William's position reflects that embraced by the
Aesthete in Kierkegaard's very first publication: "Another Defense of
Woman's Great Abilities," a very short piece issued in 1834 in *Kjøben-
havns Flyvende Post* (see *EPW*, 3–52).[11] Making his first appearance in
this grotesquely ironical essay, A sneers at bluestockings and paints exaggerated pictures of the transformations that, in his opinion, are likely to

occur in the wake of female liberation. He resorts to ridicule (to what Marguerite Duras, aiming to denounce precisely such a condescending attitude, would in our century call "the defense of the weak") and pokes fun at the woman presumptuous enough to cross the boundaries naturally allotted to her sex (Duras 1980, 113). Dramatizing through derision the scene of her transgressive behavior, he shows her busily brooding over abstract concepts, judging philosophical disputations, and so forth, while, like a medieval knight, the male thinker of her choice wears her colors (SV, XIII, 8). In the revulsion with which thoughts of the self-asserting woman and of woman's emancipation fill each one of them, neither A (the Aesthete), nor B (Judge William), nor C (Constantin) hesitates to sacrifice logic to the strength of prejudice. Nor do these male pseudonyms object to resorting to fantasies far more delirious than those they patronizingly deplore in the "fair sex" (det smukke Kjøn). Ironically, on the evidence of such portrayals, foolhardy would be the attempt to praise the powers of abstraction, or the coolheadedness of these male personae!

Kierkegaard, speaking in his own name in *Works of Love*, echoes on this point the sentiment of his aesthetic and ethical pseudonyms. Overwhelmed by "what battles there have been to establish women on equal terms with men in the secular world," the philosopher declares himself proud to have fought for no emancipation whatsoever—be it (in a derisive association recurrent throughout the production) that of the Jews, or that of women (WL, 48; AN, 50; CUP, 1:430). In the same work, he expresses his disapproval of well-meaning Christians who, extending their enthusiasm for humanity to all, seek to influence women and to modify their status: "Foolish men have foolishly busied themselves in the name of Christianity to make it obvious to the world that women have equal rights with men—*Christianity has never demanded or desired this*" (WL, 80, 139–140; my emphasis). In keeping with a tradition in whose name the masculine has arrogated to itself rights from which it has been careful to exclude women, Kierkegaard, for whom the emancipation of women is the "invention of the devil," mercilessly propounds that she, whose flesh is at fault, be mortified in the flesh (JP, 4:4992)!

But, it must be asked, what are the dangers, in the eyes of author and pseudonyms, likely to ensue in the wake of woman's liberation? One of the negative aspects of this eventuality is explicitly identified by Kierkegaard; it appears to stem from a generous impulse: the "sympathetic anxiety" that animates him at the thought that woman's upbringing would make her feel compelled (just like man) to realize herself in the noise

and bustle of outward existence and to launch upon the struggle for life
on the model of men.

> There is really something to it that in the last resort women are a
> bit more self-sacrificing. It is probably because they live more qui-
> etly and withdrawn and thus a bit closer to ideality. They are not
> as likely to acquire the market-price standard the way a man does,
> who from the outset is on the go in life. The saving factor for
> women (which is why one still sees in them the traces and expres-
> sions of individuality, the boldness to grasp a single thought and
> to dare hold on to it) is the distance from life which is granted
> her for a period. This quieter life has the result that she becomes
> somewhat more herself than does a man, who already even as a
> lad is demoralized by having to be like the others, and as a youth,
> to say nothing of the adult, is completely demoralized by learning
> how things go in practical life, in actuality. This very knowledge
> is the ruination of him. If girls were brought up the same way—
> then good night to the whole human race. (JP, 4:4992)

Judge William, on whom equally weighs the nineteenth-century bourgeois dichotomy between domestic or private female space and eco-
nomic-political or public male space, also opposes the notion that women
should become the emulators of men. Yet—more offensively patronizing
than his maker—he argues that, by doing so, a woman would expose
herself to "irreparable" loss and place herself "completely in his [a man's]
power, abandoned to his conditions . . . a prey to his whims" (EO, 2:312).
If the aesthetes pitied woman's overall condition, William sanctimoniously deplores the plight of the overreaching female—a further instance of (a) man relishing the luxury of expressing compassion for a
creature who can only lose when she tries to improve her lot.

Another stereotypical rationale adduced by the Judge is that female
emancipation would weaken the whole structure of society. Biblical considerations are also invoked; namely, the fear that, once freed from masculine domination, woman would be condemned to work, "man's sour
sweat" (SLW, 166; Genesis 3, 17–19). In Genesis, God's punishment of
Adam and Eve, and beyond them, of every man and woman in every
generation, has the sexual division of labor resting on divine authority.
Adam's toil is to produce the goods of society by the "sweat of his brow,"
an expression that, in man, allies muscular and mental work. Eve's labor,

meanwhile, consists of reproducing the species in pain and subservience to Adam. But the woman daring enough to seek emancipation from universally/masculinely defined conditions would be working by the sweat of her brow—thus confusing everything. Likewise, Kierkegaard, struck by the spreading of the work ethic to women in Protestant countries, was puzzled by the "observation" that such callous "pedestrianism" tends to proliferate in northern countries. This, in his opinion, "warps the feminine nature" by advancing that "a woman is a person who is useful and profitable," whereas, "originally it was not so; originally woman was designed to be a luxury: a companion, an adornment, a decoration. Only in the North does she have to prove herself to be useful, and therefore it is only in the North that the question of her emancipation has to arise" (*JP*, 6:6904).

Another negative correlative of liberation—adduced sometimes as effect, sometimes as cause—is the masculine indifference that, bound to follow in its wake, will entail the marginalization of the woman involved. By her unwillingness to conform to masculine expectations, a woman dooms herself to incurring sexual and social depreciation: Having barred herself from her "true" destiny, she will never experience the ordinary satisfactions of female life. When she becomes a bluestocking with an itch for scribbling, a woman chooses to forsake man, hence, his respect and his attentions. Contrasting with the traditional definition of woman as passive and "feminine," the intellectually assertive woman not only condemns herself to remaining an untalented scribbler, she is excoriated as anomalous, unnatural, monstrous, and so forth; in other words, as threatening to the surrounding culture. In brief, she is, if not a man, at least not a "real" woman.

To understand that such is the fate that, not only in the ethicist's view but also in Kierkegaard's, awaits the independent, intelligent female, all the reader has to do is consult the letters that Kierkegaard addressed to some well-known female contemporaries. In an 1849 missive, he accuses Frederika Bremer, the Finnish-Swedish journalist, of being a "smug spinster" and a "silly tramp" unable to find a husband (*JP*, 6:6493). There is also the case of Clara Raphael, the pseudonymous author of *Twelve Letters* (*Tolv Breve*), a book written by Mathilde Fibiger, the first Danish feminist. As an intellectual, Clara has, in his opinion at least, crossed over into realms foreign to her natural habitat where, left gasping with the ineffectuality of a fish out of water, she is bound eventually to succumb to personal asphyxia. Desperate for something to do, it occurred to her, still according to Kierkegaard, to latch onto an idea, namely, that of the emancipation of women. Yet she did not do so, he comments in an unpublished review of her book, because of delight in the exercise of her mental powers; no, she did so only because of her lack of interest in marriage (*JP,* 6:6709). Of Clara's grotesque transgression of Nature's boundaries he sees further evidence in her desire for a brother-sister relationship with her husband. Unmistakable are the implications: If a woman uses her intellect, she does so, not by choice, but merely because she has missed her particular calling, or because Nature has made her neither fish nor fowl, neither man nor woman; literary or philosophical potentiation in the "other sex" is systematically equated with sexual frustration.

Given the presumption that woman neither is, nor should be, active or reflective, the exception to the rule is perceived as altogether alien to the category "woman" and as therefore unfit for romance. Underlying the pernicious imagery of ugly bluestockings and dried-up spinsters is the familiar dualism of mind and body, a key component of Western patriarchal ideology. Once incompatibility has been assumed to exist between feminine/bodily fulfillment (through another) and masculine/intellectual achievement (through oneself), a female will offend the males' sense of decency precisely to the extent to which she appears to realize herself independently. In "their" books, as Hélène Cixous would write more than a century later, "either woman is passive or she does not exist" (Cixous and Clément 1986, 64).[12] The harder a woman works at autonomy and intellectual independence, the more she is made to feel freakish (both in the acceptations of "unsexed" and of "fallen"), anomalous, alien, alienated, and likely to lose everything.

That Kierkegaard had a tendency to show little patience for his female critics, that, in their case, he was not beyond arguing *ad feminam* is further exemplified by his answer to a fairly sober letter from feminist author Lodovica de Breteville. Even though Lodovica was perhaps one of his most articulate and systematically minded correspondents, the philosopher inveighs against her with a testiness reminiscent of that manifested by Judge William each time the issue of women's liberation is broached. Undercutting Lodovica's innocuous remarks, Kierkegaard quips as one personally offended: "It is typically feminine, whenever one has ventured too far in self-reflection, then to cry out to another person, 'Restore me to myself!'" (*LD,* 372). Not just content with putting her back in her place, he finds shocking that she could voice opinions different from his own and concludes hence that she must be hysterical to do so.

So superfetatory are the rationales, so interlocked the motivations—conscious and unconscious—that what these males hope to accomplish by barring women from work and by scaring them with the abomination of the single life can only be tentatively assessed. Whether liberation is blamed on the northern mentality, on Protestantism, on sexual appetite, or conversely on sexual frustration, the difficulty begins when (a) woman does not stay in the place (allegedly) befitting her sex, within the limits (allegedly) assigned to her by Nature.[13] What happens, of course, is that, by preventing women from decking themselves out as a bastard gender and from denying their "natural" destiny (as companions for men, as mothers, and so forth), a male perpetuates, or ensures, his own dominance and the Other's submission. The impression everywhere given is that woman cannot do without man. More realistically, however, when a male "explains" that a woman cannot assert herself as an autonomous individual without threatening and betraying the feminine ideal, when he pharisaically claims to be defending her, he is only betraying *his* fear—the fear of an emancipated damsel who might refuse to worship at his altars![14] What in effect annoys him is the thought that a woman could become deficient in qualities he holds to be supremely desirable in a subordinate: What of the poor man—think!—left to fend for himself? The hope is that woman, seduced by the assumed ease of her condition, will not seek to modify a status quo that has hitherto served the "first sex" rather well: By being protected *from* man, she is in fact protected *for* him. Because a man's pleasure manifestly lies in the receiving, hers, it is "naturally" assumed, lies in the bestowing. Woe then to the female exception who does not abide by certain standards of obedience and unquestioning dumbness! No one has perhaps expressed the feeling with greater accuracy than Bernick when, in Ibsen's *Pillars of Society* (1877), he exclaims: "People ought not to think of themselves first; women least of all" (Ibsen 1911, 5:368). Self-servingly, (a) man—an ethicist to boot—keeps on maintaining that this secondary being remains preponderant, that she has the upper hand, while denying her the right to exist as an individual and taking care that she does not enter the domain he regards as his own.

Furthermore, inasmuch as a woman is supposed to think and write about certain things in a certain way, a male is bound to deem improper or indecent her expressing something—anything at all—about a subject that might involve discussion of the sexual relation.[15] That this was one of Kierkegaard's fears can be seen in his blind acceptance of the traditional argument about feminine loquacity: "Everything revolves around woman. Charming, but then one can also be sure that everything revolves around chatter, trivialities, and in a refined way, around sexual relations" (JP, 4:4998). Two corollaries of the fear are the interdict that, weighing upon women's upbringing, forbids their concerning themselves with sexual problems; from a more general point of view, any curiosity in these matters is considered unwomanly and the sign of a sinful disposition. But there is more, as Victor Eremita makes plain at the end of his speech in "In Vino Veritas": there is a certain lack in woman's nature that "makes it impossible for woman to state man's nature" (SLW, 65). This discovery of a lack is no accident; it is clear that any discussion of sexuality would entail a concomitant glance at man and his role in the whole business. Since a woman's "nature so obviously is as it is," and since man's consists in the denial of all that makes up her life, she could not understand a man without eliminating her femininity, without denying herself as a woman, with the consequence that "an erotic relationship with her would be unthinkable" (SLW, 65)! Similarly bent upon emphasizing the necessity for woman to remain in her place, the green, but strangely cocksure, Young Man of Stages, in yet another classical example of the double bind, hands his fellow symposiasts a vatic looking-glass that shows how unsettling such (un)feminine exceptions would be. To make his point, he adduces the examples of two women whose knowledge on the subject of love would match his own. One would find erotic love (Elskov) comic, as he does, while the other would have discovered its tragic nature, as he apparently also has. Knowing too much, the first woman could not possibly understand him; as for the second one, not only would she not understand him, but—more tragically—she would in addition lose her powers of seduction and "be destroyed" in the process (SLW, 46–47).

In sum, the fear of feminine achievement and self-affirmation is no less than the fear of feminism, namely, the fear of women (putatively) daring enough not to hold themselves in contempt and bold enough to stand up defiantly to the men. What the portrayal of female overreachers as alienated through the embracing of virile values and as doomed in their sexuality underscores is the males' inability to dissociate sexuality from power and authority—prerogatives they were and are certainly intent on preserving. Thus, whether they spurn woman for being what she is, or deny her access to anything else, the males—through their endorsement of traditional sex roles—discourage her access to authority, with the consequence that, in this instance as well, the assessment they have initially made of her inferiority finds itself retroactively justified. Whether they deny her advantages that, they maintain, do not count, or beg her to leave all the *tedium vitae* to them, the men ensure that their own interests continue to be served and that their sex, identified with the universal, be allowed to go on exploiting the Other('s) in good conscience.

Espied in fear and trembling is the possibility that feminism— traditionally equated with the masculinization of women and women's appropriation of the masculine realm—may educe not only a change in the men, but also a change in their conception of themselves as men. If rivalry between husband and wife, between men and women is to be prevented at all costs, it is because it primarily concerns men among themselves. Although the causal link manifestly established by Judge William and Kierkegaard is that between female genius/autonomy and sterility, it is not difficult to surmise that it may after all be a lie by which a fear disguises itself as its opposite. Behind Johannes the Seducer's predilection for young girls over women lay, we recall, the fear of a woman whose powers would equal or surpass his own, of a woman in whom sexuality and autonomy would be identified—an assimilation that, in the Seducer's opinion, is only legitimate when applied to his own gender (*EO*, 1:324). A lustful, oversensual creature would represent a dark—both contaminating and threatening—side of sexuality insofar as, free from shame and inhibition, she would have bartered her femininity for pleasure; more threateningly for the Seducer, she would have created for herself a situation analogous to his own.[16] The direction of the vector is irrelevant; what is significant is that both Johannes and William betray the terror inspired by a being whose self-assertiveness threatens man in his essence as well as in his sexuality. The perception of sexual activity as manifesting itself in inverse ratio to mental activity betrays the fear that too active a mind would trouble the sexual order, would lead woman, not to sterility and isolation, but to adultery or corruption. What this linking of the two poles of intellectual independence and sexuality (asserted or repressed) reveals is the likelihood that the fear is not *for* the woman, but *of* the woman.

But there lurks perhaps something else behind the alarm. As we have just seen, Judge William's opinion is that the autonomous woman, who has renounced the feminine side of her nature by being too much of a person, merely succeeds in appealing to effeminate types, namely, to men who, he suspects, have sunk into a state of emotional dependency upon women—to men who, he thinks, physiologically and psychologically have been made, or have made themselves, "womanish." Does not the depth of the homophobic panic induced in William by these mixed categories, made of the pseudovirile women and of the pseudofeminine males by whom they are encouraged, identify his fundamental fear as that of a general effeminization or of a contamination of the masculine by the feminine? Indeed, as Freud has well shown in "The Taboo of Virginity" (1918 [1917]): What man fears is "being weakened by the woman, infected with her femininity and . . . then showing himself incapable" (Freud 1955–74, 11:198–99). If it is degrading to be a woman, it is even more degrading to be *like* one! Or could it be that—even more shockingly—the source of the fright is other than the one explicitly described? Could it be that the alarm a male experiences at the thought of woman's emancipation has in fact very little to do with woman herself—that it comes from elsewhere? Could it be that the ambivalence, whereby Judge William deems himself confronted upon imagining these ill-defined borders, comes in fact from within?

Although Kierkegaard definitely appears to be in agreement with his Judge both on the antagonism manifested toward women's liberation and on the assumption of the existence of essential differences between the sexes, further assessment of his "true" feelings on these questions would certainly be presumptuous until the place assigned to woman by the highest existence-sphere is thoroughly examined. In defending marriage, Judge William, for whom men and women (their differences notwithstanding) are internally, transcendentally alike, means to defend women; yet, it is clear from the above that his success with respect to the latter is far from evident. But, since other pseudonyms are yet to come— pseudonyms higher than the Judge—by whom the universal obligation to marry will be contested, it is necessary to exercise caution and to refrain from assuming total congruence between author and pseudonym regarding these matters. As some feminists have suggested, Kierkegaard's unwillingness to grant women liberation may after all be a temporary roadblock, a sign both of the ambivalence he discerns in the ethical treatment of the "other sex" and of his conviction that women's equality and autonomy are only conceivable beyond the sphere of the ethico-universal—in which case his misogamy would have its source in a gynophilia bent on defending women both from men and from themselves.[17] Conversely, it could be that professing belief in the virtual/abstract equality of both sexes will only place women at a vertiginous distance from the acquisition of rights without which their actual lives will never be enhanced.

But, uncertain at this point of the conclusions of the religious, let us turn to our profit the lessons of the ethical. When, guided by the pen of his author, Victor Eremita, the general editor of *Either/Or*, decides to conclude his own preface with a "word to the reader," he lets Judge William speak in his stead:

> Go out into the world. . . . Visit an individual reader in a favorably disposed hour, and if you should encounter a reader of the fair sex, then I would say: My charming reader, in this book you will find something that you perhaps should not know, something else which you will probably benefit by coming to know it. Read, then, the something in such a way that, having read it, you may be as one who has not read it; read the something else in such a way that, having read it, you may be as one who has not forgotten what has been read. (*EO*, 1:14–15)

Although the serial ventriloquism has been interpreted in ways so varied that their examination would mandate a study unto itself, "the something" that, according to Judge William, "the charming reader" ought not to know has usually been understood as pointing to the aesthetical writings of the first volume of *Either/Or*—particularly "The Seducer's Diary." As for "the something else" that she should not forget, it has been commonly identified with the ethical writings of the second volume, namely, the Judge's letters. Could it be that William has something else in mind? Could it be that "the something" that woman "should not know" is that which would empower her to contest the place assigned to her by patriarchy and "the something else" she should remember that which would enable his sex to retain its hegemony? Even if compliance is assumed, there remain, however, a possibility and a hope for "the reader of the fair sex": the possibility and the hope that, having read "the something," she neither will, nor can, be ever again "as one who has not read it."

Notes

1. Anna Nielsen (1807–50), a favorite of critics, became a member of the Royal Theater company in 1821. She was famous for portraying the Danish woman from her early youth to her later years. She was married to N. P. Nielsen, an actor and director. See Letter 170 (*LD*) and *JP*, 1:152.

Let us bear in mind that, even though the actress makes a project of herself, she essentially acts to nourish her narcissism, namely, her self as seen by others, her self as Other. Her triumph lies precisely in her alienation. Therefore, whether women identify with the image of themselves reflected in the eyes of an adoring public (all actresses are women), or in those of an admiring lover (all women are actresses), it is all the same to the masculine gaze, whose presumptions find themselves validated either way. If actresses are so convincing on stage, is it not because throughout history women have tended to be perceived first of all as narcissistic, that is, as existing in re-presentation? Conversely, if women have succeeded as actresses as they have in no other professions, is it not because masculine strictures do not mind seeing their hysterics indulge a bit of public, hence publicly condoned, histrionics?

2. In the very same breath in which Kierkegaard—like William—addresses to woman the problematic praise of being a beneficial "corrective" for man, he adds: "And for the sake of the cause, a woman may lift the burden just as well as a man *precisely because she has fewer ideas*, and also fewer half-ideas, *than the man, and thus more feeling, imagination, and passion* (*JP*, 6:6531; cf. "The Woman Who Was a Sinner," with *Training in Christianity*, 261–62; my emphasis). The philosopher also feels that, in sharp contrast with a man who thinks first and then acts when he opts for a lifestyle, a woman, unable to summon the help of rational powers before coming to a decision, acts first and then attempts to justify the randomness of her behavior (*JP*, 6:6709).

3. Prompted by an analogous conviction, the preacher of *Thoughts on Crucial Situations* is careful not to stir complex thoughts in the female members of his congregation, lest the ensuing strain should upset their precarious emotional and intellectual balance (*TDIO*, 44).

4. That weakness presented as strength is nothing but weakness is evident from Climacus's remark that, because of his having "only a woman's strength, which is in frailty," Jacobi (compared here to Lessing) was "not the stronger but the weaker" (*CUP*, 1:101).

5. In the same vein, Constantin emphasizes in *Stages* the distinction that makes woman have her being in relationships—that is, be "relational," or relative to another's existence—whereas man acts absolutely, expresses the absolute, *is* the absolute. The dichotomy explains why Kierkegaard's experimental psychologist subsumes woman under the category of "jest," a category that by his own definition, is only "embryonic[ally] ethical" (*SLW*, 48).

6. In parallel fashion, Quidam, not just content with declaring in " 'Guilty?'/'Not Guilty?' " that "the religious movement of infinity may not be *natural* to her individuality," adds that in fact "it is not essential for a woman" (*SLW*, 302, 306; my emphasis). The sentiment already occurs in *Fear and Trembling*, 36.

7. Similarly in *Prefaces*, N. N., the mock eponymous Dane, equates his wife's "reasoning" with an "incantation" so irresistible in fact that it can be resisted by none—least of all by him who shares her life (*P*, 24).

8. Anti-Climacus, who stresses, in *The Sickness unto Death*, the need for the Christian to believe that "for God everything is possible," will no doubt find it easier for woman—this selfless and confident creature who "in a decisive sense (does not possess) intellectuality"—to effect the transition from the lowest to the highest sphere (*SUD*, 38–39, 49 n).

9. In her compelling study, "Is Female to Male as Nature Is to Culture?," anthropologist Sherry Ortner (1974) observes that "the psychic mode associated with women seems to stand at both the bottom and the top of the scale of human modes of relating" (86).

10. Although Sandra M. Gilbert and Susan Gubar (1979a) investigate the dichotomy throughout their trilogy, see most particularly the first volume, *The Madwoman in the Attic*, 17–31, 34, 44, 46, 48, 68, 78–79, 194, 196, 203, 219, 240, 244, 314, 321–23, 345–46.

11. The 17 December 1834 article was in response to "Defense of the Superior Origin of Woman," the satiric picture of women drawn only a few days earlier (4 December) by P. E. Lund in the same newspaper (*SV*, XIII, 5–8). See Watkin (1996).

12. See also Jacques Lacan's remark concerning woman's complaint of having been excluded from the nature of things/words, in *Feminine Sexuality: Jacques Lacan and the école freudienne*: "Only they don't know what they are saying, which is all the difference between them and me" (Mitchell and Rose 1985, 144).

13. Far from us, however, to suggest that Kierkegaard was alone to make such claims in the nineteenth century. Our intent is not to incriminate a particular writer with respect to the woman question, but to show how his stance is typical of patriarchal strictures, how he is a product, albeit perhaps a paroxystic one, of his time, culture, and gender. As in the case quoted by Wendy Martin and retold by Sandra M. Gilbert and Susan Gubar: "In the nineteenth-century this fear of the intellectual woman became so intense that the phenomenon . . . was recorded in medical annals. A thinking woman was considered such a breach of nature that a Harvard doctor reported during his autopsy on a Radcliffe graduate he discovered that her uterus had shrivelled to the size of a pea" (Gilbert and Gubar 1979a, 56. See Wendy Martin, "Anne Bardstreet's Poetry: A Study of Subversive Piety," in Gilbert and Gubar 1979b, 13–31).

Not uncharacteristically, some male Kierkegardian critics, in complicity with the fantasy which they (occasionally) try to expose, betray their vestigial sexism by glossing over this unfair treatment of women. Thus Gregor Malantschuk could, as late as 1976, congratulate Kierkegaard for having "*resist*[ed] the attempts to establish sexual equality in the external, secular sense" (Malantschuk, 61; my emphasis).

14. As Virginia Woolf (1929) points out in *A Room of One's Own*: "The history of men's opposition to women's emancipation is more interesting perhaps than the story of that emancipation itself" (57).

15. Cf. *Les Voleuses de langue* (The tongue snatchers), where Claudine Herrmann (1976) remarks: "With the beginning of her teen years, the female adolescent experiences limitations in her ability to acquire vocabulary. This comes not only from her being excluded from terms that have something to do with sexuality, but even from those that present an analogy—were it only a sound analogy—with such terms" (11; my translation).

16. In his November 1939–March 1940 *Carnets de la drôle de guerre*, Sartre (1983) expresses much the same thought, to wit, that a frankly sensuous woman "would have disconcerted and shocked me, imparting a kind of necessity to some contingent preferences manifested by the masculine structure" (345).

17. Such is, for instance, Birgit Bertung's interpretation. According to the Danish critic, over against Judge William and Hegel who defend marriage, Kierkegaard's attacks on this institution, along with his vituperations against women, represent the best [indirect] way the philosopher had at his disposal to communicate a message of equality at a time "when the official marriage ritual said that the wife should be submissive to her husband" (Bertung 1989, 16). See also Bertung 1987.

References

Bertung, Birgit. 1987. *Om Kierkegaard Kvinder og Kaerlighed—en Studie i Søren Kierkegaards Kvindesyn*. Copenhagen: C. A. Reitzel.

———, ed. 1989. *Kierkegaard—Poet of Existence*. Copenhagen: C. A. Reitzel.

Brontë, Charlotte. *Shirley*. First issue of this edition, 1908; reprint, 1911, 1914. London: Dent and Sons; New York: E. P. Dutton.

Cixous, Hélène, and Catherine Clément. 1986. *The Newly Born Woman*. Translated by Betsy Wing. Minneapolis: University of Minnesota Press.

Duras, Marguerite. 1980. "Smothered Creativity." Translated by Virginia Hules. In *New French Feminisms: An Anthology*, edited by Elaine Marks and Isabelle de Courtivron. Amherst: University of Massachusetts Press.

Fibiger, Mathilde. 1851. *Tolv Breve*. Edited by J. L. Heiberg. Copenhagen.

Freud, Sigmund. 1955–74. *The Standard Edition of the Complete Psychological Works of Sigmund Freud*. 24 vols. Translated from the German under the General Editorship of James Stratchey. London: Hogarth.

Garside, Christine. 1971. "Can a Woman Be Good in the Same Way as a Man?" *Dialogue* 10:534–44.

Gilbert, Sandra M., and Susan Gubar. 1979a. *The Madwoman in the Attic: The Woman Writer and the Nineteenth-Century Literary Imagination*. New Haven: Yale University Press.

———, eds. 1979b. *Shakespeare's Sisters: Feminist Essays on Women Poets*. Bloomington: Indiana University Press.

Herrmann, Claudine. 1976. *Les Voleuses de langue*. Paris: Des femmes.

Howe, Leslie A. 1994. "Kierkegaard and the Feminine Self." *Hypatia* 9, no. 4:131–57.

Ibsen, Henrik. 1911. *The Works of Henrik Ibsen*, 6 vols. Edited and translated by William Archer. Boston: Scribner.

Léon, Céline, 1977. "The Validity of Judge William's Defense of Marriage." In *The Ethical Aesthetic: Essays and Perspectives on Kierkegaard's Either/Or*. Edited by David Humbert. Atlanta: Scholars Press.

Mackey, Louis. 1971. *Kierkegaard: A Kind of Poet*. Philadelphia: University of Pennsylvania Press.

Malantschuk, Gregor. 1980. *The Controversial Kierkegaard*. Translated by Howard V. Hong and Edna H. Hong. Waterloo: Wilfred Laurier University Press.

Mitchell, Juliet, and Jacqueline Rose, eds. 1985. *Feminine Sexuality: Jacques Lacan and the école freudienne*. Translated by Jacqueline Rose. New York: Norton.

Ortner, Sherry B. 1974. "Is Female to Male as Nature Is to Culture?" In *Woman, Culture, and Society*, edited by Michelle Zimbalist Rosaldo and Louise Lamphere, 67–87. Stanford: Stanford University Press.

Pope, Alexander. 1979. *The Rape of the Lock*. In *The Norton Anthology of World Masterpieces*, 4th ed., 2 vols., general editor, Maynard Mack. New York: Norton.

Sartre, Jean-Paul. 1983. *Carnets de la drôle de guerre*. Paris: Gallimard.

Watkin, Julia. 1998. "Serious Jest? Kierkegaard as Young Polemicist in 'Defense' of Women." In *International Kierkegaard Commentary: Early Polemical Writings*, edited by Robert L. Perkins. Macon: Mercer University Press.

Woolf, Virginia. 1929. *A Room of One's Own*. New York: Harcourt, Brace.

6

An Aparté on Repetition

Sylviane Agacinski

How does the thunderstorm happen, in other words, repetition, the event, which is also to say, a tear, a rupture? Something, perhaps, blows or blows up, pops, pierces, opens and shows up. There it was, and now here it is. It happens.

Repetition: what does it produce, give (back), duplicate, yield, deliver, conceive, return, engender?

A child at the same time as his father and mother.

"Oneself," as Constantine's correspondent says. His last letter refers to repetition as being at the same time auto-engenderment, auto-conception, and loss of self.

My Silent Confidant:
    She is married . . . I am myself again. Here I have repetition, I

understand everything, and life seems more beautiful to me than ever. Let life reward her as it will, let it give her what she loved the most; it also gave me what I love the most—myself . . .

Isn't that a repetition, then? Did I not get everything double? Did I not get myself again and precisely in such a way that I might have a double sense of its meaning? Compared with such a repetition, what is a repetition of worldly possessions, which is indifferent toward the qualifications of the spirit? Only his children did Job not receive double again, for a human life cannot be redoubled in that way (*fordoble*). Here only repetition of the spirit (*Aandes Gjentagelse*) is possible, even though it is never so perfect in time as in eternity . . .

I am myself again; the machinery has been set in motion. The inveiglements in which I was entrapped (*Sonderhugne ere de Besnaerelser*) have been rent asunder; the magic formula that hexed me so that I could not come back to myself has been broken. There is no longer anyone who raises his hand against me. My emancipation is assured; I am born to myself, for so long as Ilithyia folds her hands, the one who is in labor cannot give birth. (R, 220–21)

Repetition is distinguished from reproduction—to which, however, it bears a metaphorical resemblance—in that it does not add to the number of the living. It is an ideal impregnation: of the Idea, by the Idea—"I belong to the Idea" (*Ideen tilhorer jeg*). The Idea's delivery. This is actually how *Repetition* already began, with the feminine aptitude for an impregnation by the Idea. But the fact that this aptitude is characterized as "feminine" obviously does not mean that woman is capable of it. "The inveiglements have been rent asunder," says the young man. What can it actually mean to tear apart (symbolically) these inveiglements?

"But what can it actually mean to tear this symbolical veil. . . . If this birth-veil was torn, then he saw the world and was re-born. . . . The necessary condition of his rebirth was that he should have an enema administered to him by a man. . . . Here, therefore, the phantasy of rebirth was simply a mutilated and censored version of the homosexual wish-phantasy. . . . The tearing of the veil was analogous to the opening of his eyes and to the opening of the window. . . . The wish to be born of his father . . . the wish to present him with a child—and all this at the price of his own masculinity . . . in them homosexuality has found its furthest and most intimate expressions . . ."

This fragment from Freud's *Wolf-Man* (*An Infantile Neurosis*, 17:100–101)[1] can be found in a note to Derrida's "The Double Session" (*Dissemination*, 269), a session that, beyond Freudian analysis, draws the reading here toward whatever links *Repetition* to dissemination and carries it out of the reach of the dialectical reappropriation that is, nonetheless, also at work in it. The birth to himself of the young man in the thunderstorm appears as a *resumption* since the word *Gjentagelsen* can also have that meaning (the French translator, Tisseau, even sees in it an intimation of the "resumption" of relations with Regine). A thematic reading would of course show that reappropriation, reflexivity, idealization can also be found in *Repetition*. But it is not that simple: the young man is "liberated" (and first of all from a bond: "No one coaxes out of my being an explanation that not even I myself can give to another" [R, 221]—what is this an explanation of, if not of his [first] birth?). However, this is not in order finally to arrive at the kind of masterful self-knowledge that is required by the other. On the contrary, it is in order to abandon oneself all the more, to let oneself get carried away to the *abyss*, the *infinite*, the *stars*, through the "poetic" activity of writing. It is not his identity he meets up with again but a kind of brilliant explosion, a dispersal with neither return nor revenue: "three cheers for the dance in the vortex of the infinite, three cheers for the cresting waves that hide me in the abyss, three cheers for the cresting waves that fling me above the stars!" (R, 222). Through writing, he finds his deliverance and his loss.

The abyss here is not only a lyrical theme for the poet: it is above all the abyss of repetition itself, of the text that bears this title several times over. For if repetition does not allow for resumption, this is because the book is already divided and split. Through the repetition of the title, *Repetition*, on the inside of the book, it opens at least twice, thus placing *Repetition en abyme*.[2] The repetition of the same title at the heart of the text can indicate neither a simple starting over again nor another section: it shows that *Repetition* is not a *single* book. I can't help being struck by the quiet assurance of the [French] translators who note: "The resumption of the title indicates that repetition is to be henceforth understood in its religious sense." Likewise, it is not possible to ignore the *mise en abyme* of the author: the words of the young man are merely staged, mouthed by a (pseudonymous) author who effaces himself before the poet he has produced (perhaps out of himself), "just like the midwife in relation to the child she has delivered" (230). There is no taking hold of *Repetition*.[3] Let's say about it what "The Double Session" says about dissemination: "*repetition* affirms the always already divided generation of meaning" (268).

Were we to destroy the scenarios one by one, there would be no more repetition, no more book.

Just like the mime, like *Mimique*,[4] repetition, also understood as a text, turns the event into an abyss without adding anything to it. And if nothing is repeated or represented by it, this is not because it would present "it-self."

It is like the theater where, in the middle of his "story," Constantine goes looking for repetition.

Haven't we all wanted at one time or another to be actors? Mistakenly, perhaps, lured by a false image of the double, tempted by a toned-down form of repetition. . . . Every "young man," admits Constantine, would like to enjoy all the possibilities he feels within himself by becoming all those he is capable of becoming: "There is probably no young person with any imagination who has not at some time been enthralled by the magic of the theater and wished to be swept along into that artificial actuality in order like a double to see and hear himself and to split himself up into every possible variation of himself, and nevertheless in such a way that every variation is still himself" (R, 154). A "taste for the theater" is a passion for the possible: an idle dream no doubt, but perhaps momentarily necessary on account of its very futility, since "it is just as salutary for the adult to have something in his past life that he can laugh about as something past that draws his tears" (R, 155). We will finally laugh, then, about that desired illusion, or illusioned desire, a desire for shadows, reflections, doubles, masks, fleeting scenes where "the frothing foam of words that sound without resonance" (R, 156). But repetition is not a numerical multiplication; out of one it does not make several.

The actor is not all the roles, he is merely an actor, and that is his only identity.

Just as a theatrical event does not take place several times, nothing gets repeated in it. Constantine learns this when he returns to the Königstädter in Berlin. His memory of this theater was as sharp as if he had just come out of it, and he was hoping once more to find a certain *Stemning* (mood, atmosphere, disposition). But when he attends a new performance, nothing is repeated: he can find neither the same box nor the same girl out in the audience nor the same laughter. "Beckmann could not make me laugh." Able to stand it no longer, he leaves the theater after half an hour: "There is no repetition at all. This made a deep impression on me" (R, 169). Of all he had known in Berlin, nothing was reproduced. His apartment had changed, and even the coffee is no longer to his liking.

"I perceived that there was no repetition" (R, 171).

The impossibility of repetition reveals itself in the very place where it had seemed to be the rule: at the theater.[5]

From writing to woman, from woman to repetition, to the theater and back again to writing, there are several courses to follow in every direction, and each intersects with the others.

Woman seems to have been Kierkegaard's first reason for writing. P. E. Lund, a friend of K.'s, had published an article entitled "Defense of the Superior Origin of Woman" on 4 December 1834. On 17 December K. publishes a "New Apology for the Superior Nature of Woman." The title is obviously ironic. Unless—and this would amount to the same thing—it is one of those discourses that glorify woman's Christian qualities, like the one in *The Sickness unto Death*: "the feminine nature is devotedness, abandon, and it is unfeminine if it is not that" (49–50). True woman, the only one who is any good, is the one who is herself only by *not* being herself, her own self. She has to be lost, offered up: in this way she realizes her happiness. "She loses herself in her abandon (devotion), and only then is she happy, only then is she herself; a woman who is happy without devotion, that is, without giving herself, no matter to what she gives it, is altogether unfeminine" (50). Her suffering, her particular despair, is not to realize her loss, it is to be deprived of that to which she wants to abandon herself. If a man abandons himself, it is never *properly speaking* (this term does not apply to him), if he happens to abandon himself, "his self remains behind as a sober awareness of devotion."

When a woman realizes the full extent of her nature, of her abandon, she becomes a model of Christian living—this is Mary Magdalene. And yet, she remains essentially *less* religious than man since "in most cases the woman actually relates to God only through the man." Woman is ultimately less religious than man in her abandon: this is perhaps because, abandoned *by nature*, she always gives up less than he does. . . . It is as though man were capable of being *more* of a woman, a *better* woman than woman: in other words, religious.

This is because it is not before God that woman submits herself, that she must submit herself, but rather before man. Man is to woman what God is to man. Silence, the mark of submission and obedience—that silence God imposes on Job—silence will be woman's lot, and it is in this way that she will be exemplary. "Let your women keep silence in the churches: for it is not permitted unto them to speak; but *they are commanded* to be under obedience, as also sayeth the law." And then this: "And if they will learn anything, let them ask their husbands at home; for it is a shame for women to speak in the church" (1 Cor. 14:34–35). The law of this silence would thus have been written, in black and white, for all time. But this is a silence before man, it is only a figure of silence, a human image for the religious position. But then, if woman, "in most cases," relates to God only through man, would she ever be directly involved with the religious?

There is a woman in K.'s texts, just one, who incarnates at once the essence of femininity and the absolute submission of Christianity, and this is "The Sinner Woman"—perhaps the most beautiful of the *Edifying Discourses*.[6] She provides a lesson for Simon and the others: she weeps at the feet of Christ, in silence. "A dumb personage from one end to the other of this scene." "What is it, then, that this woman from whom we are supposed to learn—did? The answer is: Nothing, she did nothing at all; she practiced the high, rare, exceedingly difficult, genuine womanly art of doing nothing at all" (268). "No doubt man has many more thoughts than woman . . . and no doubt man is stronger than weak woman" (262). This is not ironic: *of course*, man's superiority is not in question here, but woman, this woman, possesses the rarest, the most difficult, virtue—perhaps difficult for man—weakness; she is weakness itself. But from the religious point of view the affirmation of weakness signifies its opposite: "a prodigious strength."

". . . but then again woman has one—one what? Why, just one, the fact that *one* is woman's element. One wish, not many wishes—no, only one wish, but that with the whole soul put into it; one thought, not many thoughts—no, only one thought, but that a prodigious strength by the power of passion, one sorrow, not many sorrows—no, one sorrow, but so deep in the heart that one sorrow is certainly infinitely more than the many" (262).

Such is the case of Mary Magdalene. If such is woman, then it would seem that she is more naturally religious than man; but precisely because she is so more *naturally*, she is always *less* so than he. True Christianity requires virility—K. will always put a great deal of stress on this. "Naturally" passive, weak, mute, woman cannot know true religious castration. Which is why woman can be a *model* of religiousness without being truly religious, without ever being so as much as man, who is not religious naturally.

All things considered, it is only a matter of the image, of the idea of woman. "In most cases"—notably in the majority of cases in K.'s texts— woman is woman insofar as she signifies the opposite of this submission: she is the terrifying, voracious she-lion, egotistic, loving only herself through her progeny.

Mary Magdalene alone is complete frailty, complete submission; she is the "total impotence" required for forgiveness. She weeps, she is silent. She has understood or believed that the forgiveness of Christ, as God or man, is obtained only by not seeking to obtain it. A doctrine of grace.

Grace is what she has in fact: she is beautiful.

(I think I may have seen her, painted by Füssli. She is sitting with her legs crossed, her head resting on her bosom, her hair falling to her feet and hiding her whole face. Her arms are hanging down, too, folded elegantly over her feet, while her spreading fingers trace out, though just barely, a graceful gesture. It is called *Silence*. It could be an eternal silence, or just a pause.)

She does *nothing*, says K.: but this is not exactly true. Like the unknown man at Bethany, in Matthew's gospel, she *squanders*. Along with her tears, she pours out an expensive ointment over Christ's feet. And in the opinion of Judas, she squanders "indiscriminately." But that is because she understands that this is a festive occasion, and she knows how to spend for it. "Let us not, however, forget the festive occasion; as she for her part did not forget it" ("The Sinner Woman," 267). She pours out her tears over Christ, along with her hair and her ointment. "She weeps"—"she is silent": words incessantly repeated in the *Discourse*. All of these repetitions produce an effect of fascination; she must be fascinating to be able to appear fascinated in this way—"She anoints Christ's feet with ointment and wipes them with the hairs of her head, she weeps."

Thus, she does absolutely *nothing*. And why doesn't K. talk about the kisses with which she also covers the feet of Christ?

" 'Simon,' he said, 'you see this woman? I came into your house, and you poured no water over my feet, but she has poured out her tears over my feet and wiped them away with her hair. You gave me no kiss, but she has been covering my feet with kisses ever since I came in.' . . . Then he said to her, 'Your sins are forgiven' " (Luke, 7:44–49).

The sexual difference divides every scene, organizes the distribution of all the roles, and provides the hierarchy for all the positions and oppositions. Every alternative seems to be part of the one that is most pressing of all: "Am I a man or a woman"—each of these terms dividing itself on its own, endlessly. This is not even an alternative, then, since every choice turns out to be unstable. But there is a choice only because woman is not (merely) the name for a natural being but also the name for a position, even several of them that, as such, represent a number of possibilities for man. Perhaps, even, these are his only possibilities. There are at least two of them, and they correspond to the two types of woman, to the double "nature" of woman. What if man could choose only between two ways of being a woman?

Woman is always the woman of a couple—no matter which couple— and in the couple she is able to stand for herself *as well as* her opposite: in others words, castration *or* its opposite: the power of (re)production.

—Castrated, she is the wife as well as the son: that is the Christian position. But there is a conflict here because castration is enjoyable whereas Christianity is supposed to entail suffering.

—Powerful, she is the mother but she's also virile and paternal. So she takes the father's place, reappropriates it for herself, competes with God. She is guilty . . . unless it could be shown that she begets only in pain, that she suffers.

The conflict, then, could also be written in this way: How is it to marry a woman, take on a virile superiority, become a father, something that, insofar as I am a son, I cannot do without laughing? But neither can I remain a son without being the feminine wife of the Father. But if by writing I become father, thus giving birth to myself, then I become a mother, a virile woman, who is neither Christian nor man. And even if I choose to be God's bride, my enjoyment enters into contradiction with his law, which requires me to suffer. And if I choose the paternal maternity of writing, I'm still betraying the Father's law.

In any case, femininity shows itself along with all of its enjoyment. It would be necessary to reject the feminine positions one by one, to cleave them, deny them, always to separate the good femininity from the bad. . . . And finally to give back to man the good femininity. This is never simply possible. The Christian has to be wrested from the passive enjoyment of the mother. This is not possible short of denying to woman *true* submission (Christian, not natural), short of denying to woman *true* (spiritual) maternity.

I'm not going to reconstruct all the scenes in which the question is asked, "Am I a man or a woman?" Nor is it necessary to isolate or privilege *one particular* phantasy. There are several series of contradictions and compromises, or attempts at compromise. Each series is only a link, as Freud would say, in a chain of associations, and it would be necessary, in order to resolve just one symptom, to provide the case history of a "patient" in its entirety. Where would we find this entire case history? And what is the illness? It is no use diagnosing a case of hysteria, for instance, if it does nothing but reveal, only in a more acute manner, a constitutional bisexuality. In general, it is no use even giving it a name. If such a constitutional bisexuality actually exists, then trying to define what is masculine and what is feminine is already a first symptom of it, the second being the urgency of the need to be situated with reference to these definitions. Still another would be the multiplicity and contradictory character of the responses to it.

K. will make the rounds of all the possible and impossible responses, taking time to stop at each paradoxical compromise: virile childbirth, virile castration, feminized and feminanimalizing erection . . .

Freud: "In one case which I observed, for instance, the patient pressed her dress up against her body with one hand (as the woman), while she tried to tear it off with the other (as the man)" ("Hysterical Phantasies and Their Relation to Bisexuality," 9:166).

The eminently Christian solution to these conflicts, the one Kierkegaard will eventually settle on, is the rejection of sex in its entirety, of sexuality as such—let it be rejected, pushed off entirely onto one or the other of the sexes, thus eliminating the difference and the alternative. Faced with the anguish produced by bisexual fantasies, with the impossibility of a choice or compromise, the question is denied: there is no sexual difference. It is enough just to deny one of the two sexes, it is enough to take away from what is called "man" or "woman" the sexual, differential determination, for the difference to disappear (therefore sex itself), for there to remain only a sovereign indifference. To neutralize the opposition is to push the hierarchy that governed it to the limit of its violence. The old hierarchy lives on endlessly after its abolition: what remains, the indifferent, is always man—no matter what side "sex" was at first placed on.

If sex is originally and exclusively masculine, then woman represents the resurgence of a difference, due to degeneration, a fall, or a depravation of sex itself that divides and cuts itself off from itself. Man is original indifference. If woman is the fallen sex, then castration would be the establishment of difference here.

If sex is feminine, it signifies a setback, or animality, and man represents the indifference acquired through choosing castration. Castration, then, is the establishment of *in*difference.

In any case, it is the woman that differs, therefore it is always through *her* negation that indifference is reestablished. The desire to neutralize the opposition here is once again subject or accomplice to the desire to reinforce it.

A double desire, always, to abolish the difference while preserving it, to occupy all the positions in the opposition, and to enjoy it.

I want to be a man—I don't want to be just a man.

What we could call "the argument of the unique masculine *and* indifferent" sex is, curiously enough, attributed to Plato: "Even Plato recognizes that, at bottom, man's state of perfection is sexual indifference. He believes that in the beginning there existed only the male (without the female, sexual difference is obviously undifferentiated), but that due to deprivation and degeneracy the female appeared. He thinks that evil and cowardly men become women when they die, though not without the hope of eventually being raised again to the status of males. In a perfect life, he believes that the male, as in the beginning, would be the only sex and that, therefore, there would be sexual indifference" (*JP*).

A surprising reading of Plato: it obviously cannot be in reference to the androgynous myth told by Aristophanes in *The Symposium*—besides, the Androgyne is not a man. Perhaps this comes in roundabout fashion from the speech of Pausanias? He does, in fact, distinguish two Aphrodites: the *Common* one, the daughter of Zeus and Dione, who mostly inspires a bodily love, an ephemeral love for women as well as for men; and the *Heavenly* one, the goddess of a kind of love whose attributes "are altogether male." This Aphrodite, who is called "Urania" if she is the same one Hesiod refers to, is also a goddess *with no mother* since she is born from the frothing testicles of Uranus, which were cut off by Cronus and thrown into the sea by him. In *The Concept of Irony*, the speech of Pausanias receives the following commentary: "The one love is the motherless daughter of Uranus, the heavenly; the other love is much younger, has as its basis the difference between the sexes, and is the common. He then discusses the significance of that species of heavenly pederasty which loves the spiritual in man and is not degraded or debased by the sexual" (*CI*, 79). By combining various elements of the Platonic myths (Androgyne, The Heavenly Aphrodite, the transmigration of souls), we could trace all the elements in K.'s dream. But to go from there to attributing to Plato the idea that sexual indifference is the state of perfection is after all quite a big step.

The positions that at first seemed specifically feminine—submission, renunciation, or the labor of childbirth—will have to be, each one of them, divided, doubled, in such a way as to signify *virility itself* on the one hand, and the most brutish sensuality, the most feminine (beastly) stupidity (*la bêtise*) on the other. Reproduction, then, in the sense of procreation, becomes the object of the most injurious deprecations: the mother represents unenlightened selfishness, devotion to the progeny of flesh; she is "the lioness," indeed the "sow and her litter" . . . whereas man's share is the "spiritual" form of reproduction: repetition and dialectical reduplication.

By the same token, feminine submission is devalorized. When it is feminine, renunciation remains a mediocre calculation, it remains finite—whereas sacrifice, martyrdom, infinite renunciation belong properly to man, who alone is capable of choosing the absolute renunciation. This man of renunciation is the Christian: the Jew portrays his effeminate and brutish caricature.

To woman, the Jew, the animal, belong: sex, sensuality, enjoyment, children, number, life, immediacy, the finite, temporal world.

To man, the Christian, belong: virile castration, spirit, dialectical reduplication, the ideal, infinite sacrifice, suffering, solitude, eternity.

This basic division appears clearly in the last fragments of the *Journal*, where woman takes on a more and more threatening, more and more terrible, figure, to the point of becoming the enemy, the devourer whose sole aim is to "destroy man insofar as he is spirit." The determination of sex as *uniquely* feminine carries the day and it is *qua sex* that woman goes to war with spirit.

". . . that is why she is also called the sex: woman is the sex" (*JP*, 3:456).

The voice of the *Journal* is amplified here, is perhaps becoming delirious. It is no longer a question of choosing, the voice is now defending itself against an enemy on the outside: the conspiracy of sex is worldwide, historical, finding its allies in the state, the church. The world is thus split in two: those who plot among themselves to devour the others, to take advantage of them, kill them, eat them; and those who ask nothing better than to die and to suffer but who refuse to nourish the living off their death. They do not want to be robbed of their death, to have their sacrifice recuperated, to have its exemplary meaning perverted. In the service of this historical conspiracy of the living against the dying the most powerful institutions are at work: the Protestant Church, the family, the state, all of them serve feminine reproduction, all of them labor to kill spirit, to *bring back* to life what is actually the work of death, the only true "production," the work of spirit.

We can make out resonances of Blake's voice in *The Meaning of Heaven and Hell* here, too. It tells of the same kind of split—but the enemy forces there are united by their common need for one another: "Thus one portion of being, is the Prolific. The other, the Devouring: to the devourer it seems as if the producer was in his chains, but it is not so, he only takes portions of existence and fancies that the whole. But the Prolific would cease to be Prolific unless the Devourer *as a sea* received the excess of his delights."

All of K.'s voices can also be heard in Blanchot: it is enough to follow *Faux Pas*, for instance, and in the following order: "The Journal of Kierkegaard"—"Meister Eckhart"—"The Meaning of Heaven and Hell," and so forth.

Woman is infernal because of her "selfishness."

This means that the function of woman, her desire, is reappropriation, always. She has no relations with her children or her husband except in view of this reappropriation. In the general conspiracy, her role consists in humiliating man, destroying him, cutting him off from his spirituality, enfeebling him. The institution of the family is her instrument for this. She does not believe in marriage any more than man does, but it serves her ends and she does not seem to suffer from the lie. She feels "comfortable" with the lie and imposes it on man, for whom it is "degrading." Like him, she knows that marriage is condemned to degenerate, she is aware that it brings neither fulfillment nor happiness, but she pretends to believe in it, she acts "as though." Through the lie she imposes on him, she submits man to her law. He is also ensnared by the woman-mother, he does not see that, "as wife, as mother—well, here is an egoism of which the man has no intimation. Society has licensed it under the name of love—good heavens, no, it is the most powerful egoism in which woman most certainly does not love herself foremost but through (egotistically) loving her own she loves herself" (JP, 4:576).

That is her economy. As mother of the family, and this is not anything new, woman *is* economy, in other words, finite calculation. She loves herself through her children and she also wants, *in them,* to abolish the singularity of the husband. She never gives herself except in order to preserve (herself) better, to preserve her children, and in them to preserve the (dead) father. Woman is the sole *end* of the family.

This economic law of reappropriation, this sort of *Aufhebung,* does not seem to be the law of *the family* as such (as the site of the sublation of sexual difference), but rather only the law of woman.

From this perspective it would be possible, though at the risk of a crude comparison, to say that *Spirit* has nothing to do with the family *here,* except insofar as it fiercely resists the family, and also insofar as the family is established in order to destroy it. Or else: if the family accomplishes only the law of woman, if reappropriation is always feminine, then it would be necessary to say that, for K., the Hegelian dialectic is feminine.

If woman goes to war against spirit insofar as she is naturally sex and life, then there is no more sexual *difference* properly speaking. Virility (or spirituality) is the renunciation of sex. *Virile* would be equivalent to *castrated.* Because man alone has the possibility of castrating himself, that is where his power lies.

When it is feminine, sex constantly takes on the figure of a *tail.* That is the sign of the animal, who himself represents, as always, the "level below man." Man, man's model, is Christ: *ecce homo.* Whoever fails to recognize his kinship with him loses his kinship with God and men, and "redescends" to the level of an animal. Now who is Christ? The crucified, the sacrificed, the castrated—more precisely, the castraterect.

Judge for yourselves with the help of this portrait: "In this very instant the family of man is debased beneath what it is to be a man and is essentially animal. A humorist would say that poetic justice requires that man, in memory of the event, be decorated with a tail, and he must insist that this tail stand perpendicularly from the body in such a way that it would be impossible for any tailor's skill to hide it, and also that it could not be chopped off inasmuch as it would have the remarkable capacity of immediately growing again" (JP, 1:33).

Apparently, the tailor is invoked only to clothe, hide, cover, adorn the ornament and thus to conceal it, but what follows is still of interest to him since he is just as much the one who sews as the one who cuts. The incapacity to attire or protect (*parer*: to adorn, embellish, defend, parry) is thus always the tailor's. He can attire or protect (*parer*) neither by sewing or weaving—supplemental ornaments—nor by cutting off this bizarre ornament that stems as much from the vegetable as from the animal realm. He can neither prune nor graft.

In fact, perhaps you have to be something of a "humorist" to understand how this upright tail, as though triumphant, becomes the sign or the signifier of impotence. This is because the individual who holds it, or upholds it, condemned in spite of himself to an erection, constantly hands over for castration the ornament which he exhibits and which he cannot *not* exhibit. It is perpetually exposed, threatened, offered to a cutting he cannot control. Such an erection is therefore, paradoxically, impotent, and thus is by no means a genuine erection—one of those on the contrary that one must be able to deprive *oneself* of in order to ward off (*parer*) every other castration. Genuine castration, then, would be auto-castration. This is why the martyr—who alone chooses and provokes his sacrifice—is the only one to hold himself up (he must be something of a humorist), in other words, to castrate himself: therein lies his force and his virility. He alone is man, only man is Christian: "Christianity is earnestness. Obviously therefore the criterion is applied to the man; the Christian requirement is related to the man, to God's very conception of what this means; the man is the human" (*JP*, 3:476).

Virility and Christianity are one and the same: provided virility is determined as the possibility of castration. The "perversion of Christianity" is to believe that this is a woman's affair, to lose sight of the "virile ideal," the human ideal. An unexpected "proof" for this thesis is offered by the historical origins of Christianity: where does Christianity come from?—from the Orient.

"What was the relationship there? There the man was the human; women and children were almost a kind of domesticated animal" (*JP*, 3:477).

Notes

1. *The Standard Edition of the Complete Psychological Works of Sigmund Freud.* 24 vols. Under the General Editorship of James Strachey. London: Hogarth, 1955–74.

2. *TN. Mise en abyme* was first used in its current sense by André Gide. Based on an analogy with the procedures of heraldry and Flemish painting, it is a kind of story within a story that tells what the text itself is actually about. While it is helpful here to point to the familiar example of the Quaker Oats box that shows someone holding a Quaker Oats box that shows someone holding a Quaker Oats box, etc., we should try to remember that this is merely a pictorial analogy for a strictly linguistic structure. A more technically precise definition of the *mise en abyme* would be a text that ends up becoming an example of its own statement. Thus, in the present case, the text that is about repetition is itself a form of the repetition it tries to describe. In such an instance it becomes impossible to determine where *Repetition* as statement and *Repetition* as example begin and end, open and close.

3. *TN.* Translation, like repetition, precludes our taking hold of what is being repeated or translated in this passage. The words Agacinski uses here for "resumption" (*la reprise*), "mouthed" (*repris par*), and "taking hold" (*on a pas de prise*), *repeat* each other in a way that English cannot hope to reproduce in a comprehensible manner.

4. *TN.* A short text by Mallarmé, one of the disseminating pivots in "The Double Session."

5. *TN.* The word *répétition* is not only the equivalent of the English "repetition" but also names the theatrical practice of "rehearsal."

6. *EN.* In English, see *Training in Christianity and the Edifying Discourse which 'Accompanied' It*, tr. Walter Lowrie (Princeton: Princeton University Press).

7

The No Woman's Land of Kierkegaardian Exceptions

Céline Léon

Since many a male pseudonym in Kierkegaard's authorship protests of his lasting interest in the Other('s) sex, and since the two volumes of *Either/Or* explicitly acknowledge the disjunction as the alternative between the aesthetic rapport of seduction and the ethical relation of marriage, it seems reasonable to assume that an ethical man will, at the conclusion of a proper engagement, choose permanent union to the betrothed. Striking therefore is the realization that, despite Kierkegaard's emphasis on the ethical character of an engagement, and despite the fact that Judge William and Nicolaus Notabene, the two ethicists of the authorship, must have been engaged at one time, the production, in strict parallel with the author's biography, limits itself to aborted relationships, fictitious moves, engagements that lead nowhere. Although there is no dearth of fiancés—

the Young Man of *Repetition* (1843), Quidam of *Stages on Life's Way* (1845), and Kierkegaard himself—none of the engaged parties ever actually walk to the altar.[1] This sundering between man and the realization of his proffered wish of union to the beloved is effected by means of the idiosyncratically Kierkegaardian concept of "the exception," whose status, as Constantin Constantius contends in the letter to the reader with which he concludes *Repetition*, is achieved in a "dialectical battle" with the universal (*R*, 226–28). The Young Man, Constantin's correspondent in that book, is "the exception," yet qua poet, he is only so in a restricted—relative and transitory—understanding of the term. For the more significant "exceptions," the "truly aristocratic" ones, Constantin forewarns, it is necessary to wait for the "religious exceptions," whose prototype, carefully delineated by Johannes de Silentio in *Fear and Trembling* (1843), is Abraham, the knight of faith, ready to sacrifice his son, Isaac. Because I have dealt with the former/lower exception elsewhere (Léon 1995), I shall, after a brief summary of the dissimilarities existing between Quidam and the Young Man, concentrate here on the latter/higher exception—most particularly on what Quidam's differences from the justified exception and from "the Father of faith" signify for woman (the woman in and out of his life) and the relation between the sexes.

The distinction between Quidam and the Young Man, the two pseudonymous fiancés of the authorship, has to do with what motivates these men to reconsider their resolution to marry. In his letter at the conclusion of *Stages*, Frater Taciturnus, the pseudonymous editor of Quidam's Diary, reminds the reader that, in the case of *Repetition*, the Young Man's collision—that between (1) becoming a poet because of a *girl* and being therefore unable to become her husband, and (2) marrying the *girl* and not becoming a poet—remains within the sphere of the aesthetic (*SLW*, 402). *Stages*, however, evinces a refinement that indicates progress in the direction of the religious, thanks to Quidam, whom the Frater describes as "a hero much too advanced for [a merely aesthetic collision]" (*SLW*, 403). Not only is Quidam separated from Quaedam by insuperable differences, as is the Young Man of *Repetition* from the Young Woman, but the higher collision experienced by the later/higher pseudonym is owing to the existence of a secret that Quidam finds himself bound either ethically to share with her, or religiously to keep to himself. Quidam's love, encountering in itself a stumbling block, is ethico-religious, hence dialectical (*SLW*, 415–16). The discrepancy between the Young Man and

Quidam is further accentuated by the fiancés' motives in initiating the rupture: Whereas Constantin's protégé would have broken the engagement for his own sake, the Frater's would have done so with the *girl* in mind, in the conviction that, had the engagement led to marriage, there would have ensued a lifelong torment for the beloved.

For an elucidation of that something to be said which Quidam cannot say, the reader can expect very little from *Stages*, but a great deal from *Fear and Trembling*, a book whose initials significantly anticipate those of Frater Taciturnus. Through a series of ethico-religious conflicts, Johannes de Silentio (John of Silence) investigates the connection that ties speech to the married life in its contradistinction to that whereby silence is bound to the single life. Not only are the stories probed unified by this set of oppositions; they are also linked by a threatening something, whose advent would expose the secret's nature. It is hoped that a thorough examination of the moment crucial—at least, in Johannes de Silentio's opinion—for the self-preservation of one, or both, of the partners about to be united will yield something of the secret that inhabits the Frater's protégé and of its significance for woman, the being whose (co-)existence it precludes.

The Sexual Difference

It must first be noted that no more than the Young Man of *Repetition* is Quidam kept from marrying his beloved by inflexible parents, incompatible backgrounds, or any such adventitious reason. Although no external obstacle prevents the young people from being united, there is, we are told, in either instance a barrier that hinders the establishment of a genuine relationship of love—an insurmountable apprehension, on the young man's part, of the absolute dissimilarity of the categories within which he and his beloved exist. In the words of Constantin, the radical difference that lies between the lovers stems from the "unusual" character of the Young Man's "mental powers" (*R*, 183). Troubled by the young woman's lack of intellectual independence in relation to his views and by the devotion (*Hengivenhed*) with which she flings herself at him—a devotion he finds himself unequipped to handle—Quidam himself acknowledges, echoing Constantin's words: "A girl is different from a man" (*SLW*, 312; also 373, 427, 433). In his imaginary psychological construction titled

" 'Guilty?'/'Not Guilty?' " the Frater projects a situation parallel to that of the Young Man. In spite of their love for each other, Quidam and Quaedam constitute "two heterogeneous individualities" (*SLW*, 420). If they fail to "understand each other," it is, Quidam assumes, because his "consciousness has one more extension" (*SLW*, 374). He even expresses the desire of becoming a woman "for half a year so that [he] could learn how she is dissimilar to man" (*SLW*, 302). Although the brevity of their intercourse has been such, he concedes, as to prevent the colossal misrelation from showing forth: "Alas, alas, we have been united too briefly to have any differences," he continues nonetheless: "We have nothing between us, and yet we have a world between us, exactly a world" (*SLW*, 216). So vast a distance between human beings is tantamount to no less than a "language difference" (*SLW*, 314, 433).

In his concluding "Letter to the Reader" in *Stages*, a letter much more extensive than that with which Constantin brings *Repetition* to a close, the Frater takes the measure of that distance, unambiguously displaying the comic incongruity that would result from the union of partners between whom lies so unsurmountable a gulf: (1) Whereas Quidam is "inclosingly reserved" (*indeslutted*), Quaedam is open and lighthearted; (2) whereas he is depressed, she is "full of the joy of life" (*SLW*, 429–31). Besides, should it befall her to become depressed, her depression would not only be at variance with his, it would also be unlike, hence inferior to, that of any male aesthete. This is because, still according to the Frater: "There is a difference between depression and depression. There is a depression that for poets, artists, and thinkers is the crisis and with women can [only] be an erotic crisis" (*SLW*, 429, 430); (3) Quidam is first and foremost a thinker, spiritually qualified; Quaedam, in sharp contrast, is naive, spontaneously cheerful and endowed with no talent whatsoever for reflection; (4) while he is ethically dialectical, she is aesthetically immediate; (5) lastly, nothing could be further from his masculine sympathy than her feminine, delectable loveliness, that is, the weak, innocently self-loving immediacy that characterizes her being (see also *Prefaces*, xxiii, xxiv).

Not even the way in which each one loves the other is exempt from such a grievous inscription of difference: While Quaedam apprehends their love "esthetically," he understands it "ethically"—so much so in fact that, the Frater contends, "the two individualities relate inversely to each other" (*SLW*, 421, 436, 423, respectively). In a passage from " 'Guilty?'/'Not Guilty?' " the section of *Stages* where he carefully retraces his day-by-day relation to Quaedam, Quidam emphasizes the tragicomic discrepancy that, he feels, exists between him and his beloved: "I cannot keep my soul in the immediacy of falling in love. I am well aware that she is lovely, in my eyes indescribably so. . . . I am most unhappy when she is most beautiful. Then it seems to me that she has such an indescribable claim upon life; I cannot comprehend that every human being has a claim upon life—I alone do not. I wish that she were ugly—then everything would go better" (*SLW*, 221–22).

More disturbingly perhaps, either she does not have the slightest intimation of what is going on inside him, or she does: In the former case, their marriage would constitute a misalliance; in the latter, they both would be unhappy, since each one would seek to shield the other (*EO*, 2:117). Either way, their union would be a fraud, "a deception that marriage does not tolerate" (*SLW*, 375; see also 355, 374). Should marriage come to pass, the male spouse would either embrace, or reject, the reassuring statements of a wife worried by his melancholy stance; yet, either way, he would be unfaithful to her—by betrayal in the former instance, by plain callousness in the latter (*SLW*, 375). As with the aesthetic objections to the ethical pondered by Judge William, the dissimilarities that make Quidam and Quaedam incompatible would show most prominently on the occasion of a wedding, when the male partner would most painfully be made aware of what he knew all along, to wit, that "we are not united . . . we are separated," and worse, "precisely in that which should bind us together" (*SLW*, 355).[2] Indeed, what could be more disturbing to an ethico-religious consciousness than the realization, as the Frater points out, that "the wedding ceremony," in fact, "performs the strange service of becoming the separating factor" (*SLW*, 434)?

These two essentially mismatched entities are further separated by their failing to achieve a common expression for their sorrow—a sorrow whose origin lies in Quidam's decision to break off the engagement. When he did so, it is, he claims, out of sympathy for her; meanwhile Quaedam, out of an instinct for self-preservation, in an innocent sort of self-love, tried to bind him by taking advantage of the ethical element in their relationship. In this instance as well, while his suffering, begotten by guilt and responsibility, is ethical, hers, bound up with the consideration of results, is illusory, hence, merely aesthetic, with the consequence that (still according to Quidam): "It is unethical for her and for me to sorrow jointly in this way" (*SLW*, 302; cf. 303, 204). Furthermore, because where she is concerned, it is (still in his opinion) "out of sight, out of mind," her most critical and dangerous moments are in the actuality of seeing him. With him, however, it is the exact opposite, insofar as nothing helps him to reconstruct or re-create (the Frater says: "create") the scene with the other so much as her absence (SLW, 424). Therefore, whereas his absence assists her in freeing herself from him, hers hinders him. Magnified, enlarged by the distance of unreality, she becomes a ghost, but the problem with "a ghost" is that it "is always terrifying" (SLW, 423, 424; PAP, V B 148:8). Because barriers function to increase rather than reduce desire, Quidam, like Johannes de Silentio's knight of resignation, "does not need the erotic titillation of seeing the beloved," with the paradoxical consequence that apparently nothing succeeds in eroticizing the "plot" so much as the strategic absence of the girl (FT, 44). It is perhaps not without significance that a young man "virtually inexperienced with regard to the opposite sex" should feel so strong in the presence of the girl, yet experience no difficulty in pushing her away (SLW, 423).

Of particular import is the remark that, far from inscribing the differ- ence(s) between two individualities, such divergences in fact express the essence of the sexual difference. Indeed most women in Kierkegaard's authorship are "young girls" in love with someone imbued with a sense of his own egregious superiority. It is also noteworthy that, in his "Re- flections on Marriage"—the essay immediately preceding Quidam's Diary in Stages—Judge William, Kierkegaard's paradigmatic married man, should, with the relationship between Goethe's hero and Frederikke in mind, ponder the difference between man and woman and ascribe to ethics the problem of determining whether or not "there is an intellec- tual existence so eminent that in the profoundest sense it cannot become commensurable with the erotic" (SLW, 151; see also 169–84; Goethe, "Aus meinem Leben, Dichtung und Wahrheit," 26:5–39, 120–23). That it is not just Quidam who stresses how "dangerous it is for a thinker to be in love, to say nothing of being married and having daily arguing from a woman," that it is not just Quidam who, in the words of the Frater, "did not understand the distinctive characteristic of a female existence," is also made plain by the realization that the dreaded possibility of day-to- day commerce with a woman infiltrates as abstract a book as the algebraic Philosophical Fragments (SLW, 305 and 456; PF, 25; and SLW, 432, where the same phrase is used by the Frater). Johannes Climacus, the book's pseudonym, for whom it is well-nigh impossible to conceive of two such heterogeneous beings as belonging to the same species, reads the prodi-

gious disparity in their mental faculties as emblematic of the sexual difference: "We may well assume [between man and woman] an intellectual
difference that makes understanding impossible" (*PF*, 27; see *SLW*, 355).

In sum, if a male flees the opposite sex, it is because, as in the relation
between Socrates and the state alluded to by Kierkegaard in *The Concept
of Irony* (1841), he is unable to "find a likeness in this unlikeness" and,
with a more direct allusion to the incongruity inherent in the heterosexual union: "It is always comic when two things that cannot possibly be
related are placed in relation to each other" (*CI*, 195). For, as Quidam
argues:

> *Like loves only like.* If she were unhappy, it would help. But this
> childlike happiness, this buoyancy in the world, which I cannot
> understand and with which I cannot deeply and essentially sym-
> pathize (because my sympathy with it is through sadness, which
> indicates precisely the contradiction)—and my battle, my cour-
> age (to say something positive about myself), my buoyancy in
> dancing over abysses of which she has no idea whatsoever and
> with which she can sympathize only unessentially, as with a
> dreadful story one reads and whose actuality one cannot conceive,
> that is, through the medium of imagination—what will come of
> this? (*SLW*, 222; my emphasis)

As summed up by the same pseudonym, one of his problems—perhaps
his major problem—with the other sex comes from the realization that
"Other is not like" (*SLW*, 221). The self-diagnosis is confirmed by Frater
Taciturnus, in whose opinion the pair does "not have a common viewpoint, he [Quidam] does not form a contiguous angle with her [Quae-
dam]. Neither from his viewpoint nor from hers is it *like for like*" (*SLW*,
457; my emphasis).

But since, after all, the disparity existed all along, the question must
be asked: What prompts Quidam—when confronted with the alternative
of either maintaining a relationship while keeping something from the
beloved, or reconsidering the decision to marry while remaining concealed—to choose precisely the option of reneging on the promise made
and—as if this were not humiliation enough for the beloved—to abstain
from providing (directly, at least) the explanation that would account for
his altered behavior? As there is apparently no change of heart, the
change in attitude that eventuated in the rupture must be ascribed—

rather than to a shift in Quidam's feelings—to the presence of a secret, the "one thing" that deeply troubles him and that, like Abraham, "he cannot say," but "which would explain everything" (FT, 113, 115).

Speech and Marriage versus Silence and the Single Life

Because, as Kierkegaard specifies in his journal, the intent of Johannes de Silentio is to show that, although totally in love with the girl, the lover "humanly speaking, cannot possibly get her," we may do well to turn to the appropriately named pseudonym of Fear and Trembling for an attempt at elucidating why a man cannot marry the woman from whom he must keep a secret (JP, 6:6598). Relying on the scriptural teaching that at the time of the Last Judgment everything shall be revealed, John of Silence believes it to be a fundamental axiom of ethical existence, hence a duty for every man, to become transparent, public. In his view, the Christian wedding ceremony exacts complete openness between the pair to be married (FT, 82). In the last section of the book, titled "Problema III," the same pseudonym scrutinizes the legitimacy of being an exception; that is, of breaking with the universal, not only in the case of Abraham's testing (on which the whole work is centered), but also in that of individuals who, because of either a deficiency in their nature, or of a specific historical situation, have been confronted with an ethico-religious conflict, or—to avail ourselves of the terminology used in the text—been set outside the universal (FT, 82–120). From the version of a marriage affair in Delphi—a story loosely adapted from a passage in Aristotle's Politics— through the legend of Agnes and the merman, through the story of Sarah and Tobias in the book of Tobit, through Shakespeare's Richard III, to the drama of Faust, John of Silence probes the nature of, and the circumstances surrounding, a love-relation between a (mer)man and a woman. In all these tales where the dichotomy of silence/disclosure figures prominently, Johannes carefully delineates the alternatives. Either the hero or protagonist speaks, or he does not. If he speaks, as Johannes assumes is required of the ethical, "the whole thing"—as explained in the first and fifth stories—"becomes an unhappy love affair," with the result that everything is thrown into disorder (FT, 91, 110, 111). If he does not speak, it is either because of his unwillingness, or because of his inability, to do otherwise. Whereas in the former instance, he is lost in the demonic paradox, in the latter, he is saved in the divine paradox where, like Abraham, the knight of faith, he, "the single individual," "stands in an absolute relation to the absolute" (FT, 120; also 93, 106, 113). In a further ramification of the disjunction, by refusing to disclose himself, the hero or protagonist may, or may not, let matters (the wedding, the seduction) proceed as intended. By going on with things as planned, by choosing to marry, as the first story has it, he would "offend the girl"; it cannot be doubted that, had she known the truth she would never have given her consent. Concomitantly, once the crisis occurs, she will be entitled to anger and resentment over his silence (*Taushed*; FT, 90–91). By not marrying, however, he commits "an offense against the girl and the reality of their love" (FT, 91).

In the case of Abraham, as it cannot be a question of introducing any external argument (*anagnorisis* = recognition), and as the collision brought about by the crucial moment makes impossible a return to the aesthetic, the choice has to be between an ethical existence where one bares oneself, and a religious one where one, albeit in pain and sorrow, bears one's secret. The dichotomy, it is true, is not exactly new in the production; already in *Either/Or*, reference was made by Judge William to a secret that would justifiably prevent an individual from giving his life the kind of expression marriage requires: "If in some way or another you have swallowed a secret that cannot be dragged out of you without costing your life—then never marry" (*EO*, 2:117; see also the Antigone-motif in *EO*, 1:153–64 and *JP*, 5:5569 and the middle of the third letter in *R*). As far as "the father of faith," this paradigm for the religious, is concerned, it is clear that it is not only his choice of silence over speech but in effect his whole existence that signifies a suspension of the universal; it is also clear that his problem is that "he *cannot* say that which would explain everything" (*FT*, 117, 115; my emphasis). But does a young man— Quidam, for example—have the right to break off his engagement on grounds that he himself regards as higher than those of honoring his commitment? According to Johannes de Silentio, the only way in which an individual can receive authorization for his silence (that is, qualify as a legitimate exception) is by becoming directly responsible to the power that is higher than the universal and by acknowledging that he, "as the single individual," has "been placed in an absolute relation to the *absolute*" (*FT*, 93; Johannes's emphasis). Put somewhat differently, a human being encounters the paradox, enters the category of the absurd, when he is forced by God to renounce God's command: "If any one comes to me and does not hate his own father and mother and wife and children and brothers and sisters, yes, and even his own life, he cannot be my disciple" (Luke 14:26; FT, 72). But, before going further, it becomes necessary at this point to orient ourselves a bit with respect to the category of "the (higher) exception."

The Religious Exception

It is indeed remarkable that, as early as his two letters to the Aesthete in the second volume of Either/Or (the volume that, let us not forget, was written first), Judge William, the apologist and defender of matrimony, should, as Johannes Climacus observes in Concluding Unscientific Postscript, contemplate a stance that radically clashes with his own ethico-universal standpoint and feel "compelled to make concessions in the direction of the religious" (CUP, 230, 450 n; EO, 2:328–32). More striking even than the Judge's willingness to admit the possibility of a legitimate exception to the universal is the realization that he is the pseudonym who paradoxically ends his "Reflections on Marriage" with a list of the psychological conditions required for an individual to bypass the ethico-universal. The criteria William sets can be summed up as follows: (1) The exception must be "really in love" (SLW, 176–77); (2) because "the person who wants to break with actuality must at least know what it is he is breaking with," he must have had to break the relationship at the price of his honor (SLW, 177); (3) he must be a married man who thus "places life in contradiction with itself, places God in contradiction with himself" (SLW, 178); (4) he must love life with an enthusiasm unfound in others (SLW, 178); (5) "he must look upon the afterpains of the break as punitive suffering" (SLW, 179); (6) he must have become an "enemy of the sensate" (SLW, 180); (7) he must be forced to the rupture by something that happens from without; (8) he can explain neither himself, nor his plight, to others, since no one can understand a man who has broken with the universal (SLW, 180); (9) he can never know definitely, at least in this life, whether he qualifies as a justified exception (SLW, 181–83).

Since Quidam is not married and since he hardly appears to be fond of life, it is immediately obvious—as Sylvia Walsh (1994) points out in Living Poetically: Kierkegaard's Existential Aesthetics—that, from William's point of view, he lacks the requirements for becoming an authentic religious personality (183). From the perspective of Frater Taciturnus and of his protégé, it is of course another story, inasmuch as Quidam, this "demonic figure oriented to the religious," this figure for whom silence or inclosing reserve is identified with "the teleological suspension of the duty to speak the truth," may very well be on his way to becoming legitimately exempt from realizing the universal (*SLW*, 484, 230; cf. 222). In fact, it is precisely insofar as he fears that a merely ethical existence would prevent him from consecrating himself to something higher than the highest *telos*, to wit, Christianity, that Quidam can claim a religious justification for the breach of his love-relationship. Kierkegaard likewise spoke of having had to let the loved one go "in order to love God" (*PAP*, XI¹ A 226, SV XIV 197; *JP*, 4:5000, KAUC, 163). Let us not forget, however, that a highly significant feature of *Fear and Trembling* is Johannes de Silentio's conviction that Abraham believed all along that he would get his son back and *in this life* (my emphasis). Therefore, if we are to pursue the comparison with the story of Abraham and Isaac, as the very importance of *Fear and Trembling* enjoins us to do, the question must be asked as to when (if?) Quidam expects to get back what he is relinquishing.

Because, after all, the secret—like the sexual difference—must have been there all along, what may be of greater import are the unforeseen circumstances that have conferred upon it a renewed and decisive significance. It is therefore imperative to take a closer look at the determining factor, the "crucial moment" at which, as Johannes puts it in his first tale, "the hero [the bridegroom] obtains information" (*FT*, 90). As one learns from Johannes's many variations on the theme of speech versus silence, a painful concreteness is suddenly given to that which, up to that point, had been but an abstraction. More pregnant therefore than the investigation of the existential or essential elements that separate the male protagonists from the realization of the universal may be the similarities by which each one of them is linked to the others because of either circumstances or (even more tragically) nature itself. If critics have occasionally remarked on the associations existing between some of these accounts and Kierkegaard's own situation in relationship to Regine Olsen, his onetime fiancée and lifelong preoccupation, neither have they sufficiently remarked on the insistent commonality of the tales told, nor have they convincingly probed the particular relevance of these tales for Quidam and, beyond him, the biographical pattern.

The Crucial Moment

It is immediately striking that in not a few of these narratives the decisive factor happens to be either (ethically) the proximity of the wedding night, or (aesthetically) the imminence of the seduction. Thus, in the story borrowed from Aristotle: *"The bridegroom, to whom the augurs prophesied a calamity that would have its origin in his marriage, suddenly changes his plans at the crucial moment when he comes to get the bride"* (FT, 89; Johannes's emphasis; *Politics*, V, 4, 1303 b–1304 a). Bent on obviating this fate—a fate more terrifying than death— "[when] the door of the temple opened," the bridegroom "walked past *her* door" (FT, 90; my emphasis; *Politics*, V, 4, 1303 b–1304 a). In the biblical story from the book of Tobit, Tobias, undaunted by the fact that seven suitors before him have perished in the bridal chamber, persists in wishing to marry Sarah. Sarah herself knows that her bridegroom will be killed on the wedding night (FT, 102; Apocrypha, 6:8). The time of the wedding comes. The two marry and dreadful consequences follow: "When the door was shut . . . the bridegroom rose from the bed and said: Rise up, sister, and we will pray that the Lord may have mercy upon us" (FT, 103; 8:4). Now Sarah could be a man, Johannes de Silentio continues. Then what? The male Sarah, to whom it has been told that "if he loves a girl an infernal spirit will come and murder the beloved on the wedding night," chooses the demonic and "inclose[s] himself up in himself," telling himself that he can "in fact be a Bluebeard" whose "delight" consists of "seeing maidens die on their wedding night" (FT, 104–5). Similarly aware that the crisis will be the wedding night, Quidam entertains the thought that either he or the girl "would die before evening" (SLW, 375; cf. SLW, 227). In other words—as we must assume some anterior knowledge on his part—*she* will be crushed by discovering something that will render their marriage a nightmare.

Therefore, should a male protagonist opt for silence and marriage rather than the advocated alternatives of marriage/speech or silence/the single life, circumstances, namely, the wedding night, would declare him a monster not averse to letting his beloved share his tragic fate. In the story of Agnes and the merman, the merman is either a seducer who cannot seduce Agnes or any other *girl*, or—according to Johannes's subsequent treatment of the legend—he "has a bad conscience about girls and does not dare to approach them" (FT, 95*). By turning the plot around, the latter version is more incriminating for the *girl*, insofar as it proclaims that—even when a merman is involved—there is no safeguard against feminine pursuit and that "generally, it is pure nonsense and game-playing and an insult to the female sex to imagine a seduction in which the girl is utterly, utterly, utterly innocent" (FT, 95). In this case, "inflamed" by Agnes, he soon—because, it can safely be assumed, of her role in the seduction—grows "tired" of her, with the consequence that she becomes a mermaid (FT, 95*). In an entry dated from 1843, the year of the publication of both *Fear and Trembling* and *Repetition*, Kierkegaard gave the fantastic tale of seduction a little matrimonial—and undoubtedly more personal—twist by declaring that "the Church cannot give the marriage its blessing," because the merman can neither initiate Agnes into his tragic existence, nor let her know that he is a monster at certain times (JP, 5:5668). Indeed, through all three versions of the tale, the reader is reminded that, as early as 9 December 1840, that is, at the time of his engagement to Regine, Kierkegaard was comparing himself to the merman at the bottom of the sea, that is, to an inadequate, desexed, dehumanized being. Either literally, or metaphorically, what is shown is the way in which frustrated culture handles (physical) nature, or as Johannes de Silentio puts it with unwitting irony, the way in which "so-called culture protects a girl from seduction" (Kierkegaard's letters to Regine, no 26; FT, 95).

As if the unflattering metaphor were not enough, thoughts of the misshapen Richard III impress themselves on the mind of the unphilosophical author of *Fear and Trembling*:

> I, that am rudely stamp'd, and want love's majesty
> To strut before a wanton ambling nymph;
> I, that am curtail'd of this fair proportion,
> Cheated of feature by dissembling Nature,
> Deformed, unfinish'd, sent before my time
> Into this breathing world, scarce half made up,
> And that so lamely and unfashionable
> That dogs bark at me as I halt by them—.
> (*King Richard the Third*, 1:1)

Once again, it is no coincidence that, in *Stages*, a book so closely tied to *Fear and Trembling*, Quidam, set at variance with the universal, should compare himself to erstwhile Gloucester, "the cripple," "the desperate one." Like the Shakespearian protagonist, and in anticipation of Zarathustra's evocation of the "reversed cripple, who had too little of every-thing and too much of one thing," it is "by the power of the spirit that he wanted to scoff at nature, which had scoffed at him; he wanted to hold nature up to ridicule together with its invention of erotic love and love of the beautiful, for he . . . wanted to demonstrate, despite language and all the laws of life that he could be loved" ("On Redemption," *Thus Spake Zarathustra*, 152; *SLW*, 352). Running the risk of being explicit to the point of self-betrayal, Quidam turns to yet another Shakespearian character: " 'What is honor?' says Falstaff, 'Can it put on a leg?' " (*Henry IV, Part 1*, 5.1.133–43; in Shakespeare 1936, 17:575). But Quidam adds, "it can do the opposite if it is lost, it can take off a leg" (*SLW*, 353). Painfully derisive is the pseudonym's characterization of himself as the boy on "crutches" who disguises his plight by pretending to be as healthy as the others, the "wounded" man, the "disabled soldier" whose "leg has been taken off," the lover with "an artificial leg," eager "to conceal from other people that it is an artificial leg" (*SLW*, 196, 353, 203, 248). Can such a man be a true fiancé, a "proper" lover? "Yes," answers Quidam, but only "by virtue of the artificial leg I use" (*SLW*, 248). What is of course amazing is that—given this impediment—anything should have begun at all. The problem with Quidam, as the Frater sees it, is that "He sees the girl, has an erotic impression of her. . . . Time passes . . . but the erotic has not received its due at all" (*SLW*, 435). Understood in this light, the legend of Faust, which deals with a genius and appears at first to be quite different from all the stories that involve a monster, is tied to the others by the fact that he too "sees" the *girl* (Margaret) "in all her adorable innocence," but—at least according to Johannes de Silentio's version of Goethe's drama—can go no further (*FT*, 109).

Could it be that in all these aborted and tragic love affairs the trouble comes from a "veil"—a veil "more delicate, lighter, and yet more con-cealing" than all the bride's adornments? (*FT*, 89). Or, as indicated by Johannes de Silentio's subtle transition from "the door" to "*her* door" in the first story, could it be that, like the city's wall, the bedroom door metaphorically signifies the hymen, the gateway to the *girl's* body (*SLW*, 210)? Could the fear be (analogous to) that elicited by Sarah, who "still has a young girl's beatific treasure, her prodigious, enormous mortgage on life, her '*Vollmachtbrief zum Glücke*' (full warrant for happiness)—[the capacity] to love a man with all her heart" (*FT*, 102)? Of this, of course, a *girl* knows nothing, and yet, as the Seducer—that other Johannes—declares in "In Vino Veritas," in *Stages*, "her modesty possesses an instinctive presentiment; she is separated from man, and the partition of modesty is more decisive than Aladdin's sword that separates him from Gulnare, and yet the devotee of erotic love who, like Pyramis, places his ear against the partition of modesty senses dim intimations of all the passion of desire behind it" (*SLW*, 78).

Likewise, Kierkegaard—as early as 1843—incriminates nature: "I wanted it [marriage] but was incapable of it," and again, ten years later: "To be healthy and strong, a complete man . . . this was never granted to me" (*JP*, 5:5663; *JP*, 6:6837, respectively). He, who agonized over never having been young, over never having been like the others, is the exception lurking behind the legitimate cases adduced by Judge William and Johannes de Silentio—the bearer of a secret that could only be extirpated at the price of his life. Could his corporeal deficiency, what he described as his "major leak," be repaired? He consulted his physician to see whether by sheer power of the will he could overcome what nature had rendered inoperative. The man shared his feeling that "the outcome of the repair job would be very doubtful" (*JP*, 5:6021). In an 1846 entry, five years after having broken off his engagement to Regine, he complained of "a misrelation between my soul and my body" (*et Misforhold mellem mit Sjael og mit Legeme*) and one can easily surmise the layers of reticence he had to cut through before bringing himself to write the following:

> I therefore asked my physician whether he believed that the structural misrelation between the physical and the psychical could be dispelled so that I could realize the universal. This he doubted. I asked him whether he thought that my spirit could convert and transform this misrelation by willing it. (*JP*, 6:5913; see also *JP*, 6:6603)

But against his "thorn in the flesh" (*min Pael i Kjødet*), against the thorn of his flesh, nothing could be done:

> He [my physician] doubted it; he would not even advise me to set in motion all the powers of my will, of which he had some conception, since I could blow up everything. (*JP*, 5:5913; cf. *PV*, 68)

Two years later, during Easter week (19–24 April) 1848, Kierkegaard, contemplating once more the possibility of speaking, approached his physician with similar questions (*JP*, 5:6131, 6133). On his deathbed, he complained one last time of his "thorn in the flesh," making explicit to his lifelong friend, Emil Boesen, the connection between this impediment and his breaking off of the engagement (*PAP*, VI A 133). "With respect to being human," he lamented in 1850, "what I lack is the animal-attribute"; to those who "take brutish joy in demanding of me what has been denied me," he directs the following plea: "Give me a body, or if you had given me that when I was twenty years old, I would not have been this way" (*JP*, 6:6626). In *Kierkegaard: The Indirect Communication*, Roger Poole, the British critic for whom the reason why Kierkegaard opted in favor of the rupture is to be found in this misproportion, surprisingly argues that the philosopher contradicts himself when he contends, on the one hand, that the difficulty is permanent and, on the other, that it can be healed either by a supreme act of will, or by divine intervention (Poole 1993, 184). But what contradiction is there in believing that, when ordinary human means fail, extraordinary—human, more often divine—resources can be resorted to? Does the journal not echo in this Judge William's and Johannes de Silentio's common belief that "For God all things are possible (*For Gud er Alt muligt*) (*JP*, 5:6135; *EO*, 2:315; *FT*, 46, 115, 119)? As for the question of deciding whether or not the problem was a psychical, or "merely a physical one," which so puzzles Roger Poole, it is certainly not difficult to understand that, in a man of Kierkegaard's mental and spiritual powers, no problem—even an essentially physical one—could have been perceived in isolation from soul (*Sjael*) or the psychical (*det Psychiske*) (Poole 1993, 186–88).

But for now, let us ponder what it might have meant for Quidam/Kierkegaard to be God's chosen. What is to pseudonym/author the faith of Abraham? Could it be that, more significant than the question of Quidam's lack of conformity to the exception as it is delineated by Judge William, is that of the difference that possibly lies between the Frater's young man and the "father of faith"?

Quidam/Kierkegaard: Knights of Faith or Knights of Resignation?

Lacking the extraordinary faith of Abraham, Kierkegaard feels melancholy each time he reflects that the breach of his engagement is owing to his "not [having] dared believe that God would lift the elemental misery of my being" (*JP*, 5:6135). A glimpse of how different his situation would have been, had he had the faith of Abraham, is provided by the passionate 17 May 1843 Berlin entry where, alluding to his having begun " 'Guilty?'/'Not Guilty?' " he declares: "If I had had faith, I would have stayed with Regine" (*JP*, 5:5664). Although the ripped page in the middle of the entry leaves unclear the referent of the "it" in the sentence with which the philosopher resumes his writing—contending that "*it* would surely have happened"—the impression given by this "If I had had faith," the theme of *Fear and Trembling*, is that, since for God all things are possible (*For Gud er Alt muligt*), Kierkegaard still believed at this point in the possibility of a repetition with Regine (*JP*, 5:5664; *FT*, 49–64, and more particularly, 57). This "repetition" was of course out of the question; precisely at that time, back in Copenhagen, Kierkegaard's former fiancée was engaging herself to Fritz Schlegel.

In his plan for Quidam's diary, Kierkegaard, considering the eventuality of the pair coming together, remarks: "Nearly all the entries in the last part at midnight shall deal with meeting again in eternity" (*PAP*, V B 97:34). Like the *passive*, despairing, or effeminate self described by Anti-Climacus in *The Sickness unto Death* (1849), Quidam is unwilling, or unable, to hope for the removal of his temporal cross, "his thorn in the flesh" (Kierkegaard's emphasis; *SUD*, 78). Indeed at no point does Quidam's faith appear to be the extraordinary faith of the knight of faith who could say: "I have faith that I will get her—that is, by virtue of the absurd (*i Kraft af det Absurd*)," by virtue of believing that "for God all things are possible" (*For Gud er Alt muligt*) (*FT*, 46; also 99, 115, 119). In his despair, he is no more than a knight of "resignation"; that is, an individual determined

> to make the eternal suffice, and thereby to be able to defy or ignore suffering in the earthly and the temporal. The dialectic of resignation is essentially this: to will to be one's eternal self and then, when it comes to something specific in which the self suffers, not to will to be oneself, taking consolation in the thought that it may disappear in eternity and therefore feeling justified in not accepting it in time. (*SUD*, n. 70)

Put another way, Quidam has just enough faith to be a knight of resignation who is ready to sacrifice a beloved being, but not enough to be a knight of faith (*Troens Ridder*) who believes, like Abraham, that the Lord will give him back that individual. In brief, Quidam's prayer for a post-mortem reunion with the beloved rests on the knowledge that he, the "deformed" person, "heal[ed]" once his life relation has passed into eternity, will at long last be spared the vicissitudes of the sensuous (*SLW*, 391, 334, 383, 390; also *PAP*, V B 98:7). Like the inverted Sarah, like the merman, like Richard III, Frater Taciturnus's young man owes his suffering to having had "his omnipotence [reduced] to impotence," for, who could deny that, in his case as in theirs, "feminine attractiveness has a claim that demands precisely what he lacks" (*FT*, 107; *SLW*, 457)? As Kierkegaard concedes: "With respect to marriage it is not true here that everything is sold in the condition 'as is' when the hammer falls; here is a matter of a little honesty about the past" (*JP*, 5:5664). Despite the angst that, he claims, takes hold of him each time he thinks that Quaedam might marry someone else, Quidam does not so much reveal the bitterness experienced by Kierkegaard when Regine embarked on her own repetition, as betrays his, or his author's, fear and "true" desire: "In a certain sense that is what I want, what I am working for" (*SLW*, 227). The loss is a gain, to the extent to which, unlike Abraham, it is precisely by losing the object of his affection that Quidam gets everything back.

But even when it is understood that—insofar as he did not have the faith to believe that he could become disclosed and yet be saved by Quaedam—Quidam is no knight of faith, no Abraham, just a tragic hero like Agamemnon, the question remains open of his feelings within the context of the first scene, to wit, the engagement (*FT*, 79, 99, 115). His admission in " 'Guilty?'/'Not Guilty?' " that "a No suits me better [than a Yes from the *girl*]" makes plain that, if he does not wish to get the *girl* back, it is because he did not want her in the first place (*SLW*, 306). Only three days after his engagement, was he not already lamenting: "Is this how it is to be engaged? . . . Is this the way it is?" (*SLW*, 215). Even more tellingly, his first morning entry—where, as in all morning entries he recollects what happened on this day in the course of the preceding year, that is, even before the actual beginning of the affair—includes, not, as one might have expected, a declaration of love, but, instead, a remark on his awareness of the "many anomalies" that make such a step as marriage "a most difficult task" (*SLW*, 195; see also 197, 268; also repeated throughout Frater Taciturnus's concluding "Letter to the Reader"). In the course of the next morning entry, Quidam alludes to his fear of a "counterorder," likely to show that he "should not have presumptuously intervened disturbingly" in relation to the *girl* (*SLW*, 202; also, 261). In brief, all along he was saying no to the *girl*. By saying yes to her in eternity, he says no to her in this life. Where the *girl* is concerned, despite Quidam's protestations to the contrary, *his* alternative becomes *her* destiny—a no-win situation that consists of either being lied to within marriage, or being forsworn out of it (*SLW*, 402).

In fact, matters only get worse for the *girl* who, discarded on the pretext that a wedding would eventuate into a murder or a monstrous affair, finds herself incriminated. Thus, when Quidam protests: "Woe to the woman whose look moved me in this way," it is undeniable that, like Richard III, whom he quotes as one who "himself hated, and yet aroused erotic love," he cannot help experiencing a dislike, an antagonism for the Other in whom (he feels/fears) are aroused desires he deems himself powerless to satisfy (*SLW*, 352; *Richard III*, 1.2.43–223, in Shakespeare 1936, 792–94). With a duplicity reminiscent of that used in the second version of the legend of the merman, he reverses the situation by deflecting the blame away from himself and projecting it onto the powerless woman; jettisoning the *girl* on the pretext that she herself is a seductress allows him to justify his indifference by pinning it on her desire (*SLW*, 328–29). The modulation, the distortion of reality brings to mind Sarah Kofman's reflections on Freud's interpretation of Irma's dream: "It is always the ladies' fault. . . . The dream is a thoroughgoing plea in favor of Freud's innocence: it piles up reasons for excusing him"; hence inescapable is the conclusion that "if Freud has such an urgent need to excuse himself, it is because he knows perfectly well that he himself is the criminal" (Kofman 1985, 46–47).

More often than not, however, the male is quick to reappropriate the capacity to seduce with which he has invested (the) woman. Thus, doubling the affront constituted by the bridegroom's refusal to marry the *girl* in the story adapted from Aristotle, Johannes de Silentio suggests a romantic alliance between the young man and his intended; yet, no sooner has he made the suggestion than he takes it back, alleging the *girl's* respectability (*FT*, 91 n). The merman likewise brags of his own powers, claiming that "he can seduce Agnes, he can seduce a hundred Agneses, he can make any girl infatuated" (*FT*, 94–95). Quidam, who oddly interprets the absence of external obstacles as proof of potency, also protests: "It is certainly true that I have desired her, indeed, that I do desire her" (*SLW*, 338). He too talks of circumventing the wedding by way of an "erotic arrangement" and does not hesitate to brag of possessing powers of seduction so formidable as to be able "easily [to] elicit the seduction from her [Quaedam]" (*SLW*, 358). Nor is Kierkegaard averse to presenting himself as the desiring subject—as attested to by the following passage from the nonpseudonymous *For Self-Examination*, published six years after *Stages*:

> So, imagine someone who has fallen in love! He saw the object; it was thereby that he fell in love, and this object became for him the delight of his eye and the desire of his heart! And he reached for it—it was the delight of his eye and the desire of his heart! And he reached for it; he held it in his hand—it was the delight of his hand and the desire of his heart! (*FSE*, 78)

But it is all talk; the Frater's young man does protest too much, indirectly revealing his fear—a fear in direct proportion to the *girl's* proximity—what he calls her "actuality":

> A year ago I escorted her home in the evening. There was no one else who could be asked to do it. In the company of several others, I walked happily along at her side. And yet it seemed to me that I was almost happier in my hiding place; to come so close to actuality, yet without actually being closer, results in distancing, whereas the distance of concealment draws the object to oneself. What if the whole thing were an illusion? Impossible. Why, then do I feel happier in the distance of possibility? (*SLW*, 205)

When Quidam breaks his protracted silence, the outburst, the "unexpected and passionate" outpour of words, suggests defloration, yet it prevents its actuality by remaining in the medium of aural transaction: "When the castle gate has not been opened for many years, it is not opened noiselessly like an inside door that turns with springs. When the door of silence has been shut for a long time, then the word does not come out like the hello and goodbye of a quick tongue" (*SLW*, 210). Only tympani are ruptured by the din made during rehearsals that, keeping the performance in abeyance, defer it ad infinitum. Frightened vessels make indeed the most noise!

Unable to live ethically with a woman, Quidam chooses the religious: "I have been religiously crushed . . . but I cannot be erotically crushed" (*SLW*, 276, 222). In spite of Quidam's denegations, in spite of his claim that religiousness can force an individual so far back in inwardness that he experiences (increasing) difficulties in reaching actuality, remarks made by himself or by Frater Taciturnus lead the reader to surmise the likelihood that the converse is true: The impossibility to reach actuality introduces the religious, retroactively legitimizing the failure to finish what has already begun (*SLW*, 351). Once his desire became "stranded on [an] impossibility," Johannes de Silentio's knight of resignation[1] let it be "turned inward" by allowing his "love for the princess" to "assume a religious character" and to "be transfigured into a love of the eternal being, which true enough denied the fulfillment" (*FT*, 44, 43). As for the princess herself, she could only disturb the knight; once the latter has made the movement of infinite resignation, she is "lost" with respect to the earthly fulfillment of her love (cf. *FT*, 44). In such a context, it is certainly easy to take at face value the Frater's allegation that "as a lover, the male character would hardly succeed in the world" and that, with his "singularity and unerotic behavior," Quidam is bound to "make a girl feel strange" (*SLW*, 400, 399 n; see also 266, 430, 431, 435 and *PAP*, V B 148:34). Nor is Quidam totally unrealistic regarding the effect which he produces on the other sex: "An existence such [as mine] is utterly incongruous with a feminine existence, it cannot engross a woman, far less incite her" (*SLW*, 273). If the Frater so adequately conveys Quidam's reticence, is it not because he shares his disciple's inexperience and apprehension regarding matters of love? Indeed, for him as well, "the erotic and the erotic relationship are of minor concern" and it is evident that men with this disposition do not "chase after women" (*SLW*, 436, 493). Roger Poole rebukes Henning Fenger for propounding that, "when things went seriously wrong, Kierkegaard was quick to rationalize the disaster into something that had been intended from the start" (Poole 1993, 20). What Fenger in effect writes is that Kierkegaard "wishes to break off before matters come to that [the seduction]. Kierkegaard is afraid of the erotic, anxious lest he not be man enough to meet the situation. . . . It is difficult not to see a fear of sexuality as a main factor in the break with Regine" (Fenger 1980, 208). After having heard in July 1843 of Regine's engagement to Schlegel, "it is altogether understandable from a psychological point of view," Fenger further explains, that Kierkegaard "now leaps into faith and glorifies his 'sacrifice': his renunciation of Regine becomes a religious act in the service of higher powers" (Fenger 1980, 219). Kierkegaard's own assessment that "I dared not believe that the fundamental misfortune of my being could be resolved: and so I grasped eternity" certainly allows for such an interpretation (*PAP*, VIII[1] A 650;

JP, 5:6135). So does his contention that "if . . . I had been in any ordinary sense a man, then I should certainly have forgotten Christianity entirely. . . . But the very simplest requirements for being a man, those are the very ones which have been denied me. . . . Oh, but particularly in my earthly youth, what would I have not given to be a man for half a year!" (*PAP*, X² A 61; *JP*, 6:6500) Thus, when a love affair with an unhappy ending unilaterally decided upon by a reluctant fiancé discharges a man into the religious, there is some basis to the argument that his expressed intention of celebrating the happiness of heterosexual love is little more than a cover(-up) for that which he finds himself unable to experience in actual life.

Writing (Off) the Feminine

But, what is a woman to do when her rejection—a rejection allegedly effected for her greater good—signifies that her universe has been destroyed? How will Quaedam's existence unfold in the wake of her release? Hypothetically, at least, Quidam and his mentor are willing to grant her options in all three spheres: (1) either she will—aesthetically—(a) resign herself to a new love, or (b) be heightened to something "great and exceptional" in temporal existence; (2) or she will ethically resume the interrupted relationship; (3) or, unwilling to remain in the sphere of aesthetic immediacy, she may relinquish her wish to become united to her lover and effect a transfer in the direction of the religious analogous to Quidam's (*SLW*, 228, 236, 246, 301–3, 309, 357, 456; see *JP*, 1:632, 649, 653; *JP*, 5:5865). In effect, however, the pattern of existence-possibilities is soon made to shrink dramatically. As for option 1b, insofar as she is an intellectual nonentity, Quaedam is given little hope regarding the possibility of aesthetic self-transcendence. Concerning option 2, namely, the ethical or conjugal alternative, it is difficult to see how it could be enacted once the *girl*'s fiancé has singlehandedly decided against the concretization of their love. As for option 3, Quidam's own preference clearly lies with the religious solution, by virtue of which the *girl* would agree to a reduplication (*Fordoblese*), namely, a difficult tightrope walking of the mind whereby she, in emulation of him, would "remain at the pinnacle of the wish"; that is, at once give up, and maintain, the hope of union (*SLW*, 426; cf. *SLW*, 302, 303; *JP*, 4:5007). Tellingly, however, no sooner has Quidam granted her this last possibility than he takes it away: For one thing, he views the movement of infinity as not "natural to [an] individuality" who exists in a relationship of ontological inferiority to him; for another, in the unlikely event of such an expansion, she would be unable (precisely because of it) to understand the moment decisive with regard to the fulfillment of her wish—should that moment ever come (*SLW*, 302; *FT*, 36). More forthright, however, is his admission that, "as soon as she begins to venture along the narrow way to a religious movement, she is lost to me" (*SLW*, 302; cf. *JP*, 5:5723). In the end, once jilted by a proto-religious man, a *girl* is given no better alternative than option 1a, namely, that of union to another man—a possibility that once realized, will (conveniently for the jilter) prove the illusory character of both her love for the new man and her sorrow for the former one. "One often hears that a girl could not live without a man, and it was true, but it was not that man but another man"; again, she "acquires for herself a new partner in the dance of life—if a person [a woman] cannot have the one, then [she] takes the other" (*SLW*, 392 and 456; also, 304, 357, 227).

Let us not forget the fifth, perfectly repugnant possibility that Quidam patronizingly grants her as a privilege! A woman, he contends, can become insane, and this can happen in two ways: one, sudden and petrifying, the other, slow and gradual. The pseudonym deems the latter eventuality more likely, but also less dangerous, insofar as it demands reflection, an aptitude that a *girl* does not possess, and that he makes sure she will never acquire: "She was . . . almost not reflective at all, [yet] just a tenth of the reflection-possibilities I have set in motion . . . would be sufficient to disturb a feminine head" and "I have done everything to make reflection disgusting to her . . . one can suck poison out of another person . . . in order to divest another person of reflection" (*SLW*, 270, 271; also, 274). Even then, loath to empathize with her plight, he fends off all likelihood of reappropriation on her part: "If insanity does come, then it would have to be an offended feminine pride over being rejected, which, despairing of taking revenge, inclosed itself within itself until it lost its way" (*SLW*, 271). In this instance as in so many others, the attribution of blame is turned around, as Quidam reduces this possibility to being nothing but "an ugly falsehood on the part of self-love against me" (*SLW*, 273). Tellingly, when Kierkegaard thinks of taking up the notion in his papers, he alludes—not as the Frater does—to Quidam's "story of suffering," but instead to the possibility of a "psychological construction of feminine insanity" (*PAP*, V B 97:33). Although she at once loses the

object of her attachment, her dignity and—at least in the immediate—
chances to recover herself through purposeful activity, the victim, paradoxically and cynically incriminated for her executioner's suffering, must
pay for the crime with which she is charged either by forcing him to
sacrifice her, or by willingly sacrificing herself (*JP*, 6:5865). Like Ophelia,
her mistake is to have involved herself with an individual whom she
could not comprehend and whose monotonous and inescapable conclusion is that she must be bruised. Once again, the male gets his way; the
female takes the rap. Adam's self-exonerating voice can be heard. Said to
have been created for the punishment of man, for his suffering, Eve's
daughter is nevertheless made to suffer when she (allegedly) does just
that.

The Femininity of Writing

In a paradox that is only apparent, the (discarded) woman *without* is
never quite so frightening as the woman *within*: "If only," Quidam be-
seeches, "she is outside, really outside me," then the terror is somewhat
less (*SLW*, 228). Far more dreadful to the Frater's pupil is the thought of
having to deal, not with the *girl* "as an actuality outside himself," but
with "only himself" and his nameless passion (*SLW*, 425). Of what goes
on inside, Frater Taciturnus offers a glimpse through his depiction of the
delights of intercourse with the invaginated folds, the involuted orificia-
lity of Danish, the living, maternal language:

> I feel fortunate to be bound to my mother tongue, . . . bound as
> Adam was to Eve because there was no other woman. . . . I am
> happy to be bound to a mother tongue that . . . with its sweet
> tones sounds voluptuously in the ear; a mother tongue that does
> not groan, obstructed by difficult thought; . . . a mother tongue
> that does not puff and sound strained when it stands before the
> unutterable; . . . a language [which] in its happy relation to
> the object . . . goes in and out like an elf; a language that is intense
> and emotional every time the right lover knows how to incite
> masculinely the language's feminine passion, is self-assertive and
> triumphant in argument every time the right master knows how
> to guide it. (*SLW*, 489)

Being joined in body with the maternal tongue—a tongue that will obey the expert hand that guides it—will enable him, if only for a while, to break with the paternal law that kept him at a distance from the feminine. As Sarah Kofman (1973) puts it in "Un Philosophe 'unheimlich,' " in *Ecarts*: "The voice of truth is always that of the law, of God, of the father. The metaphysical logos has an essential virility. Writing, that form of disruption of presence, is, like woman, always put down and reduced to the lowest rung. Like the feminine genitalia, it is troubling, petrifying—it has a Medusa effect," which may turn a man dumbfounded into stone (125–26). Faced with the realization that, far from being outside the masculine, the feminine inhabits it as otherness, as difference, as disruption or anomie, a proto-religious individual, like Quidam, or—as I have shown elsewhere—a poet, like the Young Man of *Repetition* (Léon 1995), strikes out against woman because, as Freud has well shown in *The Taboo of Virginity*, she is "different from man, forever incomprehensible and mysterious, strange and therefore apparently hostile" (1918/1957, 11:198). If a man—religiously, or religiously bound—feels that he must tear from himself every shred reminiscent of what woman stands for, if his upper-handedness expresses itself at her expense, it is because she (the being outside himself) reminds him of the unavowed, shameful side of his nature, of the part (within) which he must sacrifice. In conformity with what Freud describes in "Analysis Terminable and Interminable" as man's "repudiation of femininity" (1937/1964, 23:250), as his "struggle against his passive or feminine attitude," Kierkegaard had in Regine a welcome screen against the feminine side of his nature—a screen whereby his own split otherness, his own division, his own castration were conveniently concealed. Simultaneously, however, she could not help embarrassing him by making him explicitly aware of the feminine side of his primordial, androgynous essence. Painfully, achingly, in Julia Kristeva's words, she reminded him "of the essential struggle that a writer has to engage in with what he calls demonic only to call attention to it as the inseparable obverse of his very being, of the other (sex) that torments and possesses him" (Kristeva 1982, 208). Terrified by being made to confront the dilemma of being feminized, he had to castrate the woman without so as not to be reminded of the vulnerability within.

Imagining a Dane, a "countryman," who would conclude his book by damning him, along with all poets, as "the most dangerous sort of seducer," Frater Taciturnus pleads "not guilty" to the accusation of literal seduction. Not too surprisingly, we recall, the Frater "does not crave the favor of any woman, and this indifference is not a cover for a secret passion, far from it; he is pursuing no girl. . . . He does not go to dances with girls . . . nor does he chase after women" (*SLW,* 491, 492), hence the irony of the praise he lavishes on Greece for being "so fortunate in its beautiful girls" (*SLW,* 484 n). Nevertheless, like Kierkegaard who regarded himself as a great eroticist, he claimed to be a seducer. Since "ordinarily one thinks of a seducer in connection with women," he is, he concedes, "a seducer in a different sphere" (*SLW,* 491, 492). This (in)different seducer, seduced by language, in turn seduces listeners whom "with his imagination he lures on into seductive ideals" (*SLW,* 491). But who are those whom he seduces? "*Girls,* little misses" who, deprived of speech, deprived of a (mother) tongue, barred from sharing with others who speak their language, have no choice but to "listen" to the male poet who, having feasted with the mother tongue, consuming a language that is inexhaustible and never stops miraculously renewing itself, endlessly speaks of himself and of his own sex—either directly, or by translating into his own the Other's thoughts (*SLW,* 492).

Notes

1. It is not impossible to assume that the Young Man, who resurfaces in "In Vino Veritas," in *Stages,* is the same young man who, under the pseudonym of Quidam, appears in " 'Guilty?'/ 'Not Guilty?' " Both pseudonyms would correspond to Kierkegaard: Whereas the first one would record his feelings before he has fallen in love, the second one would describe him in the throes of his disengagement from the relationship.

2. See most particularly "Some Reflections on Marriage in Answer to Objections" (*SLW,* 87–184).

References

Fenger, Henning. 1980. *Kierkegaard, The Myths and Their Origins: Studies in the Kierke-gaardian Papers and Letters.* Translated from the Danish by George C. Schoolfield. New Haven: Yale University Press.

Freud, Sigmund. 1918/1957. "The Taboo of Virginity (Contributions to the Psychology of Love III)." Translated by Angela Richards. *The Standard Edition of the Complete Psychological Works of Sigmund Freud,* 11:191–208. London: Hogarth.

———. 1937/1964. "Analysis Terminable and Interminable." Translated by Joan Riviere. *The Standard Edition of the Complete Psychological Works of Sigmund Freud,* 23.209–53. London: Hogarth.

Goethe, Johann Wolfgang von. 1828–42. *Aus meinem Leben. Dichtung und Wahrheit, Goethe's Werke. Vollständige Ausgabe letzter Hand.* Vols. 1–55. Stuttgart: Tübingen.

Kofman, Sarah. 1973. "Un Philosophe 'unheimlich.' " In *Ecarts: Quatre Essais à propos de Jacques Derrida*. Paris: Fayard.

―――. 1985. *The Enigma of Woman: Woman in Freud's Writings*. Translated from the French by Catherine Porter. Ithaca: Cornell University Press.

Kristeva, Julia. 1982. *Powers of Horror: An Essay on Abjection*. Translated by Leon S. Roudiez. New York: Columbia University Press.

Léon, Céline. 1995. "Either Muse or Countermuse: The Neither/Nor of the Second Sex in Kierkegaard's Aesthetics." *Arachne* 2, no. 1:16–49.

Nietzsche, Friedrich. n.d. *Thus Spake Zarathustra*. Translated by Thomas Common. New York: Random House.

Poole, Roger. 1993. *Kierkegaard: The Indirect Communication*. Charlottesville: University Press of Virginia.

Shakespeare, William. 1936. *Richard III*. In *The Complete Works of Shakespeare*, edited by George Lyman Kittredge. Boston: Ginn.

Walsh, Sylvia. 1994. *Living Poetically: Kierkegaard's Existential Aesthetics*. University Park: The Pennsylvania State University Press.

8

Almost Earnestness?

Autobiographical Reading, Feminist Re-Reading, and Kierkegaard's *Concluding Unscientific Postscript*

Mark Lloyd Taylor

Perhaps your first reading of Søren Kierkegaard resembled mine: twenty-five pages in a college philosophy textbook. After a brief summary of "the bare facts of Kierkegaard's life," the author of the textbook directed me to "the facts about Kierkegaard's inner life," which he held to be "more interesting, and also more difficult to fathom" than the "externals" (Jones 1969, 209). His account of this inner life began with the twenty-two-year-old Kierkegaard's confession of a need "to find a truth that is true *for me*, to find *the idea for which I can live and die*," followed by discussion of a series of sixteen ostensibly autobiographical statements, organized around Kierkegaard's relationships to his father and to his fiancée, Regine.[1] My author effected a transition from Kierkegaard's life to his writings by suggesting that "his huge literary and philosophical production should be read" in terms of the "double task" he set for himself: "becoming a Christian" and "bringing to the attention of others what is involved in becoming a Christian" (Jones 1969, 213). The reading that emerged over the next twenty pages depended heavily upon a single book of Kierkegaard's, *Concluding Unscientific Postscript* (hereafter *Postscript*), for fifteen of twenty-three excerpts came from *Postscript*, a total of eight from four other books. Marginalia indicate that a passage from *Postscript* also made the strongest impression on my twenty-year-old sensibilities. Many of you could probably recite the passage I underlined so boldly. It begins: "*An objective uncertainty held fast . . .*"; although I reserved the inscription of a big blue star for the end of the quotation: ". . . holding fast to the objective uncertainty, so as to remain out upon the deep, over seventy thousand fathoms of water, still preserving my faith" (Jones 1969, 224). Without assessing its adequacy, I suggest that my first reading of Kierkegaard was typical in two respects: the meaning of his writings was located within an autobiographical framework and *Postscript* was granted a place of special privilege in the interpretation of the writings.

Perhaps the path you traveled from a first reading of Kierkegaard toward a feminist re-reading does not resemble mine at all. Abstracting, inappropriately of course, from actual women in my life, I would point to the following landmarks along my path: reading Mary Daly during graduate school; finding books by two medieval women, Catherine of Siena and Margery Kempe, foundational to my teaching of Christian life and thought; encountering such contemporary feminist writers as Luce Irigaray, Judith Butler, and Carol Adams. The work of two other women has helped connect these resources to my interest in Kierkegaard: Caroline Walker Bynum's (1987, 1991) account of the differences between the ways medieval Christian men and women write or dictate their lives and Camille Paglia's assessment of the masochistic and misogynist self-feminization of nineteenth-century male writers. As a result, a different sensibility now guides my reading, namely, the importance of taking the body of a male writer's texts earnestly and attending to how he figures gender. Why not, therefore, work toward a feminist re-reading of Kierkegaard by beginning again where I and other readers began, with *Postscript*, this time approaching the book as exemplary of the gendered body of his writings.[2]

Postscript as Johannes Climacus's Autobiography

Despite his reliance on *Postscript*, the author of my college textbook failed to inform me that not one but two names appear on its title page: Johannes Climacus, who writes *Postscript*, and S. Kierkegaard, who serves as Climacus's editor. Kierkegaard ends *Postscript* autobiographically, or, rather, appends to it a "First and Last Explanation" in which he acknowledges being the author of a series of pseudonymous books published between 1843 and 1846, including Climacus's six-hundred-page *Postscript* as well as the one-hundred-page *Philosophical Fragments* (henceforth *Fragments*) to which *Postscript* serves as a postscript (*CUP*, 1:625–30). Climacus begins and ends *Postscript* autobiographically with a preface and an appendix in which he muses on the fate of his *Fragments* among the reading public and seeks to come to an understanding with the reader of his present book (*CUP*, 1:5–8, 617–23). Between the preface with which he begins and the appendix with which he ends, Climacus writes frequently and in some detail about himself. When he does, gender figures prominently.

Attention to the autobiographical texture and architecture of Climacus's text is rare in the scholarly literature. That is to say, *Postscript* is not often read as an autobiographical piece by its pseudonymous author. It has been read as inscribing something of Kierkegaard's autobiography, albeit less frequently than has been the case with other pseudonymous books.[3] But if my practice of attending to the gendered body of a text is sound, then the otherwise implausible jest of reading *Postscript* as Climacus's autobiography might merit earnest consideration. I hope to sidestep all theoretical controversy about what constitutes autobiography by stipulating a simple definition: the autobiographical includes any writing about one's own self, one's life, and one's writing. My initial task, then, is to identify those places in *Postscript* where Climacus writes about himself, his life, and his writing.

A common way of writing about one's self is to write one's proper name. Climacus does so six times in the body of *Postscript* (*CUP*, 1:15, 17, 109, 280, 617). A consistent self-portrayal appears in these passages. Climacus denies that he is a Christian, identifying himself instead as a humorist: more precisely, "an imaginatively constructing humorist," that is, one who engages in thought experiments (*CUP*, 1:619). With what does he experiment? Why, with his own self. "In the isolation of the imaginary construction, the whole book is about myself, simply and solely about myself" (*CUP*, 1:617). As befits a humorist, his self-experimentation, his *Postscript*, has to do with becoming the very person he is not. " 'I, Johannes Climacus, now thirty years old, born in Copenhagen, a plain, ordinary human being like most people, have heard it said that there is a highest good in store that is called an eternal happiness, and that Christianity conditions this upon a person's relation to it. I now ask: 'How do I become a Christian?' . . . I ask solely for my own sake. Indeed, that is certainly what I am doing or, rather, I have asked about it, for that is indeed the content of the book" (*CUP*, 1:617–18). He dubs this question about "the individual's relation to Christianity" the "subjective issue" and distinguishes it from the "objective issue" of the "truth of Christianity" (*CUP*, 1:17). While he insists that "the [subjective] issue pertains to me alone," Climacus believes that "if properly presented" the question of how he might become a Christian "will pertain to everyone in the same way," for the "highest good" promised by Christianity "awaits me just as it awaits a housemaid and a professor" (*CUP*, 1:17, 15). And yet he worries that readers in the "world-historically concerned" nineteenth century will find his "attach[ing] such importance to one's own little self [*Jeg*]" inappropriately vain. Climacus's only defense is that Christianity itself attaches such importance "to my own little self and every ever-so-little self" insofar as it wants to make all persons eternally happy (*CUP*, 1:16). Hence, the inscription of his own proper name serves to articulate what I will call Climacus's own proper problem, the issue of how he (and all others) might become a Christian.

The autobiographical makes a second appearance in *Postscript* when Climacus writes about his development as a thinker. He recounts how, after his student days, he came reluctantly to the conclusion that his own proper problem "was not being advanced but suppressed" by a series of influential men: his teachers, an orator, and a systematician well versed in speculative thought (*CUP*, 1:11–14). At first, Climacus blamed himself for the lack of a solution to the issue, given his own "insignificance" and the "deserved renown" of the other thinkers. Eventually, Climacus acquired sufficient "dialectical intrepidity" to be able "to render unto Caesar what is Caesar's—his admiration unto the renowned person" and still "hold fast to his issue despite all celebrities." At last, Climacus the maturing dialectician met a famous thinker, Lessing, who did not disappoint him. An entire section of *Postscript* expresses his gratitude to Lessing (*CUP*, 1:61–125). Some additional figures to whom Climacus compares and contrasts his thinking are named: the duo of N. F. S. Grundtvig and J. C. Lindberg, Hegel, Socrates (*CUP*, 1:34–46; 331–33; 201–10). Others remain nameless: a speculative thinker, a revivalist, and an orthodox believer (*CUP*, 1:212–34; 505–7, 565–67, 614–15; 594–613). But the relationship between Climacus and Lessing takes precedence.

The two resemble each other. Climacus admires the fact that Lessing avoided becoming "world-historical or systematic with regard to the religious"; he understood, to the contrary, that "the religious pertained to Lessing and Lessing alone, just as it pertains to every human being in the same way, understood that he had infinitely to do with God, but nothing, nothing to do directly with any human being" (*CUP*, 1:65). Lessing's own self figures centrally in his writing as does Climacus's in *Postscript*, for Lessing possesses a "nimbleness in teasingly employing his own I [*Jeg*]" (*CUP*, 1:69). Most important, Climacus portrays Lessing as a humorist. "All of this, is it earnestness?" he asks. Is it earnestness that Lessing "conducts himself the same way toward everyone, although differently in form," so that neither the attackers nor the defenders of Christianity can determine if he is on their side? Is it the "outcome of an earnest man's life, that his parting words are just as enigmatic as all the rest," so enigmatic that his companion Jacobi "does not even dare vouch for the salvation of Lessing's soul?" (*CUP*, 1:70). "No," Climacus says, "Lessing was not an earnest man. His entire presentation is devoid of earnestness" (*CUP*, 1:69). Unless, that is, "it would be impossible to understand earnestness if one does not understand jest," unless there were a "dialectical reciprocity between jest and earnestness" (*CUP*, 1:70–71). But "if Lessing is not an earnest man, what hope is there for the person," Climacus himself, "who relinquishes so very much, the world-historical and contemporary systematics, in order to have recourse to him?" (*CUP*, 1:71).

In addition to tracing the influence of other persons on his thinking, Climacus identifies two fortuitous events that led to his becoming a writer. The passages narrating these two events stand out from their surroundings and show formal connections one to the other. Both come in the middle of earnest discussions that Climacus interrupts by saying, "This sounds almost like earnestness" and "This almost seems to be earnestness" (*CUP*, 1:183, 234). Both events take place on Sundays, four years prior to the writing of *Postscript*, the second two months after the first. Both occur in gardens: a public park, Frederiksberg Gardens, which represents a "queen's recollection of her late lord [Frederik VI]," and a cemetery, "the garden of the dead" (*CUP*, 1:185, 235). Idly smoking cigars in a café in the first garden on the first Sunday, Climacus decides to devote his idleness to "mak[ing] difficulties everywhere," as his contemporaries "by virtue of thought systematically make spiritual existence easier and easier," so much so that there is a danger that "it would become all too easy" (*CUP*, 1:186–87). In the cemetery, Climacus overhears an old man speaking to a boy of ten at the grave of another man, the boy's father, the old man's son. The deceased lost his Christian faith under the deleterious influence of speculative philosophy. The old man binds the boy with an oath in the name of Jesus Christ not to make the same fatal mistake. Deeply moved, Climacus resolves to use his dialectical skills to explore the relationship between speculation and Christianity. Or, linking the formal task set by the first garden scene to the material content provided in the second, Climacus the humorist will make becoming a Christian more difficult by locating the misunderstanding between speculative thought and Christian faith.

Third, the autobiographical emerges in *Postscript* when Climacus writes about his own writing. What a humorous career! Repeatedly, just as Climacus stands poised to publish a book, he discovers that another writer has already accomplished his goals. First, Victor Eremita, then Johannes de Silentio, Constantin Constantius, Vigilius Haufniensis, Nicolaus Notabene, and even one Magister Kierkegaard steal Climacus's thunder. With *Fragments*, he finally manages to get a book in edgewise, although while he is planning *Postscript's* yet another book appears, *Stages on Life's Way* (hereafter *Stages*). In a substantial review of these books (*CUP*, 1:251–300), all of which Kierkegaard acknowledges as his own in the "Explanation," Climacus clarifies his motives and methods as a writer.

Because *Postscript* is first of all a postscript to *Fragments*, Climacus writes about his own writing throughout the entire book. The title of *Fragments* appears on *Postscript's* title page. Both prefaces make autobiographical use of the same classical quotation. Moreover, Climacus begins the introduction to *Postscript* by referring to an apparent promise made at the end of *Fragments* to write a sequel. He refuses to grant any earnestness to this remark, inasmuch as he claims to have accomplished the more difficult task in his first book, leaving a simpler matter for the sequel. Any seminary graduate could "clothe the issue in historical costume," the sequel's stated task, while he doubts many could have "present[ed] the issue" with the "dialectical rhythm" and "dialectical clarity" he achieved in *Fragments* (*CUP*, 1:10). What issue? The one posed on the title page of *Fragments*: *"Can a historical point of departure be given for an eternal consciousness; how can such a point of departure be of more than historical interest; can an eternal happiness be built on historical knowledge?"* (*CUP*, 1:15). With the addition of his own proper name this becomes the subjective issue of *Postscript*, Climacus's own proper problem: How can I, Johannes Climacus, become a Christian? And so, Climacus admits, *Postscript* "is really more than the promised sequel as a clothing in historical costume, since this costume is provided merely by mentioning the word 'Christianity.' " The brief first part of *Postscript* disposes of the sequel, whereas the second part, the bulk of the book, represents "a new approach to the issue of *Fragments*" (*CUP*, 1:17). In the longest single unit of *Postscript* Climacus both writes most explicitly about "The Issue in *Fragments*," as the title of the chapter has it, and rehearses most vigorously his central autobiographical claim, that he is a humorist, not a Christian (*CUP*, 1:361–586).

Women (and Men) in Climacus's *Postscript*

If a feminist re-reading of Kierkegaard's writings might begin with attention to the body of *Postscript*, to its autobiographical texture and architecture, then such an interpretation would be advanced by an analysis of the construction of gender present in the text. I proceed, therefore, to consider what Climacus has to say about women (and men) as he writes about himself, his life, and his writing. A complex pattern emerges.

A *Portrait of the Dialectician as a Young Man*

As I indicated, Climacus tells of his intellectual development by describing his relationships to renowned (male) figures. What I did not indicate, however, is that he portrays his youthful self as a woman or girl in love with a man. For instance, the orator "speaks, he carries away" young Climacus "and the listener loses himself in the depiction." Climacus's "admiration for the distinguished orator" causes him "to surrender with feminine abandon [*gjør ham qvindeligt hengiven*]; he feels his heart pounding; his whole soul is moved" (*CUP*, 1:12).[4] This womanly demeanor can also be described as childlike. The orator "revives the troubled one, wrests him out of the terror as the mother her child, who feels reassured by the most affectionate caresses." But the "poor dialectician" does not find his issue "even presented, much less solved" by the orator and so Climacus "goes home dejected," possessing only the "unhappy love of admiration" (*CUP*, 1:12–13).

As soon as he has "freed himself from the orator's domination," Climacus falls under the influence of the systematician who asserts that "not until the end of it all will everything become clear" and yet "treat[s] everything as completed" (*CUP*, 1:13). An older Climacus can look back and smile at such a systematician, for "if the conclusion is lacking at the end, it is also lacking at the beginning," and "if the conclusion is lacking at the beginning, this means there is no system." But with "youthful decorum," the immature Climacus "abstains from every conclusion concerning the lack of a conclusion—and full of hope he begins his work," his systematic reading of the systematician's writing. "Admiration holds him captive; he submits himself to a superior power." Climacus puts the "entire awesome [*sværmerske*] trust of youth in the renowned person," for "like a maiden [*en Pige*] who has only one wish, to be loved by that someone, so he wishes only one thing—to become a thinker" (*CUP*, 1:13). Once again, he is disappointed in his love.

What Climacus says about youths enamored of Hegel describes his own break with the systematician. A young man who "despair[ed] of himself . . . in order not to abandon [*at opgive*] Hegel" when doubts arose concerning Hegel's accomplishment, "has a right to demand the nemesis of having laughter consume in Hegel what laughter may legitimately claim as its own" once the youth "comes to himself again" (*CUP*, 1:118). Such a "doubting youth" will "write a dreadful epigram on Hegel" when he seeks "the truth for existence" in "Hegelian positivity" (*CUP*, 1:310). Not that he will "attack" Hegel, let alone be "capable of overcoming" him. Rather, the "satire on Hegel" consists precisely in the youth's "admiration, his enthusiasm, and his limitless confidence in Hegel," his being "willing to submit unconditionally to Hegel with feminine devotedness [*qvindelig Hengivenhed*]," while having "sufficient strength also to stick to his question" (*CUP*, 1:310–11). His disappointment at the hands of the orator and the systematician teaches Climacus enough dialectical intrepidity to avoid the weakness of an enraptured girl in his relations with academic theologians and clergymen. He may feel "safe to abandon [*hengive*]" himself "to admiration" for a scholar's philological expertise, but Climacus denies he could "build [his] eternal happiness" on such objective, critical scholarship (*CUP*, 1:25–26). Likewise, although he "cannot but remember with gratitude and admiration the splendid accomplishments" of Grundtvig, Climacus "does not exactly feel any pain in the moment of parting, nor does he exactly feel abandoned [*forladt*] at the thought of being in disagreement with this thinker" (*CUP*, 1:45–46).

When Climacus meets a renowned thinker who advances his work on his own proper problem, he also discovers that he cannot relate to this new figure as he did the others. He is unable to approach Lessing as an adoring girl would a man, for one cannot "abandon oneself [*hengive sig*] to Lessing with the same confidence" demanded by systematic thinkers with their "genuine speculative earnestness" (*CUP*, 1:91). Such womanly abandon must be given up as immaturity. Climacus criticizes Jacobi for failing in this regard. "Jacobi did not understand how to discipline himself"; he was "enamored of Lessing," but required direct assurances from Lessing concerning the religious and so, in Climacus's mind, was "not the stronger but the weaker" having "only a woman's strength, which is in frailty" (*CUP*, 1:101). Jacobi "wants to sweep Lessing off his feet" and convince him he is not really a Spinozist (*CUP*, 1:101–2). Employing irony, Lessing manages to avoid Jacobi's company (or interference in his relationship to God). "Lessing reposes in himself and feels no need of companionship; therefore he parries ironically and slips away from Jacobi on his old legs." For "despite all his enthusiasm for others," Jacobi "is self-seeking. That he by all means wants to convince Lessing is precisely his need" (*CUP*, 1:103). Climacus distances himself from the weakness of Jacobi's womanly ways, but also refuses to attribute to himself the domineering power "of a ruler or a conqueror." Instead, he claims "the only power I have is the power to restrain," which is a "power only over myself" (*CUP*, 1:164–65). Climacus does not know exactly how to relate to Lessing, for he acknowledges "how difficult it is to approach Lessing with regard to the religious. If I were to present a few thoughts and then by rote ascribe them directly to [Lessing]," he says, "if I were to clasp him affably in admiration's embrace as the one to whom I owed everything, he would perhaps withdraw with a smile and leave me in the lurch, an object of laughter" (*CUP*, 1:71).

The distance Climacus has traveled from his youthful, womanly attachment to renowned male figures becomes even clearer after (and because of) his relationship to Lessing. Climacus confesses "something about myself, something regrettable," that may account for his inability to think as others do (*CUP*, 1:161). While "most people are by nature such good people [*Mennesker*]; first they are good children, then good young people, then good husbands and wives," this, he admits, "is not the case with me, . . . I am a corrupt and corruptible man [*Menneske*]." Because "my father is dead and I no longer attend school," and because "I have no wife to tell me that God knows I am a good man [*Menneske*]," Climacus feels "obliged to grapple alone with myself." A man with no woman in his life, he discovers that the "only one who consoles me is

Socrates" (*CUP*, 1:161). And so Climacus's dialectical efforts replace both an adult male relationship to an actual woman as well as his girlish demeanor toward other men. Upon returning home from the decisive scene in the cemetery, Climacus reports he "thought as follows: You are quite bored with life's diversions, bored with girls, whom you love only in passing; you must have something that can totally occupy your time" (*CUP*, 1:241). The project of seeking the misrelationship between speculative thought and Christianity becomes his alternative to loving a woman. Similarly, in recounting the first garden scene, he describes his well-developed "indolence" as a power that "continually constrained me, captivated by its persuasions" (*CUP*, 1:185–86). This indolence differs from "the vehement craving of erotic love" and "the intense incitement of enthusiasm." Instead, it resembles "a woman in the house [*en Hustru*] who constrains one and with whom one gets on very well—so well that one never dreams of wanting to marry" (*CUP*, 1:186). By the time of the events in the two gardens, Climacus has left behind his tendency to give himself hence to another as a woman would, cultivating instead a single life, a life of self-restraint. He receives support not from a woman, but from two other men, Lessing and Socrates. Yet these men do not allow him to get too close or give himself hence to them. Climacus chooses erotic language only to describe his mature relationships to abstractions, not to actual women. He speaks, for example, of twilight, of "evening's taking leave of day," as a beckoning invitation, "as if rest were to be found only if one remained out for a nocturnal rendezvous, not with a woman but, womanlike [*qvindeligt*], with the infinite" (*CUP*, 1:235).

If Climacus calls attention to his being a single man who does not need or want a woman and to his becoming a writer instead of a husband, then as a reader of other male writers he also tends to ignore or abstract from women. This is evident in his review of the pseudonymous books. Climacus insists that he does not intend to offer "a detailed account of [their] contents" (*CUP*, 1:299). He wants to show, rather, that the authors of these books experimentally and humorously explore issues prefatory to his own proper problem. But the contents he abstracts from are precisely women and men's relationships to them. He mentions with approval Constantius's use, in *Repetition*, of an unhappy love affair to get at what it means to exist. The reasons why the Young Man breaks his engagement, however, reasons tracing back to gender difference and the ambiguity of the young man's sexual identity, remain undisclosed. A reader could surmise from the review that the Judge of *Either/Or* writes on marriage, but would not realize that the entire book, both volumes 1 and 2, deals with the nature of woman and of erotic love. Climacus refers by name to one of the sections of *Either/Or*, Part I, "Silhouettes," in order to show that A, the aesthete, is characterized by a "depression [*Tungsind*]" that "deceptively occupies itself with the sufferings of others," without ever mentioning that the lives whose silhouettes A studies are those of three women (Marie Beaumarchais, Donna Elvira, and Margarete) who suffer at the hands of men (Clavigo, Don Juan, and Faust) who seduced and/or abandoned them (*CUP*, 1:253). Only at the very end of his discussion of *Stages* does Climacus hint at the centrality of gender in that book when he says: "Johannes the Seducer ends with the thesis that *woman is only the moment*"; and then, "where Johannes the Seducer ends, the Judge begins: *Woman's beauty increases with the years*" (*CUP*, 1:298–99).

Critique of Woman

Throughout *Postscript*, Climacus makes critical comments concerning women. Several times he portrays them as an integral constituent of comfortable bourgeois life, a life he contrasts to authentic Christian faith with its linkage of an individual's "infinite interest in his own [eternal] happiness" to the "interest with which he hates father and mother" and "makes light of systems and world-historical surveys" (*CUP*, 1:16). For instance, Climacus imagines that if a man in his day and age were to worry "that it was not quite right to call himself a Christian," his wife would say to him: "Hubby, darling [*lille Mand*], where did you ever pick up such a notion? How can you not be a Christian? You are Danish, aren't you? . . . Don't you tend to your work in the office as a good civil servant; aren't you a good subject in a Christian nation, in a Lutheran-Christian state? So of course you are a Christian" (*CUP*, 1:50–51). Or he opposes the capacity "to believe against the understanding" involved in being a Christian to the way a man oriented to the world of the probable "thanks [God] when for a wife he finds a girl both beautiful and congenial," whose beauty "in all probability will last a long time" and who "is built in such a way that in all probability she will bear healthy and strong children" (*CUP*, 1:232–33). Climacus does not know "whether [to] laugh or weep" when people place the highest good alongside lesser goods: "a good job, a beautiful wife, health, the rank of a councilor of justice—and in addition an eternal happiness"; or when a man "who is situated with a wife and children in a good living, cozily indoors, and is a councilor of justice, a 'serious man' . . . wants to do something for his eternal happiness," even spend "ten rix-dollars on it," if only the "duties of his office and his wife and children permit it" (*CUP*, 1:391, 395). He likens the lack of "ethical striving" in such persons to "a soft, effeminate embrace [*et blødagtigt, qvindeligt Favnetag*]" (*CUP*, 1:138). Climacus also sets the Christianity that was an "offense to the Jews and foolishness to the Greeks" over against that of an orthodox believer who "continually talks about childhood faith, what is learned as a child, a womanly heart [*Qvindehjertet*], etc.," but who "has managed to mix up Christianity with the childlike," who "now longs for childhood, and whose longing is especially distinguishable by a longing for the loving tenderness of the pious mother" (*CUP*, 1:598).

Climacus ridicules what he considers the unruly, yet transient, emotions of women. "If the dialectical is skipped" in a religious discourse or a presentation of Christianity, "then it becomes woman-chatter and old wives' blather [*Fruentimmer-Vrøvl og Qvinde-Vræl*], for, as is known, Jews and women blather in one minute what a man [*Mand*] is unable to do in a lifetime" (*CUP*, 1:430). The "endurance in inwardness" that would make a person a hero from "the ethical and religious point of view" differs from both a "lively chap who is able to take everything lightly" and "a half hour of feminine screaming [*fruentimmeragtig Vrælen*]" (*CUP*, 1:266). Similarly, he distinguishes the perseverance in suffering that is an "essential expression of existential pathos" from the "immediate person" whose passion is ludicrously disclosed in "momentary feminine squealing [*fruentimmeragtig Vrælen*] that is forgotten the next moment" (*CUP*, 1:443). Climacus even complains about how women write. He applauds the (male) authors of the pseudonymous books for not giving readers direct assurances concerning the erroneous standpoints of their characters, "as if an existence-deviation were amended by being brought to a final decision, such as insanity, suicide, and the like, which female authors [*Fruentimmere . . . som Forfattere*] in particular do, and so speedily that they almost begin with it" (*CUP*, 1:252). Authors who insist on providing the "trustworthiness of a severe lecture or an unfortunate outcome (for example, madness, suicide, poverty, etc.)" in order to show that a "standpoint is in error" write "effeminately [*fruentimmeragtigt*] for childish readers" (*CUP*, 1:296).

A similar attitude toward women permeates the second garden scene. "Inwardness," Climacus claims, "is untrue in direct proportion to the ready availability of external expressions in countenance and bearing, in words and assuring protestations" (*CUP*, 1:236). On the other hand, for someone "to have no direct expression for his inwardness, none, and yet to stand by his word—that is true inwardness." Then he casts this contrast in terms of gender:

> Praised be the living person who externally relates himself as a dead person to his inwardness and thereby maintains it, not as the excitement of a moment and as a woman's infatuation [*Be-daarelse*], but as the eternal, which has been gained through death. Such a person is a man [*En saadan er en Mand*]. It is not unlovely for a woman to bubble over in momentary inwardness, nor is it unlovely for her to forget it again very soon—the one corresponds to the other, and both correspond to the feminine nature [*det Qvindelige*] and to what is ordinarily understood by inwardness. (*CUP*, 1:236)

Although impressed by what he overhears the old man say to the boy, Climacus obeys his own strictures, acts the part of a man, and chooses not to "rush forward and emotionally express my sympathy to the old man" (*CUP*, 1:239). For "the feminine approach [*det Fruentimmeragtige*] is always dangerous. A tender handshake, a passionate embrace, a tear in the eye are still not exactly the same as the quiet dedication of resolution. Inwardness of spirit is indeed always like a stranger and foreigner in a body—why, then, gesticulations" (*CUP*, 1:239–40). He even employs the notion of a giving hence (*Hengivelse*) of the self, which, as was shown earlier, represents the definitive mark of a woman, to describe such deficient forms of inwardness. Imagine an enthusiastic learner who "in the strongest terms proclaims his praise of the teacher and thus, as we say, lays bare his inwardness; his inwardness is not inwardness but a spontaneous devotedness [*den umiddelbare Hengivelse*], because the pious, silent agreement, according to which the learner personally appropriates what is taught, distancing himself from the teacher because he turns inward into himself—precisely that is inwardness" (*CUP*, 1:242).

In his comments on the third part of *Stages*, a long piece by an experimenting psychologist called Frater Taciturnus, Climacus adds one final specification of the nature of womanly inwardness: it is directed outward toward another person. Quidam, the male subject in Taciturnus's experiment, is "distinguishable by his having his inwardness defined by the contrast within himself, by his perceiving as comic that which neverthe-less is in him with all the passion of inwardness. A feminine [qvindelig] inwardness as devotedness [Hengivenhed] is less inwardness, because the direction is obviously outward, toward [hen til], whereas the presence of the contrast specifically signifies the direction inward [ind efter]" (CUP, 1:291).

A Vindication of the Rightness of Woman

But perhaps we should not take Climacus's earnest criticism of women with complete earnestness, for our single male dialectician humorously commends a reappropriation of womanly qualities, while rejecting inap-propriate male demeanors. His very first mention of women's writing might make us suspicious. With reference to the promise of writing a sequel to *Fragments*, Climacus says: "It is therefore quite in order that it be fulfilled in a postscript, and the author can scarcely be accused of the feminine [fruentimmeragtigt] practice of saying the most important thing in a postscript." Then he jestingly undercuts his own statement: "that is, if the whole matter is of any importance at all. In essence, there is no sequel" (CUP, 1:11). Has Climacus avoided the female trait of writing the most important matters in a postscript only by doing something even further removed from earnest male writing: simultaneously re-presenting and revoking the accomplishment of a brief jesting (earnest?) book, *Frag-ments*, in a long earnest (jesting?) postscript, *Postscript?* Although he warns that worldly goods such as erotic love, marriage, and family can lead a person to forget one's highest good, Climacus, in his criticism, focuses on the values of husbands, not the attitudes and behaviors of wives. He contrasts the male lover who "can 'venture' everything for his love" to the "married man, who," although "in possession of his beloved, ventures nothing for her, even if with her he endures everything," and thereby "insults his wife if he uses the expression ["venture"] that is the lover's loftiest enthusiasm" (CUP, 1:425 n). Moreover, Climacus relativ-izes marriage in light of Christian faith. "It is a matter of indifference," he claims, "whether one has been married or not, just as it is a matter of indifference whether one is Jew or Greek, free or slave." The indifference of one's marital status derives from an essential equality of men and women before God. "Marriage is still a jest, a jest that must be treated with all earnestness, except that the earnestness does not therefore in-here in marriage itself but is a reflection of the relationship with God, a reflection of the husband's absolute relation to his absolute *telos* [end] and of the wife's absolute relation to her absolute *telos*" (*CUP*, 1:456). Women may be characterized by weakness or softness, but Climacus employs these same terms to describe the dominant male culture of mid-nineteenth-century Europe. "So the immorality of our age could very easily become a fantastic-ethical debilitation, the disintegration of a sensual, soft [*blødagtig*] despair, in which individuals grope as in a dream for a concept of God" (*CUP*, 1:544). When he comments on the way "an immediate enthusiast," a male religious figure, "bawls out [*vræler*], . . . pester[ing] people with his enthusiasm," Climacus selects the verbal form of the word he used to ridicule the screaming (*Vrælen*) of women (*CUP*, 1:504).

Finally, women and womanly qualities are associated by Climacus with two figures in whom he shows intense interest: the Christian and the humorist, the two that figure so prominently in his autobiographical statements. He analyzes in detail the self-related inwardness exemplified by Quidam in *Stages*, calls it hidden inwardness, and contrasts it sharply with Christian faith. In fact, the inwardness associated with the Christian resembles what Climacus earlier dismissed as womanly inwardness, an inwardness directed outward toward another person. In Christianity this other person is Jesus Christ, the paradox of God existing in time and space. "To be infinitely interested and to ask about an actuality that is not one's own is to will to believe and expresses the paradoxical relation to the paradox. . . . Faith's analogy to the ethical is the infinite interested-ness by which the believer is absolutely different from an aesthete and a thinker, but in turn is different from an ethicist by being infinitely inter-ested in the actuality of another (for example, that the god actually has existed)" (*CUP*, 1:323–24). Of course, Climacus has consistently denied being a Christian, preferring to be known as a humorist. But gender cate-gories also become strangely mixed in his descriptions of the humorist. In a footnote in which Climacus attributes to the humorist, himself per-haps, a typically male withdrawal from others and into one's own self ("just as one can voluptuously pull the eiderdown quilt over one's head and let the world go hang, so the humorist with the aid of immanence hides himself away in recollection's eternity and smiles sadly at temporal existence with its brief busyness and illusory decision"), he also bestows upon this humorist qualities of a woman (*CUP*, 1:270–71 n). For while honoring the "moral and for his part [doing] everything as best he can," the humorist remains "femininely infatuated [*qvindeligt forelsket*] with immanence, and recollection is his happy marriage and recollection his happy longing" (*CUP*, 1:271 n).

Climacus closes the long section of *Postscript* in which his disavowals of being a Christian and testimonies to being merely a humorist become ever more frequent with another scene from his own life. He describes "a young married woman [*en unge Kone*]" who at a social occasion "expressed her pain over life, that it keeps so very little of what it promises"—"a happy childhood or, rather, the happiness of a child." Falling silent, she "bent down to a child fondly clinging to her, and patted the little one's cheek. One of the group, whose emotion was clearly in sympathy with the young woman, continued, 'Yes, and above all the happiness of childhood to be spanked' " (*CUP*, 1:551). The recollection of this exchange initiates a comparison of irony and humor. While many hearing the remark about being spanked took it to be ironic, Climacus understands it to be humorous. The difference? "In irony there is no sympathy; it is self-assertion, and its sympathy is an altogether indirect sympathizing, not with any one person, but with the idea of self-assertion as every human being's possibility" (*CUP*, 1:553). On the other hand, "because there is always a hidden pain in humor, there is also a sympathy." The "remark was not rude teasing," Climacus explains, "on the contrary, it was sympathetic"; the humorist means to say that the sad longing for childhood in the midst of "financial difficulties" or an "unhappy marriage" is "not nearly as sad as to long for it" in the midst of the "eternal recollection of guilt" (*CUP*, 1:552 n). Then he proposes a gendered account of irony and humor: "One often finds humor in women, but never irony. Any attempt at it on her part is unbecoming, and a purely feminine nature [*en reen qvindelig Natur*] will consider irony to be a kind of cruelty" (*CUP*, 1:553).

All this makes difficulties for Climacus's gendered assessment of himself, his life, and his writing. He claims to have advanced beyond a girlish giving hence of himself to others and to have achieved self-restraint and dialectical intrepidity through his relationships to Lessing and Socrates, both of whom are explicitly identified as ironists. Indeed, in the discussion of the young woman's remark about childhood, Socrates is cited as the chief example of irony and his reply to a man's confiding a secret to him is juxtaposed to the humorous remark "a young girl [*en Pige*]" might make to the same man (*CUP*, 1:552–53 n). Climacus insists he is a humorist, not a Christian. He makes it clear that his mature identity is that of a single male. However, both the Christian he denies being and the humorist he professes to be manifest womanly traits. The gendered texture of Climacus's text thus raises the question of the earnestness of his most basic autobiographical claim.

From Climacus's *Postscript* Toward Kierkegaard on Women (and Men)

On the basis of my reading of *Postscript*, I now want to make some assertions pertaining to the role of gender in Kierkegaard's writings and pose some questions about its significance. In so doing, I am cognizant of two things. First, mine is only one among many ways a feminist re-reading of Kierkegaard could be ventured. Second, in the limited space available I can only call attention to representative passages and central themes, not treat them adequately.[5]

Some Assertions

A feminist re-reading of Kierkegaard is needed in order to arrive at an adequate reading, for gender matters as much throughout his writings as it does in Postscript.

Although I encountered one woman, Regine, in my first reading of Kierkegaard, her presence was restricted to a few pages dealing with his life. In fact, an attentive reading of the body of Kierkegaard's writings discloses the centrality of gender. While he may write about a host of issues, Kierkegaard consistently fleshes them out through stories of women and men in relation to one another.

The very first piece of writing Kierkegaard published is a satiric article concerning women's intellectual abilities (*EPW*, 3–5). In his first book, he compares Hans Christian Andersen's work as a novelist unfavorably to that of an anonymous female author (*EPW*, 53–102).[6] Gender is absolutely pervasive in the pseudonymous books of 1843–46. *Either/Or* and *Stages* consist almost entirely of essays, aphorisms, letters, and diaries by male writers concerning women, men, seduction, engagements, marriage, happy and unhappy love, faithfulness and betrayal, as well as literary, theatrical, and musical expressions of these themes. In other books, relationships between men and women lead male characters and authors to consider topics such as the Book of Job and the meaning of writing a book (*Repetition* and *Prefaces*). Not surprisingly, the author of a dialectical lyric relies upon stories of men and women to make his points (*Fear and Trembling*). One might be surprised, however, that a learned treatise on original sin would be grounded so firmly upon an interpretation of sexual difference and the human body, soul, and spirit (*Concept of Anxiety*). I have already explored the role of gender in *Postscript* and will do so for Kierkegaard's upbuilding and Christian discourses over the next few pages. Given the gendered texture of the body of his writings, I must conclude that a reading of Kierkegaard not informed by feminism, at least in the minimal sense intended here, represents a misreading.

The portrayal of women (and men) in Postscript *is typical of that presented throughout much of Kierkegaard's published writings.*

For Climacus, a woman is defined primarily by her relationships; her inwardness or subjectivity requires another to whom she gives herself hence. He views this essential relationality both as the weakness and the peculiar strength of women. A similar characterization can be found throughout all phases and facets of Kierkegaard's work as a writer. In the first paragraph of his dissertation (1841), he says it is "fitting for the phenomenon, which as such is always *foeminini generis* [of the feminine gender], to surrender [*at hengive sig*] to the stronger on account of its feminine [*qvindelige*] nature" (*CI*, 9). In the last written piece to be published in his lifetime (1855), after portraying a Christian as one who dies to the world and a man as one who maintains his ethical principles at all cost, he asserts that a woman is "essentially determined by the conception of her emotion [*Følelse*]" so that "one sorrow" can "determine her way of life for a whole lifetime," so that "the death of her beloved or his unfaithfulness" can lead her to understand "it as her task to be lost for this life" (*KAUC*, 265–66).

In the pseudonymous books, Johannes the Seducer elaborates a theory of woman as "being-for-other"; her defining characteristic is "pure virginity" or "absolute devotedness [*Hengivelse*]" (*EO*, 1:429–32). The chief pseudonym employed after Climacus, Anti-Climacus, proposes a gendered account of the two forms of conscious despair: the "despair in weakness," which is "feminine despair [*Qvindelighedens Fortvivlelse*]," and despair as "defiance" or "masculine [*Mandlighedens*] despair"

(*SUD*, 49). He expresses his understanding of gender this way: "However much more tender and sensitive [*ømt- og fiintfølende*] woman may be than man, she has neither the egoistical concept of the self nor, in a decisive sense, intellectuality" (*SUD*, 49 n). Instead she is defined relationally. "The feminine [*Qvindens*] nature is devotedness [*Hengivenhed*], givingness [*Hengivelse*], and it is unfeminine [*uqvindeligt*] if it is not that" (*SUD*, 49–50 n). In an early upbuilding discourse, Kierkegaard writes of a woman in the Gospels who exemplifies the female nature perfectly. She "found rest at Jesus' feet, she forgot herself in her work of love. As she wept, she finally forgot what she had wept over at the beginning; the tears of repentance became tears of adoration. She was forgiven her many sins, because she loved much" (*EUD*, 75–76). And in a later discourse concerning this same woman, he concedes that "sure enough man is stronger than the weak one [*den Svage*], woman [*Qvinden*], man has more ways out, knows much better how to take care of himself." But then he praises the unity and simplicity of woman's inner life, concluding: "Let man with respect to thought have more earnestness; with respect to feeling [*Følelse*], passion [*Lidenskab*], decision [*Afgjørelse*], with respect to not creating an obstacle to oneself and to the decision by thoughts, proposals, resolutions, with respect to not disappointing oneself by coming quite near to the decision but without making a decision, in this respect woman has more earnestness" (*SV*, 3d ed., 17:13–14; my translation).

While neither Kierkegaard nor his pseudonyms theorize about man quite the way they do about woman, they assume that if her nature is to feel and love, then his is to think. Greater attention is paid to an aberrant form of male intellectuality, the attributes of which are just the opposite of female relationality. Climacus, for instance, must outgrow or break with his girlish dependence upon others in order to become a thinker and a man. Yet he recognizes in the hidden inwardness of Quidam an exaggeration of his own dialectical intrepidity. Indeed, Quidam best exemplifies the aberrant male thinker. In his first diary entry, he asserts: "Depression [*Tungsind*] is my nature" (*SLW*, 195). Taciturnus agrees, describing him as "ethical-dialectical," "essentially a thinker," "depressed [*tungsindig*]," and "inclosingly reserved [*indesluttet*]" (*SLW*, 427–32). To underscore the heterogeneity of Quidam and his beloved, Taciturnus claims: "His reserve [*Indesluttethed*] is shipwrecked on [her] devotedness [*Hengivenhed*]" (*SLW*, 427). Similarly, Judge William takes A, the aesthete, to task for his lack of female qualities: "This is how it is with you, and you will also see how egoistical your enjoyment is, and that you never give of yourself [*hengiver Dig*], never let others enjoy you" (*EO*, 2:24–25). Anti-Climacus identifies the "most intensive form" of male despair as "inclosing reserve [*Indesluttethed*]" or "inwardness with a jammed lock" (*SUD*, 72–73).

The portrayal of women as relational (and men as intellectual) gets put to three primary uses in Postscript *and throughout Kierkegaard's writings.*

Climacus makes the following evaluative judgments based on his understanding of women. First, he criticizes women as emblems of the complacency and comfort of bourgeois existence, although as I argued above the critique of woman can and should be viewed as a critique of bourgeois man and his values. Second, Climacus hints that the difference between men and women is relativized by their common human relationship to God. Third, in religious contexts he understands typical female qualities to represent the norm for all human beings, men as well as women. A similar pattern of critique, relativization, and commendation of women appears throughout Kierkegaard's writings.

The rejection of women, marriage, family, and career as bourgeois comforts antithetical to Christian faith, what I will call Kierkegaard's sociopolitical asceticism, becomes much more thoroughly marked out in the works that follow *Postscript*. For example, Anti-Climacus asserts that "even the more profound person [*Menneske*] can have many weaker moments when to him it is as if Christianity were misanthropy [*Menneske-fjendskab*], because in the weaker moments he wants to coddle himself, whimper, have an easy life in the world, live in rather quiet enjoyment" (*PC,* 117). Such weakness can be related to gender. "This is the effeminacy [*det Qvindagtige*] in a human being, and therefore it is also quite certain and true that Christianity has an uneasiness about marriage and also desires to have among its many married servants an unmarried person, someone who is single, because Christianity is well aware that with woman and erotic love etc. also come all the weaker, softer elements in a person" (*PC*, 117). If a married man fails to discover these weaker, softer elements for himself, "the wife ordinarily represents them with an unconstraint that is extremely dangerous for the husband, especially for the one who is to serve Christianity in the stricter sense." As did Climacus, so Anti-Climacus puts the tempting words of compromise and comfort in the mouth of a woman who asks her husband: "Why do you want to expose yourself to all those annoyances and efforts and all that ingratitude and opposition? No, let us two enjoy life in coziness and comfort. . . . The teaching that wants to tear a person out of the world in that way is misanthropic and is least of all Christianity"; it is an "invention of some sallow, grumbling, misanthropic hermits who have no sense for the feminine [det Qvindelige]" (PC, 117–18). A convoluted, gendered condemnation of the male leadership of the Danish Lutheran church runs through Kierkegaard's "attack upon Christendom." He castigates pastors and bishops for deceptively clothing themselves as women (KAUC, 144–46, 174–77); seducing (male) seminarians as if they were innocent girls (KAUC, 128–29, 146); working as matchmakers, if not pimps, to bring men and women together (KAUC, 162–63, 217–22); colluding with the midwives to breed herds of Christians in order to maintain their own comfortable livings (KAUC, 157–58, 164–65, 188–90, 212–16). It may be, Kierkegaard writes, "that only in the soft arms of a blameless wife does true felicity reside" and "that in those soft arms one forgets the world's alarms," but the real "question is whether there is not also something else one can only too easily forget in these soft arms—namely, what Christianity is" (KAUC, 145).

Judge William anticipates Climacus's relativizing of gender difference; he argues that when a man and a woman become husband and wife they each take on an attribute ordinarily associated with the other sex. "The individuals became free—he from false pride, she from false humility . . . and the religious pushed in between the two lovers, who held each other so tightly encircled, not to separate them, but so that she could give herself [hengive sig] with an exuberance that she had not previously suspected and so that he could not only receive [modtage] but give himself [hengive sig] and she receive [modtage]" (EO, 2:61). Taking a crucial New Testament passage on gender as his text, Galatians 3:23–29, Kierkegaard writes that by virtue of faith every human being can say: "when people disdained me, I went to God; he became my teacher, and this is my salvation, my joy, my pride" (EUD, 12). "Every person may say it," he insists;

> whether his forehead is almost as flat as an animal's or arches more proudly than heaven, whether his arm is stretched out to command kingdoms and countries or to pick up the scanty gifts that fall from the rich man's table, whether thousands obey his beck and call or not one soul pays any attention to him, whether eloquence blossoms on his lips or only unintelligible sound passes

over them; whether he is the mighty male [*den kraftfulde Mand*] who defies the storm or the defenseless female [*den værgelose Qvinde*] who only seeks shelter from the gale—this has nothing to do with the matter, my listener, absolutely nothing. (*EUD*, 12–13)

A central claim in *Works of Love* is that the Christian "doctrine of love for the neighbor" implies an "equality [*Ligheden*] of all persons [*Mennesker*] before God" (*WL*, 140). This means, for Kierkegaard, that all human differences, including the gender difference, are "a disguise." For "in being king, beggar, scholar, rich person [*Riig*], poor person [*Fattig*], man [*Mand*], woman [*Qvinde*], etc., we are not like [*ligne*] each other— therein we are indeed different. But in being the neighbor we are all unconditionally like each other" (*WL*, 88–89).[7]

Anti-Climacus's discussion of male and female forms of despair marks the transition from the second use of gender categories, the relativization of difference, to the third, the commendation of women and womanly qualities as exemplary. After a lengthy account of woman's essence as the giving hence of herself (*Hengivenhed* or *Hengivelse*), he limits the scope of its applicability. "But it is to be borne in mind that this does not refer to devotion [*Hengivelse*] to God or to the God-relationship. . . . In the relationship to God, where the distinction of man-woman vanishes, it holds for men as well as for women that devotion [*Hengivelse*] is the self and that in the giving of oneself [*ved Hengivelse*] the self is gained. This holds equally [*ligeligt*] for man and woman" (*SUD*, 50 n). Consistent with this judgment, Kierkegaard employs female figures in his books to illustrate the proper human relationship to God, for example, the older woman who convinces Judge William that women should always officially represent the Christian congregation at baptisms and weddings (*EO*, 2:313–16) and Anna, witness to the dedication of the infant Jesus, upon whom Kierkegaard bestows the title of prophet even though this is "a name rarely given among the Jews to a woman because in the view of that people women are regarded as more imperfect than men" (*EUD*, 218). Most significant, however, are four women from the Gospels whose stories Kierkegaard takes up in a dozen discourses published from 1843 to 1851: the woman caught in the act of adultery (John 8); the female sinner (*Synderinden*) who came uninvited to Jesus as he sat at table in the home of a Pharisee, washed his feet with her tears, and anointed them with ointment (Luke 7); Mary, Martha's sister, who sat at Jesus' feet listening instead of helping with the housework (Luke 10); and Mary of Bethany, Martha's and Lazarus's sister, who anointed Jesus' feet (John 12). If *Postscript* is one of the most widely read (or at least mentioned) books of Kierkegaard's, then these discourses would have to be among his most infrequently read works. I believe, however, that they are crucial not only to my purposes here, but to an understanding of the entire published authorship.[8]

Precisely as women in their relationships to Christ Jesus, not in spite of their womanliness, these four women exemplify faith. In one of the discourses Christ himself is portrayed in language otherwise used of women. Kierkegaard says that with his arms outstretched at the altar, Christ very literally hides a multitude of sins. "When one human being places himself in front of another human being and covers him entirely with his body so that no one, no one, can lay eyes on the one who is hidden behind—so it is that Jesus Christ hides your sin with his *holy body*" (SV, 3d ed., 17:45; my translation). He likens Christ to a hen covering her chicks and then chooses familiar (female) terms. "As the night spreads itself concealingly over everything, so he gave himself hence [*gav han sig selv hen*] and became the covering behind which lies a sinful world that he has saved. . . . He gave himself hence as a covering for the whole world, for you as much as for me" (SV, 3d ed., 17:46). But to the women of these discourses themselves, Anti-Climacus writes of Mary of Bethany: "Indeed, with the exception of the apostles, that woman very likely was one of the few who understood [Christ]" (PC, 170). The crowds "misunderstood" it all, Christ's teaching and miracles, "his association with sinners and tax collectors," "his renunciation of everything," "his prediction of his suffering and death." Mary demonstrated her understanding by "anoint[ing] him with costly ointment," although in so doing "she misunderstood him nevertheless, for she did not understand that she did it, anointed him, for his death" (PC, 168, 170). According to Kierkegaard, the female sinner becomes for Christ "a picture [*et Billede*], a parable" shown or told to his Pharisee host and should function similarly for the hearer of her story. "This woman was a sinner—yet she became and is a pattern [*et Forbillede*]; blessed is the one who resembles [*ligner*] her in loving much!" (SV, 3d ed., 14:197–98; my translation) However out of place she may have been at the Pharisee's banquet, she is properly situated "between the confessional and the altar" as the faithful prepare to receive communion; there "she is far from being a forbidding picture; she is, to the contrary, more encouraging than the incentives of all speakers, when it concerns following [Christ's] invitation that leads to the altar: 'Come unto me, all ye that labor and are heavy laden'; for there she leads the way, she who loved much, she who therefore also found rest for her soul in loving much, that is, in the fact that her many sins were forgiven her" (SV, 3d ed., 14:199).

In another discourse, Kierkegaard goes a step further. He declares that the presentation of a woman "as a teacher, as a pattern [Forbillede] of piety" ought not to "surprise anyone who knows that piety or godliness [Fromhed eller Gudelighed] by its nature is womanliness [Qvindelighed]" (SV, 3d ed., 17:13, my translation). However, a re-reading of the Pauline injunction that " 'women are to keep silent in the congregation' and thus not teach" becomes necessary, such that, paradoxically, "precisely this keeping silent before God belongs essentially to true godliness, and thus you must be able to learn it from woman." The silence of the female sinner should teach us two things: "to become, like her, indifferent to everything else" except "find[ing] forgiveness"; and to understand "what she understood," namely, "that with respect to finding forgiveness she herself could do nothing at all" (SV, 3d ed., 17:14, 18). Kierkegaard also commends her for *not* behaving the way a woman might have been expected to behave.

> She went festively then to the banquet—truly, who would have guessed what her errand was, or what her entering that house meant to her! But she understands completely that she herself is able to do nothing. Instead, perhaps, of giving herself hence to self-torment [at hengive sig til Selvplagelse], as if thereby she would be more pleasing to God, and thereby come closer to God, instead she *squanders* (that was indeed Judas' opinion), she squanders *frivolously* (that is indeed the self-tormentor's opinion), she squanders on what had to do in an earthly sense with festivity. She takes with her an alabaster cruse of ointment in festive correspondence with the banquet. She enters. She understands completely that she herself is able to do nothing. She does not therefore give herself hence [hengive sig] to a passionate expression of self-accusation, as if this would bring salvation nearer to her, or make her more pleasing to God. She does not overdo it, truly, no one can accuse her of that. No, she does nothing at all, she keeps silent—she weeps. (SV, 3d ed., 17:18–19)

This woman does not adopt the conventional female role of excessive, empty emotion. She does indeed weep, but eschews showy guilt. She refuses to give herself hence to self-torment or self-accusation. In so doing, she does right. By not doing anything, she allows Jesus to do all, to forgive her. And therein she provides a pattern for all Christians, male and female.[9]

Some Questions

What value does a feminist re-reading of Kierkegaard have for contemporary thought and practice?

Kierkegaard's treatment of gender is ambiguous. He shows some recognition of the socially constructed character of gender, which would imply that gender arrangements can be criticized, relativized, even deconstructed and reconstructed. Yet he also insists on natural differences and inequalities between men and women. Does such ambiguity signify theoretical inconsistency? A lack of moral integrity? Or might Kierkegaard's ambiguity prefigure the unsettled state of our own discussions in which the socially constructed and the naturally given no longer seem so easy to differentiate? How we each evaluate Kierkegaard's treatment of gender may depend on the sense we make or fail to make of his view that Christianity effects an absolute equality of men and women *before God,* transforming everything *in inwardness,* while also leaving the old order outwardly intact.

Does the sociopolitical asceticism of a male Christian writer like Kierkegaard liberate or oppress women (and men)?

Kierkegaard writes as if one cannot separate the human body from human society, as if Christian renunciations of the body may be motivated by opposition to a particular sociopolitical order. But in his polemic against compromised, bourgeois Christianity, he figures the body, even the male-dominated social body, as female. Does not such misanthropy inevitably invite misogyny? Or is the reverse true? Could a rigorous Christian asceticism liberate both men and women from the oppressive possibilities of gendered selfhood? Does the embrace of Christian asceticism represent a man's refusal to inscribe himself in a violent and violating social body? Or is it just one more version of despairing male intellectuality, where inclosing reserve (*Indesluttethed*) and melancholy (*Tungsind*) signal a man's estrangement from his own body?

Does the approach of a male Christian writer like Kierkegaard to the body of Christ Jesus, an approach made through a female figure, liberate or oppress women (and men)?

Kierkegaard argues that all human beings should embody a giving hence of themselves in relationship to God. But his primary examples of such humanity are female. Women provide access to Christ Jesus' body by anointing his feet and by leading the way to the altar. What are we to make of the lack of particularity that characterizes these women? The female sinner's namelessness, silence, and ability to do nothing impress Kierkegaard as eloquent testimony to Christ's ability to do everything for every sinner, male or female. Where does Kierkegaard's female sinner lead female sinners? Out of or into despairing namelessness, silence, and inactivity? What are we to make of a male Christian writer who attaches himself to a woman as the pattern of how one approaches The Pattern, Christ Jesus? What are we to make of Kierkegaard and the nameless female sinner (or Alan of Lynn and Margery Kempe, or Raymond of Capua and Catherine of Siena)? Has he matured enough genuinely to give himself hence to another? Or is he still immaturely feminizing himself, that is, autoerotically projecting on to a woman the giving hence (*Hengivelse*) of the self he fails to embody?

Could almost earnestness, humor, represent the proper rubric under which to consider not only Kierkegaard on gender, but also gender itself?

Such questions keep me re-reading Kierkegaard.[10]

Notes

1. I say ostensibly autobiographical because of a footnote concerning an intoxicated young man's visit to a prostitute: "Like so many of Kierkegaard's self-revelations, this was recorded as if it were the sketch of a plot for a novel. But there is little doubt that it had a real-life basis" (Jones 1969, 212 n. 2). Henning Fenger (1980) disputes just this claim, thereby raising doubts about the usual account of Kierkegaard's life and writing. Incongruously, after arguing that many of the early journal entries do indeed belong to an abandoned epistolary novel, Fenger concludes with an impassioned attack on Kierkegaard the writer because of Kierkegaard the man's alleged cruelty to Regine.

2. For a re-reading of an American contemporary of Kierkegaard, see my essay on Herman Melville (Taylor 1992).

3. Interpretations of Kierkegaard's writings that center on their relationship to his life range from the solicitous Christian reading of Walter Lowrie (1938) to Louis Mackey's (1986) brilliant, torturous postmodern assessments. For *Postscript* as in some sense an autobiographical text by Kierkegaard, see Sylviane Agacinski (1988) and Josiah Thompson (1967). My favorite discussion of Kierkegaard's life remains Thompson's (1973). Kirmmse's (1990) is a marvelous study of the social, literary, and religious world in which Kierkegaard lived and of the writings that followed *Postscript*.

4. Although I believe the new translations by Howard and Edna Hong sometimes blur the sharpness of Kierkegaard's language concerning gender, I have adhered to them scrupulously. As in the sentence just cited, however, I shall often indicate the crucial terms used in the original Danish. I shall also provide my own translations of passages from works not yet available in the series *Kierkegaard's Writings*.

5. I am grateful to Wanda Warren Berry, Kimberly Chastain, Marcia Robinson, Vanessa Rumble, Vanina Sechi, and Sylvia Walsh for conversations, letters, formal responses to my papers, and papers of their own, all of which have enlivened and disciplined my work on gender in Kierkegaard.

6. The author is Thomasine Gyllembourg, to whose writings Kierkegaard returns in *A Literary Review*. He dedicates his book to her as a "nameless, yet so renowned, author" (*TA*, 3).

7. We should attend, however, to Kierkegaard's careful circumscription of this equality. Christianity, he says, "makes [the woman] *in inwardness before God* absolutely equal with the man" (*WL*, 138; my emphasis). "Inwardly everything is changed" and yet "outwardly," in marriage for instance, "the old more or less remains. The man is to be the woman's master [*Herre*] and she shall be subservient to him."

8. I find it humorously fitting that the abbreviations system contributors to this collection were encouraged to use does not include the books in which English translations of three of these discourses appear, for they are older volumes now superseded by *Kierkegaard's Writings*. In order of original publication, the twelve discourses can be found as follows: *EUD*, 55–68; *EUD*, 69–78; *EUD*, 125–58; *TDIO*, 7–40; *WL*, 280–99; *CD*, 297–303; *CD*, 371–77; *CD*, 379–86; *PC*, 167–79; and, until such time as new translations become available, Kierkegaard, 1850/1947, 255–71; Kierkegaard, 1851/1944, 7–16 and 17–25.

9. Complex as it is, the foregoing fails to survey fully Kierkegaard's treatment of gender. Three additional attitudes toward women appear in his writings, although not in Climacus's *Postscript*: first, a harsh attack on women as weak by (male) aesthetes, hermits, and seducers in the early pseudonymous books, coupled with a construal of the giving hence (*Hengivelse*) of herself as sexual intercourse (*SLW*, 47–80; *R*, 143–44, 184–86; *EO*, 1:341–42, 367–68, 429–33); second, Judge William's defense of women as humble, not weak, as both closer to God and more solidly grounded in temporality, finitude, and concrete actuality than men (*EO*, 2:50–62, 92–93, 113–14, 306–16; *SLW*, 124–47, 165–69); third, an unqualified rejection of women's emancipation (*EO*, 2:22, 311–13; *SLW*, 55–56; *WL*, 138–39).

10. Special thanks to my special colleagues Debra Sequeira and Les Steele for their eleventh hour readings of this essay.

References

Adams, Carol. 1990. *The Sexual Politics of Meat: A Feminist-Vegetarian Critical Theory.* New York: Continuum.

Agacinski, Sylviane. 1988. *Aparté: Conceptions and Deaths of Søren Kierkegaard.* Translated by Kevin Newmark. Tallahassee: Florida State University Press.

Butler, Judith. 1990. *Gender Trouble: Feminism and the Subversion of Identity*. New York: Routledge.

Bynum, Caroline Walker. 1987. *Holy Feast and Holy Fast: The Religious Significance of Food to Medieval Women*. Berkeley and Los Angeles: University of California Press.

————. 1991. *Fragmentation and Redemption: Essays on Gender and the Human Body in Medieval Religion*. New York: Zone Books.

Catherine of Siena. 1980. *The Dialogue*. Translated by Suzanne Noffke, O.P. New York: Paulist Press.

Daly, Mary. 1973. *Beyond God the Father: Toward a Philosophy of Women's Liberation*. Boston: Beacon.

Fenger, Henning. 1980. *Kierkegaard, The Myths and Their Origins: Studies in the Kierke-gaardian Papers and Letters*. Translated by George C. Schoolfield. New Haven: Yale University Press.

Irigaray, Luce. 1985. *Speculum of the Other Woman*. Translated by Gillian C. Gill. Ithaca: Cornell University Press.

Jones, W. T. 1969. *A History of Western Philosophy*. 2d ed. Vol. 4, *Kant to Wittgenstein and Sartre*. New York: Harcourt, Brace and World.

Kempe, Margery. 1985. *The Book of Margery Kempe*. Translated by B. A. Windeatt. New York: Penguin.

Kierkegaard, Søren. 1851/1944. *For Self-Examination and Judge For Yourselves and Three Discourses, 1851*. Translated by Walter Lowrie. Princeton: Princeton University Press.

————. 1850/1947. *Training in Christianity and the Edifying Discourse Which "Accompanied" It*. Translated by Walter Lowrie. Princeton: Princeton University Press.

Kirmmse, Bruce. 1990. *Kierkegaard in Golden Age Denmark*. Bloomington: Indiana University Press.

Lowrie, Walter. 1938. *Kierkegaard*. Oxford: Oxford University Press.

Mackey, Louis. 1986. *Points of View: Readings of Kierkegaard*. Tallahassee: Florida State University Press.

Paglia, Camille. 1991. *Sexual Personae: Art and Decadence from Nefertiti to Emily Dickinson*. New York: Vintage Books.

Taylor, Mark Lloyd. 1992. "Ishmael's (m)Other: Gender, Jesus, and God in Melville's *Moby-Dick*." *Journal of Religion* 72:325–50.

Thompson, Josiah. 1967. *The Lonely Labyrinth: Kierkegaard's Pseudonymous Works*. Carbondale: Southern Illinois University Press.

————. 1973. *Kierkegaard*. New York: Knopf.

9

On "Feminine" and "Masculine" Forms of Despair

Sylvia Walsh

Of the two forms of conscious despair delineated in *The Sickness unto Death*, despair in weakness (not willing to be oneself) and despair in defiance (willing to be the self one wishes to be rather than the self one essentially is), the first is characterized by the pseudonymous author, Anti-Climacus, as "feminine" despair, the second as "masculine" despair (*SUD*, 49). This distinction between the forms of despair in terms of sexual categories figures importantly in Anti-Climacus's analysis of selfhood and despair in woman and man, but it has received little or no attention in studies of Kierkegaard's writings.[1] For a generation grown skeptical of sexual stereotypes, such a distinction is quite questionable and calls for critical examination. Beginning with a brief account of what Anti-Climacus has to say about feminine and masculine despair, the following analysis will focus on two areas of concern: (1) the congruence of his views with the general structure of selfhood and analysis of despair presented in the work; and (2) the compatibility of his perspective with recent findings on sexual differences and personality development. From a determination of these correlations we can more readily assess the significance and appropriateness of the sexual categories employed in Anti-Climacus's analysis of despair.

As if anticipating objections to his classification of despair as feminine and masculine, Anti-Climacus appends a lengthy note to the text that introduces this distinction, defending and commenting upon it in some detail. He claims that his classification is conceptually correct as well as true in actual life, although in exceptional cases masculine despair may occur in women, and conversely, feminine despair may appear in men (*SUD*, 49). The distinction is thus an ideal one that holds true largely, but not entirely, in actuality. It corresponds on the whole with the ways despair is generally experienced in human life. Women are more apt to manifest despair in weakness, while men are more prone to despair in defiance.

Anti-Climacus goes on in this note to give a brief account of despair in weakness or feminine despair in women. Woman's nature, he says, is characterized by devotedness (*Hengivenhed*) or giving of herself in submission and abandonment to others (*Hengivelse*). Lacking a selfish concept of self and not possessing intellectuality in any decisive sense, woman is blessed by nature with an instinctive insight into that to which she ought to give herself. While she can be coy and particularly hard to please, her womanly nature first comes into existence through a metamorphosis or transfiguration of her boundless coyness into feminine devotedness (*SUD*, 49–50). Substantively, then, woman gains herself by losing herself; that is, she becomes a woman by giving herself in devotedness to others. Only when she gives herself thus is she herself, and only then is she happy.

Not intending to demean woman by this characterization, Anti-Climacus lauds her sensitive instinctiveness, against which, he says, "the most eminently developed male reflection is as nothing," and he hails her devotedness as a "divine gift and treasure" (*SUD*, 49). Nevertheless, later on in the main text he states that femininity constitutes a "lower synthesis" than does masculinity, which alone falls within the qualification of spirit (*SUD*, 67). The reason for this, presumably, is that woman lacks the reflectiveness and internal orientation of man. As indicated in the note, she becomes herself instinctively, by giving herself to someone or something outside herself.

The crucial point in Anti-Climacus's characterization of woman is that the devotedness (Hengivenhed) that is her nature also constitutes for her a mode of despair. If I read the Danish text correctly on this point, devotedness in itself is not despair, nor is the lack or loss of devotion, as is suggested by the new Princeton translation, which reads: "woman, with genuine femininity, abandons herself, throws herself into that to which she devotes herself. Take this devotion away, then her self is also gone, and her despair is: not to will to be oneself" (SUD, 50). The word "devotion," however, does not appear in the Danish version of the second sentence quoted above; only the demonstrative pronoun dette (this) is used, which grammatically refers to the det (that) to which woman devotes herself in the previous sentence, not to devotion.[2] The meaning of the text, therefore, is that in abandoning or throwing herself altogether into that to which she devotes herself, woman tends to have a sense of self only in and through the object of her devotion. When that object is taken away, her self is also lost. Her despair, consequently, lies in not willing to be herself, that is, in not having any separate or independent self-identity.

Anti-Climacus further points out that man, like woman, gives himself (and "he is a poor kind of man who does not do so," Anti-Climacus remarks), but his self, unlike hers, is not defined by devotion; rather, it is constituted by a "sober awareness" of his giving that remains behind when he gives (SUD, 50). Thus, man does not gain his substantive or sexual identity by giving himself, as woman does, but already possesses and retains a sense of self apart from it. His despair, therefore, is quite different from hers, as it is characterized by an unwarranted self-assertion rather than by self-abandonment. In relation to God, however, sexual distinctions disappear, and it holds that for both woman and man selfhood is constituted by devotion to God, although Anti-Climacus observes that "in most cases the woman actually relates to God only through the man" (SUD, 50).

I

When these views are considered in relation to the general structure of selfhood and analysis of despair presented in The Sickness unto Death, a number of questions, problems, and issues arise. In the classic description of the self with which the work commences, a human being is viewed as becoming a self by relating itself to itself as a synthesis of the finite and the infinite, the temporal and the eternal, necessity (limitations) and freedom (possibility). Since the human self is established by a power other than itself, it becomes itself by relating itself not only to itself but also to the power which establishes it, that is, God. No distinction is made between man and woman in this description. Since the general term for human beings (*Mennesker*) is used, the basic structure of selfhood is presumably the same for both sexes. From Anti-Climacus's note on feminine and masculine despair, however, it would appear that substantive differences nevertheless exist between woman and man within this general structure. Woman's being, we may recall, is centered in relatedness, in self-giving, while man's is characterized by a self-awareness sustained apart from relations to others. Although he gives to others, his self-identity is not constituted by giving.

It should be noted that giving or relating to others is not a constitutive factor in Anti-Climacus's general description of a self either, as that includes relating to oneself and to God but says nothing about relations to others as forming an essential ingredient in the structure of the self. Anti-Climacus's characterization of man's being thus corresponds more closely to the general description of a self than does that of woman, as it stresses self-consciousness or relating to oneself rather than relating to others.

The absence of a relation to others in Anti-Climacus's general description of the self is rather puzzling inasmuch as, only a year prior to the appearance of *The Sickness unto Death,* Kierkegaard published *Works of Love* (1847), which focuses on relating to others through self-renouncing love and envisions a triadic structure (the lover, the beloved, and love of God as a third party) of existence in love (*WL*, 121). One must conclude either that there is a serious inconsistency in the authorship, or that Kierkegaard does not follow through with a systematic and integrated development of his thought, or that the insights of the earlier work are somehow implied in the later one. If the last alternative is accepted, it is possible to interpret the general description of a self in *The Sickness unto Death* as incorporating a social dimension in and through the relation to God or as a component in the self-relation, under the rubric of giving the eternal concrete expression in love, faithfulness, and so forth.[5] Still, one wishes that Anti-Climacus had addressed the matter of relatedness to others more directly in defining the structure of the self.

If self-renouncing love is included in the structure of the self, the resulting character of selfhood would correspond more to the feminine devotedness associated with woman than to the self-conscious masculinity
of man.[4] That, however, would contradict Anti-Climacus's contention
that only the latter falls under the qualification of spirit; males, or at least
those persons who are predominantly masculine in character, presumably
have more spirit or self because they possess more self-consciousness ("the
more consciousness, the more self") than do most females (SUD, 29).

Further problems appear in connection with Anti-Climacus's claim
that devotedness constitutes the proper mode of relating to God. Woman,
as represented in the Gospels by the woman who was a sinner (Luke
7:36–50), is presented by Kierkegaard in an edifying discourse as the
model of religiousness because of her absolute submission to God.[5] Yet,
as Sylviane Agacinski has perceptively pointed out, woman is not considered truly religious, or at least not so religious as man, because she abandons herself by nature, whereas man does not; ironically, therefore, it
seems "as if the man were capable of being more and better a woman than
the woman: that is to say, religious."[6] Since the self has its ground in the
eternal, which consists essentially in love, and one's chief task in life is
to actualize that quality, it would seem too that devotion to the eternal
would properly be given expression in and through one's relations to
others. That, in fact, is how Anti-Climacus sees it commonly working in
woman's existence, but not in man's, which sustains a separate, direct
relation to God.

When Anti-Climacus's distinction between feminine and masculine
despair is considered in the context of his analysis of the two types of
conscious despair, some incongruences can also be noted in relation to
the despair in weakness. As delineated in the text, this despair occurs in
two basic forms: despair over the earthly (the totality of worldly things)
or over something earthly (the particular), and despair of the eternal or
over oneself. The first of these is "the most common form of despair,"
Anti-Climacus says, and is immediate in nature, containing no (or only
a measure of) reflection (SUD, 57). In it there is no infinite consciousness of the self nor any awareness of despair as being despair. One seemingly suffers as a result of external circumstances, so that one's despair is
not at all self-activated from within. With an increase in reflection, this
form of despair becomes more internally motivated, and a greater distinction is made between oneself and the environment. As consciousness of
the self increases, despair in weakness becomes despair over one's weak-

ness, in which one shuts oneself off from the self (*Indesluttethed*) but becomes preoccupied with it, confessing in solitude one's weakness in willing to be that self.

Anti-Climacus characterizes despair in weakness as feminine, but in his illustrations of it mostly male examples are used.[7] Indeed, if it is the most common form of despair, one would assume that it is more typical of males than is despair in defiance. Yet the latter is primarily associated with male experience, while despair in weakness is supposed to be representative of women. Anti-Climacus's description of the first form of despair in weakness corresponds closely to his characterization of woman as instinctive, that is, immediate and unreflective, in contrast to man as self-consciousness and intellectuality. At the more conscious and intensive stage of despair in weakness, however, the introversion that occurs concerns the masculine mode (one's relation to oneself) more than the feminine mode (one's relation to others). Thus his characterization of despair in weakness as feminine is not altogether consistent.

As Anti-Climacus moves on to an analysis of defiant despair, it is seen as presupposing a still higher level of self-consciousness and awareness of despair; but here the feminine mode is projected as the appropriate way to selfhood: "through the aid of the eternal the self has the courage to lose itself in order to win itself" (*SUD*, 67). Earlier this paradox was seen as characterizing woman's existence, but not man's. Now it is related to masculine or defiant despair in that the self "is unwilling to begin with losing itself but wills to be itself" (*SUD*, 67). Defiant despair thus results from an individual's unwillingness to adopt a feminine mode of selfhood.

In what sense the self is expected to lose itself is not stated in the text. Essentially, however, despair in defiance comes to expression when one seeks to become the self one wants to be instead of the self one is intended to be by God. The distinctiveness of this mode of despair lies in the fact that one will not recognize one's contingent or derived status as a self; rather, the self wishes to create itself, to be its own master. Fundamentally, then, this form of despair has to do with one's relation, or more precisely misrelation, to God and to oneself in the expression of an inappropriate form of self-assertion.

The pathway to selfhood thus includes both masculine and feminine modes of relating, and the possibility of going astray on this path eventuates in corresponding forms of despair. Feminine despair reflects a lack of self-consciousness (the masculine mode), while masculine despair indicates a need for the feminine mode (submission to that which is the ultimate source of life). While woman's self is lost or misplaced in a finite object of devotion outside herself, man's self is internally misplaced in himself. If being a self were only a matter of relating to oneself, and thus only a question of willing to be oneself, there would be only the possibility of despair in weakness. But since the self is constituted not only by its relation to itself but also to the divine power that establishes it, one can only become a true self through orienting oneself in (devoting or submitting oneself to) that power. Thus the feminine mode is inextricably involved in the process of becoming a self. How much that includes relatedness to other human beings in self-giving remains unclarified in *The Sickness unto Death*. Inasmuch as masculine self-consciousness provides individuality or a sense of separateness and consciousness of the eternal, it also plays an important and indispensable role. These modes and their corresponding forms of despair in woman and man are not altogether integrated in Anti-Climacus's thought, but they indicate a complementary wholeness toward which he aims.

II

Although the inclusion of both masculine and feminine categories in Anti-Climacus's analysis of despair is preferable to defining selfhood in terms of one sex only, the appropriateness of the sexual distinction itself remains a matter of debate. While definite physiological differences obtain between men and women, it is now widely recognized that psychological characteristics distinguishing them tend to be culturally rooted rather than biologically determined.[8] Indeed, many apparent differences turn out upon inspection to be mythical, the product of cultural stereotyping, rather than real. Thus far, psychological measurements devised for determining sex differences have shown only four such differences clearly to exist: males exhibit more aggression, better quantitative skill, and greater spatial visualization, while females excel in verbal ability.[9] There is no evidence supporting a gender difference in general intelligence, particularly the frequently held notion that women are less intelligent than men.

Anti-Climacus's views on woman and man reflect traditional stereotypes of the sexes; and, to the extent that these continue to shape cultural perceptions and patterns of social development, his characterizations are compatible with popular viewpoints in contemporary society. Yet that does not necessarily make them valid or acceptable; indeed, his views on woman's intellectuality and spirituality, or lack of these, are highly questionable.

Insofar as woman's being is typically characterized by devotedness, as Anti-Climacus claims, it may well not be an innate feature of her nature, but what she has been culturally conditioned to become (generally at the expense of forming her own separate identity). Similarly, the egocentricity that Anti-Climacus sees in males could be due to excessive encouragement of the individuation process in them, at the expense of developing a sense of relatedness to others.[10] Thus many social critics view the identification of woman and man in terms of conventional sex roles and characteristics as inhibiting their full blossoming as human beings, for these sex roles permit only a one-dimensional development of personality. Instead, social critics point to "psychological androgyny" or cultivation of both "feminine" and "masculine" characteristics in women and men as contributing to higher self-esteem and positive social adjustment.[11]

In substance, Anti-Climacus's analysis of feminine and masculine despair is in line with that of proponents of androgyny inasmuch as he diagnoses woman's despair as a lack of masculine self-identity and man's despair as defiance against feminine devotedness and submission in relation to God. Ironically, however, his use of stereotyped characterizations of the sexes contributes to the perpetuation of cultural identifications of women and men in terms of those stereotypes and thus reinforces the very despair which his analysis is designed to counteract. Insofar as Anti-Climacus's analysis is congruent with the views of contemporary advocates of androgyny, it offers a philosophical perspective that may be helpful in elucidating a common structure of selfhood in terms of the basic components of individuality (masculinity) and relatedness (femininity).[12] In at least two important respects, however, some contemporary social theorists differ from Anti-Climacus. First, over against his interpretation of despair as being essentially internally motivated or self-activated, they emphasize the need for, and impact of, change in the external structures of society so as to provide better opportunity for fuller personality development.[13] Second, whereas Anti-Climacus analyzes masculine despair only in terms of man's relation to the divine, they point to man's need to develop more receptivity, intimacy, commitment, and giving in relatedness to other human beings, especially in relation to woman.[14]

It should be noted, too, that there is considerable disagreement among women concerning the notion of androgyny and its appropriateness for women's development. While some emphasize the need for women to be self-assertive and independent like men, others acknowledge and seek to preserve a distinctive character in woman. Labeling androgyny as a patriarchal construct that results in a pseudointegrity in women, the radical feminist philosopher Mary Daly thinks woman can create a sense of selfhood that is not male-defined and that will manifest genuine differences from man, not those of traditionally defined femininity but of a kind yet to be determined, by spinning "threads of connectedness" with her sisters.[15]

Closer in line with Anti-Climacus's association of femininity with devotion, psychologist Carol Gilligan identifies "a different voice" of women evident from the centrality of attachment and care for others in their lives and from the importance of relationships for the formation of their identity.[16] Claiming that "we know ourselves as separate only insofar as we live in connection with others," she finds in women's development a fusion of separation and attachment, identity and intimacy.[17] If that is true, Gilligan provides an important corrective to Anti-Climacus in pointing to an interdependence of self-identity and relatedness in women.

Although Anti-Climacus stresses devotion to others in woman's being, he views it as a potential mode of despair for her in that she tends to lose herself in the object of her devotion. Certainly that can and often does happen, but the possibility of despair does not negate the importance of relatedness in forming self-identity. It is the integral intertwining of these two components of selfhood that Anti-Climacus does not sufficiently recognize and incorporate in his analysis. He rightly sees a need for both separateness and relatedness, but for him they appear to be separate categories, so that he fails to perceive the actual interconnection between them. Although Gilligan finds such an interconnection typifying women's development, this possibility can be extended to males, for with them also identity and relatedness are undoubtedly connected, even if perhaps in a somewhat different way. Thus, without negating sexual differences, one can ultimately look beyond them to a common model of selfhood not defined by gender. Since Anti-Climacus carries out much of his analysis of selfhood and despair without regard to the sexes and in other works emphasizes our common humanity, the thrust of his analysis is in this direction.

How, then, shall we finally assess Anti-Climacus's use of sexual categories in the analysis of human despair? While a distinction between the forms of despair can be made without them, they enable Anti-Climacus to bring more concreteness and specificity into his analysis, as well as to account for what he perceives as differences between the sexes in the experience of despair. Insofar as it is historically true that the lives of males and females have been characterized by patterns traditionally associated with masculinity and femininity, he provides an astute analysis of the connection between the forms of despair and these modes of sexual identity. In particular, his linking of despair with submissive self-abandonment on the part of women and defiant self-assertiveness by men illumines some of the dangers and limitations of traditional feminine and masculine modes. His pointing in the direction of androgyny within a common structure of selfhood for the sexes provides a conceptual basis for a fuller development of individuality and relatedness in both sexes. We can further appreciate the depth to which Anti-Climacus's analysis goes in showing a fundamental connection of despair in woman and man with a misrelation to the divine. The idea of a relation to God coupling a high level of self-consciousness with devotion or self-giving establishes an ultimate matrix within which to affirm both individuality and relatedness in woman and man.

Despite these positive features, there are several aspects of Anti-Climacus's analysis that remain unsatisfactory. First, it perpetuates stereotyped views of woman and man that are in some cases erroneous or unsubstantiated, in others perhaps historically accurate but largely the product of cultural conditioning unfavorable to the full development of both sexes. Second, it does not take sufficient account of the influence of external factors in occasioning and potentially overcoming despair. On a more theoretical level, his analysis fails to incorporate clearly or adequately relations to others besides God in the general description of a self and in particular as an essential dimension of male self-identity. Furthermore, it does not recognize the integral interdependence of individuality and relatedness to others in the formation of the self, particularly in female development. Finally, we may wonder whether feminine devotedness provides an appropriate model for the relation to God inasmuch as it traditionally involves a form of submissiveness that is often made the basis for male dominance over women. Indeed, another pseudonym, Johannes Climacus, points to a less hierarchical model for the divine-human relation, and thus also for human relations, in *Philosophical Fragments*, where in the parable of a King and a Maiden (*PF*, 26–35), the two are made equal in love.

Notes

1. Recent studies of selfhood and despair in Kierkegaard's writings that do not treat the distinction between masculine and feminine despair include Mark C. Taylor, *Kierkegaard's Pseudonymous Authorship: A Study of Time and the Self* (Princeton: Princeton University Press, 1975) as well as his *Journeys to Selfhood: Hegel and Kierkegaard* (Berkeley and Los Angeles: University of California Press, 1980); J. Preston Cole, *The Problematic Self in Kierkegaard and Freud* (New Haven: Yale University Press, 1971); essays in Joseph H. Smith, ed., *Kierkegaard's Truth: The Disclosure of the Self* (New Haven: Yale University Press, 1981); Kresten Nordentoft, *Kierkegaard's Psychology*, trans. Bruce H. Kirmmse (Pittsburgh: Duquesne University Press, 1978); Jann Holl, *Kierkegaards Konzeption des Selbst: Eine Untersuchung über die Voraussetzungen und Formen seines Denkens* (Meisenheim am Glan: Anton Hain, 1972); Vincent A. McCarthy, *The Phenomenology of Moods in Kierkegaard* (The Hague: Martinus Nijhoff, 1978); John Elrod, *Being and Existence in Kierkegaard's Pseudonymous Works* (Princeton: Princeton University Press, 1975); Alastair Hannay, *Kierkegaard* (London: Routledge and Kegan Paul, 1982). Libuse Lukas Miller, in *In Search of the Self: The Individual in the Thought of Kierkegaard* (Philadelphia: Muhlenberg, 1962), notes the distinction between "manly" and "womanly" despair but does not explore it in her analysis. Several studies of Kierkegaard's view of woman and man touch on or are relevant to the discussion of this distinction: Howard P. Kainz Jr., "The Relationship of Dread to Spirit in Man and Woman, According to Kierkegaard," *Modern Schoolman* 47 (1969): 1–13; Christine Garside, "Can a Woman be Good in the Same Way as a Man?" *Dialogue* 10 (1971): 534–44; Gregor Malantschuk, "Kierkegaards Syn paa Mand og Kvinde," in *Den kontroversielle Kierkegaard* (Copenhagen: Vintens Forlag, 1976), 30–61; Birgit Bertung, "Har Søren Kierkegaard foregrebet Karen Blixens og Suzanne Brøggers kvindesyn?" *Kierkegaardiana* 13 (1984): 72–83; Peter Thielst, *Søren og Regine: Kierkegaard, Kærlighed og Kønspolitik* (Copenhagen: Gyldendal, 1980) 129–31. Sylviane Agacinski, *Aparté: Conceptions et morts de Søren Kierkegaard* (Paris: Aubier-Flammarion, 1977), also contains some pertinent reflections on Kierkegaard's view of woman and sexual differences (see especially 152–62).

2. The Danish text reads: "Qvinden aegte qvindeligt styrter sig i, styrter sit Selv i Det, til hvilket hun hengiver sig. Tages nu Dette bort, saa er ogsaa hendes Selv borte, og hendes Fortvivlelse: ikke at ville være sig selv" (*Samlede Værker*, 3d ed. A. B. Drachmann, J. L. Heiberg, and H. O. Lange, 20 vols. [Copenhagen: Gyldendal, 1962–64], 15:106–7).

Emanuel Hirsch's German translation, *Die Krankheit zum Tode. Søren Kierkegaard/Gesammelte Werke*, 24–25 (Dusseldorf: Eugen Diederichs, 1957), interprets the text as I do: "das Weib echt weiblich sich, ihr Selbst hineinstürzt in das, daran sie sich hingibt. Wird nun letzteres fortgenommen, so ist auch ihr Selbst fort, und ist es ihre Verzweiflung, dass sie nicht sie selbst sein will." The older German translation by Hermann Gottsched (Jena: Eugen Diederichs, 1911) interprets it similarly. Walter Lowrie's English translation, *Fear and Trembling and The Sickness unto Death* (Princeton: Princeton University Press, 1954), unfortunately omits the crucial second sentence of the text quoted above, as well as an earlier phrase identifying devotion as a mode of despair, so that on the basis of his translation it is impossible for the reader to determine wherein woman's despair lies.

3. John Elrod in "Kierkegaard on Self and Society," *Kierkegaardiana* 11 (1980): 178–96, also notes that Kierkegaard's pseudonymous works "pay no attention to the ontological and

the epistemological roles played by the other in the development of a concept of the self." He sees *Works of Love* and all the later literature as being concerned with that deficiency, so that Kierkegaard discovers in them "a social conception of human beings based on the phenomenon of love" (181). Elrod makes a similar point in his book, *Kierkegaard and Christendom* (Princeton: Princeton University Press, 1981), treating *The Sickness unto Death* as part of the earlier pseudonymous literature even though it actually appears after *Works of Love* (131–32).

4. An important qualification should be noted here, however. Instead of devoting oneself exclusively to one other, as is the tendency in erotic love relations, in Christian self-renouncing love one is devoted to all, bestowing love equally on the basis of our common humanity. One must give up the type of devotion and boundless abandon that characterizes erotic love; such devotion, Kierkegaard maintains in *Works of Love*, is nothing more than a "devoted self-love" (cf. *WL*, 55).

5. See "The Woman That Was a Sinner," published in English with *Training in Christianity*, trans. Walter Lowrie (Princeton: Princeton University Press, 1941), 261–71.

6. Agacinski, *Aparté*, 153–55. For a similar interpretation of Kierkegaard, see Garside, "Can a Woman be Good in the Same Way as a Man?"

7. See *SUD*, 53, 56, 59, 63–65. However, excellent examples of females who manifest despair in weakness as described in *SUD* can be found in *Either/Or*, Part I, in the characters of Marie Beaumarchais, Donna Elvira, and especially Margaret in Goethe's *Faust* (*EO*, 1:176–215).

8. Janet T. Spence and Robert L. Helmreich, *Masculinity and Femininity: Their Psychological Dimensions, Correlates, and Antecedents* (Austin: University of Texas Press, 1978), 4–10, 121–22; Janet Shibley Hyde and B. G. Rosenberg, *Half the Human Experience* (Lexington, Mass.: Heath, 1976), 7 (emphasizing an interaction of biological and environmental factors); Janet Saltzman Chafetz, *Masculine/Feminine or Human? An Overview of the Sociology of Sex Roles* (Itasca, Ill.: F. E. Peacock, 1974), 4, 27.

9. Eleanor Emmons Maccoby and Carol Nagy Jacklin, *The Psychology of Sex Differences* (Stanford: Stanford University Press, 1974), 349–55.

10. This possibility is suggested also by David Bakan in *The Duality of Human Existence: Isolation and Communion in Western Man* (Boston: Beacon, 1966), 107–9.

11. J. H. Block, "Conceptions of Sex Roles: Some Cross-cultural and Longitudinal Perspectives," *American Psychologist* 28 (1973): 512–26; June Singer, *Androgyny: Toward a New Theory of Sexuality* (Garden City, N.Y.: Anchor, 1977); Barbara Lusk Forisha, *Sex Roles and Personal Awareness* (Morristown, N.J.: General Learning, 1978), 30–36; 87–105; Spence and Helmreich, *Masculinity and Femininity*, 109–110 (with references to others favoring an androgynous or dualistic approach); S. L. Bem, "The Measurement of Psychological Androgyny," *Journal of Consulting and Clinical Psychology* 42 (1974): 155–62; Judith M. Bardwick, *In Transition: How Feminism, Sexual Liberation, and the Search for Self-Fulfillment Have Altered Our Lives* (New York: Holt, Rinehart and Winston, 1979), 153–69, 177–78 (although retaining an appreciation of gender identity and differences).

12. Although working primarily out of a Whiteheadian perspective, V. C. Saiving, "Androgynous Life: A Feminist Appropriation of Process Thought," in *Feminism and Process Thought*, ed. Sheila Greeve Davaney (New York: Edwin Mellen, 1981), 11–31, seeks to develop a general model in which both individuality and relatedness are included. In an earlier, ground-breaking article, "The Human Situation: A Feminine View," published in *Journal of Religion* (April 1960) and repr. in Carol P. Christ and Judith Plaskow, eds., *Womanspirit Rising* (New York: Harper and Row, 1979), 25–42, Saiving analyzes masculine and feminine experience in a manner very similar to Anti-Climacus's, although without specific reference to his analysis of despair. Anti-Climacus's analysis is explicitly discussed and appropriated in a feminist context in Wanda Warren Berry, "Images of Sin and Salvation in Feminist Theology,"

Anglican Theological Review 60 (1978): 25–54. See also my discussion of individuality and relatedness in "Women in Love," *Soundings* 65 (1982): 352–68.

13. Hyde and Rosenberg, *Half the Human Experience*, 275–78; Bardwick, *In Transition*, 170–82. Critical of the dualistic origin of the term "androgyny" but endorsing the notion of wholeness associated with it, Rosemary Reuther, in *New Woman, New Earth: Sexist Ideologies and Human Liberation* (New York: Seabury, 1975), emphasizes the need for social, economic, and political change (24–31, 204–11). See also Maccoby and Jacklin, *Psychology of Sex Differences*, 374; Dorothy Dinnerstein, *The Mermaid and the Minotaur: Sexual Arrangements and Human Malaise* (New York: Harper and Row, 1976).

14. Bardwick, *In Transition*, 97–99, 125–29; Eugene C. Bianchi and Rosemary R. Reuther, *From Machismo to Mutuality* (New York: Paulist Press, 1976), 84–85, 96, 120; Nancy Chodorow, *The Reproduction of Mothering* (Berkeley and Los Angeles: University of California Press, 1978), 218.

15. Mary Daly, *Gyn/Ecology: The Metaethics of Radical Feminism* (Boston: Beacon, 1978), xiii, 382, 387. To Daly androgyny conveys an image of "something like John Travolta and Farrah Fawcett-Majors scotch-taped together" (xi). Naomi Goldenberg, in *Changing of the Gods: Feminism and the End of Traditional Religions* (Boston: Beacon, 1979), finds some value in the figure of androgyny if it is used to inspire the imagining of a plurality of sexual styles, but she envisions a distinctly feminine form of religion and identity for women in the return to Goddess worship (78–81).

16. Carol Gilligan, *In a Different Voice: Psychological Theory and Women's Development* (Cambridge: Harvard University Press, 1982). See also Saiving, "The Human Situation: A Feminine View."

17. Gilligan, *In a Different Voice*, 63, 156, 159, 164. See also Christine Downing, *The Goddess: Mythological Images of the Feminine* (New York: Crossroad, 1981), which envisions for woman an "Aphroditic consciousness," that is, a "loving consciousness" and a "being conscious in relationship" (202–7).

10

Kierkegaard and the Feminine Self

Leslie A. Howe

Kierkegaard's writings offer us a rich and often devastatingly insightful analysis of human selfhood; indeed, it could well be argued that the core of the Authorship, which includes all those works that Kierkegaard published under his own name and under the names of various pseudonyms, is built around the question of how one becomes one's true and best self, considered in ethical and religious terms. There is, however, an ambiguity in much of Kierkegaard's writing regarding how women fit into this picture. On the one hand, he appears to be elaborating a distinctly egalitarian or even androgynist ideal; on the other, he appears to be excluding women from the possibility of attaining full selfhood. Thus he argues in the same work that, essentially, there is no distinction between man and woman (SUD, 49 n) and also that woman is constituted by a "lower synthesis" than that of man (*SUD*, 67). What are we to make of this? Is this simply a rather banal expression of culturally conditioned attitudes, inadequately overcome by a more considered reflection, or are we really seeing the indications of a much more deeply embedded, and even systematic, philosophical misogyny?

In this essay, I explore Kierkegaard's views on the nature of the feminine self, and I offer some answers to the question of just how women fit into Kierkegaard's analysis of human selfhood. In the process, I consider the question of whether Kierkegaard does, in fact, present us with an androgynist ideal. This question arises for a number of reasons. First of all, given the ways he distinguishes "feminine" and "masculine" characteristics, this may be his one escape from the charge of misogyny; that is, if what he is really arguing for is the recognition of the necessity for each human being to put together in herself or himself a balance of very different, though equally essential, human characteristics or capacities. And, on the face of it, his remarks concerning the essential similarity of man and woman would seem to lend support to such an interpretation.

From a more general point of view, whether a feminist philosophy of religion would necessarily be concerned to establish such an ideal is certainly open to a great deal more discussion. However, we might well be disposed to consider the appropriateness of androgyny as an ideal of selfhood if we also happened to favor two basic assumptions. First, that the differences between women and men that at the present seem to be so obvious are in some ultimate sense unessential or unimportant—in other words, that all human beings are, as such, and in all the ways that finally matter, fundamentally the same kind of creatures. This sort of claim may well make more sense in a religious context (or, more specifically, certain kinds of Christian context) than in a secular one, as it is precisely the contrast of the human with the divine that is supposed to show the vanity of human distinctions. Second, one would have to be inclined to suppose that these distinctions are worth overcoming, particularly if doing so allows one to perfect one's relationship to the divine.

These, suffice it to say, are large assumptions that themselves raise a number of additional issues. For example, exactly what human characteristics or capacities are important in developing the God-relation? This becomes at once a more pressing and a more difficult question if one also accepts that most or all such characteristics and capacities are contingently acquired. I do not propose to explore all of these issues here. But it should be pointed out that the two assumptions just stated have a particular pertinence to the Christian context within which Kierkegaard pursues his discussion. Insofar as the relationship to the divine is the most important one that a human being can have, and is that which determines the boundaries of ideal selfhood, the contingently human has its significance primarily as that which is to be overcome in favor of this relationship. Consequently, Kierkegaard's understanding of the self, and of what is required for a human being to become a true and fully developed self, depends upon a particular understanding of the divine, and of the nature of the relation in which human beings stand to the divine.

Having said all this, however, one of the things I argue in the following is that, although Kierkegaard does seem to make the previous two assumptions, it is also the case that he makes a number of other assumptions concerning the respective natures of men and women that conflict with the former. Thus, I show that, in fact, Kierkegaard does not present us with an androgynist ideal of selfhood, though he does provide us with some important foundations for such an ideal.

I

The human self, for Kierkegaard, is a synthesis of several pairs of complementary elements: finitude and infinitude, possibility and necessity, the temporal and the eternal. What this means for a human person in more practical terms is, in the first case, that one can exercise the infinity of one's will, feeling, and imagination in order to extend oneself beyond the finite limitations of one's actual physical being while yet remaining anchored within them. That is, we can have knowledge and awareness of things that we have never ourselves experienced directly. Thus, we can understand another person's situation; we can write and appreciate fiction and poetry; we can invent new devices, and so on. In the second case, one exists in the natural world, subject to the necessities of physical causes and influences, the whole complex of natural inevitabilities, but at the same time, not all of one's existence is determined by forces outside of one's own control; one has possibility beyond the statistically predictable. So, even if it should be the case that our life or death, poverty or prosperity, is in the hands of others, still we ourselves determine what meaning this has for us as the particular individuals that we ourselves are. Finally, each person has a temporal history, but, for each of us, our existence expresses more than merely an extended spatiotemporal location. Our definition, our peculiar identities, amount to more than the immediately traceable details of our historical, geographical, and sociological itineraries. This "more" is the eternal in us, and it can be represented in us by love, the good, ethical life, or the search for God. As individuals we are not simply units, making up a discrete quantity of a species; our significance includes, but also transcends, the biochemical transience of temporal existence.

These elements are said to be held in relation to each other by spirit, and this relating of one element to another can be either unconscious (where spirit is said to be "dreaming" [CA, 41–44, 48–49, 91]) or self-conscious (the self relates "itself to itself in the relation" [SUD, 13]). This question of the consciousness of spirit is absolutely crucial, since in the former case one does not really have a self in the proper sense of the word, and it is only in the latter case that one can even begin the task of becoming one's ideal self, the existential task that confronts every human being. It is also in the latter case that spirit manifests itself as spirit—an expression that needs some explanation. "Spirit," of course, is not a *thing* (like some kind of ghost, if ghosts are things); it is a relation. Spirit is, essentially, freedom. When spirit expresses itself, the self has now become aware of itself as a free (as well as actual) being. That is, the self becomes conscious for the first time of its own relation to itself, of its parts to each other, and thus of both its actual existence (the way it is) and its possible existence (the way it might be): it is free, which it can only be if it is self-conscious. And freedom, in the first instance, is simply this awareness/consciousness of the relation between actuality and possibility in oneself. In the second instance, it is the attitude one takes to this consciousness. Only at this point can an individual become an ethical being. Thus spirit/freedom, self-consciousness, and ethical existence are inseparable.

The self-conscious person is able self-consciously to affect the relationship, or balance, of the elements constitutive of the synthesis. One can self-consciously lose oneself (one's everydayness) in imagination (infinity), and so on. But this sort of thing can also happen unconsciously. That is to say, consciously or not, one can get out of balance with oneself. Instead of an equilibrium of essential elements or capacities, the self leans to one side or the other of its constitutive synthesis: too much necessity, not enough possibility, for example. In the terminology of Anti-Climacus, the pseudonymous author of *The Sickness unto Death*, this amounts to despair. Clearly the psychologically healthy self, the self that is constituted as it ought to be, is one that is in perfect equilibrium—a state that will also require self-consciousness to be attained and maintained. All the forms of despair that Anti-Climacus enumerates involve the failure of human individuals to keep in equilibrium their actual and ideal selves.[1] He makes a number of distinctions, but only one concerns us here, namely, that between "masculine" and "feminine" despair.

"Masculine" despair, as Anti-Climacus defines it, is despair in defiance, it is "in despair to will to be oneself" (SUD, 67), whereas "feminine" despair is despair in weakness, or "in despair not to will to be oneself" (SUD, 49).[2] These designations of "masculine"/"feminine" hinge, in the first instance, on the characterizations of these two kinds of despair as involving in the one case self-assertion or egocentricity, and, in the other, weakness or (self-)flight. In the second instance, of course, they hinge on the association of these characteristics with men and with women, respectively.

Anti-Climacus himself expresses some reservations about this association and offers the observation that some women may, in exceptional cases, manifest masculine despair, and vice versa. He is describing ideal categories, and ideals are rarely encountered in the real world (SUD, 49 n). Nevertheless, he goes on to argue, there *are* characteristics definitive of woman and of man that are distinct and that justify these designations: "However much more tender and sensitive woman may be than man, she has neither the egotistical concept of the self nor, in a decisive sense, intellectuality. But the feminine nature is devotedness, givingness, and it is unfeminine if it is not that. . . . Devotedness is the one unique quality that woman has, and that is also why nature took it upon itself to be her guardian" (SUD, 49 n). Man is characterized by reflection, by spirit (SUD, 67), and fulfills himself by taking hold of himself; that is, by self-assertion, putting himself apart from the immediate. Woman, by contrast, is characterized by the natural, that is, by instinct and the immediate, and by a need to fulfill herself, to become her true self, through devotedness. Woman becomes herself by giving herself:

> In devotion she loses herself, and only then is she happy, only then is she herself; a woman who is happy without devotion, that is, without giving her self, no matter to what she gives it, is altogether unfeminine. A man also gives himself—and he is a poor kind of man who does not do so—but his self is not devotion (this is the expression for feminine substantive devotion), nor does he

gain his self by devotion, as woman in another sense does; he has himself. He gives himself, but his self remains behind as a sober awareness of devotion, whereas woman, with genuine femininity, abandons herself, throws her self into that to which she devotes herself. (*SUD*, 49 n)

As Sylvia Walsh's discussion of feminine and masculine despair points out, the two classes of despair correspond less to separate categories than to a continuum of despair, one that begins with the most rudimentary consciousness of despair and ends with the most profound (and demonic) defiance of God. At each period in this continuum the self has a more intense awareness of self and its despairing condition. Greater intensity corresponds to greater self-discernment and self-individuation (or as Anti-Climacus would have it: "the more consciousness, the more self" [*SUD*, 29]). Feminine despair is associated with the earlier portion of this continuum, where there is a relative lack of individuation; masculine despair is associated with an *excess* of this self-differentiation. This leads Walsh (1987) to the observation that, whereas "feminine" despair (the failure to will to be oneself) is a lack of "masculine" self-assertion (i.e., in effect, willing oneself), "masculine" despair—defiance—"results from an individual's unwillingness to adopt a feminine mode of selfhood" (128). The defiant individual asserts himself, or rather, the self he wishes to make himself into, against God, refusing to accept himself as the self that God made him to be. The cure is for him to learn to yield that self that he wills to be, to submit himself to God, and allow God to teach him what he is to will for himself. He needs to become more "feminine," less "masculine."[3]

As Walsh puts it, the "pathway to selfhood thus includes both masculine and feminine modes of relating, and the possibility of going astray on this path arises in corresponding forms of despair. . . . Thus the feminine mode is inextricably involved in the process of becoming a self" (1987, 128–29). Or, as we might also express it, the equilibrium necessary for the psychological health of the human self includes a balance of both feminine and masculine "modes of relating" to oneself and to one's environment. As it happens, Anti-Climacus describes the condition of not being in despair, that is, faith, as follows: "In relating itself to itself and in willing to be itself, the self rests transparently in the power that established it" (*SUD*, 14, 49). This formula seems clearly to incorporate both the assertive self-choice associated with the "masculine" and the self-less confidence that characterizes the "feminine." Hence it would appear that the ideal of human selfhood presented in *The Sickness unto Death* is one of psychological androgyny, which holds both feminine and masculine qualities to be equally valuable and equally necessary for a fully developed and healthy human individual, of either sex.

Although this is in many ways an attractive conclusion, however, there are at least two major reasons to suspect its validity. The first has to do with the weight of the characterizations of woman and the feminine throughout the Authorship; the second has to do with the two-tiered structure of the process of acquiring ideal selfhood, that is, the fact that one has two relations to effect: that to oneself and that to God. As I shall show, there is reason to suspect that, if woman in reality bore any close resemblance to the way in which she is characterized in the Authorship, she could never carry out the full task of selfhood—or, at least, not nearly so well as man.

Anti-Climacus himself observes that femininity constitutes a "lower synthesis" (*SUD*, 67). This characterization is not explained in *The Sickness unto Death*, though we can surmise that he is perhaps referring to the relative lack of consciousness present in the kind of despair that is designated as "feminine." It should be noted that woman does not, on this analysis, lack spirit altogether. To be a synthesis at all requires spirit (see *SUD*, 13–17), but it would appear that, for Kierkegaard, spirit in woman does not manifest (or rarely manifests) itself *as spirit:* spirit in woman stays dreaming. This also means that woman never (or rarely) becomes a truly self-conscious self, one that is fully aware of itself in reflection, and thus one that can participate in ethical society as a full and equal member. Woman is, in effect, nature's innocent (even when she strays). Consequently, as we have seen, although "feminine" despair, like "masculine" despair, requires some degree of consciousness, the consciousness involved could be quite minimal. The important point is that the degree of consciousness *increases* with "masculine" despair.

If we explore the rest of the Authorship, we find a near-constant set of associations between woman and the feminine, on the one hand, and absence of spirit and consciousness, especially self-consciousness, on the other. The pivotal association, however, is with *nature*.

II

In those works written early in Kierkegaard's authorship dealing extensively with aesthetic themes there is a good deal of talk about woman,

much of it of perhaps questionable sincerity. Aside from the circumstances of Kierkegaard's personal life, the poetic character of the pseudonyms who are the fictional authors of these works renders the status of
their remarks hypothetical. After all, it could be argued: "Of course Johannes the Seducer says *that* about women—he's a *seducer!*" Poetic li-
cense aside, however, there is a high degree of substantive agreement
among the pseudonyms and Kierkegaard himself regarding the nature of
woman, although there is some disagreement on the subject of just what
significance woman and her nature have for man.

We find in these works that the aesthetic, and "the aesthetic stage of
existence," are associated as metaphysical categories with certain other
such categories. The most important of these, and the one that has the
most profound significance for the aesthetic mode of existence, is immediacy. Those who are immediate in their existence are governed by mood,
feeling, beauty, sensuousness, passion, and the like. They are, at one extreme, wholly determined by their environment; they *react* immediately.
This is not to say that such persons are mindless automata, but they are
incapable of determining their own actions independently of contingent
circumstances. The idea of *mood* is invaluable here: if one's surroundings
determine one's mood, and whether one acts in such and such a way is
dependent on one's mood, then one is not significantly separate from
one's environment or milieu. The motives for a person's actions then
come fundamentally from outside that person, and are not *self*-deter-
mined. If it were not that they may also be highly cultured human beings,
functioning smoothly in an environment of advanced civilization, it
would be hard to distinguish such persons, metaphysically (and ethically), from nonhuman animals: they are, in a significant sense, *natural*
creatures, at least insofar as they are in terms of identity not separable
from nature; they act from nature, never contrary to it; they are expressions of nature. Thus, Don Giovanni, who is archetypal for such a personality, is described by the admiring aesthete A, the pseudonymous author
of the first part of *Either/Or*, as being at least as much a force of nature as
an individual (*EO*, 1:96).

Immediacy is contrasted with reflection. Don Giovanni does not reflect
on his nature, on his actions, on the question of whether he ought to act
in one way rather than another; he simply acts. Although all aesthetes
seek the immediacy of experience that such creatures as Don Giovanni
enjoy, it is not the case that all aesthetes lack reflection in this way.
Indeed, it requires reflection deliberately to seek out immediate experi-

ences, although, since one is reflective and not purely immediate, those experiences will (perhaps) never have quite the same depth of *immediacy* as they would if one were not so reflective. A is just such a reflective aesthete, as are Johannes the Seducer, Constantin Constantius, and Victor Eremita. So, although immediacy and reflection are, as such, mutually exclusive, the aesthetic can, and usually does, include both (at least for the aesthete). Reflection permits the aesthetically inclined individual to appreciate the object of his admiration in a particular way, but also to arrange or affect that which he enjoys so that he can enjoy it even more deliberately. Thus his enjoyment is also heightened in a certain respect. This is something that the individual who lacks reflectiveness is never able to do.

Reflection is also essential for ethical existence, although reflection in and of itself can never make one into an ethical being.[4] The ethical requires a decision, which is essentially an act of passion, although one that runs counter to all that the aesthete stands for. For a person to be able to carry out a decision, that person must already have attained sufficient reflectiveness to be able to separate his or her own existence from the environment/milieu, to be able to understand himself or herself as a distinct self that is capable of acting and choosing independently of all environmental factors and influences. Even the reflective aesthete is reluctant to act independently to the requisite degree; hence the aesthetic individual never acts in a decisive way. Or, as it might also be expressed: the aesthetic individual never fully becomes *spirit*. The "decision to decide," which is at the very basis of the ethical, is the act of "positing oneself as spirit"; that is, a free and responsible being, a self aware of itself as a self. Thus, to the same degree that reflectiveness and immediacy are opposed, so also are the ethical and immediacy.

Now, woman is described by the aesthetic personalities in terms that place her definitively within the realm of the immediate, the natural, that which is to be enjoyed on an aesthetic level. Perhaps the most striking example of this is an extended passage in "The Seducer's Diary," in *Either/Or*, Part I, where Johannes explains that both femininity in general and all of nature are being-for-other, in the sense that by itself neither has meaning, until apprehended by something that can put an interpretation upon it, put it into relation to itself:

> So she is being-for-other. Here in turn, from a different angle, we must not let ourselves be disturbed by experience, which teaches

us that very seldom do we meet a woman who is truly being-for-other, since the great majority usually are not entities at all, either for themselves or for others. She shares this qualification with all nature, with all femininity in general. All nature is only for-other in this way, not in the teleological sense, in such a way that one specific segment of nature is for another specific segment, but the whole of nature is for-other—is for spirit. It is the same again with the particular. Plant life, for example, in all naïveté unfolds its hidden charms and is only for-other. Likewise, an enigma, a charade, a secret, a vowel, etc. are merely being-for-other. This explains why God, when he created Eve, had a deep sleep fall upon Adam, for woman is man's dream. The story teaches us in another way that woman is being-for-other. That is, it says that Jehovah took one of man's ribs. If he had, for example, taken from man's brain, woman would certainly have continued to be being-for-other, but the purpose was not that she should be a figment of the brain but something quite different. She became flesh and blood, but precisely thereby she falls within the category of nature, which essentially is being-for-other. Not until she is touched by erotic love does she awaken; before that time she is a dream. But in this dream existence two stages can be distinguished: in the first, love dreams about her; in the second, she dreams about love. (EO, 1:430)

By itself such being has no direction; it is purposeless (dreaming) until directed by spirit—which comes from outside. And hence woman, as he says, is characterized by virginity, which is in itself an abstraction, which has meaning only in relation to something else (EO, 1:430–31).

The association of woman with nature is especially underscored by Johannes's repeated likening of her existence to that of plants. Thus, "Woman's being (the word 'existence' already says too much, for she does not subsist out of herself) is correctly designated as gracefulness, an expression that is reminiscent of vegetative life; she is like a flower, as the poets are fond of saying, and even the intellectual is present in her in a vegetative way" (EO, 1:431). What is really significant about this association, however, are the conclusions he draws from it. In particular, because woman "belongs altogether to the category of nature," she is "free only aesthetically" (EO, 1:431). By this he would appear to mean that she is free to follow her moods as she pleases. True ethical freedom, by contrast, involves being able to decide independently of one's moods, feelings, and environment. Insofar as one does not control the environment that determines one's moods (and this external control is precisely the aim of the seducer), one is only minimally free; one does as one pleases, but one is not free to determine for oneself what that is which pleases. "Aesthetic freedom," then, is a kind of false consciousness, which in this case is also a deliberately deceitful construction.

But, for aesthetes such as Johannes, the falsity is entirely justified by the end that is to be achieved—an aesthetic ideal of beauty, which, being an ideal (and hence reflective) construction, lifts woman out of the realm of the purely natural, the vegetative. This gives her a significance she would not otherwise have. Indeed, woman *should not* have any reflective qualities of her own; the aesthetic demands that she come to the situation unformed, a *tabula rasa*, in effect. A girl should not be interesting in her own right, as this implies reflection, and hence individuality and spirit—distinctively masculine qualities.[5] Reflection and the interesting involve an engagement of the intellect that is inappropriate in girls as they are to be enjoyed aesthetically. The interesting is something that is produced in her by the male's reflectiveness acting upon her. A female reflectiveness (brought about by associating with other girls) unsettles this relationship, and makes her unsuitable for the role of male companion (*EO*, 1:339–40).[6]

Intellect [*Aand*] is, in some sense, opposed to beauty. Thus the Seducer opines that a man cannot conquer a woman with masculine beauty, but only with intellect, which, as it is nothing to her and negates her entire womanly existence, generates anxiety, which in turn generates the interesting (*EO*, 1:362).

Woman's distance from reflection, and closeness to anxiety, is elaborated on by the pseudonym Vigilius Haufniensis in *The Concept of Anxiety* (see especially 63–67). The degree of sensuousness in a person, it seems, is proportional to that of anxiety, and vice versa. Woman is more anxious than man because she is more sensuous, and she is more sensuous because she is, among other things, derived. Both man and woman are created beings, and each subsequent individual in the continuing history of the human race is derived from those who arrived before, but, since Adam was first and Eve derived from Adam, woman is "more" derived than man (*CA*, 63–64). The relationship of generation, then, imparts a "more" to the subsequent individual that is a "more" of sensuousness, and of anxiety, as well as a quantitative accumulation of the history of human sinning in the context of which the individual must endeavor to avoid personal sin.

Vigilius thinks that the fact that woman is more sensuous than man is evident in her physical structure—an observation that he chooses not to explain further. However, he also argues that, "viewed ethically, woman culminates in procreation," which indicates that she is more sensuous (CA, 64, 66). According to Vigilius, at the moments of conception and of childbirth, the woman is at one extreme of the synthesis, and consequently spirit (which holds the two "ends" of the synthesis together, and which therefore has nothing to do at this time) is pushed to the side, or "suspended." Both events are extremes of sensuousness, thus, for Vigilius, extremes of anxiety (72). Why these events should be the culmination of woman's ethical task, however, is unclear. Unless, that is, we also assume that woman is constitutionally unsuited (by her sensuousness) to the tasks of spirit.

That woman is more sensuous than man is also exemplified by the particular nature of woman's beauty. "When beauty must reign, a synthesis results, from which spirit is excluded" (CA, 65). Thus, Vigilius argues, inspired by the Greeks, a woman is most beautiful when represented as sleeping, as this is a state in which spirit is absent, whereas for a man, who is characterized by spirit, this would be the most unattractive mode of representation.

What we have here, then, is a fairly consistent identification of woman with the physical or natural (including instinct), and of man with spirit or reflection (consciousness).[7] Despite the occasional association of woman with the infinite, she is most often put in relation to the finite. This is especially evident in Judge William, whose response to the aesthete A constitutes the second volume of Either/Or, and who describes woman as having been created to deal with, indeed to save man from having to deal with, minutiae (EO, 2:68). He describes her as being in harmony with time (306–7), as having an innate ability to explain the finite (310), as Nature's mistress, associated with the earth, as man is with heaven (310–13).[8] Vigilius's emphasis on woman's procreative role is echoed by William in his praise of mother love: a woman's development is not complete until she is a mother (SLW, 131–35).[9] Also, William too identifies woman with the aesthetic and, consequently, thinks that her natural immediacy (including the tendency to romanticism) gives her an edge in getting to faith; for her it is an easy transition from the first to the second immediacy, without reflection (166–67). Of course, this therefore also suggests that woman does not attain the degree of reflection that man does, which William otherwise holds to be a necessary intermediate stage for man to get to the ethical.

What all of these authors agree on is woman's comparative lack of consciousness. William, for example, puts a (perhaps unwholesome) stress on woman's childlike qualities (*EO*, 2:310), and argues that she does not and should not have reflection the way a man does (*SLW*, 166). As previously noted, Johannes argues that, for the sake of the aesthetic ideal, a girl should be isolated from other girls, lest she develop an unseemly (masculine) reflectivity (*EO*, 1:339–40). He also argues that it is precisely woman's innocence, her lack of self-consciousness, that is alluring: "This is how woman tempts" (*SLW*, 78). Moreover, she wants to be seduced; she is better off for being seduced.[10] Finally, she does not die as a man does; she dissolves, as a dream, since that is what she is (*SLW*, 77–80). Constantin regards woman as fundamentally irrational, and Victor Eremita as completely unaware that her entire existence is a negative one (*SLW*, 52–56, 56–65). And, as we have recently seen, Vigilius argues that a woman's proper beauty is best represented by one who is asleep, that is, unconscious.

This lack of consciousness has, of course, important consequences. The first of these is that a woman cannot become an ethical individual, as this requires reflection, and especially a reflection that effects in the individual a fully adequate concept of self. But if woman does not possess the basic requirements for becoming an ethical individual, it is also true that she does not become a self in any profound sense, as the requirements are the same: self-consciousness. Hence William's comments concerning woman's easy transition to the religious show the degree to which this pseudonymous personality misconceives the religious as well as the ethical: Throughout the second volume of *Either/Or* he argues the compatibility of aesthetic immediacy with ethical existence (specifically, the civil institution of marriage) through a religious movement (thanksgiving to God). There are many things wrong with William's views in the Kierkegaardian context alone, but the error here involves the notion that one can, first of all, retain an essentially unaltered immediacy while performing a self-conscious resolution (that defines the ethical), and second, relate oneself to God without having a self to relate.

Woman's relativity is occasionally referred to directly, but more often it is implied. Notice, for example, in "The Seducer's Diary," that Cordelia's reactions to Johannes are inevitably a reflection of his relation to her: she resonates, reacts *to him;* she never acts independently. In his attack on the emancipation of women in *Either/Or,* Judge William remarks that in trying to find her perfection through the definition of man, woman only becomes "a prey to his whims, whereas as woman she can be everything to him" (*EO,* 1:310–13). But, of course, in being everything to him, she still has her definition in relation to him.

This brings us to the question of whether there is really any significant difference between William's views and those of the other pseudonyms. It is true that William prefers to praise women and objects strongly to the critical aesthetic attitude to woman. William's celebration of woman involves seeing her "imperfections" as perfections; that is, he argues that her natural condition is to be appreciated for what it is, not altered as Johannes would do, for the sake of some artificial aesthetic ideal. As nature, finite, she is the necessary complement of man, who is, by himself, "an unstable spirit"—hence the importance of marriage to provide equilibrium (see *EO* 2:313; also *EO* 2:66–67).

But, although William rejects Johannes's instrumental alteration of women for the sake of aesthetic enjoyment, he too regards them as instrumental in providing both aesthetic enjoyment and ethical opportunity. In effect, they are still objects—the difference is whether the man needs to alter them first to make them into more enjoyable or more worthy objects. Woman is conceived, by the aesthetes and by William, as first and foremost a "helpmeet" to man's existence: she enhances his life in one way or another, but thus she is always seen as an instrument, an addendum, whether aesthetically, or as the occasion for an ethical decision on *his* part. Like disease or wealth, woman is a factor in the environment within which man develops. Woman has no decisive significance save in relation to man, whether this relation is positive or negative: just like the rest of the natural world.

III

In the acknowledged works, those that Kierkegaard published under his own name, we see two apparently contradictory trends in the attitudes expressed toward woman and the feminine. One of these continues in much the same vein as the aesthetic works, gradually increasing in the level of its hostility, until in the "attack" literature and the late Journal entries we have evidence of a particularly pronounced misogyny. The other, however, puts forward woman as the pattern for all Christian life. Once again, these two trends are not so far apart as they might seem. As before, the nature of woman is not seriously in dispute; only whether that nature is a good thing, and in particular, whether it is compatible with the demands of Christianity.

At this point, we are concerned not only with the first relation the fully realized self must effect—that is, that to itself—but also with the second: the relation to God. When the self becomes conscious of itself, one of the things it discovers is that it is a created being that must also relate itself to its creator, namely God (*SUD*, 13–14). In this God-relationship, according to Anti-Climacus, "the distinction of man-woman vanishes," and "it holds for men as well as for women that devotion is the self and that in the giving of oneself the self is gained" (*SUD*, 49 n). Thus, it appears from this that full selfhood not only is open to man and woman equally, but also actually requires feminine qualities of both—at least at the level of the God-relation. I shall return presently to the very interesting question of why these two relations should appear to have differing requirements, but for the moment, let us concentrate on this second set.

Two separate discourses on the same subject, "The Woman That Was a Sinner," put forward this woman's example as the appropriate pattern for Christian worship—for the God-relation that is required to complete the task of true selfhood. It is important to realize that there is nothing in the description of woman in these two discourses that is either at odds with, or even very different from, anything we have seen so far. Her association with love is repeated and deeply accentuated. The quality that woman has, and man has too little of, is passion, the ability to act without getting sidetracked by questions, further considerations, and technical details. Woman has a capacity to be single-minded in a way that man's capacity for reflection makes difficult for him. As Kierkegaard remarks, "*One* is woman's element. One wish, not many wishes—no, only one wish, but that with the whole soul put into it."[11] So, when it comes to the question of her relationship to her sin, which is crucial for getting rightly related to God, woman can concentrate all her attention on this, and thence to God. Thus concentrated, gaining forgiveness for her sins becomes the only thing of concern to her. In this way she becomes a pattern for man, as every human being must relate to God in this way.

The other significant obstacle that man faces in his God-relation is his self-assertion—his defiant selfhood. Man has to learn to be more like "the woman that was a sinner," and submit his self and his own ideas about what his self should be to God. The woman annihilates herself, which allows her to receive herself again from God; she loves God more than she loves herself, and in loving God she forgets herself (CD, 379–80, 382). She admits that of herself she can do nothing at all in terms of getting this relation right; she must let God do it.[12] If she were to imagine that there was something she could do herself, she would in fact be asserting herself against God, as if she did not really need him: she would be in defiance of God. Thus, the cure for the "masculine" despair of defiance is for the man to become like "the woman that was a sinner," to acquire those qualities that woman has by nature: devotedness, submission, self-abnegation, and so on.

Woman's love in this instance is praised, as it exemplifies a religious ideal. But this is not always the case. Woman's love also exemplifies the earthly, and all that is dangerous and deluded about purely human conceptions of what is ideal for human beings. The love most often associated with woman is erotic love.[13]

Kierkegaard has a number of objections to erotic love, many of which apply equally to friendship. Erotic love (as well as friendship) is partial; it separates out some small set of persons from the rest, and loves only them, to the exclusion of all others; hence it is the antithesis to neighborly love, which is the specifically Christian love (WL, 52–57). Erotic love is "a desire for this life"; it lacks the eternal quality of religious faithfulness; it "has the sadness of temporality and thus the inspiration for the poet" (WL, 311, 312). In other words, it is aesthetic, and insofar as woman's love is identified with the erotic, it is also identified with aesthetic existence—which lacks spirit and is therefore incapable of effecting a true religious relation. That Kierkegaard does make this identification is shown by the way he puts together the feminine and the distinctly human conception of what it means to love. Thus,

> In relation to what the natural man, who loves himself selfishly or loves himself in a womanly way, regards as love [Kjerlighed], friendship, and the like, Christianity resembles a hatred of what it is to be a human being, the greatest curse and torment upon what it is to be human. Indeed, even the more profound person can have many weaker moments when to him it is as if Christian-

ity were misanthropy, because in the weaker moments he wants
to coddle himself, whimper, have an easy life in the world, live in
rather quiet enjoyment. This is the effeminacy in a human being,
and therefore it is also quite certain and true that Christianity has
an uneasiness about marriage and also desires to have among its
many married servants an unmarried person, someone who is single, because Christianity is well aware that with woman and erotic
love [*Elskov*] etc. also come all the weaker, softer elements in a
person, and that insofar as the husband himself does not hit upon
them, the wife ordinarily represents them with an unconstraint
that is extremely dangerous for the husband, especially for the
one who is to serve Christianity in the stricter sense. (*PC*, 117)

Here the feminine and the feminine conception of love are clearly associated with an attachment to the things of the world, to the easy way out,
compromise, and complacency. What also comes out in this passage is
the dangerousness of a woman's love for a man who wishes to relate
himself properly to God. This notion appears in a relatively mild form in
Works of Love, where Kierkegaard offers the following admonition: "Not
only shall the person who totally belongs to God's calling not belong to
a woman, lest he be delayed by wanting to please her, but also the person
who in love belongs to a woman shall first and foremost belong totally to
God, shall not seek first to please his wife but shall first do his utmost so
that his love may please God" (*WL*, 112–13). Further along, he asks:
"How many a one has not been corrupted, in the divine sense, by a girl's
love because he, defrauded of his God-relationship, became all too faithful to her, while she in turn was inexhaustible in her eulogies of his
love?" (*WL*, 128). And in the *Instant*, we find an extended attack on the
institution of marriage (*KAUC*, 219–22).[14]

Woman's love, then, is presented in two quite different ways: it can be
the pattern for man's religious existence, and it can be a hindrance to
that very existence, interfering with a man's ability to adopt the pattern
in his own life. How can these two very different visions be reconciled?
In a sense, they do not need to be. When woman's love is praised, and
exalted as a pattern, what is praised is simply one aspect of it: the single-
mindedness, the utter devotion to the task of love. But for Kierkegaard,
what woman (ordinarily) sees as the task of love is misconceived. Woman
can only love in her characteristically immediate and possessive way; she
cannot follow the man into the dialectical realm of true Christian exis-

tence, so she ends up holding him back (see *JP*, 4:5007 [XI² A 192]). Kierkegaard's praise for woman's love, then, is *selective*; his use of it as a pattern is comparable to his use of "the birds of the air": we should be like the birds of the air in the sense that we should trust in providence—not in the sense that we should build nests of twigs and eat worms.

However, *Works of Love* in particular also develops the notion that in the relationship to God, man and woman are essentially equal. But, once again, what we see in this argument is that, insofar as what woman (or man) strives for is equality in *earthly* or *purely human* terms, she (or he) departs from what is decisively Christian. The contrast is between the purely human and the Christian. Thus those who strive to establish earthly equality completely miss the truly Christian relationship of equality before God, where each individual is answerable to God for his or her relationship:

> What abominations has the world not seen in the relationships between man and woman, that she, almost like an animal, was a disdained being in comparison with the man, a being of another species. What battles there have been to establish in a worldly way the woman in equal rights with the man—but Christianity makes only infinity's change and therefore quietly. Outwardly the old more or less remains. The man is to be the woman's master and she subservient to him; but inwardly everything is changed, changed by means of this little question to the woman, whether she has consulted with her conscience about having this man—as master, for otherwise she does not get him. Yet the conscience-question about the conscience-matter makes her in inwardness before God absolutely equal with the man. . . . In the name of Christianity, fatuous people have fatuously been busy about making it obvious in a worldly way that the woman should be established in equal rights with the man—Christianity has never required or desired this. It has done everything for the woman, provided she Christianly will be satisfied with what is Christian; if she is unwilling, then for what she loses she gains only a mediocre compensation in the fragment of externality she can in a worldly way obtain by defiance. (*WL*, 138–39)

God is the essential middle term in any human relationship (*WL*, 107–13). God "really becomes the sole object of love, so that it is not the husband who is the wife's beloved, but it is God. . . . The merely human view of love can never go beyond mutuality. . . . Christianity teaches that such a love has not yet found its true object—God. The love-relationship requires threeness: the lover, the beloved, the love—but the love is God" (121). First one relates oneself to God, in one's conscience, and only then to the other—who is then first and foremost the neighbor, which each *human being* is *essentially* (140–41). Thus it is God who teaches each of us how we should love wife or husband, and not the husband the wife or the wife the husband (112–13). In this way, it seems that each human individual is on the same footing with respect to God, at least, if not to each other in a secular sense (given that man remains woman's "master"). This would be the case if it were true that woman actually does relate to God on her own recognizance, as it were, and not only *through the man*.[15]

But then, what are we to make of the more spiteful and vitriolic attacks on women and the indirect condemnations of the feminine character that we find in the writings of Kierkegaard's final period (the journals of 1854–55 and the *Instant*)? In the *Instant* he carries on his assault on the "effeminacy" of contemporary Christendom, particularly the Danish Lutheran Church and its ministers. Under this heading he includes such traits as untruth, coquetry, duplicity, and equivocation (see esp. *KAUC*, 176). In the attack, it is clear that these are characteristics that he attributes to women. Hence the crime that these men commit against Christianity is that of feminizing it when they should be deepening the spiritual basis of Christian belief.

In the journals the criticism of official Christianity or Christendom continues hand in hand with a rejection of feminine qualities and concerns. First among these is marriage, which is condemned as one of the trivialities that fill one's life (along with one's job, children, and position) and that Christianity demands that one be willing to break with. The decadence of contemporary Protestantism is demonstrated by the fact that now "everything revolves around woman," and so around chatter, trivialities, and sexual relations (*JP*, 4:4998 [XI¹ A 141]). Indeed, the "whole business of man and woman is a very intricate plot or a practical joke intended to destroy man *qua* spirit. . . . And it follows as a matter of course that once man enters this company he is essentially lost for everything higher" (*JP*, 4:5000 [XI¹ A 226]). In other words, marriage is a devious trap in which woman "corrupts" man, by "finitizing and mediocritizing" him (*JP*, 4:5003 [XI¹ A 281]). "Man was structured for eternity; woman leads him into a side remark" (*JP*, 4:5005 [XI¹ A 426]). Marriage introduces man to an egotism that he would not otherwise know (*JP*, 4:5000 [XI¹ A 226]), and to an existence of lies, pretending that marriage is the true happiness:

> Constantly lying like this is extremely degrading to the man. It is different for a woman; she is once and for all a born virtuoso in lying, is really never happy without a little lying, just as it is *a priori* certain that wherever a woman is there is a little lying. In a sense she is innocent in this; she cannot help it. It is not possible to get angry about it: on the contrary, we find it very attractive. She is in the power of a natural disposition which uses her with extreme cunning to weaken the man. (*JP*, 4:4998 [XI¹ A 141])

Thus, at the start and at the end of Kierkegaard's writings, woman appears as a barely conscious locus of natural forces.

Now, as Julia Watkin (1991) rightly points out (89), this later Kierkegaardian polemic is *not* specifically an attack on woman per se (perhaps none of Kierkegaard's remarks on the subject form part of such a deliberate attack), but it is in fact directed at those (the Judge Williams of the church, as it were) who would, in his view, turn Christianity into a complacent comfy-bourgeois compromise with the world. As such, his comments are consistent with the whole of his religious project, and do not represent any radical shift in attitude. Nor, as we can now see, do they represent any very significant shift in attitude to women. What is rejected first and foremost is a preoccupation with the earthly, with purely human distinctions, and whatever distracts one's attention from one's spiritual relationship to God and the truths of Christianity. Strictly speaking, woman is not the problem; spiritual vacuity is. However, having said this, it cannot be overlooked that woman is nevertheless deemed by Kierkegaard to be an appropriate stick with which to beat his opponents. Whether she is his target or not, the association *is* made, by Kierkegaard, between spiritual degradation and woman.

And yet, we also have Kierkegaard's (and Anti-Climacus's) claims to the effect that, before God, man and woman are essentially similar. As remarked earlier, the two relations involved in human selfhood appear to have differing requirements. It is time now to examine more closely the relationship between these two relations.

IV

Why is it that, in the God-relation, man and woman are essentially un-important distinctions, whereas no such claim is made for the first rela-tion of ordinary self-consciousness? One fairly obvious answer is that in the first relation, an individual learns about the self that he or she actu-ally is, here and now, and comes to a realization of what is possible for him or her. One of the things that we inevitably are (so such an explana-tion might run) is male or female, and which of these we happen to be does make a certain amount of difference not only for what each of us is now but also for what we might become, in short, for the way in which we relate to ourselves. On the ordinary, secular level, sex matters.

However, in relation to God, such differences are meaningless. These distinctions, like those between rich and poor, powerful and weak, shrink into insignificance in comparison with the gulf that separates God from the merely human. The Word of God cuts through these distinctions to lay a command upon each human being, to which each must respond, in the ways open to him or her.

Now, while it is true that sex matters at the secular level, what is not clear is how deeply it matters, at least for Kierkegaard. That is, does he regard the difference as surmountable, at either the secular or the reli-gious level? Sylvia Walsh (1987) seems to suggest that Kierkegaard's anal-ysis of the self and of masculine and feminine despair could allow us to interpret the situation something like this: the fact that the first relation of selfhood neither requires nor expects equality of men and women while the second presupposes it merely reflects the difference between the essential nature of human beings as metaphysical and moral equals and the actuality of their existence as historically constrained and cultur-ally conditioned beings (129–34). Thus, men and women being what they are, or have been made into, culturally and sociologically, it is a contingent fact that each is prone to develop in one way rather than another, thus justifying the designations "masculine"/"feminine" for each type of behavior. Men and women relate differently to themselves, suc-ceed better or worse at the project of becoming selves, because history and society have joined forces to make them that way, not because God fashioned them from different molds. In the relationship to God these differences are fundamentally irrelevant and without meaning: here all humans are essentially similar, because here what is at issue is what humans are *essentially*, underneath all the contingent conditioning. In fact, the ideal human self is one that overcomes the traditional stereotypes, and moves away from the excessive "masculinity" of defiant despair and the "feminine" egolessness and identification with the other characteristic of the despair of weakness, toward the equilibrium of an androgynist combination of modes of relating.

On an account such as this, all that condemnation of "effeminacy" in the attack literature, as well as the ridicule of woman in the early aesthetic works are really a rejection of the *stereotype*, of the deficient creature that society has made, not of woman herself.[16] The difference, then, is surmountable at the religious level, and possibly also at the secular, though this would require a society rather different from any that Kierkegaard experienced or perhaps even envisaged. It has to be admitted that this question of whether Kierkegaard was talking about women in general, or whether he was only criticizing the women *of his time* as contingently unrealized selves, is crucial. It makes all the difference for whether he was a common misogynist or some sort of ironical feminist. But a number of obstacles stand in the way of the latter interpretation. First of all, Kierkegaard's expression gives every indication of being absolutist: woman is essentially as he describes her. Individual histories may vary in their details, not the category "woman" (or "man"). There is a dearth of positive evidence to support the notion that Kierkegaard entertained the view that under some alternative sociocultural regime woman either could or should be significantly different from the way in which he describes her. (At least, that is, in terms of her basic *nature*; it is plain that Kierkegaard demands as much a change in *behavior* from women as he does from men.) Indeed, there is plenty of evidence to show that he thought the attempt to alter the prevailing structures to border on the perverse, though it must also be said that the main thrust of his criticism of such efforts is that they tend to miss the point existentially (in effect, making us bean-counters of rights, instead of existentially responsible human beings) (see *EO*, 2:311–13; *TA*, 77–96; *WL*, Part 2, chap. 7). Clearly, he thought the difference surmountable at the religious level, but it takes a highly imaginative reading of Kierkegaard to find this happening at the secular level. Moreover, Vigilius's references to the biblical account of the creation of Eve in support of his statements about the nature of woman, as in *The Concept of Anxiety*, would seem to offer some (admittedly indirect) support for the contention that Kierkegaard's views on the subject of women are essentialist, not accidentalist.

More important, however, it is questionable whether such an account can get around a more serious problem with Kierkegaard's analysis of the self. And that concerns the matter of whether woman, equal with man in the God-relation, can in fact carry out this relation on her own behalf. In other words, whether the sexual difference is truly surmountable at the religious level. This is a problem precisely because there are *two* relations involved, and this is the *second* one.

Recall Anti-Climacus's remark that femininity is a "lower synthesis." Although, on the one hand, "essentially" man and woman are the same, in that both are constituted by a synthesis of complementary factors held together by spirit, on the other (as Vigilius explains), woman's synthesis is naturally heavily tilted to one side, to the "more" of sensuousness and the comparative absence of conscious spirit. Woman's existence is determined by nature and instinct to a far greater degree than is man's. Of course, this "more" would not by itself have to mean that woman is a less worthy self. On the contrary, the "more" translates into a tougher struggle for woman to become a self, but precisely for that reason, if she succeeds, she becomes a more perfect self (see CA, 64, 72; Bertung 1989)—though the difficulty involved might mean that fewer women succeed than men.[17]

However, insofar as the "lower" quality in the feminine synthesis is explained by women's *biology*, it is difficult to see how the general failure of women to become selves could be put down to purely historical circumstances and cultural expectations. For Kierkegaard, this could hardly have seemed sociologically contingent. Furthermore, insofar as this "more" of sensuousness and instinct also entails a lack of *consciousness*, woman is not, generally speaking, self-defining. She is relative, while man is absolute.[18] Woman's existence is defined by her relation to another (usually man), but the same is not true for man who is defined by his relation to his self (which he has independently) (see SUD, 49 n). Woman may well provide the occasion for his effecting this relation, but she is not the essential factor in it (as the man is for her).

This, then, leaves us with an apparently irresolvable difference between man and woman in terms of the latter's possibility/possibilities for selfhood: how she becomes a self, and even whether she can become a self. If, when Kierkegaard or Anti-Climacus says that woman becomes herself (devotedness) by instinct, author or pseudonym means that this self she becomes is her true self, in the sense of the self she ought to be, then it is clear that woman becomes the self she ought to be *by instinct*. If self-consciousness is otherwise held to be crucial for selfhood (which does seem to be the case),[19] and if woman becomes what she ought to be without it, then (although *some* women may become themselves self-consciously) the self that woman ought to become is a significantly different kind of self that that which man ought to become. And this difference is more than simply one of sex: woman is not so fully developed a self as man. If, indeed, she is properly speaking a self at all, she is, in one important respect at least, a lesser self.

Man, being self-conscious, has to learn to give himself in devotion to God; he has to *learn* to do self-consciously what woman does by instinct. Could all this simply mean that man and woman have each their different, but equally valid, "modes of relating" to God? Not if self-consciousness is itself a superior "mode of relating" to oneself and the world than instinct. If so, the man's devotion to God is superior to woman's, even though devotion is what characterizes woman's nature and is what man must learn from her; man fulfills woman's task better than she can herself.[20] In this case, woman cannot have a relation to God that is comparable to man's, either because she does not have a self to relate or because she just cannot do it as well (see also Garside 1971).

Now, if man and woman do not relate the same way to God, then it is difficult to see what sense there is in saying that in the God-relation the distinction vanishes. Clearly, if the foregoing is true, man and woman are not equal before God. Or, they are only equal in the purely formal way that a peasant and an aristocrat are equal before the law: both are subject to the rule of law, but, in concrete terms, they face quite different sets of laws. In this context, we can see that the claim that Kierkegaard makes in the *Journals* to the effect that Christianity is a man's religion[21] is not particularly at odds with the implications of the rest of his writings.

Finally, I wish to make a few observations about the androgynist ideal that Kierkegaard seems at times to be putting forward. Given that the God-relation can be expected to transform one's ordinary human relations, one could expect that a religious ideal that was fundamentally androgynist might well motivate a restructuring of such relations. Such a relationship between the religious and the ethical is certainly evident in *Works of Love*. Thus, if Kierkegaard had held a truly androgynist ideal we might expect to see evidence of such a restructuring. However, the most we could say of the ideal presented in *Works of Love* (and this might be too much, for the reasons just presented) is that it is egalitarian, not that it is androgynist. As I have already argued, when Kierkegaard praises the feminine character, he does so *selectively*. The feminine quality (i.e., devotedness) that man needs to cultivate for the sake of his individuated soul is only one aspect of woman's existence. He is not otherwise asked to make himself "feminine"; this, in fact, he is warned against. It is also worth noting that, whereas there is much stress placed on his developing devotedness and submission of his self to God, there is comparatively little emphasis on woman developing the masculine qualities of self-individuation and self-assertion. Rather, she is simply advised to find the object of her devotion in God rather than man. Moreover, we should expect a properly androgynist ideal to operate not only at the religious but also at the secular level, that is, "masculine" and "feminine" qualities ought to be shared by persons of both sexes in their relations not only with God but also with each other. Yet, there is no indication that a man is supposed to display devotedness (or any other supposedly feminine quality) toward woman, or other men, much less that woman is to show masculine qualities with respect to either men or women.

Many of us (though by no means all) would also reject the kind of close and exclusive associations that Kierkegaard makes between woman and nature on the one hand, and man and reflection on the other. Kierkegaard is just plain wrong about the essential nature of woman (and man, for that matter), supposing for the moment that talk about the essential nature of either sex makes any sense.[22] If Kierkegaard is wrong about what women and men are really like, then he is certainly also wrong about a number of consequences of these assumptions, not the least of which is that woman is a lesser self. This suggests another reason why the most "positive" assessments of woman that we find in the Authorship (as in Judge William, *Three Discourses at the Communion on Fridays*, and *An Edifying Discourse*, among others) are not much of an advance over the negative ones: Devotedness may well be a good thing (though we cannot say so without qualification), but it is questionable praise to say of any person that they are essentially this. Woman is not *one* thing; nor is man. We are complex beings, with many "essential" qualifications. To say that a person, male or female, is just this one thing, whether it is otherwise considered good or bad, is to diminish, not to celebrate, that person.

This, in turn, suggests a possible response to the problem before us.

An extraordinarily large part of Kierkegaard's writings is concerned with putting together the complementary aspects of human existence. The aesthetes try to realize the (aesthetic) ideal in actual persons, while William argues at length about how the immediacy of the aesthetic can be incorporated with the abstract demands of the ethical: that the universal can be made concrete in one's own existence. In *For Self-Examination*, Kierkegaard argues that we must be not only hearers of the Word, but doers of it: the unity of word and deed becomes an important theme in the later acknowledged works. Indeed, Kierkegaard has a reputation for stressing the importance of inwardness and the isolation of the individual from all around him. Yet, he also argues the importance of turning faith into *practice*: loving one's neighbor is not just having warm feelings. Hence, the "attack" on "hidden inwardness" in *Practice in Christianity* (*PC*, no. III, v). In *Two Ages*, as well, we find the notion of a "genuine association" that puts together the individuality of its members with their union in an ideal (*TA*, 62–63). And, of course, we have the dichotomies of time and the eternal, necessity and possibility, the finite and the infinite, which appear not only in *The Sickness unto Death*, but throughout the pseudonymous works. A true self is a complete self, one that gets all these elements in balance in its own existence. Why, then, should these not include the masculine and the feminine?

First of all, it should be noted that, in any case, the equilibrium that is sought is not one in which both elements participate in *exactly* the same way. For example, in the case of passion and reflection, Kierkegaard argues, in effect, that passion is a vital motive force without which the human individual is lost in the sterility and aimlessness of reflection. But passion must be filtered through reflection first, in order to be able to serve as the proper antidote to excessive reflectiveness.[23] To begin with, we have passion as an immediate, primal, impulse; then, reflection superimposed upon passion; finally, reflection motivated and intensified by passion—but a passion that has itself been altered by its encounter with reflection. The passion that forms one half of this pair is *not* the same passion that is initially overcome by reflection; it could not be, insofar as any immediacy that is brought into relation with consciousness is necessarily changed by that relation into something other than it was. Meanwhile, reflection itself does not appear to be altered, though clearly the human self that has effected this equilibrium within itself must be profoundly transformed.

Much as Kierkegaard values passion in relation to reflection, it seems clear that he regards reflection as being in some sense a *higher* achievement. Passion has to be transformed by reflection in order to be able to participate in a relationship of equilibrium. This suggests that underlying Kierkegaard's psychology of equilibrium is a metaphysics of hierarchy, in particular, one which devalues the natural and the instinctual in favor of consciousness, reflection, and so forth. Thus, to the extent that woman is defined by the natural, and for this reason is assumed to be relatively incapable of the higher achievements of consciousness, it is inevitable that she should fail to become a fully developed self. It is woman's association with the natural, *combined with* the devaluation of nature, which makes her a second-class self.

This, then, is the crucial point for those who wish to find the basis of an androgynist ideal of selfhood in Kierkegaard. For any such ideal, *all* the terms involved in the constitution of the self must stand on equal ground. Consequently, any attempt to reappropriate Kierkegaard for this purpose must also include a reinterpretation or redefinition of the more fundamental relationships of the terms involved. "Masculine" and "feminine" cannot indicate the complementary components of an equilibrium if these terms are understood to mean what Kierkegaard understands them to mean, not only because this is descriptively inaccurate, but because the characteristics and capacities so designated are assumed from the outset to have a relationship to each other that renders a true equilibrium impossible.

This, of course, leaves aside the question of whether it even makes any sense to talk about "masculine" and "feminine," in anything other than a provisional sense, in the context of androgyny. If such an ideal is a valid one, then no characteristics or capacities are properly "masculine" or "feminine," only human, and talk about an equilibrium in which the "masculine" and the "feminine" are ideally balanced in a single human individual is at best an expedient, though perhaps pernicious, fiction; the complementary pair "masculine"/"feminine" ultimately has no place in a fully human self. But, again, this is because all the fundamental constituents of the self must weigh equally in the balance, and not be subject to depreciation on the basis of some spurious association.

So, the question remains, Does Kierkegaard offer an androgynist ideal of selfhood? Clearly, no. Could, however, Kierkegaard's account of the self provide the basis of such an account? The answer to this, I think, is yes—with a lot of reservations. What Kierkegaard's example points out to us is what we might loosely term the ecology of metaphysical presuppositions. The problem here, after all, may be less in Kierkegaard's attitudes to women than in his attitude to the natural; not so much misogyny, or androcentrism, as (perhaps) anthropocentrism. However this may be, if we want to rehabilitate or reappropriate Kierkegaard's views on the self in such a way as to include all of us as potential selves, it is the hierarchical assumption that must be done away with. If this is abandoned, then, it seems, the misogyny no longer has any philosophical basis. The big question is whether this can be done without doing violence to the rest of Kierkegaard's theoretical structure, and the answer to this is unclear. This does still leave us with questionable characterizations of men's and women's "natures," but simple failures of description are more easily remedied than fundamental distortions of the metaphysical framework.

If we look at the situation positively, however, what we find is that Kierkegaard does give us an otherwise highly useful analytic structure for understanding the process of acquiring selfhood, particularly where selfhood is itself understood as a combining and a balancing of the different (sometimes opposed, sometimes complementary) aspects of our existence, and especially where this existence is assumed to involve a relation to God. Moreover, despite the reservations noted, Kierkegaard's analysis of the many and varied ways in which we fail to become ourselves is second to none in the brilliance of its insight into the human psyche. Quite simply, there is too much of value here to allow us just to dismiss Kierkegaard as an irretrievable misogynist. On the contrary, given that Kierkegaard's own analysis starts out with terms that are in fact common to all human beings and that extend to the full compass of human existence, we have here much of the necessary conceptual apparatus to begin to build a new account of the self that is fully human, and that thus may well also be androgynist in some sense.

But should we still call such an account Kierkegaardian? Our problem here is much the same as the one faced by nonbelievers, or non-Christian believers, in confronting Kierkegaard. Although some would like to argue that, for Kierkegaard, what counted most was simply faith, and that what exactly happens to be the object of one's faith, whether the Christian God-in-time or a wooden idol, is irrelevant,[24] this seems to be an ultimately untenable reading of Kierkegaard's views. For Kierkegaard, the only and final remedy for the human existential condition is submission in devotion to the God of the New Testament. All other solutions fail adequately to orient the individual in self-consciousness and in the God-relation. Just as we must accept the fact that Kierkegaard himself was a political conservative, and a misogynist, we must also accept that he was, so to speak, a religious imperialist: you do not get Kierkegaard without the Christianity. Yet it also seems deeply false to conclude on that basis that he has nothing to say to those who remain steadfast nonbelievers.

The issue is the authorship of the process of reappropriation. If we derive from Kierkegaard an account of the self that completely neglects a specifically Christian point of view, or that eliminates the hierarchical relationship between instinct and reflection, then it would be both fair and accurate to say that such an account is *not* Kierkegaardian in the sense that it is not *Kierkegaard's*, but is in fact contrary to *Kierkegaard's* own express position. Happily, however, philosophy is not a static discipline, and *inspired* by Kierkegaard, *fueled* by his observations and conceptual techniques, we can recommence the project of defining the human self. But we must also recognize that in doing so we are speaking with our *own* voices, and not Kierkegaard's.

Notes

1. Note that "ideal" can have two senses in talking about the self: what one *can* be (a possible self that one projects for oneself, which may or may not be optimal for the self one actually is) and what one *ought* to be (the self that is one's true self; a perfect balance of actual and possible selves).

2. These distinctions are echoed in *UDVS* ("Purity of Heart is to Will One Thing").

3. Cf. Judge William's comments to A concerning his wife's assessment of the latter's character: "She sees very well that you lack a certain degree of womanliness. You are too proud to be able to devote yourself" (*EO*, 2:326).

4. See *CUP* (vol. 1, esp. Part 2, sec. 2, chap. 1 ["Becoming Subjective"]); see also Part 1, chap. 1, § 1.

5. "An interesting girl may very well be successful in pleasing, but just as she herself has surrendered her womanliness, so also the men whom she pleases are usually just as unmasculine" (*EO*, 1:339).

6. See also *SLW*, 166, where William remarks that "a feminine soul does not have and should not have reflection the way a man does." It follows from this that she does not have an ethical understanding either.

7. An apparently inconsistent association is also sometimes made between woman and the eternal. The key to the explanation for this is to be found here in the complementary association made between man and spirit: spirit permits decisiveness, activity, and these in turn permit the possibility of history (*CA*, 66). Insofar as woman lacks spirit, she also lacks the differentiation inherent in having a history; woman is an infinitude of possibilities—being nothing definite, she can be anything. Thus she has a kind of backdoor connection with the eternal, which some of the more hostile aesthetes of the early pseudonymous works (Victor Eremita, Constantin Constantius, the Fashion Designer) might instead express as the fantastic. But this is perhaps the reason why woman is also described (often by the same personalities) as having an idealizing effect on man (see *SLW*, 56–63). And it is consistent with her associa-

tion with imagination (see *R*, 182; *EO*, 1:392), or with love—which might be either sensuous or eternal, or both at once.

8. Note that Johannes also describes a young girl as "nature's *venerabile*" (*EO*, 1:391).

9. It should be pointed out that, for William, the male is just as bound by life to marriage as is woman (*SLW*, 145), though not nearly so much is made of fatherhood as of motherhood.

10. In *Either/Or*, Part 1, it is claimed that the women whom Don Giovanni seduces are raised to a higher level of consciousness—in a sense, they are improved (*EO*, 1:98, 100, 108–9).

11. "An Edifying Discourse," in *Training in Christianity and the Edifying Discourse which "Accompanied" It*, trans. Walter Lowrie (Princeton: Princeton University Press, 1941), 262. That this attitude is supposed to be essentially feminine is further supported by the sort of comment which we find in *UDVS* ("Purity of Heart"), 95, the basic sentiment of which is frequently repeated: "Just as a mother carrying her beloved child asleep in her arms along a difficult road is not worried about what may happen to her but fears only that the child may be disturbed and disquieted, so he [who truly wills the Good] does not fear the world's troubles for his own sake."

12. "An Edifying Discourse," 266–69.

13. Mother love also appears frequently, but it is mentioned to illustrate one of two things: either feminine single-mindedness, or (in a non-gender-specific parental analogy) God's love for man.

14. See also *JP*, 4:4998, 5000, 5003, 5005 [XI¹ A 141, XI¹ A 226, XI¹ A 281, XI¹ A 426].

15. "It is probably true that in most cases the woman actually relates to God only through the man" (*SUD*, 49 n).

16. Birgit Bertung gives a particularly persuasive and subtle version of this sort of explanation.

17. Note that, when Anti-Climacus says that woman relates to God through the man, he does say "in most cases" (*SUD*, 49 n).

18. Cf. *SLW*, 48, where Constantin says, "It is the man's function to be absolute, to act absolutely, to express the absolute; the woman consists in the relational."

19. "The self is the relation to oneself" (*SUD*, 17).

20. See Walsh (1987), 126–27. If woman's devotion is instinctively based, rather than self-conscious, one supposes that she might be more likely to make mistakes with respect to her object—much the way beavers do who, driven by instinct to build dams over running water, have apparently been known to build damlike constructions over loudspeakers carrying the sounds of running water.

21. "Christianity as it is found in the New Testament has such prodigious aims that, strictly speaking, it cannot be a religion for women, at most secondhand. . . . The essentially Christian task requires a man, it takes a man's toughness and strength simply to be able to bear the pressure of the task. . . . So it is with everything essentially Christian. Only man has from the hand of Governance the toughness to be able to endure the dialectical" (*JP*, 4:5007 [XI² A 192]).

22. Which I assume it does not, but this is an argument for another place.

23. "Considerable reflectiveness is the condition for a higher meaningfulness than that of immediate passion, is the condition for it" (*TA*, 96). "The prerequisite for acting more intensively is the thorough kneading of reflection" (*TA*, 111).

24. As in Johannes Climacus's discussion in the *Postscript* concerning the *what* and the *how* of religious belief (*CUP*, 1:201–3). Yet it is in the same work that it becomes clear that, for Climacus, only the paradoxical truth of Christianity can restore the individual to existential harmony.

References

Bertung, Birgit. 1989. "Yes, a Woman *Can* Exist." In *Kierkegaard Conferences I: Kierke-gaard—Poet of Existence*, edited by Birgit Bertung, 7–17. Copenhagen: C. A. Reitzel.

Garside, Christine. 1971. "Can a Woman Be Good in the Same Way as a Man?" *Dialogue* 10:534–44.

Kierkegaard, Søren. 1941. *Training in Christianity and the Edifying Discourse which "Accompanied" It*. Translated by Walter Lowrie. Princeton: Princeton University Press.

Walsh, Sylvia I. 1987. "On 'Feminine' and 'Masculine' Forms of Despair." In *International Kierkegaard Commentary: The Sickness unto Death*, edited by Robert L. Perkins, 121–34. Macon: Mercer University Press.

Watkin, Julia. 1991. "The Logic of Søren Kierkegaard's Misogyny, 1854–1855." *Kierke-gaardiana* 15:82–92.

11

The Kierkegaardian Feminist

Jane Duran

The combination of feminism and a Kierkegaardian view might be thought at best to be problematic; at worst, the two might be declared immiscible. The uses to which the concept of the feminine is put in Kierkegaard's works are multiple, and many of these uses seem to fly overtly in the face of feminist theory. In "The Seducer's Diary," from *Either/Or*, perhaps the most obvious of the problematic works, the feminine is not only the object of male seduction, but somehow in and of itself represents the sphere of the immediate, the aesthetic, and the realm of gratification. In each case, the concept is developed through the uses of categories employing females in ways that tend to trivialize or diminish the concept of woman apart from her objectification at the hands of male categorization.

But if the gynocentric, seen from the standpoint of both feminist ethics and feminist epistemology, may be thought to be that which alludes to notions of specificity, connectedness, and particularity, rather than the universal, the detached, and the normative, it may be possible to analyze at least some of Kierkegaard's authorship in terms that make it useful—perhaps extremely useful—to feminist theory. What strikes us about Kierkegaard's writings today is the extent to which they presage twenti-eth-century motifs, and the popularization of his work in the post–World War II era attests to the fact that a cultural ambiance punctuated by existentialist and angst-ridden themes readily found a place for him.

Stages on Life's Way, that quintessentially Kierkegaardian work, directs us on a path of three stages so that the life of immediate gratification—the path of sensuous eroticism, as it is detailed in "The Seducer's Diary"—is overcome. It is interesting to note that the remaining stages, usually conceptualized as the ethical and the religious, both seem to mesh more completely with aspects of feminist thought. It is with these stages that I shall ultimately be concerned in this essay.

The Aesthetic Stage: "The Seducer's Diary"

"The Seducer's Diary" poses problems for feminist theory precisely be-cause Kierkegaard seems to feel called upon to use the eroticism of the Johannes figure as the paradigm for the heightened realm of the aesthete (Jolivet 1948, 127). The contention that no other exemplar would have adequately served hardly bears weight when one thinks of the number of immediate and bodily delights that are usually available in the standard philosopher's repertory, and the uses that a thinker might make of them.[1] Not only does "The Seducer's Diary" make one sort of gratification a hallmark; it also exemplifies one sort of objectification, as the notion of reflectivity is characterized by Kierkegaard in this essay as essentially a playing of Johannes upon the personality of Cordelia. Thus Kierkegaard's introduction of a notion that later becomes important in his more obvi-ously Christian theorizing—the notion of reflectivity, used, for example, with respect to the Teacher and Disciple in *Philosophical Fragments*—revolves around the concept of a sexual seduction, use of the woman as object, creation of the objectified woman in the image of the seducer, placement of the seducer's desires in the woman's persona, and so forth (see Duran 1985, 131–37).

Another interesting aspect of "The Seducer's Diary" is its parallelism to "Immediate Stages of the Erotic," wherein Mozart's *Don Giovanni* and the importance of music as the art that best represents immediacy and immediate gratification are given free play. Kierkegaard's pronouncements on this topic go hand in hand with his construction of the Don Juan figure as one who is "exuberant gaiety" in his nonreflective natural seductiveness (*EO*, 1:101). There is little about either of these works that signifies to us that anything other than the most extreme objectification is to come of Kierkegaard's attempts to deal with notions of the feminine.

Perhaps the single most difficult aspect of the "Diary" for the female reader is the extent to which—already alluded to here—the seducer sees his victim as a creation of his own attempts at replication and, again, reflectivity. One might be tempted to say, in general terms, that it is difficult to tell the seducer from the seduced, and the point, presumably, is that Cordelia becomes Johannes's own creation. Thus the notions of agency and autonomy are denied her, and as in other works where Kierkegaard prepares us to believe that females are lacking in the kinds of traits that might promote agency (or even render it possible, such as the first part of *Either/Or*, to be examined shortly), Cordelia attains a Galatea-like status that enables the seducer/Pygmalion to think of her as entirely his created thing.

The characteristics of immanence, pliability, malleability, and lack of responsiveness that Kierkegaard routinely assigns women are seldom more manifest in his writings than in "The Seducer's Diary," but it is not simply the existence of this document alone that poses a grave problem for feminist theorizing. The importance of this document lies at least partly in its introduction of the notion of reflectivity in a way that might serve as a model for the reflectivity of the Christ figure and the Disciple at a later point in Kierkegaard's theorizing. In *Philosophical Fragments*, the Christ assumes the status of Paradox, since the Disciple is unable adequately to conceptualize the notion of God-in-flesh, and sees it as an impossibility. That the offended consciousness appropriates the paradox unto (it)self is clear from Johannes Climacus's contention that "everything it [the understanding] says about the paradox it has learned from the paradox" (*PF*, 53). Thus the Disciple is placed into a relationship with respect to the Christ that mirrors, in an odd way, the relationship of Cordelia to her seducer, and an examination of these two works and their place in the Kierkegaardian corpus supports the contention that an important development with regard to Kierkegaard's conceptual scheme takes place in the "Diary."

If "The Seducer's Diary" is, then, a major work giving us information on Kierkegaard's notions of the feminine, the feminist theorist dedicates herself to the task of clearing some conceptual ground before she can attempt to make use of any of the rest of Kierkegaard's pieces. Seduction in the "Diary" is a catalytic intellectual construct, and the Johannes figure has the piercing qualities that he has largely because of his thoughtful enjoyment of his own calculations and plans.

Johannes is able to stage the seduction of Cordelia because even in this supreme effort at objectification, the objectifying elements are addressed to a particularity. The analysis of the passages here is made doubly difficult by the fact that Cordelia does indeed embody "tendencies"—a certain sort of seventeen-year-old look, a certain sort of face—but it is these tendencies as manifested in the actual body of the physical Cordelia that move the seducer. Thus the wretchedness of the seducer's plans is magnified by the intense scrutiny of Cordelia that precedes full implementation of those plans, and his delight in making progress with Cordelia is rendered more odious by his knowledge of her.

Johannes writes, for example, of his witnessing Cordelia on one of her outings: "She has forgotten what happened—ah, yes, when one is seventeen years old, when one goes shopping in this happy age, when every single large or little object picked up gives unspeakable delight, then one readily forgets" (EO, 1:315).

Here the observations about "la giovin principiante" (the phrase employed by Kierkegaard in the epigraph to the "Diary" and taken from Mozart) are made more acute for the fictional finder and retriever of the "Diary" and also for us—inasmuch as we know that they are based on a highly particularized acquaintance with Cordelia herself. The seducer may speak in generalities, but the object of the seduction is no generalization; she is an individual, and she is selected precisely because in her individuality she exhibits in a very specific way the characteristics that the seducer has come to find desirable. The fictional owner of the "Diary" is aware of this tension, and notes it when he asserts: "Terrible it is for her; more terrible it will be for him—this I can conclude from the fact that I myself can scarcely control the anxiety that grips me every time I think about the affair" (EO, 1:310). The reliance on the particularity of the relationship to set the stage for the seduction merely underscores the extremes to which the aesthete has gone, extremes that will, in Kierke-gaardian terms, lead to despair.[2]

Specificity and particularity are, then, modes of relating to others, and these modes are hallmarks of Kierkegaard's approach to life, not only in his delineation of the stages, but in his own life as well.[3] Specificity in the aesthetic realm, particularly as illustrated in the seducer's relationship to Cordelia, leads to despair more quickly and perhaps more finally; the despair of the aesthete is the greater here because the distance between what the relationship could be and what it actually is is felt more keenly. Each instance of such a calculated seduction of someone known inti-mately in her particular relation to life kills and extinguishes that which in the seducer is capable of responding wholeheartedly to life, and leads, as Jolivet remarks, to "disgust."[4]

The feminist theorist finds this attention to particularity at every level of Kierkegaard's thought, and finds its culmination in the relationship of the Teacher to the Disciple in *Philosophical Fragments*, a relationship that, as has been commented here, mirrors the seduction by the aesthete in its reflectivity in the form of acoustic illusion. Nothing that Kierkegaard writes lacks that flavor of existential specificity and precision, and femi-nist thinkers may be galvanized into ethical theorizing just because of these features of his thought.

The Ethical Stage: "Observations about Marriage" in *Stages on Life's Way*

The transition from the realm of the aesthetic to the realm of the ethical is delineated in *Stages on Life's Way* in such a way as to suggest some further concomitance with feminist theorizing. A hallmark of reflectivity for Kierkegaard is the stepping back and distancing from a given experi-ence that are manifested in analyses of the experience and in written accounts of it. Thus the immediacy of Don Giovanni, crystallized in Mo-zart's score, lies precisely in his seductive powers as a "natural force"; one could scarcely say that Don Juan plans his seductions—they simply hap-pen. The pseudonymous author of the essay on Don Juan says, "He desires and this desire acts seductively" (*EO*, 1:99). But Johannes in the "Diary" is precisely the sort of persona who prefigures the shift to ethical catego-ries, and he leads us in this direction specifically because of his planned, calculated seductions. It is to this extent that he embodies the notion of reflectivity, also a mark of Kierkegaardian agency (Howe 1994, passim). Johannes's seduction of Cordelia is planned, and Johannes's reflection upon this seduction allows him to construct it in the way he wants, compelling us to castigate him for his cruel hedonism, a hedonism that manipulates and destroys others. This reflectivity, channeled in another direction, will, of course, become the path to the stage of the ethical. But Kierkegaard shows us precisely how this reflectivity works when he has Johannes remark: "No impatience, no greediness—everything will be relished in slow draughts; she is selected, she will be overtaken" (EO, 1:317).

Many of the most important moves that might presage a leap into the ethical are hinted at by passages from "In Vino Veritas," which precedes "Observations on Marriage" in Stages on Life's Way. If, as Jolivet (1948) has remarked, it is passion that drives the leap, then passion must be moved from the sphere of the aesthetic by the twist of reflectivity (110–24). The feminist theorist might well be intensely interested in these moves, because a kind of passionate particularity and passionate involvement seem concomitant to the leaps, even if there is reason to think that, classically speaking, androcentric distancing and detachment are often involved in ethical categorization.

This concept of passionate involvement permeates portions of "In Vino Veritas," with its odd upending of themes reminiscent of Plato's Symposium. The disgust of Johannes the Seducer for the remarks of the Fashion Designer mirrors the Kierkegaardian notion that reflective passion precipitates major change. Johannes notes that reflectivity in the aesthetic sphere brings forth new levels of enjoyment when he addresses his colleagues at the beginning of his speech: "Esteemed drinking companions . . . You certainly are talking like undertakers; your eyes are red from tears and not from wine. . . . Victor is a fanatic, Constantin has paid far too much for his intellect; the Fashion Designer is a madman" (SLW, 71, 73).

Johannes is the ideal persona with whom to end the series of speeches, for the passion-generated move into the ethical can be introduced only by someone whose investment in the realm of the aesthetic is driven by genuine interest and desire.

This leap into the ethical by virtue of altered passionate commitment is signaled in the first few pages of the second part of Stages, when the "Married Man" (Judge William) notes: "The difficulty is this: erotic love or falling in love is altogether immediate; marriage is a resolution; yet falling in love must be taken up into marriage or into the resolution" (*SLW*, 102). He goes on to make the observation that if this will becomes purely spiritual it cannot, of course, yield a human marriage; by the same token, however, this passionate will cannot remain at the stage of immediacy without becoming stagnated in the aesthetic. If, as one is tempted to claim, it is difficult to ascertain what realm might be encompassed between these two extremes, we still have a great deal of food for thought with regard to the transitional nature of the ethical—and yet this transition itself must be filled with passionate intensity.

It is, in fact, this intensity that helps to develop the notion that the feminist thinker might retrieve something from both *Stages* and Part 1 of *Either/Or*, replete though they may be with material that does not look promising. Here one does not want to be driven so much by Kierkegaard's characterization of the possibility of woman's agency (Howe 1994, 133–36), as by our contemporary notion that a sort of gynocentric connectedness might be concomitant to certain types of ethical theorizing, and that Kierkegaard has something to offer us here. The unprepared reader frequently finds Kierkegaard's work haunting or striking without being able to specify in what this striking quality consists. Implicitly understanding that the Aesthete's and Judge William's passionate intensity is about *something*, the reader may feel called upon to use his or her own passion to resolve the inevitable tension that arises between the spheres of the aesthetic, the ethical, and the religious.

In *Stages*, what is most characteristic of the commitment to the ethical is the awareness that duty and the laws of eternality have now taken precedence over the immediate and the merely temporal. Judge William refers to this as a "ledger of responsibility" (*SLW*, 117). The Judge's discourse on marriage provides us with an exemplar of the ethical move. Contrasting the notion of one who makes the vow never to marry with one who marries, Judge William writes: "[H]e is a poor wretch who goes through time with his eternal resolution but never gets it countersigned—on the contrary wherever he goes it is protested. He is an outcast of the race, and even though consoled by the eternal is nevertheless a stranger to joy, weeps, perhaps gnashes his teeth, for the person who in eternity does not wear the wedding garment is thrown out, but here on earth the wedding garment is indeed the wedding garment" (*SLW*, 112).

The conception that the married man gets his "ledger of responsibility countersigned" is intriguing, and it is this type of devoted commitment, based on a passionate devotion to a given particularity held under ethical laws, rules, and obligations that typifies the leap into the ethical. Whereas the aesthete finds that more than one night with a woman renders her intolerably boring, the Kierkegaardian ethical thinker is prepared to make a commitment for an eternity, an eternity in which he or she will have on a wedding garment.

The feminist who thinks in terms of contemporary work may find that the striking quality of Judge William's discourse comes, not so much from an emphasis on ethical laws, but from the specificity of the attachments to which it refers/defers. Kantian modes do not receive priority here; rather than writing in the mood of the Categorical Imperative, the Judge writes as an individual making individual choices. Each individual must decide for his or her own life, and this sense that an individual is connected not only to the lives of others but to his or her own eternality—in such a way that choices must be made—motivates much of what Judge William has to say in *Stages*.

The Religious Stage: Particularity and Passion in *Philosophical Fragments*

If there is particularity and passion in the stage of the ethical, then there is also a special desire attached to the stage of the religious, and *Philosophical Fragments* is perhaps the most splendid vehicle for illustrating that kind of passionate attachment. Here we can see the beginnings of an articulation of what is involved in the move to the religious; that is, a special kind of pathos. The depth of that pathos is brought home to us not only in the *Fragments* overall, but most particularly in the section entitled "Offense at the Paradox." Nielsen reformulates some of Johannes Climacus's summarization of the interaction between the Paradox and the offended consciousness as follows:

> When a human thinker encounters the Paradox [the notion that the Teacher, Christ, is simultaneously divine and human and came to us on this earth] and comes to an understanding with it, their relationship is a happy one. However, this need not happen. The thinker may instead take offense, somewhat in the manner of wounded pride. His offense is passive, a recoil occasioned by

the Paradox, even though to conceal the fact that he has suffered a wound he may outdo all the rest in self-activity. (Nielsen, 1983, 88)

Here Nielsen attempts to introduce a discussion of the point, repeatedly emphasized by Johannes Climacus, that in crossing the threshold of the religious, consciousness has only two responses to the Paradox, "either acceptance of its proposal or else offense" (89). The substance of his discussion need not detain us, but it is worth noting that, in Kierkegaardian terms, either horn of this dilemma involves a passionate form of response.

If the individual accepts the proposal of the Paradox, yielding the result of a happy relationship, then we may begin to think in terms of love. That love does indeed, in its own way, mimic the particularly involved response of earthly love and marriage, but this time there is no question of subsumption under the general law of the moral, as the realm of the moral has been superseded. Rejection of the proposal and offense yield their own sort of misery. Johannes Climacus notes that "offense has one advantage: it points up the difference more clearly, for in that happy passion to which we have not given a name the difference is in fact on good terms with the understanding" (*PF*, 54). The move from the self-contained world of the ethical into the religious cannot be made without this specifically motivated involvement, and the consciousness experiences this involvement as an involvement with him- or herself.[5] Jolivet (1948) pronounces it "interiorization," and he notes that "[it] is a struggle, and interrupted becoming, marked by qualitative . . . crises" (118). Evans (1983) notes that "there is a 'something' (reason's fundamental need to discover its limits)" that makes possible this particular move (238).

The type of interiority that personalizes struggles, rather than subsumes them under impersonal and universal laws, has been seen by many feminist theorists as a hallmark of gynocentric thinking, particularly with respect to the moral (see Gilligan 1982). But it is also seen by many feminist philosophers of religion as indicative of female-centered aspects of the religious, and it is here that those components of Kierkegaard's thought most useful to the feminist theorist may be found.[6] There may indeed be a sense of novelty with respect to these components, since, as was indicated earlier, much of the material in the Kierkegaardian aesthetic makes reference to the feminine, but in a derogatory way. Nevertheless, a broader view indicates that commitment generated by passion is so profound a part of the moves or leaps from the self-contained spheres of the stages that failure to see this does Kierkegaard's work a grave injustice. Here again Kierkegaard provides the arable groundsoil from which the enterprising feminist may reap benefits.

The notion of an individual commitment and a personalized relationship not categorizable under the notion of what-an-individual-in-the-same-situation might do appears in the very opening sections of the *Fragments*, before some of the more familiar material having to do with the nature of the Paradox is introduced. The "Thought-Project" introduces two sorts of teachers, but it is the particular relationship to the teacher that is stressed, the relationship that I-might-have-now-at-this-given-instant.

With the Socratic sort of teacher, the disciple can have but a distant and historical relationship. Johannes Climacus writes about this relationship in the "Thought-Project" as follows:

> If this is the case with regard to learning the truth, then the fact that I have learned from Socrates or from Prodicus or from a maid-servant can concern me only historically or—to the extent that I am a Plato in my enthusiasm—poetically. . . . Neither can the fact that the teaching of Socrates or of Prodicus was this or that have anything but historical interest for me, because the truth in which I rest was in me and emerged from me. Not even Socrates would have been capable of giving it to me, no more than the coachman is capable of pulling the horse's load. (*PF,* 12)

Here Johannes Climacus compares learning from Socrates to learning from a "maidservant," the point being that if, as Socrates wanted us to believe, knowledge is recollection, then the instrumental effector of that knowledge has a distant and impersonal relationship to the disciple. Again, the gynocentric and intense focus on the relationship as a vehicle for instruction, rather than the instruction itself, allows us to contrast Johannes Climacus's mode of theorizing with the Hegelian or Kantian theorizing that preceded it. But what is most striking about this section is, of course, the use to which this sort of categorization is put when the other Teacher is discussed. For here the contrast is still more apparent, and in his characteristic passionate involvement mode Climacus sets up for us the contrast with the Teacher (Paradox):

The teacher, then, is the god himself, who, acting as the occasion, prompts the learner to be reminded that he is untruth and is that through his own fault. But this state—to be untruth and to be that through one's own fault—what can we call it? Let us call it *sin*.

The teacher, then, is the god, who gives the condition and gives the truth. Now, what should we call such a teacher, for we surely do agree that we have gone far beyond the definition of a teacher. (*PF*, 15)

Here the immediacy of the situation, at least in this construal, is obvious, for it is the Teacher who prompts the Disciple to learn by providing him or her with the opportunity to appropriate the Paradox and who personalizes the relationship to such an extent that the Disciple recognizes that, if he or she is "untruth," it is through his or her "own fault." As Nielsen (1983) remarks with respect to this section, "The Moment-hypothesis thus posits a Teacher with the power to effect a humanly impossible change in the learner's relationship to the Truth" (15).[7]

There can be little misunderstanding with respect to the personalized nature of Kierkegaard's thought here and its relevance to feminist arguments that have asked us to look at strains of thought that are nonuniversalizable.[8] The relationship between the Socratic figure and the student is detached only in the sense that it lacks immediacy; otherwise, it is indeed a teacher-disciple relationship, and is personalized in the sense that *I* retrieve *my* information, according to Socratic guidelines. The relationship between the Teacher and the Disciple, expounded briefly above, is still more personalized because it is the existence of the Teacher that creates, so to speak, the conditions of the Lesson. Both relationships are personal in the sense of existential immediacy and in the sense that my relationship to a given teacher can exist only for me.

It is this personal appropriation of the given stage, whether it be aesthetic, ethical, or religious, that gives Kierkegaard's work its striking and somewhat arcane quality, and it is also this appropriation that signals to the feminist where her retrieval may begin. The ethics of the thinkers preceding Kierkegaard tended to place the individual in such a circumstance that she or he was merely one among many to whom a given set of ethical rules applied. Kierkegaard places the individual in a personal relationship with the Teacher, and from the relationship the leap or move is made.

Ironically, we are provided with a version of the relationship between the Teacher and the Learner that has at least a small feminine twist to it: the parable of the King and the Maiden. In choosing to construct this particular parable, Climacus has specifically chosen the language and vehicle of erotic love, but erotic love between beings who are vastly unequal. Here two concepts—the particularity of the Maiden in her relationship to the King, and the inequality of the relationship—illustrate the themes we are attempting to highlight. Interestingly enough, it is in Climacus's description of the Maiden, and in the very brief alteration of the Maiden analogy into that of the lily, that Climacus makes some of his most telling points. He writes:

> Then a concern awakened in the king's soul. . . . Alone he grappled with the sorrow in his heart . . . whether she would acquire the bold confidence never to remember what the king only wished to forget—that he was the king and she had been a lowly maiden. For if this happened, if this recollection awakened and at times, like a favored rival, took her mind away from the king, lured it into the inclosing reserve of secret sorrow, or if at times it walked past her soul as death walks across the grave—what would be the gloriousness of erotic love then! Then she would indeed have been happier if she had remained in obscurity, loved by one in a position of equality, contented in the humble hut, but boldly confident in her love and cheerful early and late. . . .
>
> The god does have joy in adorning the lily more gloriously than Solomon, but if understanding were at all plausible here, it certainly would be a tragic delusion on the part of the lily if, in observing the costume, it considered itself to be beloved because of the costume. (PF, 27, 29–30)

In the special particularity of the Maiden's relationship to the King— in, as Climacus writes, the possibility of her "reserve of secret sorrow," or of the lily's "consider[ing] itself to be beloved because of the costume"— the existential individuality of the decision is captured, and captured in such a way that it can never be recategorized under nomic regularity.

Finally, one last aspect of this particularity is provided in still another way in which the Divine assumes a relationship with the Learner. In "the boundlessness of love," which, "in earnestness and truth and not in jest . . . wills to be the equal of the beloved," the god assumes the form of a servant (*PF*, 32). Here the god refuses to do anything that would reveal that He is anything other than a servant, for again such a revelation would alter the reciprocity of the love and the egalitarian quality of the relationship. The form of the servant is not "put on" but is genuine, for the personalization of the relationship to the Teacher requires that each Learner be related to the Teacher in complete equality and specificity (*PF*, 33).

Conclusions: Significance for Feminist Theory

Given the emphasis on particularity that our analysis has yielded, it may be helpful to pause at this juncture for a brief overview of the notions that inform much of the commentary in contemporary feminist ethics and, indeed, feminist epistemology. At an earlier stage I alluded to specificity and particularity as hallmarks of gynocentric thinking, but further argument to support these contentions might be required.

In the area of feminist epistemology, much of the recent work establishes notions of connection, particularized thought, and a sort of epistemological communitarianism as central to anything that might be deemed to be a feminist epistemics (see, e.g., Code 1991, Duran 1991, and Nelson 1991). Whether it owes its impetus to the psychoanalytic object-relations theory articulated by Nancy Chodorow (1985) and Dorothy Dinnerstein (1978), or to contemporary analytic epistemology and philosophy of science, work done in sociology, psychology, and even anthropology supports the notion that androcentric styles of thinking have traditionally informed philosophy. Divorced, detached, and objectifying, these conceptual modes have given rise to much that is held to be classical within the Western tradition, including the somewhat solipsistic thinking of Descartes in the *Meditations*, for example (see Bordo 1978), or the ethical thought of such major theorists as Kant, already referred to here. By contrast, work that draws on gynocentric traditions of connectedness (that is, work reflective of elements in the construct of the feminine personality set out by theorists such as Chodorow) will tend to manifest less objectification and distancing, and will also exhibit a threading together of particular instances rather than an overt attempt to avoid particularity in the effort to construct a grand unifying theory.

That Kierkegaard manifests such an emphasis on particulars is part and parcel of the standard commentary upon his oeuvre, but until now this attention to lived detail has been viewed in an existentialist light. The feminist, however, may draw on other aspects of contemporary theorizing to pursue the line that attention to such detail is, in fact, gynocentric and usable in feminist theory. Still another feminist tradition, that of pragmatism, enjoins us to notice lived lives and individual choices and underscores the contention that this sort of concern, whether articulated by nineteenth- or twentieth-century theorists, is one that is concomitant with feminist thought (see Seigfried 1991 and 1992).

Philosophical Fragments, in particular, exhibits these gynocentric strains, perhaps precisely because of the fact that the relationship between the Teacher and the Disciple is one that, in Christian tradition, has been painted in broad terms. The desire to establish the catholicity of the tradition may have forced earlier commentators into an avoidance of the specific and the existential, but such avoidance also necessarily casts the commentary in androcentric terms. Kierkegaard's desire to draw a deep connectedness between *this* Disciple and *this* Teacher is at the core of his existential specificity.

Throughout this paper I have written of the uses to which a feminist might put the Kierkegaardian oeuvre, despite the fact that, at least insofar as some pronouncements are concerned, we may think of the strain of Kierkegaard's thought as misogynous. In the first two sections of this essay I was specific about those anti-woman tensions, particularly as they manifested themselves in "The Immediate Stages of the Erotic" and "The Seducer's Diary," from the first volume of *Either/Or.* Woman as objectified Other is at the heart of both of these analyses of the aesthetic, and the concept of delight based on the objectification or utilization of woman is at the center of Kierkegaard's analyses of Don Juan/Johannes the Seducer as "force of nature" and of A as reflective aesthete.

But, as already indicated, it is the relationship of Kierkegaard's personae to their others that renders the move to more advanced stages possible, and it is also these very relationships that enable an inquiring feminist to see how a gynocentric view of particulars enters into Kierkegaard's thought. The moves to the ethical and the religious require that one position oneself in a certain way with respect to otherness, and it is this specific positioning—the complete connection to the other in his or her specificity, as it were—that allows these transformations/moves to be effected.

As I claimed in my analysis of Judge William's "Observations about Marriage," the notion of a "countersigned" ledger of responsibility is one of which we can make sense only when we understand that the commitment to the other, now made under the aegis of moral law, is still a commitment to a specified other. It is, in fact, the result of the same sort of awareness of the other that permeates the "Diary" and that, as was asserted in the previous section, makes Johannes's scheming all the more reprehensible. This awareness translates, of course, into the greatest awareness of all, so to speak, when it moves to the level of the religious and when it encounters the Paradox/Teacher in all Its particularity. The attention that the aesthete focuses on Cordelia's face or that Judge William focuses on the other who is the object of the "ledger of responsibility" is now focused on the Paradox, and the dialogue with the Paradox yields, in the unhappy case, "wounded pride," and in the happy case, an ideal consummation. The wounded pride stems from the personal encounter with the irrational, and the reflectivity generated by the Paradox's meeting with the religious agent. Just as a relationship with Socrates has one character, the relationship with the Teacher has another, and in each case it is the precise qualities of the relationship that enable Kierkegaard to analyze the results of the relation in the manner that he does.

Contemporary feminist theory has asked us to make use of notions of caring and connection—notions that were traditionally left out of or deleted from many ethical theories just because they were deemed to be less developed and more primitive than the globally recognizable theses of ethicists who demanded that all persons receive the same treatment or be viewed in the same way qua persons. Failing to meet an individual in his or her specificity appears to be conceptually foreign to Kierkegaard, and for good reason. His philosophical thinking asks us to come to grips with our own lives, and to think about, as he might phrase it, the bungling in which we are enmeshed. In attempting to achieve some clarification about our bungles, errors, and mistakes, and about the various resolutions and commitments that might, once instantiated, move us away from an error-filled path, Kierkegaard repeatedly asks us to encounter an individual or particular, work through the encounter, and apply the results. The feminist, motivated by current work that encourages us to think of ethical and/or religious theorizing in new terms, can have few better friends than Kierkegaard, who saw that the intensity of Johannes's particular relationship to Cordelia was but one manifestation of the intense relationships that we have with others in the various stages of our lives.

Notes

1. The pseudonymous authorship of the "Diary" has posed problems for some, but Leslie Howe has recently argued, I think quite rightly, that there is sufficient commonality across Kierkegaard's works to prevent this type of authorial signature from being a problem (Howe 1994, 131–57). In addition, C. Stephen Evans has made the point that, were we to hypothesize that the pseudonymous authors were real individuals, there would be at least some agreement between Kierkegaard and the authors (Evans 1983, 7).

2. Jolivet (1948) notes, of this life, "Thus boredom overwhelms the aesthetician. Disgust gnaws at the pleasure-seeker. Enjoyment has a taste of death" (127).

3. Biographical work on Kierkegaard uniformly notes the importance of his relationship with Regine Olsen for his philosophy. See, in particular, Jolivet's (1948) chapter "The Betrothal to Regine Olsen," 18–29.

4. See note 2.

5. Nielsen (1983) characterizes this involvement with the statement: "How unlike each other then are the Paradox and what I think—but of course this remark, too, is a steal" (99).

6. See several of the articles in the special issue, "Feminist Philosophy of Religion," *Hypatia* 9, no. 4 (Fall 1994).

7. Nielsen (1983) also writes: "This state of Error or alienation from the truth is one of which the individual can become conscious. Since the error has to do with a difference, an opposition, between the Truth and what he thinks, it becomes error for him only when he can consciously acknowledge it as *his* own" (6). See also Roberts (1986), who asserts: "but a disciple of Jesus, if he forgets him . . . forfeits his relationship" (25).

8. Some of these arguments have occurred not only with respect to philosophy of religion and ethics, but also with respect to, for example, the place of American pragmatism in the theoretical canon of the feminist. See *Hypatia* 8, no. 2 (1993).

References

Bordo, Susan. 1978. *The Flight to Objectivity*. Albany: State University of New York Press.

Chodorow, Nancy. 1985. *The Reproduction of Mothering*. Berkeley and Los Angeles: University of California Press.

Code, Lorraine. 1991. *What Can She Know?* Ithaca: Cornell University Press.

Dinnerstein, Dorothy. 1978. *The Mermaid and the Minotaur*. New York: Harper and Row.

Duran, Jane. 1985. "Kierkegaard's Christian Reflectivity: Its Precursors in the Aesthetic of *Either/Or*." In *International Journal for Philosophy of Religion* 17, no. 2:131–37.

———. 1991. *Toward a Feminist Epistemology*. Savage, Md.: Rowman and Littlefield.

Evans, C. Stephen. 1983. *Kierkegaard's "Fragments" and "Postscript": The Religious Philosophy of Johannes Climacus*. Atlantic Highlands, N.J.: Humanities Press.

Gilligan, Carol. 1982. *In a Different Voice*, Cambridge: Harvard University Press.

Howe, Leslie A. 1994. "Kierkegaard and the Feminine Self." *Hypatia* 9, no. 4:131–57.

Jolivet, Regis. 1948. *Introduction to Kierkegaard*. New York: Dutton.

Nelson, Lynn Hankinson. 1991. *Who Knows: From Quine to a Feminist Empiricism*. Philadelphia: Temple University Press.

Nielsen, H.A. 1983. *Where the Passion Is: A Reading of Kierkegaard's Philosophical Fragments*. Tallahassee: University Presses of Florida.

Roberts, Robert C. 1986. *Faith, Reason and History: Rethinking Kierkegaard's Philosophical Fragments*. Macon: Mercer University Press.

Seigfried, Charlene Haddock. 1991. "Where are All the Pragmatist Feminists?" *Hypatia* 6, no. 2:1–20.

———. 1992. "Like Bridges Without Piers: Beyond the Foundationalist Metaphor." In *Anti-Foundationalism: Old and New*, edited by Tom Rockmore and Beth Singer. Philadelphia: Temple University Press.

12

Subjectivity Versus Objectivity:
Kierkegaard's *Postscript* and Feminist Epistemology

Sylvia Walsh

The Western philosophic/scientific epistemological tradition has been widely criticized by feminists for its objectivist emphasis on dispassionate inquiry in the search for value-free, universalizable truths. In this essay I shall argue that feminists may find in Kierkegaard's *Concluding Unscientific Postscript* (1846) both a philosophical precursor of and ally in this critique, as well as an important resource for re-visioning the concept of subjectivity in a manner that does not collapse into an isolated subjectivism, on the one hand, or into a "chummy" form of intersubjectivity that compromises the integrity of the individual, on the other.

This is not to say that the position of Johannes Climacus, the pseudonymous "author" of this text, is not subject to feminist criticism on various aspects of his understanding of objectivity and subjectivity.[1] On the contrary, as I shall point out, from a feminist perspective there are some serious deficiencies in Climacus's thought. It should be noted at the outset, however, that feminist philosophy is not monolithic in its critique and rethinking of the concepts of objectivity and subjectivity. Before turning to a consideration of the *Postscript*, therefore, I shall briefly characterize the conventional understanding of objectivity and the knowing subject that has provoked feminist critique, indicate the main objections feminists have raised to it, and sketch several feminist approaches that have emerged in the process of assessing and reformulating these concepts from a feminist perspective.

Feminist Criticisms of and Responses to the Conventional Understanding of Objectivity and the Knowing Subject

The conventional understanding of objectivity in Western philosophy is variously analyzed by feminist philosophers as having its inception in Plato (e.g., Duran 1991, 5–8; Keller 1985, 30–32; Irigaray 1985), Descartes (Bordo 1987; Hodge 1988, 152–68), and the empiricist as well as rationalist epistemologies of the Enlightenment that gave birth to modern science (Code 1991, 51; Hekman 1990, 1–10; Harding 1986, 36–57).[2] This concept is typically characterized by feminists as one that assumes a separation between subject and object, fact and value, and requires the rendering of an impartial, dispassionate, value-free, empirically verifiable, and rationally coherent account of the objective world. The concept of the knowing subject corresponding to this view of objectivity is that of an autonomous, dispassionate, detached individual who has the capacity to adopt the stance of an independent, neutral observer in relation to the external world and to suppress or eliminate personal, or merely subjective, feelings, interests, and values in coming to know and describe that world (Hodge 1988, 154–66; Code 1991, 46–52; Hawkesworth 1989, 533–57).

According to some feminists, such a view of objectivity and the knowing subject, exemplified in modern scientific method, with physics serving as its paradigm,[3] reflects a typically masculine way of relating to the world and thus actually represents an androcentric, male-biased, and male-constructed perspective rather than a gender-neutral stance toward reality (Gergen 1988, 27–48; Code 1991, 35, 117–19; Duran 1991, 5–14, 44; Harding 1991, 39–50; Nelson 1990, 189–90; MacKinnon 1987, 50, 54–55). This means that the so-called value-free descriptions of modern science and epistemology are not value-free but rather reflect the social values and interests of a specific gender. A particularly objectionable feature of this androcentric viewpoint for many feminists is that it is predicated on and perpetuates a fundamentally dichotomous form of thought in which one term is privileged, the other negated or suppressed, in the affirmation of reason against passion, mind over body, objectivity over subjective interests and values (Code 1991, 27–55; Hekman 1990, 9, 16; Ring 1991, 17–25). Since women traditionally have been associated with the devalued terms of these dichotomies, the effect has been an exclusion of women from participation in philosophic and scientific endeavors or else a denial of their female nature (assuming there is one) in the requirement that they become more like men by developing the kind of detached subjectivity or objective stance necessary for acquiring a true knowledge of the world. Another objection voiced by some feminists is that the "male gaze," or the indifferent, disinterested, and nonreciprocal objective stance associated with conventional objectivity, results in the objectification or reification and dehumanization of women (MacKinnon 1987; Haslanger 1993, 85–125; Hawkesworth 1994, 151–77).

Feminist responses to this understanding of objectivity and the knowing subject are varied but may be grouped into four major approaches: feminist empiricism, feminist standpoint theory, postmodern feminism, and a mediating, integrationist understanding of objectivity and subjectivity.[4]

Feminist Empiricism

Orienting their positions in the naturalized, contextualized epistemologies of Kuhn, Quine, and other contemporary theorists in the philosophy of science, linguistics, and analytic philosophy, feminist empiricists argue that there is no need to abandon an empirical and scientific approach to knowledge (Nelson 1990, 5–7; Duran 1991, 3–5, 19–69, 105–10; Antony 1993, 185–225). Rather, what is needed, in their view, is a new empirical science that is anti- or postindividualist in its recognition of the communal, contextual, socially constructed, nonfoundational character of knowledge and that incorporates, rather than excludes, social, political, moral, and gender values in a self-conscious and self-critical fashion in its understanding of objectivity (Nelson 1990, 5, 7, 14; Duran 1991, 3–5, 13–14, 43–69, 110–15; Antony 1993, 213; Longino 1990, 62–85, 215–25). By becoming more inclusive of the experiences and participation of women in the scientific enterprise, it is believed that empirical science will be able to give a less androcentric, more complete, and therefore more objective account of the world.

Feminist-Standpoint Theory

Feminist-standpoint theorists, like feminist empiricists, acknowledge the social-situatedness of knowledge and advocate the use of women's experiences as a basis for scientific research in the belief that they will yield a greater objectivity, or "strong objectivity," in contrast to the "weak objectivity" of objectivism or the conventional perspective (Harding 1991, 138–63).[5] Having its theoretical basis in post-Freudian object-relations theory and in a post-Marxist historical-materialist analysis of female oppression as resulting from the sexual division of labor, this position claims that "women's lives differ structurally from those of men" and provide "a particular and privileged vantage point" that is less partial and distorted than that of men (Hartsock 1983, 284; Harding 1983, 321).[6] In other words, the feminist standpoint, oriented as it is in the historical development of personality structures and modes of reasoning that foster contextual understanding, psychosomatic unity, and a sense of connectedness with other persons and nature, not only provides *greater* objectivity but also a *better* objective basis for making observations about nature, social relations, and the social order (Harding 1991, 124–33; Hartsock 1983, 298–304; Rose 1983, 73–90). Because women are "strangers" or "outsiders" both to and within the established order, their experiences provide a fresh, more distant perspective from which to test and evaluate conventional knowledge claims (Harding 1991, 124–26, 128–32).

Postmodern Feminist Epistemology

Rejecting the notion of a univocal and universal feminist standpoint, or a "women's way of knowing," as well as the masculinist, unitary conception of truth fostered by the Enlightenment tradition, postmodern feminists recognize a plurality of women's voices and interpretations of truth, none of which, in their view, is epistemologically privileged. Thus they seek to abandon the conventional categories of objectivity and subjectivity altogether, finding them a perpetuation of the masculinist, dichotomous thinking inherent in Enlightenment epistemology (Hekman 1990, 9–16).[7] In their view, both knowledge and the knowing subject are socially constituted through language or forms of discourse. The focus of their attack thus falls upon the humanist ideal of the autonomous, self-constituting subject—an ideal they find to be inherently masculinist, and thus hopelessly phallocentric, in spite of the fact that feminism historically has appealed to humanist values such as natural rights, dignity, and autonomy in its fight against female oppression (Hekman 1990, 63, 79; Jardine 1985, 44). From the viewpoint of postmodern feminists, therefore, it will not do to argue—as Simone de Beauvoir (1989) does in *The Second Sex*, for example—that women should become independent subjects like men in order to realize their self-identity; all the qualities that characterize the humanist/existentialist subject are associated with the masculine (Hekman 1990, 77). Postmodern feminists opt instead to view woman as a process whose self-identity is multiple, decentered, nonpersonal, and/or constantly deferred.[8] Although the female subject is a construct of discourse, and thus socially determined rather than self-constituting, she nevertheless has the power, they claim, to resist those modes of discourse that historically have constituted her in oppressive ways (Hekman 1990, 68, 73, 87, 189).[9] Accordingly, the possibility of fashioning new modes of female subjectivity that transgress the traditionally sharp boundaries between subject and object, self and other, is opened up.

Integrationist Approach

Many feminist thinkers, however, are unwilling to embrace postmodernism as well as some forms of feminist standpoint theory because, in their interpretation, these positions not only endorse cultural relativism but also an epistemological relativism that lapses into subjectivism or a denial of objective knowledge altogether.[10] As Sandra Harding succinctly states their objection: "One cannot afford to 'just say no' to objectivity" (Harding 1991, 160). Along with postmodern feminists and feminist theorists from the other feminist approaches, this group recognizes the fundamentally communal or contextual character of knowledge and thus denies the possibility of a pure or value-free objectivity, but not the "independent integrity" of the objective world and the possibility of gaining an objective knowledge of it (Keller 1985, 117; see also Longino 1990). Consequently, these feminist epistemologists seek to articulate a mediating position that involves an integration, interpenetration, or dialectical interplay of objectivity and subjectivity rather than a negation of them.[11] In line with the postmodernist critique of dichotomizing forms of thought, this approach envisions at least a momentary dissolution of the boundaries between subjectivity and objectivity in a mutuality of influence or intersubjectivity that affirms both separation and unity, a merging and differentiation of subject from object.[12] What is needed, then, in such a context, is a recasting or reconceptualization of objectivity and subjectivity in a nondichotomous, more harmonious relationship.[13]

Objectivity and Subjectivity in *Concluding Unscientific Postscript*

In light of these developments in feminist epistemology, let us now examine the critique of objectivity and the concept of subjectivity offered by *Concluding Unscientific Postscript*. Although the central problem for the pseudonymous author, Johannes Climacus, is a religious one concerning the individual's relation to Christianity, the text addresses this issue in the context of a wide-ranging discussion of historical, scientific, and speculative modes of inquiry as ways of determining objective truth and knowledge. Climacus's critique of objectivity primarily revolves around an analysis of two issues: (1) the presumed certainty of objective knowledge and (2) the indifferent or disinterested stance of the objective knower. He begins by making a fundamental distinction between two kinds of truth and, in correspondence with these, two modes of knowing: (1) objective truth, which is reached through a rational and/or empirical mode of inquiry; and (2) subjective truth, the truth of appropriating or making something one's own (*Tilegnelse*), attained by existing in a particular state (*CUP*, 1:21, 53–54; 2:185 n. 2). Objective truth is further subdivided by Climacus into two forms: historical and philosophical. The former, he states, is determined empirically by the historical-critical method of examining and assessing various historical reports, while the latter is established rationally by showing how doctrines that have been "historically given and verified" are related to eternal truth. (Climacus does not address here the status of nonhistorical objective truths such as logic and mathematics.) From Climacus's perspective, both forms of objective truth may be regarded as "scientific," in the broad sense in which the term was understood in the nineteenth century, inasmuch as they are purported to provide an absolute certainty of knowledge.

Far from yielding such absolute certainty, however, all objective knowledge relating to history or actuality is really uncertain and only an approximation, Climacus charges (CUP, 1:38). Historical knowledge in particular, he points out, is incomplete and always subject to doubt and revision on the basis of further observation and research (CUP, 1:30, 42, 150), but the charge is expanded to include sense-certainty and speculative philosophical truths as well in the claim that "objectively there is no truth for existing beings, but only approximations" (CUP, 1:38, 44, 218). All "positive" knowledge is therefore declared to be untrue by Climacus, and sense-certainty, historical knowledge, and speculative results are branded a delusion, illusion, and phantom respectively (CUP, 1:31, 314, 316).[14]

As Climacus sees it, the only certainty lies in the infinite and the eternal, which speculative thought in particular claims to have grasped but has not, since the knowing subject does not exist *sub specie aeterni* but is continually in the process of arriving at truth (CUP, 1:82). "Whatever is known is known in the mode of the knower"—an old saying to which Climacus appeals in his discussion—may be taken as stating a fundamental principle of his epistemology (CUP, 1:52). Thus the fact that the knowing subject is an existing subject, for whom everything historical—except one's own existence, which we shall consider in a moment—is uncertain, must be expressed in all of our knowing. Otherwise, Climacus maintains, that knowledge does not pertain to the state of the knowing subject *in existence* but to a fictive "objective subject" who does not exist (CUP, 1:81).

Climacus further points out that all objective knowledge is an abstraction from existence that gives a false rendition of actuality, which must be annulled or transposed into possibility in order to be grasped conceptually (CUP, 1:314–18). The only actuality to which one has more than a cognitive relation, or "knowledge about," Climacus claims, is one's own existence; every other actuality is known only in the form of possibility (CUP, 1:316–17). This means that the only certain historical knowledge to be had by an existing individual is self-knowledge or subjective truth—

not in the Cartesian sense of being certain of one's own existence on the basis of thought, which in Climacus's view is an abstraction from existence rather than a demonstration of it, but in the Socratic sense of being infinitely interested in relating oneself to the truth, so as to exist in it (*CUP*, 1:37, 82, 152, 153–54, 204–5, 316–17).

It is this relation of the knowing subject to the truth that constitutes the chief concern and "knotty difficulty" for Climacus (*CUP*, 1:37). Like feminists, Climacus describes the posture of the inquiring, knowing subject in objective modes of knowledge as that of a disinterested observer: "Let the scientific researcher labor with restless zeal, let him even shorten his life in the enthusiastic service of science and scholarship; let the speculative thinker spare neither time nor effort—they are nevertheless not infinitely, personally, impassionedly interested" (*CUP*, 1:21–22). Nor should they be, Climacus thinks, for in objective modes of knowledge it is the truth itself that is important, not the individual's relation to the truth, which in this context must be placed in parentheses (*CUP*, 1:27–29, 38, 47). Thus, whereas feminists fault objective modes of knowledge for failing to recognize the masculine subjective agendas that currently drive them and for neglecting to incorporate the subjective interests and values of women as well as men, Climacus accepts the essentially disinterested character of objective modes of inquiry, although he admits that in those endeavors "where one should be objective, in strict scholarship, objectivity is rare" (*CUP*, 1:43, 76 n).

But Climacus also proceeds to fault objective modes of knowledge, in company with feminists, precisely because one is required to move away from and abandon oneself in objectivity, thereby becoming indifferent to one's own existence and relation to the truth and ultimately disappearing from oneself altogether in becoming the "gazing power of speculative thought" (*CUP*, 1:56, 75, 116).[15] In Climacus's view, every human being has, or should have, an infinite interest or passionate concern about his or her own existence and eternal happiness. This passionate self-interest is understood in an ethical, not an egotistical, sense by Climacus; that is, it has to do with the cultivation of subjectivity or inwardness in the human personality—the highest ethical task assigned to every human being (*CUP*, 1:134, 151, 158, 163, 346). The adoption of an objective posture, especially in relation to ethical or existential matters, not only is incongruous with this self-interest but also renders the individual *comic* inasmuch as it requires one to move away from, rather than toward, oneself in infinite interest (*CUP*, 1:43, 54–56, 120, 124, 353). Thus, while

Climacus recognizes that there are legitimate objective disciplines, such as logic and mathematics, that bear no relation to existence or else require one to abstract from existence, in general he regards the objective tendency as "a venture in the comic" that encourages human beings to forget what they are, what it means to exist, and what inwardness is (*CUP*, 1:110–11, 124; cf. also 249, 259, 263, 269, 275 n, 287, 289). "Even if a man his whole life through occupies himself exclusively with logic, he still does not become logic; he himself therefore exists in other categories," Climacus points out (*CUP*, 1:93), and if that fact is ignored or neglected, "existence mocks the one who keeps on wanting to become purely objective" (*CUP*, 1:93). Over against a disinterested pursuit of objective truth, therefore, Climacus recommends striving for subjective truth and propounds the thesis that "[the] subjectivity, [the] inwardness, is [the] truth" (*Subjektiviteten, Inderligheden er Sandheden*) as the central tenet of his thought (*CUP*, 1:278).[16]

From a feminist perspective, however, it is important to determine exactly what subjectivity is and is not for Climacus. Subjectivity is defined as inwardness and passion—maximally a passion for eternal happiness—by Kierkegaard's pseudonym, but he does not consider it equivalent to any and every form of inwardness and passion (*CUP*, 1:33, 131, 203). In fact, Climacus takes pains to distinguish true inwardness or subjectivity from two forms of inwardness in particular: (1) "feminine inwardness" or the momentary inwardness of a "woman's infatuation" that corresponds, in his view, to the "feminine nature" and "to what is ordinarily understood by inwardness" (*CUP*, 1:236); and (2) the "chummy inwardness" of friends (*CUP*, 1:249). Let us examine each of these a bit more closely.

Associating "the feminine" in stereotypical fashion with the expression of momentary, emotional outbursts of feeling, which he characterizes elsewhere in the text as "feminine screaming," "blather," and "momentary feminine squealing" (*CUP*, 1:266, 430, 443), Climacus rejects feminine inwardness as an expression of true inwardness because in his opinion the latter is hidden and cannot be given expression in any direct or external form (*CUP*, 1:236–37, 260). Externally, the person who possesses true inwardness relates to it as a dead person: "He does not gesticulate, he does not protest, he does not flare up in a moment of inwardness, but, silent as the grave and quiet as a dead person, he maintains his inwardness and stands by his word" (*CUP*, 1:236). It is not out of mere conformity to grammatical convention that Climacus uses the third-person masculine pronoun to describe such a person; he explicitly states that "such a person is a man *(en Mand)*" (*CUP*, 1:236). It would seem, then, that only men are capable of manifesting true inwardness, while women are given to momentary excitement and external outbursts of feeling which, although "not unlovely" in them, are "always dangerous" because they frequently result in lethargy (*CUP*, 1:236, 239–40). Even more enduring expressions of feminine inwardness in the form of devotedness to others are relegated to the level of "less inwardness" by Climacus, because "the direction is obviously outward," whereas true inwardness is directed inward to the contrast or comic discrepancy between the individual's existence and the eternal (*CUP*, 1:291).

It is unfortunate that Climacus's negative opinion of women leads him here to compromise universal human claims made elsewhere in the text, such as his statement that "every human being is by nature designed to become a thinker" (*CUP*, 1:47) and the oft-repeated claim that the ethical, or the task of becoming subjective, "is the highest task assigned to every human being" (*CUP*, 1:151, 158, 163; cf. also 134). On the basis of his derogatory remarks about women and "the feminine nature" in relation to the expression of true inwardness, one must conclude either that women are excluded from the category of "human being," or else that they are constitutionally incapable of assuming the highest task assigned to them as human beings. Consequently, they must be regarded as unethical creatures who, ironically, lack subjectivity—the very quality with which they traditionally have been associated, although that quality is to be understood here quite differently from its conventional acceptation.

Climacus's relegation of feminine devotedness to the status of "less inwardness" is particularly problematic when considered in relation to *Works of Love*, a collection of deliberations published only a year after the *Postscript* under Kierkegaard's own name and therefore unequivocally reflecting the philosopher's own views as opposed to those of a pseudonym. While recognizing that there are forms of devotion that are really expressions of self-love, or a "devoted self-love," in the "enormous self-willfulness" with which one other person is loved exclusively in an "unlimited devotion" that ought to be given up (*WL*, 55), Kierkegaard sets forth in this book a Christian understanding of love based on the biblical commandment to love the neighbor, or all human beings, as oneself.[17] Although hidden in its inmost depths, having its ground in the mysterious love of God, neighbor love seeks outward expression and is made known or recognizable by its "fruits" or works of love for others (*WL*, 8–16). Optimally, the Christian view of love, as Kierkegaard understands it, is one in which one's life is "completely squandered . . . on the existence of others" (*WL*, 279). Such a view of love, however, does not square with the "hidden inwardness" of Johannes Climacus, who can find no satisfactory external expression for subjectivity or inwardness and thus cloaks it in humor as the incognito for the incongruity between the internal and the external in the religious individual's life (*CUP*, 1:461–62, 472–75, 492, 499–500).[18] In equating true inwardness with hidden inwardness, therefore, Climacus does not reflect Kierkegaard's own viewpoint, or at least not his view of inwardness as given expression in Christianity, which for him constitutes the highest form of subjectivity.

The second form of inwardness from which Climacus seeks to distinguish true inwardness is "chummy inwardness," or what I take to be a form of intersubjectivity that compromises the integrity of the individual. In contrast to the anti-individualist stance of some feminist epistemologists, Climacus emphasizes the distinctiveness and importance of the single individual or the individual subject, which every human being is and has as his or her task to become (*CUP*, 1:49, 131, 149, 355). In his view, "subjective individuals must be held devoutly apart from one another and must not run coagulatingly together in objectivity" (*CUP*, 1:79). We have already seen that, from Climacus's perspective, every actuality outside oneself can be grasped only through thought or in the form of possibility. To know another person as an actuality would require one to make oneself into the other, or vice versa, to make the actuality of the other into one's own personal actuality, which in Climacus's view is clearly impossible (*CUP*, 1:321). Even if one were able to do that, he says, the new actuality would belong to oneself as distinct from the other (*CUP*, 1:321). Ethically considered, then, "there is no direct relation between subject and subject" (*CUP*, 1:321).

This does not mean, however, that there is no communication or commonality between subjects. Like Socrates and Lessing, who closed themselves off in the isolation of subjectivity, or what Climacus calls "inclosed reserve," the subjective individual is solitary in relation to God, where "the meddling busyness of a third person" signifies "a lack of inwardness" (*CUP*, 1:65, 69, 77, 80).[19] But the subjective individual does sustain, like Socrates, a maieutic relation to others, seeking to help them acquire the same understanding he (or she) possesses through the practice of indirect communication, or the communication of subjective truth in such a way as to leave the other free to appropriate that which constitutes the essentially human (*CUP*, 1:73–79). As Climacus sees it, "[e]very human being must be assumed to possess essentially what belongs essentially to being a human being. The subjective thinker's task is to transform himself [or herself] into an instrument that clearly and definitely expresses in existence the essentially human" (*CUP*, 1:356). But Climacus goes on to point out that "to depend upon differences in this regard is a misunderstanding," for "to will to be an individual human being (which one unquestionably is) with the help of and by virtue of one's difference is flabbiness; but to will to be an individual existing human being (which one unquestionably is) in the same sense as everyone else is capable of being—that is the ethical victory over life and over every mirage" (*CUP*, 1:356). For Climacus, therefore, the art of subjectivity is to become what one essentially is, an individual human being or subject in common with others, not merely a "subject of sorts," in whom "the accidental, the angular, the selfish, the eccentric, etc." is accentuated in distinction from others. True subjectivity is rooted in our commonality as human beings, not in our individual differences, although paradoxically individuality is affirmed and cultivated precisely in and through a recognition of our common humanity in striving personally to appropriate that which constitutes the essentially human and to communicate it indirectly to others. At the most fundamental level, then, all essential knowledge, or that knowledge which pertains essentially to human existence (*CUP*, 1:197–98), is communally shared in the sense that it belongs essentially to every human being, but it is known and appropriated subjectively by each individual.

Conclusions

From this brief account of Johannes Climacus's views on objectivity and subjectivity, several conclusions vis-à-vis recent developments in feminist epistemology may be proposed. First of all, Climacan subjectivity clearly is not subjectivism, as Climacus does not deny the reality of objective truth or our ability to acquire a limited or approximate knowledge of that truth by objective means. Although he shares the postmodernist suspicion of the positivity or certainty of objective knowledge, he avoids epistemological relativism by recognizing that objective knowledge is approximate and for that reason, none other, is uncertain.

Second, we have seen that, while feminists fault the conventional view of objectivity because of its androcentric orientation, which purports to be disinterested but is not, Climacus accepts the essentially disinterested character of objective knowledge but faults it precisely because subjectivity is abandoned in objective modes of inquiry. Whereas feminist epistemologists view objectivity itself as including subjective factors, either surreptitiously (as in the masculinist concept of objectivity) or self-consciously (as in a feminist perspective), Climacus clearly separates the objective and subjective spheres. However, some forms of knowledge that currently fall under the sphere of objectivity, such as the social sciences, might qualify as essential knowledge for him if one is able to detect and appropriate an existential significance behind the numerical, quantitative analysis to which such knowledge is subjected.

Third, while Climacus would reject the anti-individualist stance of feminist epistemologists in emphasizing the single individual whose task first and foremost is to develop subjectivity or inwardness, he nevertheless affirms the concrete, contextual, and communal character of subjective truth or essential knowledge inasmuch as it pertains equally to all human beings with respect to the existential task of realizing in oneself and communicating to others that which constitutes the essentially human. Climacus would deny the communal character of such knowledge, however, if that means we learn and communicate truth through a form of intersubjectivity that blurs the distinction between self and others, as in some postmodernist and integrationist feminist epistemologies. He does not deny that individual subjects are socially constituted through relations to others, but in his view they are able to transcend human relations in the relation to God. Part of the task of subjectivity, therefore, is to assert oneself as an individual over against the determining forces of society such as family, church, and state. In this feminists may find an emancipatory pulse in Climacan subjectivity that, unlike the social determinism of some feminist positions, is able to explain why and how women are capable of resisting the social forces that historically have oppressed them.

Fourth, in emphasizing the cultivation of passion and subjectivity—capacities traditionally associated with women—Climacus can be said to be calling for the incorporation of "the feminine" into epistemology as a way of knowing. But insofar as he associates a particular form of subjectivity—momentary inwardness or emotional enthusiasm—stereotypically with women and distinguishes true inwardness from it, he compromises the feminist thrust of his insight and appears to be anti-women. Essentially, however, existential pathos is nongendered for him inasmuch as it constitutes "the pathos for everyone" (*CUP*, 1:394). Stripped of its sexist associations and narrow conception as hidden inwardness, his understanding of subjectivity or pathos could form the basis for a feminist rethinking of subjectivity in a manner that gives greater depth to the concept as it relates to women and that serves to distinguish female subjectivity precisely from the stereotyped, sexist view of feminine inwardness perpetuated by Climacus.

Fifth, while Climacus agrees with feminists in criticizing the epistemological privileging of objectivity over subjectivity, his failure to recognize the masculinist character of objectivity and his own reverse privileging of subjectivity over against objectivity would lead some feminists to conclude that he was not radical enough in his critique of the speculative-scientific mentality of his time and that his thought continues to reflect and perpetuate the very structures of the dualistic or dichotomous thinking they are intent on displacing. Inasmuch as Climacus does not question the validity of objective thought in itself, however, it would perhaps be more accurate to characterize his understanding of the relation between objectivity and subjectivity, in the manner of some integrationist feminists, as dialectical rather than dualistic or dichotomous, but dialectical in such a way as not to blur the distinction between these terms.

These conclusions suggest that Kierkegaard's *Concluding Unscientific Postscript*, often ignored by the philosophical community because of its emphasis on subjectivity, deserves a sympathetic as well as critical rereading by feminist epistemologists. They may find some viewpoints in it to reject, but also much to support and advance their own attempts to rethink and reformulate the concepts of objectivity and subjectivity in the context of the present age.

Notes

1. In "A First and Last Explanation" appended to the text of *Concluding Unscientific Postscript*, to which Kierkegaard affixed his name only as "editor" of the published version, the claim is put forth that in his pseudonymous works "there is not a single word by me" and that he is responsible for these works only "in a legal and in a literary sense" (*CUP*, 1:626–27). Therefore, one cannot unequivocally equate the views expressed here with those of Kierkegaard himself; however, inasmuch as it constitutes the central philosophical statement of his

authorship, this work undoubtedly contains much with which Kierkegaard is in agreement. On the purpose and role of pseudonymity in Kierkegaard's writings, see Walsh (1994), 10–15; Evans (1983), 6–16; and Hartshorne (1990).

2. For a concise differentiation between four senses of objectivity (absolute, disciplinary, dialectical, and procedural) in current discussions, see Megill (1994), 1–20. It is primarily the absolute sense of objectivity that corresponds to the concept of objectivity attacked by feminist epistemologists, although the disciplinary and procedural senses of the term also involve elements of the absolute sense.

3. For a critique of physics as a paradigm of scientific knowledge-seeking, see Harding (1986), 43–48; and (1991), 77–102. In place of physics, which in her view is atypical of scientific inquiry and anachronistic in its exclusion of values or social influences in explaining reality, Harding recommends that the social sciences be regarded as the model for all science. See also Code (1991), 40–41, and Hubbard (1988), 1–15, who concur with Harding's recommendation. Hubbard points out, however, that even physicists recognized early in this century that experimenters influence the outcome of their experiments, an insight expressed in Heisenberg's "uncertainty principle" (11).

4. For more extended discussions of the first three approaches, see Harding (1991), 111–87; and (1986), 36–57, 136–62; Hekman (1990), 128–35.

5. While objectivists advocate the elimination of all social values and interests in the pursuit of objective knowledge, Harding claims they fail to recognize and critically examine the historical, social position of their own background assumptions and beliefs, thus providing only a limited, partial, distorted view of reality. Strong objectivity, by contrast, "requires causal analyses not just of the micro processes in the laboratory but also of the macro tendencies in the social order, which shape scientific practices" (Harding 1991, 144, 147).

6. As Harding points out elsewhere, this position is not based on biological differences between men and women or upon essentialist claims of a distinctive "female nature," although it is often misunderstood as doing so. Rather, it is based on gender differences, or differences rooted in women's social situation and experiences, which provide an objective location from which to conduct feminist research and to criticize knowledge claims—although not an epistemological foundation for grounding knowledge claims as such, since "experience itself is shaped by social relations" (1991, 120–21 and n. 19; 123, 132–34, 137 n. 39). On object-relations theory, which accounts for the development of gender differences between males and females on the basis of how their Oedipal relation to the mother is resolved, see Chodorow (1978).

7. Hekman thus opposes a feminist epistemology that would privilege the feminine over against the masculine. As Gergen (1988) points out, the problem with the feminist standpoint theory is that it is difficult, if not impossible, to locate a common perspective on knowledge among women, as there is a variety of schools of feminist interpretation. Which among these, he asks, should be granted epistemological privilege as the feminist standpoint, and on what grounds? (32). On the abandonment of the concept of objectivity, see also MacKinnon (1987), although her critique of objectivity proceeds from a Marxist rather than postmodernist perspective.

8. For a discussion of French postmodern feminist concepts of self-identity, see Walsh (1994), 251–57, and other works cited therein.

9. Hekman (1990) appeals to Foucault's view of the constituted subject as "the subject that resists" and to Julia Kristeva's claim that the subject in process is one that has revolutionary potential, although it is not clear from either of these analyses how the subject who is constituted by discourse has the power to resist that constitution.

10. For an example of feminist standpoint theory that advocates subjectivism, see Belenky et al. (1986), 10, 52–75. For a critique of this position, see Code (1991), 253–64. Harding

(1991) argues that feminist standpoint theory advocates cultural or historical relativism but not an epistemological or judgmental relativism, as critical evaluation based on a scientific account is required "to determine which social situations tend to generate the most objective knowledge claims" (142). Hekman (1990) counters the charge of relativism in postmodernist thought by arguing that "all knowledge is contextual and historical, thus rendering the opposition between absolute and relative obsolete" (153).

11. See Ring (1991) who espouses a "minimalist dialectics" in line with the positions of Harding and Keller but places greater emphasis on the element of conflict than they do (27). On dialectical objectivity generally, see Megill (1994), 7–10. See also Code (1991), who advocates a "mitigated relativism" that is constrained by objectivity but takes subjectivity into account (251).

12. For an account of scientific practice involving such an interaction, see Keller (1983). See also Code (1991), who argues with regard to knowing subjects "that there is no stark dichotomy between interdependence and autonomy, that they are neither oppositional nor mutually exclusive" (74).

13. Feminists taking this approach do not entirely agree, however, in their reinscription of these terms. While Keller, for example, calls for a "dynamic objectivity" that includes a sense of connectedness to the objective world, thus redefining objectivity in a feminine manner that downplays (masculine) separation or autonomy (Keller 1985, 115–26), Ring (1991) retains the traditional association of objectivity with distance, detachment, and isolation, but is unwilling to concede that these characteristics are specifically male or entirely bad (54). Indeed, feminist-standpoint epistemologists appeal precisely to women's outsider or isolated status in relation to the established order as that which enables them to give a better and more objective account of the world.

14. Cf. PF, 79–84 and n. 53, where Climacus shows that, in a very fundamental way, every historical event requires an element of belief in its having come into existence, as events are always known after the fact; that is, after they have come into existence. The illusive quality of every historical event, to which we are not privy through immediate sensation and cognition, is the transition moment of coming into existence, by which the occurrence of that event is rendered uncertain. Climacus also points out—in conformity, he claims, with Greek skepticism as well as with Plato and Aristotle—that immediate sensation and cognition are not in themselves deceptive; rather, the possibility of deception arises in the *conclusions* one draws on the basis of immediate sensation and cognition. But, whereas the Greek skeptics engaged in a suspension of judgment in order to avoid error, Climacus calls for a decision or resolution (*Beslutning*), in the form of belief, that involves risk or the possibility of error, in contrast to a conclusion (*Slutning*), whose claims are those of positive or certain knowledge. Belief, like doubt, he further points out, is not a cognitive act or form of knowledge. Rather, these existential modes are opposite passions: belief constituting "a sense for coming into existence," while "doubt is a protest against any conclusion that wants to go beyond immediate sensation and immediate knowledge" (84).

15. See also Perkins (1973), where it is pointed out that "the ultimate limit of the objective way of knowing is to forget the subjective aspect, the knower, entirely and arrive at some type of fantastic knowledge without a knower. . . . Objective knowledge can and does with profit exclude the subjective, but it cannot exclude the knower" (213).

16. Although the definite article may be used enclitically to form abstract nouns in Danish, I have amended the Hong translation of this passage to emphasize its reference to the truth of subjectivity in the concrete individual rather than to the subjective nature of truth. The construal of Climacus's statement in terms of the latter meaning leaves him open to the charge of subjectivism, which is entirely unjustified. For the Danish phrase see SV 7, 237. On the need for amending the standard translation of this phrase, see Perkins (1973), 211. For an interpreta-

tion of Kierkegaard's understanding of subjectivity in terms of the concept of upbuilding, see also Perkins (1990), 7–18.

17. For more extended treatments of this work see Walsh (1988), 234–56; and (1995), 167–79. See also *SUD*, where Kierkegaard's pseudonymous Christian author, Anti-Climacus, also associates the feminine nature with devotedness and, like Climacus, regards femininity as constituting a "lower synthesis" than does masculinity, which he thinks "essentially belongs within the qualification of spirit" (50 n; 67). But Anti-Climacus nevertheless claims that in relation to God it holds for both men and women that "devotion is the self" and that "in the giving of oneself the self is gained" (50 n). This suggests that while devotedness in woman is a natural phenomenon that may serve as a mode of despair, or failure to become a self, because of a misplaced identification of the self with the object of her devotion, it is essential to the definition of a self and to becoming such in relation to God. For a more detailed discussion of devotedness as a mode of despair, see Walsh (1987), 121–34, or its revised version in this volume (Chapter 9).

18. For a more extended discussion of the role of humor in *CUP*, see Walsh (1994), 212–17. On hidden inwardness see also *PC*, 212–20, where Kierkegaard, in the persona of his Christian pseudonym, Anti-Climacus, explicitly rejects the notion of hidden inwardness because it too easily may serve in established Christendom as a ploy for claiming that all are true Christians; instead, Anti-Climacus insists upon an "inverted recognizability" of the Christian life in voluntary suffering as a result of opposition from the world.

19. Although the phenomenon of inclosing reserve is analyzed in *CA* as a demonic attempt to close oneself off from others in anxiety about the good or the possibility of freedom, Vigilius Haufniensis, the pseudonymous author of this book, also identifies a "lofty inclosing reserve," exemplified by Socrates, which he associates with earnestness and true (as opposed to spurious) religious inwardness. For a discussion of this form of inclosed reserve, which is what Johannes Climacus has in mind when he uses these terms in *CUP*, see Walsh (1994), 159–63.

References

Antony, Louise M. 1993. "Quine as Feminist: The Radical Import of Naturalized Epistemology." In *A Mind of One's Own: Feminist Essays on Reason and Objectivity*, edited by Louise M. Antony and Charlotte Witt, 185–225. Boulder, Colo.: Westview.

Beauvoir, Simone de. 1989. *The Second Sex*. Translated and edited by H. M. Parshley. New York: Vintage Books.

Belenky, Mary Field, Blythe McVicker Clinchy, Nancy Rule Goldberger, and Jill Mattuck Tarule. 1986. *Women's Ways of Knowing: The Development of Self, Voice, and Mind*. New York: Basic Books.

Bordo, Susan. 1987. *The Flight to Objectivity: Essays on Cartesianism and Culture*. Albany: State University of New York Press.

Chodorow, Nancy. 1978. *The Reproduction of Mothering*. Berkeley and Los Angeles: University of California Press.

Code, Lorraine. 1991. *What Can She Know? Feminist Theory and the Construction of Knowledge*. Ithaca: Cornell University Press.

Duran, Jane. 1991. *Toward A Feminist Epistemology*. Savage, Md.: Rowman and Littlefield.

Evans, C. Stephen. 1983. *Kierkegaard's "Fragments" and "Postscript": The Religious Philosophy of Johannes Climacus*. Atlantic Highlands, N.J.: Humanities Press.

Gergen, Kenneth. 1988. "Feminist Critique of Science and the Challenge of Social Epistemology." In *Feminist Thought and the Structure of Knowledge,* edited by Mary McCanney Gergen, 27–48. New York: New York University Press.

Harding, Sandra. 1983. "Why Has the Sex/Gender System Become Visible Only Now?" In *Discovering Reality: Feminist Perspectives on Epistemology, Metaphysics, Methodology, and Philosophy of Science,* edited by Sandra Harding and Merill B. Hintikka, 311–24. Dordrecht: Reidel.

———. 1986. *The Science Question in Feminism.* Ithaca: Cornell University Press.

———. 1991. *Whose Science? Whose Knowledge?.* Ithaca: Cornell University Press.

Hartshorne, M. Holmes. 1990. *Kierkegaard, Godly Deceiver: The Nature and Meaning of His Pseudonymous Writings.* New York: Columbia University Press.

Hartsock, Nancy C. M. 1983. "The Feminist Standpoint: Developing the Ground for a Specifically Feminist Historical Materialism." In *Discovering Reality: Feminist Perspectives on Epistemology, Metaphysics, Methodology, and Philosophy of Science,* edited by Sandra Harding and Merill B. Hintikka, 283–310. Dordrecht: Reidel.

Haslanger, Sally. 1993. "On Being Objective and Being Objectified." In *A Mind of One's Own: Feminist Essays on Reason & Objectivity,* edited by Louise M. Antony and Charlotte Witt, 85–125. Boulder, Colo.: Westview.

Hawkesworth, Mary E. 1989. "Knowers, Knowing, Known: Feminist Theory and Claims of Truth." *Signs* 14, no. 3:533–57.

———. 1994. "From Objectivity to Objectification: Feminist Objections." In *Rethinking Objectivity,* edited by Allan Megill, 151–77. Durham: Duke University Press.

Hekman, Susan J. 1990. *Gender and Knowledge: Elements of a Postmodern Feminism.* Boston: Northeastern University Press.

Hodge, Joanna. 1988. "Subject, Body and the Exclusion of Women from Philosophy." In *Feminist Perspectives in Philosophy,* edited by Morwenna Griffiths and Margaret Whitford, 152–68. Bloomington: Indiana University Press.

Hubbard, Ruth. 1988. "Some Thoughts about the Masculinity of Science." In *Feminist Thought and the Structure of Knowledge,* edited by Mary McCanney Gergen, 1–15. New York: New York University Press.

Irigaray, Luce. 1985. *Speculum of the Other Woman.* Translated by Gillian C. Gill. Ithaca: Cornell University Press.

Jardine, Alice. 1985. *Gynesis: Configurations of Women and Modernity.* Ithaca: Cornell University Press.

Keller, Evelyn Fox. 1983. *A Feeling for the Organism: The Life and Work of Barbara McClintock.* New York: W. H. Freeman.

———. 1985. *Reflections on Gender and Science.* New Haven: Yale University Press.

Lloyd, Genevieve. 1984. *The Man of Reason.* London: Methuen.

Longino, Helen. 1990. *Science as Social Knowledge: Values and Objectivity in Scientific Inquiry.* Princeton: Princeton University Press.

MacKinnon, Catharine. 1987. *Feminism Modified.* Cambridge: Harvard University Press.

Megill, Allan. 1994. *Rethinking Objectivity.* Durham: Duke University Press.

Nelson, Lynn Hankinson. 1990. *Who Knows: From Quine to a Feminist Empiricism.* Philadelphia: Temple University Press.

Perkins, Robert L. 1973. "Kierkegaard's Epistemological Preferences." *International Journal for Philosophy of Religion* 4, no. 4:197–217.

———. 1990. "Kierkegaard, A Kind of Epistemologist." *History of European Ideas* 12, no. 1:7–18.

Ring, Jennifer. 1991. *Modern Political Theory and Contemporary Feminism: A Dialectical Analysis.* Albany: State University of New York Press.

Rose, Hilary. 1983. "Hand, Brain and Heart: A Feminist Epistemology for the Natural Sciences." *Signs* 9, no. 1:73–90.

Walsh, Sylvia. 1987. "On 'Feminine' and 'Masculine' Forms of Despair." In *International Kierkegaard Commentary: The Sickness unto Death*, edited by Robert L. Perkins, 121–34. Macon: Mercer University Press.

———. 1988. "Forming the Heart: The Role of Love in Kierkegaard's Thought." In *The Grammar of the Heart: New Essays in Moral Philosophy and Theology*, edited by Richard H. Bell, 234–56. San Francisco: Harper and Row.

———. 1994. *Living Poetically: Kierkegaard's Existential Aesthetics*. University Park: The Pennsylvania State University Press.

———. 1995. "Kierkegaard's Philosophy of Love." In *The Nature and Pursuit of Love: The Philosophy of Irving Singer*, edited by David Goicoechea, 167–79. Amherst, N.Y.: Prometheus Books.

13

The Silent Woman in Kierkegaard's Later Religious Writings

Wanda Warren Berry

Introductory Note: Wresting and Jesting Silence

Feminist readers of Kierkegaard are jolted when they encounter the long apologetic for the fateful New Testament line, "women should be silent in the churches" (1 Cor. 14:33b–35), which concludes the first part of Kierkegaard's *For Self-Examination* (*FSE*, 46–51). Some Kierkegaardians may wish they could argue that the image of the silent woman here is a mere afterthought, insignificant to the main themes of one of the more often read "Christian discourses." This is ruled out by the fact that the image culminates not only the first discourse, but the overture to the whole work, the Introductory Note. The first two paragraphs of this note are dominated by issues about "speech," "oratory," "eloquence," and "preaching."[1] In this keynoting section, the authorship's central concern for what Kierkegaard elsewhere calls "subjective appropriation" (CUP) or "reduplication" (WL) is presented in terms of personal integrity in oral communication. The Note moves toward directly addressing two kinds of persons who Kierkegaard realizes are left out of such an exhortation to responsible speech acts. First, a "simple one," of whom Kierkegaard is reminded because he has been emphasizing the simplicity of the command to do what one hears (FSE, 11). Then comes the first of the discourse's three dramatic direct addresses to his female readers (FSE, 11, 46, 50): "And you, O woman, even if you are quite speechless in charming silence—if your life expresses what you heard, your eloquence is more powerful, more true, more persuasive than all the art of orators" (FSE, 11). From this direct address to the woman, the Introductory Note moves quickly to its close, by way of an amen, the "So it is" which leads the reader into a summary reemphasis upon living the truths one claims (FSE, 11).

Feminist Kierkegaardians cannot "express what they have heard" if they argue for the liberatory aspects of the authorship without addressing the lapse into romanticized patriarchy shown in For Self-Examination's image of the silent woman (see Berry, 1992 and 1995c). The literal silencing of women within the history of Western ecclesiology has come to symbolize women's lives within patriarchy. Mary Daly's (1973) call that we hear "our sisters whose voices have been stolen from them" has echoed throughout the women's movement (158). Independently influential is the voice of Audre Lorde (1984) saying, "the transformation of silence into language and action is an act of self-revelation," calling each woman "to recognize her role as vital within that transformation . . . there are so many silences to be broken" (42–44).

In his Preface Kierkegaard urges each reader of For Self-Examination to read this discourse "aloud," in order not to hear any other voice, but to "consider" only himself or herself. But both the explicit use of 1 Corinthians 14:33b–35 and the reiterated formula of direct address to "woman" obviate any possibility for a feminist to imagine For Self-Examination's words as her or his own. Even when normally preferring to interpret Kierkegaard in terms of his stated reasons for using specific literary forms, a feminist interpreter in this case must deliberately resist authorial intention. She or he here must wrest with silence, experiencing a wrenching encounter with the limitations of the very author who in other works so clearly sponsors the freedom she or he chooses for women.

Such an approach enters the discourse ready to "twist and turn by force" Kierkegaard's own sexist rationalizations.[2] Only after such wresting can a feminist suggest that we "read silence aloud," asking whether we can join Kierkegaard by "resting in silence"[3] when it symbolizes the active trust in transcendent governance that grounds what Kierkegaard calls "jest," religiously motivated ethical action.

Deliberately disobeying Kierkegaard's prefatory request that we read this discourse "aloud" so as to encounter ourselves rather than the author, this feminist interpretation first will attempt to hear Kierkegaard's own culturally relative voice articulating the image of the silent woman. It also will criticize this discourse's biblical hermeneutics and views of women. Furthermore, it will hear the discourse in terms of the authorship, noting other uses of the category of silence in Kierkegaard's later religious writings. These strategies are necessary if our hermeneutic for reading Kierkegaard is to avoid the same absolutizing approach to a text that contributes to Kierkegaard's gender-specific interpretation of the biblical command to silence. Only after these critical studies will this essay conclude by suggesting a positive comparison between Kierkegaard's use of silence and contemporary ecofeminist orientations, opening the possibility that feminists might hear themselves in reading aloud portions of these texts.

Reading Silence Silently

The Word as Mirror and Love Letter

The controlling context for the controversial passage on the silent woman in *For Self-Examination* is a beguiling presentation of Kierkegaard's biblical hermeneutic, developed as the discourse interprets the epistle lesson (James 1:22–27) through an emphasis upon the dialectic of grace and works. Kierkegaard argues that Luther's "salvation by faith" has been wrongly appropriated by a secular mentality in terms of what the twentieth century sometimes has called "cheap grace." Approving of Luther's phrase, "faith is a restless thing," Kierkegaard identifies self-knowledge as the source of his misgiving about an emphasis only on grace, saying: "I am not an honest soul but a cunning fellow" (*FSE*, 24). In the light of this knowledge he considers it important to emphasize the "minor premise (works, existence, to witness to and suffer for the truth, works of love, etc.)" rather than the "major premise": faith (FSE, 24). Thus he returns to the lesson from James with its emphasis on not only "hearing the Word, but doing it." His turn toward biblical hermeneutics is made by noting that one cannot become a "doer" of a Word that one has not "heard" or "read" (FSE, 25).

In three steps, all of which emphasize existential reading/hearing, Kierkegaard works with the imagery of mirror and "Word" to urge that the Bible be read with serious concern to hear what God wills that one do. The first, "you must not look at the mirror . . . but must see yourself in the mirror," at some length contrasts biblical scholarship with existential reading (FSE, 25). While Kierkegaard claims not to "disparage scholarship," he urges that one recognize that scholarship differs from existential reading. He calls for a religious orientation to Scripture in which the motivation for biblical scholarship is that one move through it in order to hear God's word and, in turn, to enact it.

In this context, the metaphor of the Bible "as a love letter from God" aims to convince one of the personal urgency with which the person of faith must approach texts understood to be revelatory. To see a text as Scripture is to expect it to communicate divine purpose, a purpose that when heard must be enacted. The second requirement, "to say to yourself incessantly: . . . It is I to whom it is speaking," emphasizes that such a reading happens only through a complete transition to the subjective, wherein the reader interprets each passage as addressed to herself (FSE, 35). Finally, the third requirement, if one is to hear the revelatory Word, is that one "not be a forgetful hearer," but remember how one looks in the mirror of the Word (FSE, 44). Here again Kierkegaard emphasizes the need for "honest distrust of oneself," so that one enacts what one has heard like the addict who tricks his craving not by a long-term vow, but "one day at a time" (FSE, 45).

The Silent Woman in For Self-Examination

The call "not [to] be a forgetful hearer" (FSE, 44) provides the context for the controversial passage about women and the counsel to silence (FSE, 46–51). Kierkegaard moves toward his conclusion by asking the imagined hearer not to divert energy away from the epistle lesson by turning toward criticizing "the speaker or the speech" (*FSE*, 46). Again multiplying the oral imagery, he pleads with the potential critic that he instead read the text from James "aloud" and "promptly." Then it is as if Kierkegaard suddenly "remembers the ladies" (Adams 1990, 450–51), realizing that half of the human species was barred from such "reading aloud." His nineteenth-century consciousness extends the arena of women's silence into the home, whereas in the New Testament passage the concern is with the religious congregation; this extension implicitly includes the whole of the public sphere as well:

> And you, O woman, for you it is indeed reserved to be able to be the image of the hearer and reader of the Word who is not forgetful. You comply fittingly with the apostle's admonition: Let the woman keep silence in the congregation; it is fitting. Neither does she take up preaching in the home; it is unbecoming. No, let her be silent; let her treasure the Word in silence; let her silence express that she treasures it deeply. (*FSE*, 46)

We should note that having started with direct address, by the third sentence Kierkegaard lapses into the third person, having been led by the quotation from "the apostle," "Let the woman keep silence in the congregation," into an objectifying discourse that allows essentialist categorizing.

The audience for the next direct address, "Do you not believe in silence?" is not clear. But the development of the second paragraph of the section (*FSE*, 46–47) implies that Kierkegaard no longer addresses women, but describes "woman." To an audience that apparently is imagined as male and female, Kierkegaard sets out to describe a woman of a particular kind, "a hearer of the Word who does not forget the Word" (*FSE*, 46). The overall theme of the discourse is reemphasized, then, by saying that the point of such a description is that one "not forget to become such a person" oneself. It is significant that this paragraph stresses that the woman who is not a forgetful hearer of the Word and does not speak either in the public sphere of the congregation or "talk about religion at home" has "become" silent by virtue of a conscious decision (*FSE*, 51). The question "What does this silence mean?" is asked with some slight variations six times (*FSE*, 46–47). In the fifth instance it is elaborated in such a way as to make it clear that the human ideal the woman represents is not an unthinking obeisance to the biblical counsel, but a chosen mode of religiousness. At this point the woman's husband is pictured as "straightforwardly" saying to her:

> "What does this silence mean, what are you thinking of, for there is something behind all this, something you always seem to have in mind—tell me what it is!"—she does not say it directly. At most she may say evasively, "Are you coming to church with me on Sunday?"—and then speaks of other things, or she says, "Promise to read a sermon aloud to me on Sunday!"—and then speaks of other things. (FSE, 47)

Having here hinted that the silent woman represents a person who has decided for a lifestyle that *indirectly* points others toward the Holy, the discourse itself eschews direct explanation of her silence. Instead Kierkegaard proceeds to offer the "Christian" diagnosis that "the present age" suffers from a disease in which noisy stimuli and "ever new instruments" aim to "jolt the senses" and "stir up" the crowd. The noisiness that blocks hearing God's Word is epitomized for Kierkegaard in the "rubbish" of that which is communicated through new systems of "speedy . . . overall circulation" (FSE, 48). As an antidote to this poison he calls for the "creation of silence" and promptly asserts that women have a particular power for this task (FSE, 48). The calling of "men to silence," a silence that can only be accomplished by the extraordinary man, can be achieved by "any woman" if she "wills it" in service to a higher purpose.

Of course, this essentialist definition of a peculiar talent belonging to "any woman" is premised upon heterosexuality, since the woman's power is posed in relationship to calling *men* to silence. Elsewhere I have called the tendency to express existential dialectics in male-female imagery "the heterosexual imagination" (see Berry 1995a). In For Self-Examination the cultural relativity of such imagery is especially manifest; here Kierkegaard parallels the public and domestic spheres with maleness and femaleness in ways that clearly express the economic arrangements that developed along with industrial capitalism in Europe and America and cannot be read as characteristic of all cultural frameworks (Davis 1981).

Kierkegaard's self-consciousness about emerging nineteenth-century controversies over women's emancipation motivates him in this passage to follow the introduction of his essentialism with an immediate denial that identification of women with a special sphere is "unfair" (FSE, 48). Kierkegaard argues that neither nature nor Christianity has been unfair to woman, since women are not denied humanity and power by having their lives' boundaries within a separate sphere. Women can choose to fulfill the human and feminine need for exercising power in a variety of ways. Close analysis of these lines (*FSE*, 48) reveals an interesting synthesis in Kierkegaard's inscription of the feminine between conventionally acceptable ways to women's power (through "beauty," "charm," "talent," and "happy temperament") and more surprisingly new romantic developments: e.g., "bold imagination." The way to power through this romanticized femininity is recognized as "shaky and uncertain," but it is clearly preferred to the "noisy" way, which he evaluates as "ugly and false." A fuller indication of what he sees as the "noisy" way is found in the last paragraph of this section, which moves sentence by sentence through brief indications of the dangers for women in both the aesthetic and the ethical spheres and an invocation of silence as symbol of religious existence:

> Remember the apostle's words about looking at oneself in the mirror of the Word. A woman who looks at herself in the mirror very much becomes vain and vainly loquacious. And a woman who looks at herself in the mirror of time becomes stridently noisy! Ah, but a woman who looks at herself in the mirror of the Word becomes silent! (*FSE*, 50)

Here the ethical sphere of freedom to will "world-historical achievement" is possible for women, but is identified as a "noisy" way. Kierkegaard's earlier diagnosis of the sickness of the present age as "noisiness" may explain why his language is much less negative about aesthetic vanity than world-historical effort, which in women is associated with stridency, ugliness, and falsehood (*FSE*, 48–50).

When Kierkegaard goes on in this passage to his third direct address to "woman" (*FSE*, 48), telling her to choose power by learning and teaching silence, the ensuing application of his counsel to women of all classes emphasizes in each case the "charm" that "woman" can create in her home, whatever the economic circumstances. It is interesting that Kierkegaard is self-conscious about his own bias, saying that it is the poet/the aesthete in him that sees charm as praiseworthy (*FSE* 48–49). Nevertheless, he does not try to balance this personal preference for the aesthetic feminine. While his description of the aesthetic way to feminine power emphasizes the quality of "charm" that the poet prefers, there are no comparable indications of the at least relative value of historical achievement for women:

> a woman can exercise her power in different ways—with her beauty, her charm, her talents, with her bold imagination, with her happy temperament—she can also attempt to become a power in a noisy manner. The latter way is ugly and false, but the former is shaky and uncertain. But, if you want to be a power, O woman, let me confide in you how to do it. Learn silence, and teach silence! (FSE, 48)

The main point of the whole controversial discussion of the silent woman is that women, in the separate sphere of the household, can become models of faith of particular value to the modern age. By practicing silence in the home, they can redeem an age in which "the man has so much to do, has so much, far too much, to do with the noisy world" (FSE, 50). Thinking within the framework of the nineteenth century's bourgeois dichotomies between public and private (male and female) spheres, Kierkegaard offers the possibility that a woman in her "natural" sphere can best point toward a religious orientation if she becomes silent.

Two things must be noted at this point: In the first place, while Kierkegaard identifies the essentially "womanly" with realization of the "art of making a house a home," he also recognizes that this task in itself can be accomplished either ethically, as a meritorious achievement, or religiously, through silence, "eternity's art." He says, "even if the young girl never marries, we nevertheless rank her according to this womanly merit: the art of making a house a home. But silence brought into a house—that is eternity's art of making a house a home!" (FSE, 50). In the second place, it is significant that Kierkegaard's emphasis is on the power of the presence of a woman who has chosen silence, and who therefore points others indirectly toward the transcendent, rather than on what might be called "the silence of lambs," who without freedom are sacrificed for the sake of the atonement of others with God.

Speaking Out while Reading Silently

Having read the silent woman "silently" through establishing the context of the passage as well as through an exegesis that sought to follow Kierkegaard's thinking as he developed the passage, we should now engage in a brief feminist critique of what has been revealed in this reading. The main issues center in (a) Kierkegaard's biblical hermeneutic and its use in this discourse, and (b) his lapse into essentialism when he talks about "woman."

The unsatisfactory character of Kierkegaard's use of the Bible in the discussion of the gender-specific counsel to silence reveals the limitations of the biblical hermeneutic set forth in this discourse. His call for a reading of the Bible that is motivated by existential concern invokes the central meaning of a religious reading and is echoed in most feminist biblical scholarship (see e.g., Russell 1985 and Schneiders 1991). However, the personal urgency that women bring to their reading of the Bible involves a knowledge of the deep ambiguity of biblical traditions for women. Feminists who continue reading the Bible do so, on the one hand, because the traditions flowing from it have importantly contributed to their own development. On the other hand, they cannot read the Bible simply as "a love letter from God"; they are painfully aware of the extent to which this complex collection of texts has been shaped by patriarchal culture and has been used to support women's subordination. Feminist biblical scholars have been developing careful dialectical strategies through which they aim to preserve the "hermeneutics of suspicion" as well as their ability to "hear God's word" through the Scripture of the communities they aim to reform. Kierkegaard's metaphor of the Bible as "a love letter from God" loses the dialectical tension that feminist hermeneutics require; however wonderful its reminder that Scripture should be read with existential concern, it asks for a naive reading impossible for feminists.

Kierkegaard himself, as we have noted, says he does not reject biblical scholarship; nevertheless, his "love-letter" metaphor is inadequate to correct his own cultural bias. It leads him to ignore even the most rudimentary scholarship when interpreting the gender-specific command to silence. Careful scholars long have interpreted the passage at issue (1 Cor. 14:26–36) in terms of its contradiction of other sections even of the same letter, which by calling women to cover their heads when speaking assumes their vocal activity in the congregation (e.g., 1 Cor. 11:2–16). Furthermore, a minimal requirement of scholarly reading is to interpret passages in the immediate context. To romanticize the command that women be silent in the congregation without noting that the passage goes on to legitimate the subordination of women to their husbands is at least unscholarly; an ethically sensitive and realistic interpretation would go on to notice that such an interpretation has encouraged individual and social pathologies.

Of course, the main issue feminists would have with Kierkegaard's interpretation of the gender-specific counsel to silence would be its failure to take into consideration the historical-cultural setting of the text. The premise of feminist theory in all fields is recognition of the massive distortions wrought by the historical reality of patriarchal culture. Recently, for example, historian of religions Ross Kraemer has concurred with the common view that the counsel to women's silence in 1 Corinthians is a later interpolation that was intended to silence not just women in general, but women prophets. These women participated in the ecstatic forms of religiousness practiced in the early church in Corinth. It may be significant that this spirituality apparently supported "a severing of the connections between sexuality, childbearing, and the transmission of property" (Kraemer 1992, 150).

Working through such historical-cultural and textual analysis, biblical feminists who read the Bible as a crucial record of the dialogue with God in their own historical communities in a sense employ Kierkegaard's stated method more faithfully than he does. Existential concern propels them into scholarship. They face honestly the tension between such passages and their own self-knowledge. As historical theologian Rosemary Radford Ruether says:

> The hermeneutical circle between scripture and contemporary concerns must be a two-way relationship. We must be questioned by but also be prepared to question scripture. . . . By searching in depth places where the world-view of the New Testament puzzles or confronts our assumptions, we can open up, again and again, transforming insights that expand our vision. . . . Yet we cannot abstain from coming, at times, to a provisional judgment that the world of the Hebrew Bible or New Testament falls short of values which we must affirm. There are indeed tribalistic triumphalism, sectarian rancour, justifications of slavery and sexism in parts of scripture. The text then becomes a document of human collective moral failure, rather than a prescriptive norm. (Ruether 1981, 4–5)

Such feminist biblical interpretation, then, leads to theological emphases that are consonant with aspects of *The Sickness unto Death*. When one looks at such biblical "texts of terror" (Trible 1984) as the command that women be silent, the mirror of the Scripture reveals sin. In this framework, to avoid being "a forgetful hearer of the Word" (*FSE*, 44), one might interpret the "feminine" sin as listening and the "masculine" sin as speaking, realizing that both can be reinterpreted to apply to systemic social realities as well as to individuals (see, e.g., Crites 1992).

In the second place, Kierkegaard's egregious use of the gender-specific command to be silent was caused not only by the beguiling power of the "love-letter" metaphor, but also by his tendency to lapse from religious existentialism into essentialism when talking about women (see Berry 1995b). While the existential maieutic of the authorship calls for reading the comparable lapse in *Either/Or*, Part II as a function of the pseudonym (Judge William), Kierkegaard affixed his own name to *For Self-Examination*, obviating the possibility of finding a "crotchety fiction" (Crites 1992, 144) behind the lapse into essentialism. *For Self-Examination* makes very clear the importance of remembering that this author insists he is "without authority" (*PV*, 151). One must retain authority in oneself as one moves through the authorship's existential maieutic, testing truth by one's own ability to appropriate each stage in existence. Kierkegaard encourages such reading from the outset, even in the direct discourse of *For Self-Examination*, admitting his weakness and that he may be "all too pampered" (*FSE*, 12).

Throughout the authorship, even in *For Self-Examination*, by virtue of his explicit attention to women, Kierkegaard provides a *via negativa* for women by making romanticized patriarchy manifest rather than hidden (see Berry 1995a). While I have argued that such an effect may have been consciously intended in the explicit treatment of female characters in *Either/Or*, Part I, in the direct communication of this discourse, we cannot avoid the judgment that Kierkegaard himself has lapsed into unconscious identification with nineteenth-century ideologies of the "separate sphere." The liberatory effect of his religious existentialism in the authorship as a whole can be reaffirmed only *after* this essentialist lapse into sexism has been criticized.

Those who themselves are attracted to the romanticized picture of women's peculiar affinity for the kind of domesticity that rescues us from the corrupt public world might try several self-examinations not encouraged by Kierkegaard. Imagine applying such an analysis to the existence of the African-American slave woman who, at the very time Kierkegaard is writing, labors in the field or the mines along with the male. See her in her home, which is the only arena where her work is for her own family; here she shares with the male fundamental tasks for survival (Davis 1981, 16–17), rather than being free "to spread a certain charm over [her] house" (*FSE*, 48). Try remembering the full power of Sojourner Truth's baring her muscular arm and saying, "Ain't I a woman too?" Imagine her Danish counterpart lifting and scrubbing for the privileged folk of Copenhagen. Remember that industrialization "freed" middle-class women from arduous tasks essential to the economy (agriculture, food production, spinning, weaving, and so forth) only by the creation of the proletariat woman in the sweatshop, who is encouraged to feel self-hatred and guilt when the dominant-class ideology of femininity renders her existence "unwomanly."

Some might ask: But haven't women's studies helped us to look for the meaningfulness women created throughout the centuries even under oppression? Aren't those of us "in search of our mothers' gardens" well advised to appreciate the values that women's domesticity created in the midst of the dehumanization of industrial capitalism? Isn't Kierkegaard really doing something analogous to those who now emphasize the beauty of domestic arts and crafts? Unfortunately, no. Inspired by a wrongheaded biblical hermeneutic, he romantically ignores real women's lives when he pictures "any" woman as having her task in the separate sphere. By contrast, call to mind Alice Walker's picture of her mother, who is remembered as "literally" covering "the holes in our walls with sunflowers" from the abundant gardens that she worked before and after her days in the fields (Walker 1983, 242). Walker's invocation of this "charm-spreading" is a critique of the racist-classist-sexist systems that denied African-American women the usual cultural forms of artistic expression; it does not romanticize oppression by talking of her mother's essential womanly nature.

Nevertheless, feminists who have been challenged into existence through the indirect communication of such works as *Either/Or, Fear and Trembling,* and *The Sickness unto Death* will tend to proceed beyond critique of Kierkegaard's own culturally conditioned sexist and classist essentialism to the possibility of gender-neutral interpretation, asking, "What does this silence mean?" (*FSE*, 47). We shall know at the outset how unfortunate it is that Kierkegaard was beguiled by his own sexual identity and by romanticized patriarchy into sanctioning the silencing of women. We shall greet with pain reminders that *For Self-Examination* circulated widely even during Kierkegaard's lifetime (*FSE*, xiii), as it must, then, have encouraged both the continued oppression of women and a continued separation from the religious sphere symbolized by silence in many men.[4] The danger of such consequences was lessened when this discourse was published together with *Judge for Yourself!* since the passages in the latter work on "the lilies and the birds" and the "jest" of faith make it clear that silence symbolizes important aspects of faith that must not be either distanced from or considered innately natural to the self by virtue of gender. Indeed, I believe a third major factor in Kierkegaard's advocacy of the gender-specific command to silence, perhaps more fateful even than the beguilement of the "love-letter metaphor" in causing his lapse into sexist essentialism, was his long-standing affirmation of the symbolism of silence.

Reading Silence, Silently and Aloud

Hearing Kierkegaard's own voice reading the image of the silent woman in *For Self-Examination*, therefore, must involve more than following his reasoning and noting its cultural relativity; it also requires attention to the theological import of silence as it is developed elsewhere in the authorship. Space will not allow a complete survey of such developments at this time.[5] For our purposes the most direct route to the meaning of silence in Kierkegaard is to compare its association with the imagery of "the birds and lilies" in both *Judge For Yourself!* and "The Lilies of the Field and the Birds of the Air" (CD).

What does the silence taught by "the lilies and the birds" mean? Primarily silence here means existing in terms of an immediate reliance on transcendent power and meaning: "It expresses reverence before God, that it is [God] who disposes, and [God] alone, to whom belongeth wisdom and understanding. And just because this silence is reverence before God, it is (so far as it can be in nature) worship" (CD, 328). While the three virtues taught by the lilies and the birds (silence, obedience, joy) intersect, they have distinct meanings in Kierkegaard's text. Silence specifically symbolizes recognition of an Infinite in simply being finite; this is clear when he summarizes the sections on these virtues by interpreting the conclusion of the Lord's Prayer near the end of "The Lilies of the Field and the Birds of the Air." Here silence expresses the sense of the transcendence of God; that is, that one's own existence is not to be confused with the Ultimate, the only realm that holds power and glory (CD, 355).

Since For Self-Examination is pervaded by speech imagery,[6] it is important to note that in "The Lilies of the Field and the Birds of the Air" the meaning of silence is set forth as the opposite of speech rather than sheer sound (CD, 323). Speech is unique to humans and in For Self-Examination and Judge for Yourself! is emblematic of human action. In her challenge to the "noisy" world, the silent woman, then, teaches that human activity does not "constitute itself, but is constituted by another" (SUD). Kierkegaard's analysis of the difference between the sounds of nature and human sounds emphasizes not only the "divinity" met in nature (CD, 324), but also that in it there is a "holding" of "peace" (CD, 324), something like ecological "accord" (CD, 325) in which

> each one in particular does its part so well that no one of them breaks the solemn silence, and not all of them together. The forest is silent; even when it whispers it still is silent; for the trees, even when they are most closely crowded together, hold to one another, as men seldom do, in spite of plighted promises—this being said between ourselves. (CD, 324)

Whether teaching "obedience" or "silence," the lilies and the birds have the advantage of being in nature, where one does not forget so easily that "thou art before God" as one does in the human realm through conversation: "the lily who is the teacher is profound. It does not enter into conversation with thee, it keeps silent, and by keeping silent it would signify to thee that thou art before God . . . and might become silent before God" (CD, 328).

Whereas nature simply is silent, humans must become silent. They are to "learn to keep silent," learn to "become nothing before God," seeking first "God's Kingdom" (CD, 322). In religious silence humans acknowledge the unconditioned, the infinite, as transcending all human activity. When naturally silent like the lilies and the birds, one exists by relying on the ground of being rather than one's own effort. This immanental spirituality contrasts with the restless form of religiousness expressed by Johannes de Silentio in Fear and Trembling. Johannes suffers because he feels the call of Abraham to take up finitude in the restless activity of faith-ing, but still relies on his own power to will the God-relation. By way of contrast, when one *becomes* silent, one *chooses* "to wait," trustingly holding one's activity until in "hearing God" one recognizes "the instant" (CD, 323–25). In *human* existence, silence is associated with an expectant waiting in which one rests "patiently" in temporality for the right moment to "employ" the "instant" of the eternal possibility (CD, 326). In addition to patient "waiting" and "hearing," silence before the transcendent involves acknowledging the "suffering" that accompanies finitude (CD, 327). As a consciously chosen orientation, silence expresses the synthesis of infinitude and finitude (SUD).

The special context for the discussion of "the lilies and the birds" and "silence" in *For Self-Examination* and *Judge for Yourself!* places silence into the specifically Christian category (Religiousness B). Here the context emphasizes the difference it makes to hear the teaching about "the lilies and the birds" from the Christ who is both Prototype and Redeemer. On the one hand, as Redeemer, Christ teaches a silence in which one's grateful acknowledgment of the Infinite ("serving only one Master") "mocks every human striving." On the other hand, as Prototype he jestfully "lifts up" the constant striving "with all [one's] might," which Kierkegaard has earlier emphasized as "the restlessness of faith" (JY, 153–54).

In *For Self-Examination* and *Judge for Yourself!* the images of "the lilies and the birds" and "silence" are linked by "jest" (JY, 179). The word for "jester" (*Spøgfugl*) combines jest (*Spøg*) and bird (*Fugl*) (JY, 186), thus resonating with Kierkegaard's repeated association of "birds" with "silence." The whole constellation of meanings is introduced by the image of the silent woman, who also is identified with "jest" (FSE, 47). Faith's reliance upon an Infinite that in its radiance renders all human achievement "miserable and base" is "jest" inasmuch as it is expressed in continuing immersion in striving activity. Human faith is imaged as the seamstress, who unlike the lilies and the birds *does* "spin and sew," but knows that "nevertheless" it is "really God who spins and sews" (JY, 183). The seamstress has not only "grasped the meaning of life," but "her life has in the highest sense become meaningful," because

> she understands that only when she herself is sewing will God sew for her, and therefore she becomes all the more diligent in her work, so that continually sewing she may continually understand that—what a gracious jest!—it is God who sews, every stitch, so that by continually sewing she may continually understand—

what earnestness!—that it is God who sews, every stitch. (JY, 183)[7]

In summary, the combination "silence" and "birds and lilies" points to religious existence as continual reliance upon a Meaning/Power beyond all finite achievement. When these images are constellated with "jest" and "the silent woman," as in *For Self-Examination*, the emphasis is on the ongoing finite activity of human becoming, synthesizing freedom and necessity and, at the same time, pointing not to itself but to God. In Christian silence human striving is informed by Christ both as the Proto-type and the Redeemer, who knows one's "miserable and base" efforts as sin. Silence here trusts in the Other to lift up one's effort through forgive-ness. It is interesting that the image of the silent woman adds such spe-cifically Christian meaning to the image of the seamstress: In the silent woman Kierkegaard pictures a Christian silence that chooses to partici-pate in the redemption of the world from its wrongness.

An "upbuilding" discourse of the same period, "The Woman That Was A Sinner," opens by stressing the role of the silent woman as a "teacher of piety"; but it does not link her silence with jest: "If women are to 'keep silent in the Churches' and to that extent are not to teach—well, that means precisely to keep silent before God, and precisely this belongs essentially to true godliness. . . . So canst thou also learn from a woman the right sort of sorrow for sin, from that woman that was a sinner" (TC, 261). Kierkegaard interprets Luke 7:37–50 by recognizing that the woman in the story is a teacher of "absolute sorrow for our sins" (TC, 262) and that "in relation to finding forgiveness" one can "do nothing at all" (TC, 266). He does not here stress his central concern in *For Self-Examination* and *Judge For Yourself!* that such reliance on transcendent grace gives birth to "jest," to the "striving born of gratitude" with which Kierkegaard identifies Christianity in a *Journal* entry from the same pe-riod (JP, 1:993).

In the temporal process of reading, this is the "instant" to "read silence aloud," considering the possibility that, if we could ignore Kierkegaard's culture-bound voice and hear ourselves, we might find religious truth in the image of faith as the "jest" of silence. Do feminists need this expec-tant trust in the Infinite in order to sustain our striving? Feminism has been an exhilarating contemporary recovery of immanence together with sociopolitical activity; some might think it oppressive to ask it to develop in dialogue with the talk of "transcendence" and "the Infinite" that we have found in Kierkegaard when "reading silence silently." Nevertheless, many feminists have agreed with Mary Daly's (1973) early argument that "sustained effort toward self-transcendence requires keeping alive in one's consciousness the question of ultimate transcendence . . . [recognizing] the fact that we have no power *over* the ultimately real, and that whatever authentic power we have is derived from *participation in* ultimate reality" (39). Other feminists are represented by Rita Gross (1986) who, during the period of her move toward Buddhism, called for a "mature feminism" that recognizes finitude and accepts the kind of suffering which "is simply constituent of being human," rather than a function of patriarchy (41).

Jesting Silence and Ecofeminist Hope

Indeed, there are suggestions of congruence between the themes of Kierkegaard's "jesting" silence and contemporary ecofeminism. Kierkegaard values the interconnected harmony of being that "the lilies and the birds" (nature) teach. He joins ecofeminists in criticizing the "noisy" anthropocentric hyperactivity of modern industrialization. While he lived a century too early to see the ecological crisis, he analyzed modern culture as a falsifying "noisy" consciousness in fantastical separation from natural finitude. "Nature"/"the lilies and the birds" he saw as important teachers who could recall us from this separation. Rosemary Radford Ruether explores similar themes in ecofeminist theology (see Ruether 1992) as she calls for "converting our minds to earth" (1983, 91) in terms comparable to Kierkegaard's redefinition of spirit as conscious choice of the concrete tasks of synthesizing finitude and infinitude (*SUD*). Ruether's ecofeminist hope, grounded in her identity as a Christian reformer, can be positively compared to Kierkegaard's faith and to his "jesting" interpretation of why "the rest is silence." In *Sexism and God-Talk*, Ruether (1983) offers "A Feminist Critique of Eschatology" and concludes with a formulation that seems to provide a liberation theologian's version of Kierkegaard's concern in offering the image of the diligent seamstress:

> We can do nothing about the "immortal" dimension of our lives.
> It is not our calling to be concerned about the eternal meaning of

> our lives. . . . Our responsibility is to use our temporal life span to create a just and good community for our generation and for our children. It is in the hands of Holy Wisdom to forge out of our finite struggle truth and being for everlasting life. Our agnosticism about what this means is then the expression of our faith, our trust that Holy Wisdom will give transcendent meaning to our work, which is bounded by space and time. (258)

Ruether here affirms concrete finitude as an ethico-religious task framed by hope for "transcendent meaning." Her approach is compatible with Kierkegaard's dialectical model of human existence in taking seriously the role of human freedom both in causing and in healing our current crisis. In dialogue with Kierkegaard, Ruether would more consistently emphasize his own characteristic truth criterion: concrete historical existence. She would criticize his views of nature and of women for their ahistorical romantic distortions (1983, 91). She would caution Kierkegaard about romanticizing nature, pointing out that, just as human freedom, rather than nature, has created the separate sphere of the home for women, so it now is unrealistic to picture "the lilies and the birds" as natural powers untouched by human freedom.

I believe that the feminist activism represented by Ruether's ecofeminism has much in common with Kierkegaard's "jesting" interpretation of why "the rest is silence." This is clear when she expresses an ultimate trust in "Holy Wisdom" beyond her own powers at the same time as she rejects quietistic nature romanticism, choosing instead concrete historical strivings for eco-justice. Kierkegaardian "jest" is a passionate ethical striving that consciously relies on transcendent meaning unrealizable by its own effort. And the "rest which is silence" in the jest of silence is informed by the image of Christ as Prototype and Redeemer in both Kierkegaard and Ruether. Striving with full cognizance not only of the radiance of Creation, but also of the devastation of the Fall, Ruether (1983) expresses trust that "the harmony is still there, persisting, supporting, forgiving, preserving us in spite of ourselves. Divine Grace keeps faith with us when we have broken faith with her" (266). Like other pioneering ecofeminists, Ruether wrests silence; she incarnates the refusal to accept the gender-specific command to silence into which Kierkegaard lapsed. Nevertheless, her eschatology and theology of nature show how a feminist might say that "the rest is silence," in terms of Kierkegaardian "striving born of gratitude," a jesting silence commanded for all humans.

By wresting Kierkegaard's use of the image of the silent woman before "reading silence aloud," we have found some agreement with Kierkegaard about the transcendence in which we humans trust at the same time as we "work out [our] own salvation with fear and trembling for it is God who is at work in [us]" (Phil. 2:12b–13a).

Notes

1. In the first two paragraphs of *FSE* forms of the word "orator" occur twelve times; "eloquence" occurs seven times; "speech"/"speak"/"speaker"/"speechless" occurs eight times; "say"/ "saying"/"talking" occurs eight times; "sermon" and "preaching"/"preach" as well as "babble"/ "babblers" occur twice each; "conversation," "pronounced," "discourse," "voice," "diction," "swear" each occurs at least once. Words about speech, then, occur about fifty times.

2. See the *Random House College Dictionary* on "wrest" (New York: Random House, 1979), 1520.

3. See Shakespeare, *Hamlet*, 5.2.369: "The rest is silence."

4. The layers of irony multiply, it seems, even in the Christian authorship: Whereas in *The Sickness unto Death*'s infamous long footnote, Anti-Climacus says that most women come into relationship to God through the relationship to a male, in *For Self-Examination*, the woman's separate sphere is the vehicle for religiousness for the male.

5. Some of the work has been done by others. See especially Taylor 1981, 165–88. Taylor develops an interpretation of silence in the various existential "stages on life's way," using primarily Johannes de Silentio. This leads him to argue that Kierkegaard's picture of the individual before God is inadequately conscious of the relationality fundamental to religious existence and needs correction in the direction of community/communication. It is interesting that the silent woman in *FSE* is pictured as choosing silence for the sake of teaching others, rather than for the sake of a private relationship to God.

6. See not only the Introductory Note to "What Is Required," which has been discussed above, but also, e.g., 73–74.

7. After having provided through the seamstress an image of faith as "willing to be" oneself by resting "transparently in the power" by which one was established (*SUD*, 49), Kierkegaard appears to lapse into sexism as he concludes, "She has lived: whether or not she was married is not crucial" (*FSE*, 183). This gratuitous comment suggests the patriarchal assumption that only marriage gives meaning to a woman's life. But it also could have autobiographical significance; that is, is Kierkegaard saying, "So have I lived: whether or not I was married is not crucial"?

References

Adams, Abigail. 1990. "The Adams Letters." In *Issues in Feminism: An Introduction to Women's Studies*, edited by Sheila Ruth, 450–51. Mountain View, Calif.: Mayfield.

Berry, Wanda Warren. 1992. "Finally Forgiveness: Kierkegaard as a 'Springboard' for a Feminist Theology of Reform." In *Foundations of Kierkegaard's Vision of Community: Religion, Ethics, and Politics in Kierkegaard*, edited by George B. Connell and C. Stephen Evans, 196–217. Atlantic Highlands, N.J.: Humanities Press.

———. 1995a. "The Heterosexual Imagination and Aesthetic Existence in Kierkegaard's *Either/Or*, Part One." In the *International Kierkegaard Commentary: Either/Or, Part I*, edited by Robert L. Perkins, 201–28. Macon: Mercer University Press.

———. 1995b. "Judge William Judging Women: Existentialism and Essentialism in Kierkegaard's *Either/Or*, Part II." In *International Kierkegaard Commentary: Either/Or, Part II*, edited by Robert L. Perkins, 33–57. Macon: Mercer University Press.

———. 1995c. "Kierkegaard and Feminism: Apologetic, Repetition, and Dialogue." In *Kierkegaard in Post/Modernity*, edited by Martin Matuštík and Merold Westphal, 110–24. Bloomington: Indiana University Press.

Crites, Stephen. 1992. "*The Sickness unto Death*: A Social Interpretation." In *Foundations of Kierkegaard's Vision of Community: Religion, Ethics, and Politics in Kierkegaard*, edited by George B. Connell and C. Stephen Evans, 144–60. Atlantic Highlands, N.J.: Humanities Press.

Daly, Mary. 1973. *Beyond God the Father: Toward a Philosophy of Women's Liberation*. Boston: Beacon.

Davis, Angela Y. 1981. *Women, Race, and Class*. New York: Random House.

Gross, Rita. 1986. "Suffering, Feminist Theory, and Images of the Goddess." *Anima: An Experiential Journal* 13, no. 1:39–46.

Kierkegaard, Søren. 1941/1957. *Training in Christianity and the Edifying Discourse Which 'Accompanied' It*. Translated by Walter Lowrie. Princeton: Princeton University Press. (*TC*)

Kraemer, Ross Shepard. 1992. *Her Share of the Blessings: Women's Religions Among Pagans, Jews, and Christians in the Greco-Roman World*. Oxford: Oxford University Press.

Lorde, Audre. 1984. *Sister Outsider: Essays and Speeches*. New York: Crossing Press.

Ruether, Rosemary Radford. 1981. *To Change the World: Christology and Cultural Criticism*. New York: Crossroad.

———. 1983. *Sexism and God-Talk: Toward A Feminist Theology*. Boston: Beacon.

———. 1992. *Gaia and God: Toward an Ecofeminist Theology of Earth-Healing*. San Francisco: Harper.

Russell, Letty, ed. 1985. *Feminist Interpretation of the Bible*. Philadelphia: Westminster.

Schneiders, Sandra M. 1991. *The Revelatory Text: Interpreting the New Testament as Sacred Scripture*. San Francisco: Harper.

Taylor, Mark C. 1981. "The Sounds of Silence." In *Kierkegaard's Fear and Trembling: Critical Appraisals*, edited by Robert L. Perkins, 165–88. University: University of Alabama Press.

Trible, Phyllis. 1984. *Texts of Terror: Literary-Feminist Readings of Biblical Narratives*. Philadelphia: Fortress.

Walker, Alice. 1983. *In Search of Our Mothers' Gardens: Womanist Prose*. San Diego: Harcourt Brace Jovanovich.

14

Amatory Cures for Material Dis-ease:

A Kristevian Reading of *The Sickness unto Death*

Tamsin Lorraine

In *The Sickness unto Death*, Søren Kierkegaard's pseudonym, Anti-Climacus, presents a remarkable model for selfhood. Anti-Climacus's evocation of a self that is "a synthesis of the infinite and the finite, of the temporal and the eternal, of freedom and necessity," provides a strangely contemporary image of a self struggling for unity and coherence in the face of experiences that defy conventional categorization (*SUD*, 13). Julia Kristeva also presents a model of a self-in-process by which conscious aspects of the self and the unconscious aspects of existence that would disrupt that self's coherence and continuity are mediated. I shall argue that attending to the resonances between Anti-Climacus's and Kristeva's depictions of selfhood suggests a model of selfhood that furthers the feminist project of challenging traditional gender stereotypes and envisioning in-

novative possibilities for humane ways of living and relating to one another.

The connection between Anti-Climacus and Kristeva may not be immediately obvious. After all, Anti-Climacus's views are informed by Danish Lutheranism and Kristeva's views are steeped in a Lacanian
interpretation of Freudian theory. Theology and psychoanalytic theory
have a vexed relationship. Classical Freudian theory has tended to view
God as a redundant fiction embraced by those who are unable to give up
some form of parental guidance. Freud posits God as a kind of cosmic
substitute for the all-powerful father of childhood. Thus, even after the
individual who believes in God has discovered that her or his father is
morally flawed and humanly limited, she or he still has a moral authority
and infinite ideal to which to refer when making decisions. Such an
infinite ideal may not dictate that individual's actions, but can provide a
specific orientation, and thus relieve her or him of the burden of independent thought. In *Civilization and Its Discontents*, Freud claims that the
guidance provided by religion is so restrictive that it forces people into a
state of psychic infantilism. According to Freud, every individual must
work out her or his own way of reconciling libido with the constraints
imposed by civilization. Religion's technique consists in "depressing the
value of life and distorting the picture of the real world in a delusional
manner" and is not likely to do more than spare many people an individual neurosis at the cost of intellectual intimidation (Freud 1961, 34).

Yet we know that Freud practiced a kind of intimidation of his own
and that the psychoanalytic scene is not free from encouraging psychic
regression in the name of transference. Submission both to God and to
the psychoanalytic process is supposed to effect some kind of cure for the
spiritual ills of humanity. Religion and psychoanalysis are concerned with
opening the individual to something beyond the banality of everyday
existence, to something that will revitalize the individual living in her or
his community.[1] Julia Kristeva has claimed that they both provide or have
provided opportunities for personal transformation by opening up a space
in which an individual can risk the disconcerting disorientation necessary for profound change. In addition, both religion and psychoanalysis
supply means for welcoming the changed individual back into the community; the space opened is contained and disorientation is mediated so
that the individual can find her or his way to a place more suited to that
transformed individual.

This perspective on the role of religion and psychoanalysis in mediating change raises the question of social change and the disturbing possibility that, because both organized religion and psychoanalysis can provide no more than an escape valve for subversive forces, they function only to maintain an oppressive status quo. Feminist readings of philosophers who have grappled with the question of how to go beyond the realm of the socially familiar can provide us with insight into our own, more explicitly feminist, projects. If both religion and psychoanalysis touch upon a realm of the ineffable, beyond and yet related to the mundane world of conventional living—religion through its evocation of God, and psychoanalysis through its evocation of the unconscious—then what may be made available to us through exploration of these two approaches? Kierkegaard's work presents an interesting case for a gender-inflected answer to this question; although Kierkegaard ultimately opposes a masculine self to a feminine one, his model of selfhood presses against the boundaries of a traditionally masculine self. Kristeva's work also depicts a gender-sensitive model of selfhood due to her attention to sexual difference and her elaboration of the maternal function in the pre-Oedipal phase.

The question of which cultural resources might be appropriate for facilitating feminist change is an important one. The turn to spirituality and psychology reflects a concern with providing viable models for contemporary modes of being, as well as with providing the support necessary for achieving profound transformations at a personal as well as social and political level. I propose to read Anti-Climacus and Kristeva in a way that demonstrates the resonances that exist between their accounts of the self. I believe that such models are crucial at this juncture in feminist thought; at the same time that we have become reluctant to "oppress" other women with normalizing descriptions of what women are or should be, we are still confronted with the fact of sexual difference. How we understand this difference is an important issue in contemporary feminist theory.

Over the centuries there have been many approaches to the question of sexual difference—a question that has often been posed as a question about woman's "nature" and how it compares to that of man. One approach insists that women can be "as good as" men, given equal education and opportunities. Another claims that wanting women to be like men is to accept a devalorization of what is an equally, if not more, important aspect of being human. Some using the latter approach argue for the importance of a complementary relationship between the sexes;

others argue that women need to come to the fore in order to right the wrongs committed by men with an overly masculine perspective. More recently feminists have become sensitive to the problems with trying to define woman's nature at all. But if women's differences are more salient than their similarities, then on what basis can we call for feminist solidarity? A contemporary group of feminists argues that we need to be attentive to sexual difference without assuming either that there is a binary opposition between the sexes, or that the sexual differences that can be demarcated are biologically dictated.[2] These feminists advocate attending to psychosomatic sexual differentiation as it emerges in specific social and historical configurations of power and culture. In addition to elaborating a conception of self that would valorize what have been traditionally more feminine modes of being, some of these feminists suggest that such elaboration could offer viable alternatives to traditionally masculine modes of being.

Such elaborations suggest an innovative approach to ethics at the same time that they give us new ways of understanding ourselves. Some feminists have turned to feminist spirituality in order to develop these possibilities. Others have investigated feminist psychoanalysis and psychology and/or feminist elaborations of relationships typical of the "feminine" realm of existence in the family, in particular the mother/child relationship.[3] Many feminists, however, have been uneasy about appealing to the pre-Oedipal fusional bliss of the mother/child dyad, or to a relational mode of being that values self-sacrifice over self-assertion; in addition to the question of whether or not the experiences from which these models are drawn are as blissful as they are made out to be, these feminists ask how such models could promote the feminist goal of empowering women.

Theoretical traditions of various kinds provide a rich resource for feminist conceptions of human nature and our relationship to the world. Some have argued, in a move analogous to the poststructuralist reclamation of a "feminine" Nietzsche, that Kierkegaard speaks from something like a feminine position in his use of what he calls "indirect" communication and in his sensitivity to the ineffable demands made by the God-relationship.[4] Despite the firm distinction that he maintains between "masculine" and "feminine" behavior vis-à-vis human others—a distinction that seems to be predicated upon traditionally biased notions of sexual difference—he is more attuned to "irrational" breaks that challenge conventional beliefs, and he often appeals to women for examples of what approaches his conception of the appropriate role for a human being vis-à-vis God. In addition, he develops a notion of the self in a God-relationship that articulates a more fluid, open-ended conception of subjectivity than that provided by his culture's traditional norm for (masculine) adulthood. Furthermore, this notion of self provides a contrast to the paradigm of the independent, self-sufficient self that some feminists have contested, at the same time that it resolves the problem presented by an over-"relational" self whose needs and desires are submerged into the needs and desires of a human other. In the context of a God-relationship, the self deliberately opens to the infinite and something like an experience of socially unmediated existence. Kierkegaard's acknowledgment and valorization of that which is not ordained through paternal law defies conventional ethics and provides an articulation of that which escapes the socialized norm. If this norm is patriarchal in nature, then Kierkegaard could be read as attempting to speak the repressed feminine of a culture that valorizes the masculine.

In what follows, I give a reading of *The Sickness unto Death* that presents Anti-Climacus's account of the God-relationship as an amatory discourse of self-transformation. Kristeva (1991) has suggested that it is due to the lack of such discourses (be they codes of love or religious discourse) that we are currently confronting a difficult situation: "We must live with different people while relying on our personal moral codes, without the assistance of a set that would include our particularities while transcending them" (195). Psychoanalysis, as a discourse that could help fill in this lack, "through unraveling transference—the major dynamics of otherness, of love/hatred for the other, of the foreign component of our psyche"—can be experienced as a journey toward an ethics of respect with political implications (Kristeva 1991, 182). Through the awakening consciousness of the strangers within ourselves, "that 'improper' facet of our impossible 'own and proper' "—the unconscious—we can work toward a more cosmopolitan community in which differences among people can be respected (Kristeva 1991, 191). Just as Kristeva's version of psychoanalysis represents an opportunity for self-transformation in a space in which the analysand invites and confronts the collapse of stable meaning (that, it turns out, is always in some way present to the self), so does Anti-Climacus's God-relationship represent a passionate surrender to the collapse of meaning in the faith that meaning will be restored by God. At the same time that both Anti-Climacus and Kristeva perceive the paradoxical character of subjectivity, they refuse to relinquish the spiritual hope for rebirth.

The comparison of these two discourses as codes that enable the transgression of the finite boundaries of the concrete self will suggest further possibilities for a self-transformative transcendence that confronts the always threatening risk of nihilistic dispersal. Anti-Climacus's insistence on the intertwining of the infinite and the finite in his model of selfhood opens up the traditional paradigm of the self-sufficient self at the same time that it roots that self in the concrete details of a life lived in community with others. The self he theorizes is thus both relationally fluid and yet anchored in business as usual. This model as well as Kristeva's psychoanalytic one implicate gender in a way that is problematic for a feminist cause; both seem to encourage self-transformation by way of submission to a patriarchal father—be he God, or the father of the Oedipal triangle. Reading Anti-Climacus's and Kristeva's accounts together, however, suggests a materialist reading of infinity that provides another way of reading the God-relationship, one more in keeping with contemporary feminist thought, and also one that yields important clues for getting past the limitations of a psychoanalytic framework. A Kristevian reading of *The Sickness unto Death* will not only provide a less chauvinistic reading of the God-relationship than that given by Anti-Climacus himself; it will also suggest an alternative to the psychoanalytic nostalgia for the Oedipal triangle and the lost mother. Thus, together, these two discourses present an opportunity for exploring that strange moment beyond all finite significance that is also our only hope for meaningful existence. Social categories, such as those of gender, class, race, and ethnicity, can never provide adequate descriptions of concrete individuals, but must always be existentially lived and continually reworked. Reworking these categories often brings us to the limits of conventional meaning. A better understanding of the nature of such paradoxical moments will provide insight into our ongoing struggles to encounter that which we have labeled "other" both in ourselves and in the human others with whom we come into contact.

Synthesizing Infinitude and Finitude: Anti-Climacus's Account of the Self in *The Sickness unto Death*

In *The Sickness unto Death*, Kierkegaard's pseudonymous author, Anti-Climacus, depicts the self as a conscious synthesizing activity. The open-ended project of this activity is to integrate imaginative striving toward the infinite divine with the finite limitations of embodied life. Anti-Climacus calls this process the task of becoming oneself, or becoming concrete, and claims that it requires a relationship with God as well as with oneself. As he puts it:

> The self is the conscious synthesis of infinitude and finitude that relates itself to itself, whose task is to become itself, which can be done only through the relationship to God. To become oneself is to become concrete. But to become concrete is neither to become finite nor to become infinite, for that which is to become concrete is indeed a synthesis. Consequently, the progress of the becoming must be an infinite moving away from itself in the infinitizing of the self, and an infinite coming back to itself in the finitizing process. But if the self does not become itself, it is in despair, whether it knows that or not. (*SUD*, 29–30)

After discussing several forms that despair can take (the despair of an ambitious man, a young girl in love, and an individual who wills to be himself), Anti-Climacus concludes that all despair can ultimately be traced to the will to be rid of oneself (*SUD*, 20). Human beings who become merely finite lose the infinite aspect of their selves; "to lack infinitude is despairing reductionism, narrowness" (*SUD*, 33). Such human beings absorb themselves in secular affairs and conform to the social status quo. They find it "far easier and safer to be like the others, to become a copy, a number, a mass man" (*SUD*, 34). Human beings who narrowly focus on ordinary reality lose the crucial capacity to imagine what lies beyond the everyday world. But it is equally dangerous to ignore one's contingent situation with all its obstacles and limitations. Human beings who dwell on the infinite get lost in the "fantastic"; they become so absorbed in imagining all the self's possibilities in the abstract that they lose the finite aspect of their selves. Thus, becoming conscious as self, which is for Anti-Climacus the only thing that can make one's life worth living, involves imaginative reflection on one's possibilities, as well as recognition and acknowledgment of one's concrete situation in all its particularity (*SUD*, 26–27).

A human being is a synthesis of the infinite and the finite, of the temporal and the eternal, of freedom and necessity, that relates itself to itself (*SUD*, 13). But it is not enough for a human being to be a synthesis of these opposing aspects of life; a human being cannot be a self until in addition to relating itself to itself it also relates itself to another. The most important other to whom one can relate oneself as a synthesis is God. Thus, one can become oneself only through relating the synthesis of opposing aspects of oneself to God as irreducible Other. Becoming oneself through the relationship to God involves gaining the impression that one's self exists before a God (*SUD*, 27). The belief in God involves the belief that even in the face of one's inevitable downfall, God, for whom everything is possible, will provide a way out:

> The *believer* sees and understands his downfall, humanly speaking (in what has happened to him, or in what he has ventured), but he believes. For this reason he does not collapse. He leaves it entirely to God how he is to be helped, but he believes that for God everything is possible. To *believe* his downfall is impossible. To understand that humanly it is his downfall and nevertheless to believe in possibility is to believe. So God helps him also— perhaps by allowing him to avoid the horror, perhaps through the horror itself—and here, unexpectedly, miraculously, divinely, help does come. (*SUD*, 39)

Someone who believes in God does not withdraw from the realm of the concrete when faced with imminent calamity; she or he is realistic about which options are socially meaningful and acceptable in the secular world. Even in a situation in which every option can lead only to disaster, the believer proves herself or himself to be more than a number or a representative of the mass by imaginatively reflecting on the situation in relationship to an other who is beyond all concrete situations. She or he has faith that unprecedented possibilities can emerge from the most unexpected places not only because for God everything is possible, but because God witnesses and cares about the believer's life in all its particularity. Thus, she or he can synthesize radically disparate aspects of the self in relationship to an omniscient and omnipotent Other who lovingly witnesses that process from beyond. The despair brought on by the attempts to become herself or himself that lead to excluding or denying parts of that self is thus overcome through faith in the God-relationship.

A human being with anything like a "spirit" or "self" "has an essential interior consistency and a consistency in something higher" (*SUD*, 107). The believer's consistency rests in the good. She or he therefore fears sin because it represents an infinite loss: the loss of one's consistency. It is not just the loss of consistency that is feared, but the loss constituted by a rejection or denial of some aspect of oneself because it is deemed unacceptable. Thus, faith, rather than virtue, is the antithesis of sin, because faith is "that the self in being itself and in willing to be itself rests transparently in God" (*SUD*, 82). That is, one knows that God at once "comprehends actuality itself, all its particulars" and every aspect of one's life as one struggles for synthesized consistency and yet still wills to be one's self (*SUD*, 121). Sin is "after being taught by a revelation from God what sin is—before God in despair not to will to be oneself or in despair to will to be oneself" (*SUD*, 96). That is, to sin is to know one has done wrong and to attempt to reject this act from one's synthesizing process or to let it define oneself as irredeemably sinful. To despair of forgiveness from God for one's sins is what Anti-Climacus calls "offense" because it involves diminished recognition of the abyss between God and human beings (*SUD*, 116): "The person who does not take offense *worships* in faith. But to worship, which is the expression of faith, is to express that the infinite, chasmal, qualitative abyss between them is confirmed" (*SUD*, 129).

The believer who worships in faith can thus not only believe that God will help in time of trouble against all odds, but that God will forgive one's wrongdoing, thus enabling consistency despite the conflicting aspects of one's self-becoming. Just as the belief in unprecedented possibilities in a desperate situation speaks to God's limitlessness, so does faith in God's forgiving nature speak to God's infinitude. In both cases, the individual reconciles the disparate elements of her or his situation or self in relationship to a witness who neither rejects nor denies any of those elements, and who can enable their synthesis into unprecedented possibilities for happy solutions and consistent wholeness.

Infinitude involves not merely having an intellectual conception of God as limitless, it also involves being able to reflect upon one's own possibilities before the one for whom all is possible. Merely to do or be as one is told, merely to conform, is to lack imagination, and therefore to lose one's access to the eternal. Inwardness involves an individual's confrontation with the torment presented by the contradiction between one's wish to infinitize one's possibilities and one's inability to escape the limitations of one's self as it is. Recognition of one's despair deepens one's inwardness. Despair before God is sin. Faith is the antithesis of sin and the antidote for despair. In faith, one rests transparently in God both in being oneself and in willing to be oneself. Taking God as one's criterion, existing before God, one is moved to infinitize one's possibilities without forgetting the qualitative abyss between God and human beings and the fact that it is humanity that sins and God who forgives the sinner. In accepting God's loving forgiveness, one both confronts one's finitude and accepts one's dependence on God: "The child who previously has had only his parents as a criterion becomes a self as an adult by getting the state as a criterion, but what an infinite accent falls on the self by having God as the criterion! . . . [E]verything is qualitatively that by which it is measured, and that which is its qualitative criterion is ethically its goal" (*SUD*, 79). Thus, striving for something that lies beyond the confines of conventional reality is a crucial aspect of being human, one that must be continually integrated into one's concrete life with full recognition of the ultimate impossibility of ever fully achieving such integration.

Semiotic and Symbolic Modalities of the Self: Kristeva's Account of the Subject-in-Process

For Kristeva, too, human beings are in a paradoxical situation. They are signifying processes that operate in two modalities: the symbolic modality in which the subject posits herself or himself as a unity in a certain relationship to the objects in her or his world, and the semiotic modality in which connections of the body in the process of constituting itself as a body proper are governed by a preverbal functional state that Kristeva characterizes as "analogous only to vocal or kinetic rhythm" (Kristeva 1984, 26). The semiotic modality relates to the pre-Oedipal state of symbiotic fusion with the mother from which the subject's initial body boundaries emerged. Since body boundaries can never be fixed and the subject's meaning never completed (until, perhaps, the ultimate dissolution of all body boundaries in death), the semiotic is a modality that is an ongoing and integral aspect of all signifying activity. Human beings are thus not simply subjects whose consciousness changes in dialectical interaction with their world; they are also embodied subjects engaged in dialectical interaction between the body as already signified and the material excess of those significations.[5]

In *Black Sun*, Kristeva suggests that melancholy and depression can involve a sort of vault of semiotic activity that has not been incorporated into the individual's symbolic activity.[6] Apparently, since primordial semiotic activity is linked to the maternal body, this means that one has not properly mourned or resolved one's loss of this body. Thus, one could give a Kristevian reading of Anti-Climacus, relating despair and sin to an imbalance in the semiotic and symbolic modalities of subjectivity. Too much emphasis on the former would result in an emphasis on infinitude and the fantastic—the attempt to regain the lost Thing (one's rich and varied experiences of the maternal body in the mode of primary processes) through the imaginary.[7] Too much emphasis on the symbolic modality would result in an emphasis on finitude and the secular mentality of the conforming individual who refuses to question conventional meaning. Just as Anti-Climacus concerns himself with the various forms of a lack of self and the possible collapse of self in the face of radical challenges to one's meaning, so Kristeva concerns herself with the despair of a subject reduced to being a symbolic automaton with no access to the semiotic or the possible collapse of self precipitated by a flood of semiotic affect that overwhelms symbolicity.[8]

In *Desire in Language*, Kristeva cites avant-garde literature as a kind of language that can provide opportunities for rejuvenating self-transformation. Experimental language evokes an extralinguistic response to instinctual drives and historical contradictions that the symbolic does not make explicit (Kristeva 1980, 116). In the disorienting space created by this literature, the reader is moved to undermine conventional meaning and generate new meanings on the basis of her or his reactions to the text.[9] It is the reader's own biography, her or his own desire, that will allow the breakdown of old codes and the emergence of new formulations of desire as the semiotic motility that precedes and exceeds any constitution of the subject is activated, thus prompting new investments of instinctual drive.[10] These new formulations of desire involve more than a shift in perspective due to the further development of a rational progression of thought. They involve a shattering of language and of the body that by negating any position of understanding and all previous articulations of experience allows new articulations to emerge.

Kristeva clearly values what she calls the revolutionary potential of poetic language, yet she does not think that avant-garde literature will necessarily help us achieve the ethical communities that she would herself like to bring about. In fact, in her later work she seems to suggest that amatory discourses, for example between lovers or religious discourse, might be more appropriate or more effective spaces in which to experience breakdowns in subjectivity and the reconfiguration of desire:

> In love "I" has been an *other*. That phrase, which leads us to poetry or raving hallucination, suggests a state of instability in which the individual is no longer indivisible and allows himself to become lost in the other, for the other. Within love, a risk that might otherwise be tragic is accepted, normalized, made fully reassuring. (Kristeva 1987, 4)

Kristeva claims that love, by enabling the connection of the psyche as one open system to another, can bring about renewal and rebirth. The individual in love abandons rigid fixation on a symbolic understanding of one's self in deference to one's beloved. "Libidinal auto-organization" (the semiotic modality) thus encounters "memory-consciousness" (the symbolic modality). The confusion caused by this encounter can become symbolized since the individual in love adapts to the situation in part through identification with the ideal presented by the beloved other.[11]

In psychoanalysis, transference love can elicit the same effect without the risk of loss of self that love (of the chaotic and fusional kind) can bring:

> By ensuring a loving Other to the patient, the analyst (temporarily) allows the Ego in the throes of drive to take shelter in the following fantasy: the analyst is not a dead Father but a living Father; this nondesiring but loving father reconciles the ideal Ego with the Ego Ideal and elaborates the psychic space where, possibly and subsequently, an analysis can take place. (Kristeva 1987, 30)

Thus, psychoanalysis can facilitate self-transformation by creating a space in which "fluctuations of primary processes and even bioenergetic transmissions" can be modified through a discourse that favors "a better integration of semiotic agitation within the symbolic fabric" (Kristeva 1989, 66).[12]

Religious discourse can also perform this function. Just as the analyst ensures a loving space within which the patient may risk psychic instability, Christian discourse represents Christ as a subject with fundamental and psychically necessary discontinuity. The story of Christ's relationship to his Father provides an image and narrative for the many separations that build up the psychic life of individuals. Birth, weaning, separation, frustration, castration, are all psychic cataclysms that can threaten an individual's balance:

> Their nonexecution or repudiation leads to psychotic confusion; their dramatization is, on the contrary, a source of exorbitant and destructive anguish. Because Christianity set that rupture at the very heart of the absolute subject—Christ; because it represented it as a Passion that was the solidary lining of his Resurrection, his glory, and his eternity, it brought to consciousness the essential dramas that are internal to the becoming of each and every subject. It thus endows itself with a tremendous cathartic power. (Kristeva 1989, 132)

In addition, the Christian story of God's relationship to humanity, which depicts his power to forgive, represents a powerful possibility for healing psychic breaks: "Forgiveness gathers on its way to the other a very human sorrow. Recognizing the lack and the wound that caused it, it fulfills them with an ideal gift—promise, project, artifice, thus fitting the humiliated, offended being into an order of perfection, and giving him the assurance that he belongs there" (Kristeva 1989, 216).

Kristeva suggests that it is important that this other be a father—not the prohibiting Oedipal father, but the loving, forgiving father. According to Kristeva, the break with the pre-Oedipal mother is brought about through primary identification with the "imaginary father." It is not just that the Oedipal father who represents and upholds symbolic Law prohibits incest; the imaginary father is the father who lovingly receives one despite all one's flaws. Thus, it is this dual father who is the ideal with whom one can identify—taking on the position of a speaking subject without having to relinquish the affective meaning of prehistorical identifications:

> The supporting father of such symbolic triumph [over sadness] is not the oedipal father but truly that "imaginary father," "father in individual prehistory" according to Freud, who guarantees primary identification. Nevertheless, it is imperative that this father in individual prehistory be capable of playing his part as oedipal

father in symbolic Law, for it is on the basis of that harmonious blending of the two facets of fatherhood that the abstract and arbitrary signs of communication may be fortunate enough to be tied to the affective meaning of prehistorical identifications, and the dead language of the potentially depressive person can arrive at a live meaning in the bond with others. (Kristeva 1989, 23–24)

Kristeva, despite her valorization of the feminine modality of the semiotic, indicates the need for caution in encouraging semiotic irruptions. Just as Anti-Climacus insists upon faith in God as an antidote to despair, Kristeva insists that it is through imagining the analyst as a living father who incorporates the "two facets of fatherhood" that the individual can find rejuvenation.

Going Beyond the Father: A Comparison of Anti-Climacus's Account of the Self with Kristeva's Subject-in-Process

There are obvious parallels between Anti-Climacus's God-relationship and Kristeva's depiction of a relationship to a dual father who represents an ideal with whom one can identify. Anti-Climacus's God-relationship renders a relationship to a fatherly other that could access a spiritual realm beyond conventional social meaning, beyond language, beyond possibility. In the safety of transparency before God, one could acknowledge the disturbing indications of instabilities in one's self and open one's self to the profound disorientation that acknowledgment can cause, in faith that the loving father will note and acknowledge one's transgressions as well as somehow provide for one's return to meaning and community. Thus, Anti-Climacus's God is not a rigid upholder of the Law, callously excluding those who do not abide by the Law upon which human community is founded; he is the Christian God who attends to each and every particular of each individual existence with loving care, sometimes enabling the miracle by which the excluded individual can be returned to ethical community.

Although Kristeva indicates a positive role for religious narratives, it is not clear whether she herself does not tend toward the antireligious views mentioned earlier in this paper. I suggest that whatever problems Kristeva may have with Anti-Climacus's account of the self in a God-relationship, the latter provides opportunities in self-transformation without some of the risks of her own preferred discourse of psychoanalysis. In particular, while psychoanalytic theory tends to reinforce highly gendered readings of self-transforming discourses, exploration of Anti-Climacus's views on the self, in light of Kristeva's emphasis on the body, could suggest other possibilities.

The psychoanalytic story emphasizes the originary moment of the self in the Oedipal triangle. Kristeva is, of course, right to suggest that contemporary culture associates "woman" with the body and with deeper mysteries that may relate to the ultimate mystery of living an embodied existence. She seems to think, however, that this must be the case because it is, after all, from women that we are all born. In addition, because the psychoanalytic story is an originary one, the forward impulses of an individual's existence are explained with respect to conditional causes—in this case, the biographical experiences of the individual in her or his relationship to the maternal body. The semiotic impulses of primary process, as well as the form that the ideal other takes, are thus traced to the formative experiences of individuals (although both semiotic impulses and ego ideals are not unaffected by later events). The fatherly analyst can help the analysand construct a life-narrative and self-in-process with a more satisfying synthesis of the symbolic and semiotic. Such reconstructions are implemented and stabilized within the context of the Oedipal triangle. This emphasis on personal reconstruction of one's own biography can effect the kind of liberating "cure" that concerns both Kristeva and Anti-Climacus. Anti-Climacus's story, however, depicts the God-relationship as predicated upon a genuine encounter with an infinite Other who is beyond not only all finite situation, but the Oedipal situation and the paternal law. This Other for whom all is possible can, if the situation warrants, enable the emergence of possibilities inconceivable within the boundaries of the Oedipal frame. Communication with others, for example, can bring not only new insights about our past along with reorganization of semiotic drive; it can also bring us into contact with symbolic systems and semiotic affects that are radically different from our own. In the attempt to make sense of such experiences, faith in an infinite Other could take us beyond the familiar positions constituted within the context of father/son, mother/daughter, and such relationships, to unprecedented configurations of self in relationship.

It has been suggested by more than one Kierkegaard commentator that Kierkegaard was more interested in spiritual inwardness than in a spirituality that might wreak havoc with conventional ethical orders. Certainly his chauvinism vis-à-vis Christianity would seem to suggest a low tolerance toward ethical systems other than his own. If we read the God-relationship in light of Kristeva's depiction of the contradictions presented by material existence, however, we may perceive healing possibilities for Anti-Climacus's version of Kierkegaardian faith in a broader context. The religious notion of God as that which is always other to one's own synthesizing process (God attends to finitude and yet is unlimited), and yet witnessing it in all its particularity with loving (and yet discriminating) inclusiveness, suggests a possible solution to the contemporary problem of the alienated subject. Despite the singularity of an individual God-relationship, God witnesses all of life at once in its continual unfolding. Thus, embracing this Other involves recognizing that it is not only oneself but everyone and everything in all their particularity that are witnessed by this Other. The infinite nature of such a witness—in terms of its all-inclusive attention to every detail no matter how "trivial" or nonsensical, as well as its limitless power and creativity in enabling meaningful solutions in the synthesis of that detail—encourages a responsibly creative response to postmodern confusion. Faith in such an infinite Other ensures that we will neither deny the various and contradictory aspects of our lives, nor despair of becoming more deeply ourselves[13] despite our confusion.

Believers in postmodern society are often confronted not only with ineffable aspects of their own experience that take them beyond the secular, ethical realm, they are also confronted with the clash of one or more competing ethical systems. Anti-Climacus's version of Kierkegaardian faith, when given a Kristevian reading, may involve belief that new syntheses and new meanings can emerge from ethical systems that seem in outright contradiction as well as from encounters with embodied others whose desires conflict with our own. Thus, the appeal to a loving Other who witnesses inter- as well as intrasubjective conflict could involve the refusal to reject or deny "unacceptable" persons or elements as well as the faith that meaningful connections and satisfying self-transformation in community with others could emerge from such conflict. The affective force for the emergence of new meaning would come not simply from the semiotic irruptions of relatively isolated individuals, but through the communication of subjective experience in both symbolic and semiotic modalities among individuals.[14]

While a psychoanalytic appeal to attend to and incorporate disparate aspects of ourselves that hearken back to our corporeal origins is important and useful, the religious appeal to an Other for whom all is possible and who watches over each and every one of us without discounting any individual or any aspect of particular individuals could provide a kind of transcendent ideal that could guide our attempts to build ethical community.[15] Kristeva's psychoanalytic notion of a subject-in-process encourages an Oedipal framework and an emphasis on personal biography. As important as I believe her work to be, Kristeva's emphasis on the maternal body and the inevitable association to the Oedipal triangle this entails in theorizing the body and the semiotic ruptures experienced through the body is overcautious.[16] And yet, Kristeva's attention to embodiment and her descriptions of contemporary gender-inflected subject-formation illuminate sexual difference in important ways. Anti-Climacus's religious notion of a God-relationship could take us beyond the Oedipal framework and shift emphasis to a self-in-world witnessed by an infinite Other without losing the materialist impetus of Kristeva's work. Such an approach would insist on the differences between embodied individuals. Sexual difference, as well as other differences, would be witnessed. But instead of referring sexual difference back to a retroactive story about an Oedipal triangle, new formations of that story suggesting other possibilities could be told.

Both Anti-Climacus and Kristeva are concerned with containing the dangers of a complete surrender to the infinite, the unfathomable, the uncanny underside of ordinary life, at the same time that they insist upon accessing this realm. Especially in an age where our traditional structures have lost credibility and we are inundated with so many possibilities that many of us have become unable to act at all, I appreciate their concern. The Other whom Anti-Climacus evokes in the context of a Kristevian reading is an Other who is as beyond sexual difference as the other differences that divide us. It is an Other that witnesses us all, and by so doing, provides us with the space for acknowledging multiple differences at once and so further refining our understanding of sexual difference.

Whether the rifts at issue are within the subject, or between subjects and worlds, it is through a faith that neither denies those rifts, nor despairs because of them, that ruptures in human significance and community can continue to emerge and be resolved or superseded in an ongoing and highly paradoxical process of synthesizing activity. If, as Kristeva suggests, encountering the stranger within as well as human others is an important part of a self-transformative process, and if we agree with Anti-Climacus that such a process is the only thing that makes life worth living, then faith in the miraculous resolution of that moment beyond all meaning, beyond all possibility, is indeed a faith that may be needed to face the difficult problems of our own times without despair.

Notes

1. I use the terms "religion" and "psychoanalysis" here in a rather broad sense. Although this paper will address Anti-Climacus's unorthodox reading of Danish Lutheranism and Julia Kristeva's Lacanian version of psychoanalysis, my more general comments here are meant to set the context for why a feminist might draw upon religion and psychoanalysis at all as cultural resources despite the problems they may present for a feminist project.

2. I am thinking in particular of the feminists who advocate an attention to sexual difference in the context of a strand of philosophical thought running from Hegel to Heidegger to French theorists like Derrida and Foucault. Rosi Braidotti (1991) gives a well-developed and positive account of this approach in her book *Patterns of Dissonance*. There she characterizes feminist thought as a practice that "aims to locate and situate the grounds for the new female feminist subjectivity" (3). She explains the French philosophical context for a theoretical concern with the category of the "feminine," which she believes to speak to a "rupture inside the Western order of discourse" (7), and argues that it is the attention given to sexual specificity by feminist thought that will ensure a genuine reconfiguration of thinking. Feminist thought in its focus on gender and the sexed body cannot leave the materiality of bodies or of specific social situations and everyday life behind. "The focus of my reading is the way in which feminism has put into question the corporeal nature, and above all the sexuation of the subject" (7). Rosemary Hennessey (1993) discusses this approach in a more critical way in her book *Materialist Feminism and the Politics of Discourse*.

I am also referring to feminists who have been moved by poststructuralist theory to contextualize their exploration of gender; a key article in this debate is Fraser and Nicholson (1990). In a broader sense, I include feminists from Mary Daly to Genevieve Lloyd who articulate a "feminine" mode of being without insisting upon its essential connection with human beings of the female sex.

3. Examples of those exploring feminist spirituality include Mary Daly and Carol P. Christ. The most prominent examples of those appealing to feminist psychoanalysis and/or psychology include Jessica Benjamin, Nancy Chodorow, Dorothy Dinnerstein, and Carol Gilligan. French feminists, including Julia Kristeva and Luce Irigaray, have appealed to the pre-Oedipal stage in order to elaborate an alternative ethics. Rosi Braidotti's approach is indebted to this tradition. Sarah Hoagland's (1988) *Lesbian Ethics* roots an ethical perspective in theorizing relationships among women. Sara Ruddick has elaborated an ethics based upon the mother/child relationship in her *Maternal Thinking*. The above, of course, is by no means an exhaustive list.

4. For an example of the reclamation of a "feminine" Nietzsche, see Jacques Derrida (1979). For some indication of the feminist response to this reclamation, see Kelly Oliver (1995). Some examples of readings of Kierkegaard that discuss his feminine positioning in-

clude pages 115–34 of Lorraine (1990) and Part II of Martin Matuštík (1993), esp. 130–33. Also see Sylvia Walsh (1987).

5. "The heterogeneous element is a corporeal, physiological, and signifiable excitation which the symbolizing social structure—the family or some other structure—cannot grasp. On the other hand, heterogeneity is that part of the objective, material outer world which could not be grasped by the various symbolizing structures the subject already has at his disposal. Nonsymbolized corporeal excitation and the new object of the nonsymbolized material outer world are always already interacting: the newness of the object gives rise to drives that are not yet bound and prompts their investment" (Kristeva 1984, 180).

6. "Melancholy persons, with their despondent, secret insides, are potential exiles but also intellectuals capable of dazzling, albeit abstract, constructions. With depressive people, *denial of the negation* is the logical expression of omnipotence. Through their empty speech they assure themselves of an inaccessible (because it is 'semiotic' and not 'symbolic') ascendency over an archaic object that thus remains, for themselves and all others, an enigma and a secret" (Kristeva 1989, 64).

7. "Thus the continuum of the body, which is in the process of becoming 'one's own and proper body,' is articulated as an organized discontinuity, exercising a precocious and primary mastery, flexible yet powerful, over the erotogenic zones, blended with the preobject, the maternal Thing. What appears on the psychological level as omnipotence *is the power of semiotic rhythms, which convey an intense presence of meaning in a presubject still incapable of signification.*

What we call meaning is the ability of the *infans* to record the signifier of parental desire and include itself [sic] therein in his own fashion; he does so by displaying the semiotic abilities he is endowed with at that moment of his development and which allow him a mastery, on the level of primary processes, of a 'not yet other' (of the Thing) included in the erotogenic zones of such a semiotizing *infans*. Nevertheless, the omnipotent meaning remains a 'dead letter' if it is not invested in signification. It will be the task of analytic interpretation to search for depressive meaning in the vault where sadness has locked it up with the mother, and tie it to the signification of objects and desires" (Kristeva 1989, 62–63).

8. "The excess of affect has thus no other means of coming to the fore than to produce new languages—strange concatenations, idiolects, poetics. Until the weight of the primal Thing prevails, and all translatability become [sic] impossible. Melancholia then ends up in asymbolia, in loss of meaning: if I am no longer capable of translating or metaphorizing, I become silent and die" (Kristeva 1989, 42).

9. "This heterogeneousness to signification operates through, despite, and in excess of it and produces in poetic language 'musical' but also nonsense effects that destroy not only accepted beliefs and significations, but, in radical experiments, syntax itself, that guarantee of thetic consciousness (of the signified object and ego)" (Kristeva 1980, 133).

10. "A reading, whose conceptual supports are muted, is the terrain of the reading subject's desire, his drives, sexuality, and attentiveness toward the phonematic network, the rhythm of the sentences, the particular sememe bringing him back to a feeling, pleasure, laughter, an event or reading of the most 'empirical' kind, abounding, enveloping, multiple. The identity of the reading I loses itself there, atomizes itself; it is a time of jouissance, where one discovers one text under another, its other" (Kristeva 1980, 119).

11. "The effect of love is one of renewal, our rebirth. The new blossoms out and throws us into confusion when libidinal auto-organization encounters memory-consciousness, which is guaranteed by the Other, and becomes symbolized; conversely, it arises when the memory-consciousness system abandons its fixative systematically (related to the superego) in order to adapt to the new risks of destabilized-stabilizable auto-organization. In Freudian terms, it would involve the desexualization of drive, deflecting it toward idealization and sublimation; and conversely, bringing together idealizing mechanisms with the processes of incorporation and of introjection of incorporated items" (Kristeva 1987, 15–16).

12. "There is perhaps a chance, then, for analysis to transform such subjectivation and endow discourse with a modifying power over the fluctuations of primary processes and even bioenergetic transmissions, by favoring a better integration of semiotic agitation within the symbolic fabric" (Kristeva 1989, 66).

13. Here I am assuming that becoming oneself refers to an ongoing synthesizing process contingent upon one's historical situation, rather than a process that manifests what one already is at a "deeper" level. I am also suggesting that Anti-Climacus, in saying that despair can be traced to the will to be rid of oneself, is claiming that this process requires a certain kind of honesty; one must continually strive not only for integration, but do so without excluding "inconvenient," disturbing, or contradictory, aspects of one's reality.

14. Teresa Brennan (1992) develops a theory about the energetic connections that exist between people on the basis of Freudian theory. She argues that in making the Lacanian move to a linguistic re-reading of Freud we have lost the element of the physical in Freud's thought. The notion of a psychic imprint that occurs not only between mother and child, but in later relationships, has important implications that are relevant to the kind of "semiotic" communication I refer to here.

15. I am here, of course, indicating my disagreement with the view mentioned at the beginning of this essay that the desire for a transcendent ideal (whether we call it "God" or something else) is necessarily antithetical to independent thought and action. The models of self discussed in this essay challenge the notion of a self-sufficient self, and claim that "independent" thought can only emerge through a relational process that inevitably involves an imaginative process of idealization. What I am here suggesting is that an open-ended transcendent ideal might help us to be more honest in our attempts to include all of humanity in this process.

16. There have been others who, although influenced by a psychoanalytic paradigm, have protested against its rigidity. Luce Irigaray, a philosopher and psychoanalyst working out of the Lacanian tradition, for example, holds the implicit assumption throughout her work that culture can change on both the symbolic and imaginary levels, thus releasing post–Oedipal-triangle possibilities for subjectivity. Gilles Deleuze and Félix Guattari (1983) also argue that the psychoanalytic story fixes the flux of finite existence in a conservatively arbitrary way.

References

Braidotti, Rosi. 1991. *Patterns of Dissonance: A Study of Women in Contemporary Philosophy*. New York: Routledge.

Brennan, Teresa. 1992. *The Interpretation of the Flesh: Freud and Femininity*. New York: Routledge.

Deleuze, Gilles, and Félix Guattari. 1983. *Anti-Oedipus: Capitalism and Schizophrenia*. Translated by Robert Hurley, Mark Seem, and Helen R. Lane. Minneapolis: University of Minnesota Press.

Derrida, Jacques. 1979. *Spurs: Nietzsche's Spurs*. Translated by Barbara Harlow. Chicago: University of Chicago Press.

Fraser, Nancy, and Linda Nicholson. 1990. "Social Criticism without Philosophy: An Encounter between Feminism and Postmodernism." In *Feminism/Postmodernism*, edited by Linda Nicholson, 19–38. New York: Routledge.

Freud, Sigmund. 1961. *Civilization and Its Discontents*. Translated by James Strachey. New York: Norton.

Hennessy, Rosemary. 1993. *Materialist Feminism and the Politics of Discourse*. New York: Routledge.

Hoagland, Sarah. 1988. *Lesbian Ethics: Toward New Value*. Palo Alto, Calif.: Institute of Lesbian Studies.

Kristeva, Julia. 1980. *Desire in Language*. Translated by Thomas Gora, Alice Jardine, and Leon S. Roudiez. New York: Columbia University Press, 1980.

———. 1984. *Revolution in Poetic Language*. Translated by Margaret Waller. New York: Columbia University Press.

———. 1987. *Tales of Love*. Translated by Leon S. Roudiez. New York: Columbia University Press.

———. 1989. *Black Sun*. Translated by Leon S. Roudiez. New York: Columbia University Press.

———. 1991. *Strangers to Ourselves*. Translated by Leon S. Roudiez. New York: Columbia University Press.

Lorraine, Tamsin. 1990. *Gender, Identity, and the Production of Meaning*. Boulder, Colo.: Westview.

Matuštík, Martin. 1993. *Postnational Identity: Critical Theory and Existential Philosophy in Habermas, Kierkegaard, and Havel*. New York: Guilford.

Oliver, Kelly. 1995. *Womanizing Nietzsche: Philosophy's Relation to the "Feminine."* New York: Routledge.

Ruddick, Sara. 1989. *Maternal Thinking: Towards a Politics of Peace*. Boston: Beacon.

Walsh, Sylvia. 1987. "On 'Feminine' and 'Masculine' Forms of Despair." In *International Kierkegaard Commentary: The Sickness unto Death*, edited by Robert L. Perkins, 121–34. Macon: Mercer University Press.

Select Bibliography

Adorno, Theodore W. *Kierkegaard: Construction of the Aesthetic.* Translated and edited by Robert Hullot-Kentor. Minneapolis: University of Minnesota Press, 1989.

Agacinski, Sylviane. *Aparté: Conceptions et morts de Søren Kierkegaard.* Paris: Aubier-Flammarion, 1977. (*Aparté: Conceptions and Deaths of Søren Kierkegaard.* Translated by Kevin Newmark. Tallahassee: Florida State University Press, 1988.)

Ainley, Alison. "The Subject of Ethics: Kierkegaard and Feminist Perspectives on an 'Ethical' Self." *Oxford Literary Review* 11 (1989): 169–88.

Anne, Chantal. *L'Amour dans la pensée de Søren Kierkegaard. Pseudonymie et polyonymie.* Paris: L'Harmattan, 1993.

Barfoed, Niels. *Don Juan: En Studie i dansk litteratur.* Copenhagen: Gyldendal, 1978.

Beauvoir, Simone de. *The Second Sex.* Translated and edited by H. M. Parshley. New York: Vintage Books, 1989.

Becker-Theye, Betty. *The Seducer as Mythic Figure in Richardson, Laclos and Kierkegaard.* New York: Garland, 1988.

Berry, Wanda Warren. "Finally Forgiveness: Kierkegaard as a 'Springboard' for a Feminist Theology of Reform." In *Foundations of Kierkegaard's Vision of Community*, edited by George B. Connell and C. Stephen Evans, 196–217. Atlantic Highlands, N.J.: Humanities Press, 1992.

———. "The Heterosexual Imagination and Aesthetic Existence in Kierkegaard's *Either/Or, Part One.*" In *International Kierkegaard Commentary: Either/Or, Part I*, edited by Robert L. Perkins, 201–28. Macon: Mercer University Press, 1995.

———. "Images of Sin and Salvation in Feminist Theology." *Anglican Theological Review* 60 (1978): 25–54.

———. "Judge William Judging Woman: Essentialism and Existentialism in Kierkegaard's *Either/Or, Part II.*" In *International Kierkegaard Commentary: Either/Or, Part II*, edited by Robert L. Perkins, 33–57. Macon: Mercer University Press, 1995.

———. "Kierkegaard and Feminism: Apologetic, Repetition, and Dialogue." In *Kierkegaard in Post/Modernity*, edited by Martin Matuštík and Merold Westphal, 110–24. Bloomington: Indiana University Press, 1995.

Bertung, Birgit. "Har Søren Kierkegaard foregrebet Karen Blixens og Suzanne Brøggers kvindesyn?" *Kierkegaardiana* 13 (1984): 72–83.

———. *Kierkegaard, kristendom og konsekvens.* Copenhagen: C. A. Reitzel, 1994.

————. *Om Kierkegaard Kvinder og Kærlighed—en studie i Søren Kierkegaards kvindesyn.* Copenhagen: C. A. Reitzel, 1987.

————. "Yes, A Woman Can Exist." In *Kierkegaard Conferences I: Kierkegaard—Poet of Existence,* edited by Birgit Bertung, 7–18. Copenhagen: C. A. Reitzel, 1989.

————, ed. *Kierkegaard Conferences I: Kierkegaard—Poet of Existence.* Copenhagen: C. A. Reitzel, 1989.

Bertung, Birgit, Paul Müller, and Fritz Norlan, eds. *Kierkegaard pseudonymitet* (Søren Kierkegaard Selskabets Populære Skrifter 21). Copenhagen: C. A. Reitzel, 1993.

Bigelow, Pat. *Kierkegaard and the Problem of Writing.* Tallahassee: Florida State University Press, 1987.

Brown, Alison Leigh. "God, Anxiety, and Female Divinity." In *Kierkegaard in Post/Modernity,* edited by Martin J. Matuštík and Merold Westphal, 66–75. Bloomington: Indiana University Press, 1995.

Cahoy, William. "One Species or Two? Kierkegaard's Anthropology and the Feminist Critique of the Concept of Sin." *Modern Theology* 11, no. 4 (1995): 429–54.

Caputo, John D. *Radical Hermeneutics: Repetition, Deconstruction, and the Hermeneutic Project.* Bloomington: Indiana University Press, 1987.

Carlsen, Anne Margrethe Zacher. "Æstetik og kvindelighed—brudstykker af kvindelighedens ideologi." *Litteratur Æstetik Sprog* 2, no. 2 (1984): 1–86.

Chaplain, Denise. *Etude sur "In vino veritas" de Kierkegaard.* Paris: Les Belles Lettres, 1964.

Cole, J. Preston. *The Problematic Self in Kierkegaard and Freud.* New Haven: Yale University Press, 1971.

Come, Arnold B. *Kierkegaard as Humanist: Discovering My Self.* Montreal: McGill-Queen's University Press, 1995.

Connell, George. *To Be One Thing: Personal Unity in Kierkegaard's Thought.* Macon: Mercer University Press, 1985.

Connell, George B., and C. Stephen Evans, eds. *Foundations of Kierkegaard's Vision of Community.* Atlantic Highlands, N.J.: Humanities Press, 1992.

Derrida, Jacques. "The Double Session." In *Dissemination,* translated by Barbara Johnson. Chicago: Chicago University Press, 1981.

Dewey, Bradley R. "The Erotic-Demonic in Kierkegaard's 'Diary of the Seducer.'" *Scandinavica* 10 (1971): 1–24.

————. "Seven Seducers: A Typology of Interpretations of the Aesthetic Stage in Kierkegaard's 'The Seducer's Diary.'" In *International Kierkegaard Commentary: Either/Or, Part I,* edited by Robert L. Perkins, 159–99. Macon: Mercer University Press, 1995.

Dunning, Stephen. *Kierkegaard's Dialectic of Inwardness.* Princeton: Princeton University Press, 1985.

Duran, Jane. "Kierkegaard's Christian Reflectivity: Its Precursors in the Aesthetic of *Either/Or.*" *International Journal for Philosophy of Religion* 17, no. 3 (1985): 131–37.

Elrod, John. *Being and Existence in Kierkegaard's Pseudonymous Works.* Princeton: Princeton University Press, 1975.

————. *Kierkegaard and Christendom.* Princeton: Princeton University Press, 1981.

————. "Kierkegaard on Self and Society." *Kierkegaardiana* 11 (1980): 178–96.

Evans, C. Stephen. *Kierkegaard's "Fragments" and "Postscript": The Religious Philosophy of Johannes Climacus.* Atlantic Highlands, N.J.: Humanities Press, 1983.

————. "Kierkegaard's View of the Unconscious." In *Kierkegaard Conferences I: Kierkegaard—Poet of Existence,* edited by Birgit Bertung, 31–48. Copenhagen: C. A. Reitzel, 1989.

————. *Passionate Reason: Making Sense of Kierkegaard's "Philosophical Fragments."* Bloomington: Indiana University Press, 1992.

Fendt, Gene. *Works of Love? Reflections on "Works of Love."* Potomac, Md.: Scripta Humanistica, [1990?].

Fenger, Henning. *Kierkegaard, The Myths and Their Origins: Studies in the Kierkegaardian Papers and Letters.* Translated by George C. Schoolfield. New Haven: Yale University Press, 1980.

Ferguson, Harvie. *Melancholy and the Critique of Modernity: Søren Kierkegaard's Religious Psychology.* London: Routledge, 1995.

Ferreira, M. Jamie. "Kierkegaardian Imagination and the Feminine." *Kierkegaardiana* 16 (1993): 79–93.

————. *Transforming Vision: Imagination and Will in Kierkegaardian Faith.* Oxford: Clarendon Press, 1991.

Garff, Joakim. *"Den Søvnløse": Kierkegaard læst æstetisk/biografisk.* Copenhagen: C. A. Reitzel, 1995.

Garside, Christine. "Can a Woman be Good in the Same Way as a Man?" *Dialogue* 10 (1971): 534–44.

Gouwens, David. *Kierkegaard's Dialectic of the Imagination.* New York: Peter Lang, 1989.

Grimsley, Ronald. *Søren Kierkegaard and French Literature.* Cardiff: University of Wales Press, 1966.

Hall, Ronald L. *Word and Spirit: A Kierkegaardian Critique of the Modern Age.* Bloomington: Indiana University Press, 1993.

Hannay, Alastair. *Kierkegaard.* London: Routledge and Kegan Paul, 1982.

Hartshorne, M. Holmes. *Kierkegaard, Godly Deceiver: The Nature and Meaning of His Pseudonymous Writings.* New York: Columbia University Press, 1990.

Holl, Jann. *Kierkegaards Konzeption des Selbst: Eine Untersuchung über die Voraussetzungen und Formen seines Denkens.* Meisenheim am Glan: Anton Hain, 1972.

Howe, Leslie A. "Kierkegaard and the Feminine Self." *Hypatia* 9, no. 4 (Fall 1994): 131–57.

Kainz, Howard P. "The Relationship of Dread to Spirit in Man and Woman, According to Kierkegaard." *Modern Schoolman* 47 (1969): 1–13.

Kern, Edith. *Existential Thought and Fictional Technique: Kierkegaard, Sartre, Beckett.* New Haven: Yale University Press, 1970.

Kierkegaard, Søren. *The Concept of Irony.* Translated by Lee M. Capel. London: Collins, 1966.

————. *Fear and Trembling and The Sickness unto Death.* Translated by Walter Lowrie. Princeton: Princeton University Press, 1954.

————. *For Self-Examination and Judge For Yourselves! and Three Discourses 1851.* Translated by Walter Lowrie. Princeton: Princeton University Press.

————. *Samlede Værker.* 3d ed. 20 vols. Edited by A. B. Drachmann, J. L. Heiberg, and H. O. Lange. Copenhagen: Gyldendal, 1962–64.

————. *Stages on Life's Way.* Translated by Walter Lowrie. New York: Schocken Books, 1967.

————. *Training in Christianity and the Edifying Discourse Which "Accompanied" It.* Translated by Walter Lowrie. Princeton: Princeton University Press, 1957 (originally 1941).

Kirmmse, Bruce H. *Kierkegaard in Golden Age Denmark.* Bloomington: Indiana University Press, 1990.

Lebowitz, Naomi. *Kierkegaard: A Life of Allegory.* Baton Rouge: Louisiana State University Press, 1985.

Léon, Céline. "Either Muse or Countermuse: The Neither/Nor of the Second Sex in Kierkegaard." *Arachnē* 2 (1995): 16–49.

———. "The No Woman's Land of Kierkegaardian Seduction." In *International Kierkegaard Commentary: Either/Or, Part I*, edited by Robert L. Perkins, 229–50. Macon: Mercer University Press, 1995.

———. "The Validity of Judge William's Defense of Marriage." Forthcoming in *The Ethical Aesthetic: Essays and Perspectives on Kierkegaard's "Either/Or,"* edited by David Humbert. Atlanta: Scholars Press.

Lorraine, Tamsin E. "Amatory Cures for Material Dis-ease: A Kristevian Reading of *The Sickness unto Death*." In *Kierkegaard in Post/Modernity*, edited by Martin J. Matuštík and Merold Westphal, 98–109. Bloomington: Indiana University Press, 1995.

———. *Gender, Identity, and the Production of Meaning*. Boulder: Westview, 1990.

Lowrie, Walter. *Kierkegaard*, 2 vols. New York: Harper and Brothers, 1962 (originally published in 1938 by Oxford University Press).

Mackey, Louis. *Kierkegaard: A Kind of Poet*. Philadelphia: University of Pennsylvania Press, 1971.

———. *Points of View: Readings of Kierkegaard*. Tallahassee: Florida State University Press, 1986.

Malantschuk, Gregor. *Kierkegaard's Thought*. Edited and translated by Howard V. Hong and Edna H. Hong. Princeton: Princeton University Press, 1971.

———. "Kierkegaards Syn paa Mand og Kvinde." In *Den kontroversielle Kierkegaard*, 30–61. Copenhagen: Vintens, 1976. ("Kierkegaard's View of Man and Woman." In *The Controversial Kierkegaard*, 37–61. Translated by Howard V. Hong and Edna H. Hong. Waterloo: Wilfrid Laurier University Press, 1980.)

———. *Nøglebegreber i Søren Kierkegaards tænkning*. Edited by Grethe Kjær and Paul Müller. Copenhagen: C. A. Reitzel, 1993.

Matuštík, Martin J. *Postnational Identity: Critical Theory and Existential Philosophy in Habermas, Kierkegaard, and Havel*. New York: Guilford, 1993.

Matuštík, Martin J., and Merold Westphal, eds. *Kierkegaard in Post/Modernity*. Bloomington: Indiana University Press, 1995.

McCarthy, Vincent. *The Phenomenology of Moods in Kierkegaard*. The Hague: Martinus Nijhoff, 1978.

———. "Narcissism and Desire in Kierkegaard's *Either/Or, Part One*" In *International Kierkegaard Commentary: Either/Or, Part I*, edited by Robert L. Perkins, 51–72. Macon: Mercer University Press, 1995.

Miller, Libuse Lukas. *In Search of the Self: The Individual in the Thought of Kierkegaard*. Philadelphia: Muhlenberg, 1962.

Mooney, Edward F. *Knights of Faith and Resignation: Reading Kierkegaard's "Fear and Trembling."* Albany: State University of New York Press, 1991.

Mullen, John D. *Kierkegaard's Philosophy: Self-Deception and Cowardice in the Present Age*. New York: New American Library, 1988.

Müller, Paul. *Kierkegaard's "Works of Love": Christian Ethics and the Maieutic Ideal*. Translated and edited by C. Stephen and Jan Evans. Copenhagen: C. A. Reitzel, 1993.

Møller, Per Stig. *Erotismen. Den romantiske bevaegelse i Vesteuropa, 1790–1860*. Copenhagen: Munksgaard, 1973.

Nielsen, H. A. *Where the Passon Is: A Reading of Kierkegaard's "Philosophical Fragments."* Tallahassee: University Presses of Florida, 1983.

Nordentoft, Kresten. *Kierkegaard's Psychology*. Translated by Bruce H. Kirmmse. Pittsburgh: Duquesne University Press, 1978.

Pattison, George. *The Aesthetic and the Religious*. London: Macmillan, 1992.

————. "Jung, Kierkegaard and the Eternal Feminine." *Theology* 90 (1987): 430–40.

————. ed. *Kierkegaard on Art and Communication*. New York: St. Martin's, 1992.

Perkins, Robert L. "Kierkegaard, A Kind of Epistemologist." *History of European Ideas* 12, no. 1 (1990): 7–18.

————. "Kierkegaard's Critique of the Bourgeois State." *Inquiry* 27 (1984): 207–18.

————. "Kierkegaard's Epistemological Preferences." *International Journal for Philosophy of Religion* 4, no. 4 (Winter 1973): 197–217.

————. ed. *International Kierkegaard Commentary: The Concept of Anxiety*. Macon: Mercer University Press, 1985.

————. *International Kierkegaard Commentary: The Corsair Affair*. Macon: Mercer University Press, 1990.

————. *International Kierkegaard Commentary: Early Polemical Writings*. Macon: Mercer University Press, 1998.

————. *International Kierkegaard Commentary: Either/Or, Part I*. Macon: Mercer University Press, 1995.

————. *International Kierkegaard Commentary: Either/Or, Part II*. Macon: Mercer University Press, 1995.

————. *International Kierkegaard Commentary: Fear and Trembling and Repetition*. Macon: Mercer University Press, 1993.

————. *International Kierkegaard Commentary: Philosophical Fragments and Johannes Climacus*. Macon: Mercer University Press, 1994.

————. *International Kierkegaard Commentary: The Sickness unto Death*. Macon: Mercer University Press, 1987.

————. *International Kierkegaard Commentary: Two Ages*. Macon: Mercer University Press, 1984.

————. *Kierkegaard's "Fear and Trembling": Critical Appraisals*. University: University of Alabama Press, 1981.

Poole, Roger. *Kierkegaard: The Indirect Communication*. Charlottesville: University Press of Virginia, 1993.

Roberts, Robert C. *Reason and History: Rethinking Kierkegaard's "Philosophical Fragments."* Macon: Mercer University Press, 1986.

Rudd, Anthony. *Kierkegaard and the Limits of the Ethical*. Oxford: Clarendon Press, 1993.

Rumble, Vanessa. "The Oracle's Ambiguity: Freedom and Original Sin in Kierkegaard's *The Concept of Anxiety*." *Soundings* 75 (1992): 605–25.

Silverman, Hugh J., ed. *Writing the Politics of Difference*. Albany: State University of New York Press, 1991.

Singer, Irving. *The Nature of Love*. 3 vols. Chicago: University of Chicago Press. Vols. 1 and 2, 2d ed., 1984; vol. 3, 1987.

Smith, Joseph H., ed. *Kierkegaard's Truth: The Disclosure of the Self*. New Haven: Yale University Press, 1981.

Smyth, John Vignaux. *A Question of Eros: Irony in Sterne, Kierkegaard, and Barthes*. Tallahassee: Florida State University Press, 1986.

Taylor, Mark C. *Journeys to Selfhood: Hegel and Kierkegaard*. Berkeley and Los Angeles: University of California Press, 1980.

————. "Transgression: Søren Kierkegaard." In *Altarity*, 305–53. Chicago: University of Chicago Press, 1987.

————. *Kierkegaard's Pseudonymous Authorship*. Princeton: Princeton University Press, 1975.

Thielst, Peter. *Søren og Regine: Kierkegaard, kærlighed og kønspolitik*. Copenhagen: Gyldendal, 1980.

Thompson, Josiah. *Kierkegaard*. New York: Knopf, 1973.

———. *The Lonely Labyrinth: Kierkegaard's Pseudonymous Works*. Carbondale: Southern Illinois University Press, 1967.

———. ed. *Kierkegaard: A Collection of Critical Essays*. Garden City, N.Y.: Anchor Books, 1972.

Thulstrup, Niels, and Marie Mikulová Thulstrup, eds. *Bibliotheca Kierkegaardiana*. 16 vols. Copenhagen: C. A. Reitzel, 1978–88.

Utterback, Sylvia Walsh. "Don Juan and the Representation of Spiritual Sensuousness." *Journal of the American Academy of Religion* 47, no. 4 (1979): 627–44.

Vergote, Henri-Bernard. *Sens et répétition: Essai sur L'ironie kierkegaardienne*. 2 vols. Orante: Editions du Cerf, 1982.

Viallaneix, Nelly. *Écoute, Kierkegaard: Essai sur la communication de la parole*, 2 vols. Paris: Editions du Cerf, 1979.

Walsh, Sylvia. "Forming the Heart: The Role of Love in Kierkegaard's Thought." In *The Grammar of the Heart: New Essays in Moral Philosophy and Theology*, edited by Richard H. Bell, 234–56. San Francisco: Harper and Row, 1988.

———. "Kierkegaard and Postmodernism." *International Journal for Philosophy of Religion* 29 (1991): 113–22.

———. "Kierkegaard's Philosophy of Love." In *The Nature and Pursuit of Love: The Philosophy of Irving Singer*, edited by David Goicoechea, 167–79. Amherst, N.Y.: Prometheus Books, 1995.

———. *Living Poetically: Kierkegaard's Existential Aesthetics*. University Park: The Pennsylvania State University Press, 1994.

———. "On 'Feminine' and 'Masculine' Forms of Despair." In *International Kierkegaard Commentary: The Sickness unto Death*, edited by Robert L. Perkins, 121–34. Macon: Mercer University Press, 1987.

———. "The Philosophical Affirmation of Gender Difference: Kierkegaard Versus Postmodern Neo-Feminism." *Journal of Psychology and Christianity* 7 (1988): 18–26.

———. "Women in Love." *Soundings* 65 (1982): 352–68.

Watkin, Julia. "The Logic of Søren Kierkegaard's Misogyny, 1854–55." *Kierkegaardiana* 15 (1991): 82–92.

———. "Serious Jest? Kierkegaard as Young Polemicist in 'Defense' of Women." In *International Kierkegaard Commentary: Early Polemical Writings*, edited by Robert L. Perkins. Macon: Mercer University Press, 1998.

Weston, Michael. *Kierkegaard and Modern Continental Philosophy*. London: Routledge, 1994.

Westphal, Merold. *Kierkegaard's Critique of Reason and Society*. Macon: Mercer University Press, 1987.

Contributors

SYLVIANE AGACINSKI teaches at the Ecole des Hautes Etudes en Sciences Sociales in Paris and is author of *Aparté: Conceptions and Deaths of Søren Kierkegaard* (Florida State University Press, 1988) and *Volume, philosophies et politiques de l'architecture* (Galilée, 1992), a book on architecture and the experience of space. At present she is working on the pictorial and photographic experience. In her recently published *Critique de l'Égocentrisme L'événement de l'autre* (Galilée, 1996), Agacinski sets out to deflate the universal subject of classical humanism and to deconstruct "egocentrism" by using as a model Kierkegaard—a philosopher who, because of his emphasis on individual existence and on the lived experience (*épreuve*) of the Other, has much to teach us.

WANDA WARREN BERRY, associate professor of philosophy and religion and director of affirmative action at Colgate University, is a feminist theologian and an interdisciplinarian in the humanities. She was president of the Søren Kierkegaard Society (United States) in 1994 and is a member of the Steering Committee of the Kierkegaard, Religion and Culture Group of the American Academy of Religion. Her feminist interpretations of Kierkegaard have appeared in the *International Kierkegaard Commentary* series as well as in other recent anthologies.

BIRGIT BERTUNG holds a Master of Arts degree from Copenhagen University and currently serves as secretary of the Søren Kierkegaard Society of Denmark. She is the author of two books on Kierkegaard in Danish: *Om Kierkegaard Kvinder og Kærlighed—en studie i Søren Kierkegaards Kvindesyn* (Reitzel, 1987), which focuses on Kierkegaard's view of women and love; and *Kierkegaard, Kristendom og Konsekvens* (Reitzel, 1994), an attempt to discern the logic of the philosopher's thought. In addition, she has edited/co-edited, as well as contributed to, two collections of essays on Kierkegaard.

JANE DURAN is lecturer in the humanities at the University of California at Santa Barbara, where she is also a visiting fellow in the Department of Philosophy. She is the author of *Toward a Feminist Epistemology* (Rowman and Littlefield, 1991), numerous journal articles on feminist theory, and an essay on Kierkegaard in *International Journal for Philosophy of Religion*.

LESLIE A. HOWE is assistant professor of philosophy at Bishop's University in Montreal, Canada, and has taught a range of courses in ethics, social philosophy, existentialism, and early modern philosophy in previous appointments at the University of Saskatchewan, Brock University, and Concordia University. She has published essays in *Hypatia* and *Joyful Wisdom* and has completed a book-length manuscript, *Becoming Human: Kierkegaard's Critique of Ethics*, which is under review for publication.

CÉLINE LÉON is professor of French and Humanities at Grove City College. Her publications include articles on Kierkegaard, Simone de Beauvoir, and contemporary French feminisms. She has contributed to the second volume in the series *Re-reading the Canon: Feminist Interpretations of Simone de Beauvoir* and currently is completing a book dealing with the perception of Woman, women, the feminine, and the sexual relation in Kierkegaard's three existence-spheres, *The Neither/Nor of the Second Sex: Kierkegaard on the Feminine and the Sexual Relation*.

TAMSIN LORRAINE is assistant professor of philosophy at Swarthmore College. She has published articles in Continental philosophy and French feminism and is the author of *Gender, Identity, and the Production of Meaning* (Westview, 1990). She is currently working on a nondualist account of embodied subjectivity derived primarily from the work of Luce Irigaray, Gilles Deleuze, and contemporary feminist accounts of embodiment, for a book tentatively titled *Corporeal Cartographies*.

ROBERT L. PERKINS is professor and chairperson of the Department of Philosophy at Stetson University, founder of the Søren Kierkegaard

Society (United States) and the *Søren Kierkegaard Newsletter*, and a char-
ter member of the Hegel Society of America. He edits the *International
Kierkegaard Commentary* series and is the author of published essays on
Kierkegaard, Hegel, Buber, and other nineteenth- and twentieth-century
figures and issues. Currently he is completing a book on Kierkegaard's
social philosophy.

MARK LLOYD TAYLOR is a visiting professor of theology and religious
studies at Seattle University. He taught previously at Eastern Nazarene
College, Vassar College, and Seattle Pacific University. In addition to
writing on Kierkegaard, he is the author of books and articles on God in
Hegel, Rahner, process and liberation theologies; gender and Jesus in
Melville's *Moby Dick*, burnout and grace in Christian lives and communi-
ties. He served as secretary-treasurer of the Søren Kierkegaard Society
(United States) from 1991 to 1994.

SYLVIA WALSH is an adjunct professor of philosophy at Stetson University, where she teaches feminist philosophy and history of modern
philosophy. Previously, she taught religious studies at Clark College,
where she was associate professor and chairperson of the Department of
Philosophy and Religion, and at Emory University. She has directed a
NEH Summer Seminar for College Teachers on Kierkegaard and is the
author of *Living Poetically: Kierkegaard's Existential Aesthetics* (Pennsylvania State University Press, 1994) as well as numerous articles on Kierkegaard. Currently, she is working on a book about Kierkegaard's
philosophy of love while serving a two-year term as president of the Søren
Kierkegaard Society (United States).

JULIA WATKIN is lecturer in philosophy at the University of Tasmania,
head of the Søren Kierkegaard Research Unit Australia, and secretary-
treasurer of the Søren Kierkegaard Society of Australia. Formerly, she
served as assistant director of the Department of Søren Kierkegaard Research, Copenhagen University, and taught courses on Kierkegaard at
Copenhagen University, Denmark's International Study Program, and
the Danish People's University. She is founder-editor of the *International
Kierkegaard Newsletter*, translator of *Early Polemical Writings* (Princeton
University Press, 1990) for the English edition of Kierkegaard's collected
works, and author of a number of publications on Kierkegaard.

Index